D1726949

Management of International Trade

Eun Sup Lee

Management of International Trade

 Springer

Eun Sup Lee
Division of International Trade
Pusan National University
Pusan
Republic of South Korea

ISBN 978-3-642-30402-6   ISBN 978-3-642-30403-3 (eBook)
DOI 10.1007/978-3-642-30403-3
Springer Heidelberg New York Dordrecht London

Library of Congress Control Number: 2012954775

Printed on acid-free paper

Springer is part of Springer Science+Business Media (www.springer.com)

To my family: My mother in my hometown, my wife Kee Hyang Son, my three children Suh Yeon, Sung A and Seung Woon, and my teacher Young Sook Kim, for their sacrificed dedication to me while I have worked.

Preface

The WTO multilateral trading system has increased the demand for education and training in the administrative aspect of international business transactions, from countries with both large and small economies. Under the WTO's globalized trading system, most global enterprises should consider the practical aspect of processing international business transactions to secure commercial competitive power as well as grounding those transactions in various management areas affected by globalized markets. Moreover, recent developments in communication skills make it easier and more convenient for smaller businesses and even individual persons to take part in international business transactions.

This is why most business entities need to turn their attention from general business administration practices focusing on their respective domestic markets to the management of international business transactions in the global market. In the competitive globalized market system, one of the most important factors in enterprises competitiveness is to master practical skills and capabilities to promote and complete their own international business transactions.

Considering these facts, this book aims to give upper-level undergraduates or graduate students a comprehensive understanding of the analytical skills and capabilities that are necessary in the context of real international business transactions. To reach this objective, readers of this book need to assume, albeit hypothetically, the position of personnel involved in an international trading company or of a professional trader in charge of each processing stage in the conduct of international commerce. To realize the efficient and productive processing of international business transactions, such personnel and professional traders are generally required to be equipped with the practical techniques and deepened insights needed to deal with the administrative aspects of international business transactions.

However, given the diversity and complexity of our times, it would not be efficient for an individual or the leader of a company to be equipped with all the necessary knowledge and skills to perform their tasks. Instead, it would be more productive for them to equip themselves with the capability to gather and manage the information and knowledge from internal and external sources required for their practical decisions in processing international business transactions. An exception would apply to those in specialized fields.

Upon completion of a thorough study of the concepts presented in this book, students, as potential practitioners of international trade, will be equipped with the practical skills for in- and out-sourcing information and the information gathering abilities required for managing an enterprise's international business transactions, including its exports and imports.

By mastering the administrative and practical aspects of international commerce, even if enterprises face legal, financial or managerial problems in preparing for or performing international business transactions, future practitioners will still be able to successfully perform their tasks. With the skills to solve and deal with the complicated nature of in- and out-sourcing problems, students who go on from this course to work with enterprises involved in international transactions will facilitate the increased likelihood of seeing those transactions through to completion.

To help students understand the theoretical principles and apply them to the practical fields of international trade, Chaps. 1, 2, 3, 4, 5, 6, 7, 8, 9, and 10 cover the basic principles and information to be applied to real-world international trade and Chap. 11 is designed to enhance students' capability to apply the theories and information to practical fields in international business. Students are recommended to apply the knowledge attained from this book to practice according to their own scenarios for which Chap. 11 sets out an illustrated model.

Regarding the assignments suggested within each chapter, students are required to complete and/or apply actual or assumed contracts, including international sales contracts, letters of credit, transportation contracts, and marine cargo insurance contracts. These become final reports to be submitted, together with all communications and negotiating materials including e-mailed letters or conversations over the phone made during the process of completing international business transactions. The actual or assumed transactions should meet the basic policies, marketing plan standards, and international sales contract of the company which would be established for actual or assumed transactions with a buyer in the target market. Students are required to maintain consistency in carrying out the specific transactions outlined in the following chapters to fully participate in international business transactions as if acting in real market conditions, even as they assume the business transaction under the assumed market conditions.

Students may select one item for export to their target markets. Students are required to go through the process of selecting a proper item that is suitable in the target market focusing on the possibility of making market entry and sales expansion as far as possible without disputes arising with the business counterpart. Such a selecting process will include communications and discussions with the students' partners or colleagues, as well as the planning of the systematic sale of goods. Students are required to continue to realize the business transactions with those selected items and submit their discussion and communication records to instructors along with any supplemental assignments given in the chapters.

In addition to the information in practitioners' books and articles, this publication has benefited much from: Schmittoff's Export Trade; Various Materials for

Practitioners published by Korea's Trade Association; Gason C.T. Chuah, Law of International Trade; Eun Sup Lee, Marine Cargo Insurance (written in Korean); Eun Sup Lee, Legal Environment of International Trade (written in Korean); Eun Sup Lee, International Business Transactions (written in Korean), Eun Sup Lee, Public and Private Regulation on Trade (written in Korean).

I owe a special debt of gratitude to Barbara Fess, Senior Editor at Springer, professor Tim Veach of Dankook University, Professor Klaus Oestreicher and Dr. Paul Davis at the University of Worcestershire, Professor Jane Stanfield at the University of Alabama, and Mike Wooi, CEO of the International Professional Managers Association, UK. Barbara Fess gave me invaluable feedback and ideas in designing this book, including the title; Tim Veach, Klaus Oestreicher and Paul Davis provided their expertise to heavily proofread this book; Jane Stanfield and Mike Wooi have always extended special treatment to me in doing my research for this book.

I have also been assisted by Julie Kim from Harvard University and Professor Sun Ok Kim, Dr. Ju Young Lee, Dr. Jung Mi Yang, Dr. Zhu Zhu, and Dr. Dong Wook Pung at Pusan National University, to whom I am very much indebted in writing this book.

Eun Sup Lee

Contents

Introduction

1

Learning Objectives
1. Establishment of a foreign trade department in the students' actual (or assumed) companies to increase the efficiency and productivity in conducting international trade under public and private regulation on international trade;
2. Efficient market research of the students' selected items under public and private regulations governing international trade;
3. Function of an export plan suitable for the legal environments extant in the target market and its importance;
4. Selection of the items proper to specific markets, which should be flexibly modified and adopted according to the legal circumstances of the export market;
5. Factors to be considered when enforcing international sales contracts for newly-developed and environmentally friendly products as opposed to other existing products with which consumers are more familiar;

1.1 Concepts of International Trade

International trade, in the present context, refers to international or global trading activities, distinguished from domestic business transactions which do not cross customs or territories. International trade is not limited to goods, but also encompasses the transfer of services, technology through license agreements, and even bonds and other investment vehicles. Individual countries provide support to promote international trade. By participating in international trade, countries can boost the welfare of their citizens through economic growth and development.

Individual companies seek to promote international trade in order to expand market share globally and maximize profits by pursuing profit-securing activities. In the case of smaller countries with small and open economies, however, companies often have no choice but to expand outward to international markets beyond national boundaries in order to grow and sustain their business.

E.S. Lee, *Management of International Trade*,
DOI 10.1007/978-3-642-30403-3_1, © Springer-Verlag Berlin Heidelberg 2012

International trade is a viable option for increasing market shares and profits, but it also presents risks that may not be evident to a company that limits its reach to its domestic market. First, international trade is a business transaction between parties operating businesses across different countries, meaning that there can be a significant time lag between the point at which the international business transaction is agreed upon and the point at which the transaction actually takes place.

This time lag exposes companies to a number of risks that are often not involved in domestic business transactions. For instance, parties take on credit risks concerning the delivery of contracted products and the settlement of payment. This credit risk is magnified due to the fact that multiple third parties are often involved in international business transactions, including transportation companies and foreign exchange banks. Additionally, compliance with foreign countries' public regulations that may differ from domestic regulations and differ between individual countries presents another issue to overcome.

Prior to engaging in an international business transaction, it is imperative for the participating parties to take due diligence in assessing the risks involved. After thoroughly reviewing the credit history of the potential partners to insure that payments have consistently been made to the other parties in full and on time, trade practitioners should try to engage in effective risk management throughout the whole process of international trade. For proper transactions to be made, detailed and specific sales contracts should be carefully negotiated to specify the relevant trade terms and conditions. These include the determination of the quantity and quality of the contracted items, the time and means of transportation, foreign exchange stipulations, and other safeguards with banks and insurers. Inspectors may also be required, for example, at the stage of enforcing the contract, through the pre-shipment inspection, to inspect the goods to insure that they are indeed prepared for duly contracted delivery.

Pre-shipment Inspection:

"Since the second half of the last century, private-sector buyers and sellers have resorted to pre-shipment inspection (PSI) to ensure that the quantity and quality of the goods to be traded conform to the specifications of the sales contract. However, government-contracted, comprehensive PSI service is a recent phenomenon, with the first of such contracts signed only in the 1960s. Beginning in the 1980s, it became common for a number of countries primarily developing countries to hire commercial inspection firms to verity the customs classification and value of goods destined for their markets. These companies usually operate at seaports and airports in developed countries where they examine export claims concerning the quality, quantity, price, and financing forms of the goods for export. In response to a growing concern that the use of inspection firms was impeding the flow of trade, the Uruguay Round negotiators included the Agreement on Pre-shipment Inspection (PSI Agreement). The PSI Agreement requires WTO Members that employ inspection companies (user Member) to ensure that pre-shipment inspections are conducted in a reasonable manner so as not to unnecessarily interfere with legitimate trade.

The PSI Agreement applies to all government-mandated pre-shipment inspection activities carried out on the territory of Members (i.e. in the country of export prior to exportation). PSI activities have been defined as any government or government body contracting for or mandating the use of PSI activities. The preamble of the Agreement recognizes the need for developing countries to have recourse to pre-shipment inspection as long and in so far as it is necessary to verify the quality, quantity or price of imported goods. But it also recognizes the need for the programs to be carried out without giving rise to unnecessary delays or unequal treatment. Equal emphasis is laid on the objective of transparency of the operation of pre-shipment inspection entities and of laws and regulations relating to pre-shipment inspection."

Source: Eun Sup Lee, World Trade Regulation (Springer, 2012)

According to the sales contract, an affreightment contract should be made with one or more carrying companies, while the payment method and means should be contracted with foreign exchange or commercial banks. Concluding these contracts with third parties essentially means that transaction and settlement risks are transferred to the carriers and banks from the exporter, respectively, shifting risk away from the main parties engaged in the sales contract to the third parties. Herewith, for the efficient risk management of transactions in international trade, credit and transportation risks incurred from the business transactions are required to be diversified or transferred to third parties. These include the insurance companies through maritime insurance and export/import insurance contracts.

Risks in Doing International Trade

"Effective risk management is very important in doing international trade. While all commercial transactions are accompanied by various kinds of risks, international business transactions increase additional risks to those incurred in domestic business transactions.

Transport-related risk

International transportation tends to involve greater distances, with cargo often changing hands or undergoing prolonged storage, so that there is a higher risk of damage or loss than in domestic trade. Consequently, international traders are required to make the proper transport and insurance contract to reduce and cover these kinds of risks involved in international

(continued)

transportation. Particularly, from the aspect of risk management during international transportation, it is important to make a proper cargo insurance contract considering the physical and seasonal characteristics of the transported goods.

Credit risk

Credit or non-payment risk in doing international trade is very important and required to be managed efficiently. For credit risk to be managed properly, the exporter should be serious in examining a credit record of the potential buyers when conducting market research and in establishing the provisions concerning the payment method when negotiating the sales contract. For example, payment under an irrevocable documentary letter of credit issued by the international prime banks has practically been used as a safe method to extract payment from new partners.

Quality of goods risk

Importers may find it difficult to physically examine the quality of the goods before shipment, and thus their imported goods may differ from their expectations. One way of avoiding this risk is for the importer to include provisions for pre-shipment inspection.

Exchange rate risk

If a price is determined in a particular currency in an international contract, subsequent exchange rate fluctuations will inevitably benefit one party to the detriment of the other. The easiest way to avoid this risk is simply to stipulate contractual prices in one's own currency. When it is not possible to stipulate the price in the domestic currency, international traders may make use of several kinds of foreign exchange transactions including forward exchange contracts.

Unforeseen developments or events

A strike, natural disaster or war may render delivery impossible. To be protected from these unforeseen developments or events, it is necessary for traders to be scrupulous when incorporating details regarding the specified hardships or force majeure clauses into the sales contract. For example, when firms entering into a sales contract expect that the metal prices might drasti-cally fluctuate, they should make special provisions concerning such drastic fluctuations of the mutual price in advance.

Legal or political risks

In doing international trade, exporters and importers can face legal risks, including modification of the partner country's domestic law and impossibility of obtaining an import or export license, legal disputes between the concerned parties and difficulty in determining governing law and jurisdiction. To minimize or avoid such legal risks, traders should be careful to make proper provisions when drafting the sales contract. For example, the risk arising from possible modification of the partner country's law could be minimized by drafting a specified hardship or frustration clause, and the jurisdictional risks could be minimized by drafting a commercial arbitration clause.

Investment risks

Sometimes, particularly in growing markets, exporters undertake pre-investment in the importing market to prepare for or expand exports. If exports actually decrease contrary to the exporters' expectations after making the investment, the exporter should assume the loss. To reduce or avoid such risks relating to pre-investment, the exporter should undertake serious market research and try to make use of the available insurance to cover the possible losses from such foreign investment."

See: Jan Ramberg, Guide to Export–import Basics, 19 (ICC, 2008).

1.2   Public Regulation on International Trade

1.2.1   Multilateral Regulation

Towards the end of the Second World War, a number of international negotiations were set in motion in order to create institutional structures for conducting international relations in the post-war world. One of the most important negotiating processes at the time was the United Nations Conference on Trade and Employment, held in Havana, Cuba, in 1947, after lengthy preparatory stages in New York, London and Geneva. At the end of this Conference, the Havana Charter for the International Trade Organization (ITO) was adopted. The proposed ITO was an ambitious undertaking, covering not only trade, but also employment, commodity agreements, economic development, and restrictive business practices. However, for various reasons including the failure of the United States to ratify it, the Havana Charter never entered into force. As part of the negotiations on the Havana Charter, a group of countries engaged in tariff negotiations and in 1947 agreed on substantial tariff reductions.

International Trade Organization (ITO)

"Immediately after World War II, several initiatives converged into a proposal to establish an International Trade Organization (ITO). After years of international negotiations, the 1948 draft of the Havana Charter was completed. This charter would have established an ITO to become the framework for international rules designed to prevent the kind of destructive national government 'beggar-thy-neighbor' policies many thought had contributed to the causes of the war. Despite these elaborate preparations, the effort to create an ITO ultimately failed (although an earlier effort to create monetary rules and a monetary fund – the IMF – had succeeded). The ITO effort failed largely because of the domestic constitutional and political structure of the country then economically preeminent – the United States. It failed despite the fact that the major leadership for the effort to create it had come from the United States itself. But this leadership was that of the executive branch or presidency in the United States. Under the US constitutional and legal requirements, for the government to formally accept the ITO charter, the executive branch had to get the approval of the US Congress, and this the Congress refused to give. In 1950 it was clear that it would be futile to continue trying to obtain this approval, and the ITO was stillborn."

Source: John H. Jackson, William J. Davey & Alan O. Sykes, Jr., Legal Problems of International Economic Relations, 61–62 (West Publishing 5th ed., 2002).

Pending the approval of the Havana Charter, a mechanism was needed to implement and protect the tariff concessions negotiated in 1947. To do so, it was decided to take the Chapter on Commercial Policy of the Havana Charter and convert it, with certain additions, into the General Agreement on Tariffs and Trade (GATT). To bring GATT into force quickly, a Protocol of Provisional Application was developed and entered into force in 1948. Thus, GATT was born, as a provisional agreement until such time as the Havana Charter would be ratified. The Protocol of Provisional Application, however, stated that provisions on non-tariff barriers would apply only to the fullest extent "not inconsistent with existing legislation".

Throughout its 48-year history, GATT provided the structure for a global process of steady trade liberalization through eight "rounds" of multilateral trade negotiations sponsored by its Contracting Parties, covering progressively larger volumes of international trade. This process evolved with its own dynamics, through the initial years of the Cold War, the emergence to independence of many developing countries, the creation of the European Communities, the rise of new and important trading countries, the transition of many non-market countries to market economies, the increasing globalization of the world economy, and the consolidation of the multilateral trading system through the establishment of the World Trade Organization.

This process of trade liberalization achieved: the reduction of tariff rates on industrial products in developed countries from an average of around forty percent to less than four percent; the practical elimination of quantitative restrictions; the development and strengthening of clear rules for the administration of different trade policy measures such as safeguards, subsidies, anti-dumping duties, technical barriers to trade; and development of procedures to resolve disputes. The eighth GATT round, the Uruguay Round, carried this liberalization forward.

GATT Rounds

"One of the more important roles that GATT has played during the last four decades has been its sponsorship of a series of major multinational trade negotiations. So far there have been eight such trade negotiating 'rounds'".

"The first five of these rounds focused on negotiations for the reduction of tariffs. As it turned out, the sixth round also focused on tariffs, although one of the expressed goals for the round was to deal significantly with non-tariff barriers. The seventh round was predominantly concerned with non-tariff measures, although considerable attention was still given to tariff reductions. Finally, the Uruguay Round continued detailed work on many non-tariff measures, but greatly expanded the scope of the trading system by adding services and intellectual property subjects, and, as previously indicated, created a significant new institution. Preliminary estimates of the trade affected by the Uruguay Round include $2.7 trillion for goods, plus approximately $1 trillion for services.

From the time that the new WTO organization came into being (Jan. 1 1995), this organization has endeavored to launch and complete a new round of negotiations (the ninth of the ongoing system, or the first under the WTO), but success has been difficult, as will be discussed at the end of this section."

Source: John H. Jackson, William J. Davey & Alan O. Sykes, Jr., Legal Problems of International Economic Relations, 234–235 (West Publishing 5th ed., 2002).

After the Ministerial Meeting of the GATT Contracting Parties in 1982 which could be regarded as having sown the seeds of the Uruguay Round, and the Ministerial Meeting at Punta del Este in 1986, on December 15, 1993, every issue for negotiation was resolved, including market access for goods and services.

In 1994, the Final Act embodying the results of the Uruguay Round of Multilateral Trade Negotiations was signed at a meeting in Marrakesh, Morocco, by ministers from most of the one hundred and twenty five governments participating in the Uruguay Round.

The World Trade Organization is the institutional framework of the multilateral trading system. The Marrakesh Agreement, establishing the World Trade Organization, is included in the Final Act of the Uruguay Round of Multilateral Trade Negotiations. It constitutes the principal result of the Uruguay Round and incorporates, in its Annexes, the multilateral agreements on trade including the General Agreement on Tariffs and Trade. These include the General Agreement on Trade in Services, the Agreement on Trade-Related Aspects of Intellectual Property Rights, the Understanding on Rules and Procedures Governing the Settlement of Disputes, the Trade Policy Review Mechanism, and, for those countries having accepted them, the plurilateral trade agreements.

The Uruguay Round was the most ambitious negotiating exercise ever multilaterally undertaken. The negotiations: made improvements on GATT provisions through understandings on GATT Articles; strengthened the institutions of the multilateral trading system through the creation of the WTO and the adoption of an integrated dispute settlement system; gave a more precise focus to disciplines on contingent remedy action, such as safeguards, anti-dumping and countervailing measures; modernized border regimes through agreements on customs valuation, rules of origin, import licensing procedures, pre-shipment inspection, etc.; integrated trade in agricultural products and in textiles and clothing into the mainstream of GATT rules; adapted to the process of globalization of the world economy through the adoption of multilateral rules on trade in services and intellectual property rights protection; and further liberalized world markets through market access negotiations on all products, including agricultural products and tropical products, as well as on trade in services.

Furthermore, a substantial improvement in market access conditions was achieved through an average reduction in tariffs for industrial products of about 38 percent. One hundred and twenty five countries participated in the Uruguay Round. This is another aspect of the global scope and coverage of these negotiations. Unlike the Tokyo Round of 1973–79, in which developing countries, whether or not they were members of GATT, were invited to participate fully in the negotiations with no preset conditions, participation in the Uruguay Round was open only to those countries declaring their intention to accede to GATT through the negotiations.

Tokyo Round

"The Tokyo Round is the seventh trade negotiating round which was predominantly concerned with non-tariff measures. The Tokyo Round results included, in addition to tariff reduction protocols, nine special agreements – including Technical Barriers to Trade, Government Procurement, Interpretation and Application of Articles VI, XVI & XXIII (Subsidies), Arrangement Regarding Bovine Meat, International Dairy Arrangement, Implementation of Article VII (Custom Valuation), Import Licensing Procedures, Trade in Civil Aircraft, Implementation of Article VI (Anti-Dumping Duties), and four 'understandings' – including 'Differential and More Favorable Treatment, Reciprocity and Fuller Participation of Developing Countries, Declaration on Trade Measures Taken for Balance-of-Payments Purposes, Safeguard Action for Development Purposes, Understanding Regarding Notification, Consultation, Dispute Settlement and Surveillance.'"

"The legal status of these various agreements and understandings, however, was not always clear. The nine agreements are drafted as 'stand-alone' treaties, each with signatory clauses, and in most cases with institutional measures which include a committee of signatories with certain powers, and a dispute settlement mechanism. Of these agreements, seven have sufficiently precise obligations to be called 'codes.'"

"The 'understandings', have a much more ambiguous status. These instruments mostly express goals or very general obligations, or (in the case of dispute settlement) describe procedures which arguably were already followed. These are not signed as independent agreements."

"Some of the 'codes' have titles which relate them to the GATT, such as the 'Agreement on Implementation of Article VI', and another on 'Interpretation and Application of' several GATT Articles. Again, non-signatories can argue that they are in no way bound by such codes. However, if these codes can be deemed to be 'practice' of the GATT contracting parties, they could themselves be evidence of evolving interpretation of the GATT language itself. This could be especially true if further practice in GATT develops, without protest from non-signatories of the codes, which follows a code interpretation. In these ways GATT parties who have not signed a code may find that they effectively become obligated to code terms which 'interpret' the GATT."

Source: John H. Jackson, William J. Davey & Alan O. Sykes, Jr., Legal Problems of International Economic Relations, 235–237 (West Publishing 5th ed., 2002).

The creation of the WTO and the adoption of the integrated dispute settlement mechanism provide a solid legal basis through the WTO Agreement for the multilateral trading system and for international cooperation and consultation on international trade relations. The results of the Uruguay Round constitute a global, integrated and interrelated package, which covers the interests of all trading partners irrespective of their being large or small.

Uruguay Round

The **Uruguay Round** was the 8th round of multilateral trade negotiations (MTN) established under the framework of the General Agreement on Tariffs and Trade (GATT), spanning from 1986–1994 and having 123 countries as "Contracting Parties". The Round transformed legally GATT into the World Trade Organization. This Agreement establishing the WTO is the legal instrument through which all countries participating in the Uruguay Round decided to create the WTO. The Agreement includes annexes as follows:

Annex 1A: Multilateral Agreements on Trade in Goods: GATT 1994; Agriculture; Sanitary and Phytosanitary Measures; Textiles and Clothing;

(continued)

Technical Barriers to Trade; Trade-Related Investment Measures; Application of Article VI of GATT 1994 (Anti-dumping); Application of Article VII of GATT 1994 (Customs Valuation); Pre-shipment Inspection; Rules of Origin, Import Licensing Procedures; Subsidies and Countervailing Measures; and Safeguards.
Annex 1B: General Agreement on Trade in Services.
Annex 1C: Trade-Related Aspects of Intellectual Property Rights.
Annex 2: Understanding on Rules and Procedures for the Settlement of Disputes.
Annex 3: Trade Policy Review Mechanism.
Annex 4: Plurilateral Trade Agreements: Civil Aircraft; and Government Procurement.

The new institutional and legal status of the WTO, with its integrated dispute settlement system, provides a framework for certainty, security and stability of market access conditions. This applies not only to trade in industrial products but also to trade in agriculture, in textiles and clothing, and in services, as well as a newly established coherent system to protect intellectual property rights. The overall results of the Uruguay Round are contained in more than five hundred pages of legal texts, plus over twenty-six thousand pages of schedules of concessions and commitments in market access for goods, and schedules of specific commitments on trade in services. These schedules are an integral part of the WTO Agreement.

WTO Dispute Settlement System

"The dispute settlement system of the WTO is a central element in providing security and predictability to the multilateral trading system resulting from the Uruguay Round.[1] Its aim is to secure a positive solution to a dispute. The purpose of the WTO Understanding on Rules and Procedures Governing the Settlement of Disputes (the 'DSU') is to provide for an efficient, dependable and rule-oriented system to resolve, within a multilateral framework, disputes arising in relation to the application of the Marrakesh Agreement Establishing the World Trade Organization. Throughout this description, the Marrakesh Agreement Establishing the World Trade Organization, including its annexes, will be referred to as the 'WTO Agreement', whereas the agreements composing it will be referred to as the 'WTO agreements'.

---

[1] Understanding on Rules and Procedures Governing the Settlement of Disputes, Apr. 15, 1994, Marrakesh Agreement Establishing the World Trade Organization, Annex 2, Legal Instruments-Results of the Uruguay Round, 33 I.L.M. 1125, Art. 3.2 (1994) [DSU].

The WTO dispute settlement system favors mutually agreed solutions consistent with the WTO agreements, and parties are encouraged to develop mutually satisfactory solutions, even when the matter is before a panel.[2] The WTO dispute settlement mechanism is a rule-oriented system where recommendations and rulings must aim at achieving a satisfactory settlement in accordance with the rights and obligations of the Members under the WTO Agreement. As a result, all solutions to matters formally arose under the consultation and dispute settlement provisions of the WTO agreements, including arbitration awards, must be consistent with those agreements and must not nullify and impair benefits accruing to any Member under those agreements. If it is not possible to reach a mutually agreed solution, the first objective of the dispute settlement system is normally to secure the withdrawal of the measures concerned if they are found to be inconsistent with the WTO Agreement.

The prompt settlement of situations in which a Member considers that benefits accruing to it directly or indirectly under the WTO Agreement are being impaired by measures taken by another member is essential to: the effective functioning of the WTO; and the maintenance of a proper balance between the rights and obligations of its Members. Efficiency is achieved through detailed procedural provisions, including provisions which allow a party to move forward with the case even in the absence of agreement of the other party. The procedures for dispute settlement which are laid down in the DSU have many features which make it quasi-judicial in nature. First, there is assured access to these procedures. Second, there is near automaticity in decision-making in all key issues related to settlement of individual disputes. Third, time limits are strictly stipulated for each stage of the process. And finally, there is the provision for appellate review."

Source: Eun Sup Lee, World Trade Regulation (Springer, 2012)

For the first time in history, a multilateral framework of rules was adopted for international trade in services. It consists of the General Agreement on Trade in Services (GATS), based on general rules and principles, negotiated specific commitments, and commitment to progressive liberalization through future rounds of negotiations on trade in services.

---

[2] Dispute Settlement Understanding, Art. 11.

Regulation on Trade in Services

"Services production is a core economic activity in virtually all countries irrespective of their levels of development.

In a number of countries, services have been very important for employment and employment growth, because many traditional services, including distribution, education and social services, are labor intensive. In many service sectors it has also proved more difficult to substitute capital for labor than in manufacturing. The expansion of services has been driven in particular by income-related demand shifts, benefiting for example the hotel and tourist industry; the economic stimulus results from new information and communication technologies; and the growing importance of basic infrastructural services, including transport, communication and finance, for a wide range of user industries.

New transmission technologies have overturned traditional concepts of distance – banking, education and medical services may now be provided over the Internet – and many governments have sought to open long-entrenched monopolies so as to promote efficiency and mobilize new capital and expertise.

As the share of services in international trade has steadily increased, international efforts to deal with international trade in services also have increased. It culminated in the adoption of the General Agreement on Trade in Services (GATS). GATT 1947 was concerned almost exclusively with rules on trade in goods. The Uruguay Round's banner achievements were in expanding the scope of the GATT-WTO system to include non-goods sectors, liberalizing trade in several advanced sectors, and setting the WTO Members on a course to further liberalization agreements on advanced-sector trade. With the successful conclusion of the General Agreement on Trade in Services and the TRIPS Agreement, the negotiators broke new ground by introducing core GATT disciplines to trade in services and providing effective protection of intellectual property rights. Follow-up WTO negotiations also have produced agreements on trade in information technology products, telecommunications, and financial services. Even though GATS originated from GATT with the same spirit, the particular characteristics of trade in services produces deviations under GATS regulations, in certain key respects, from the concepts and rules incorporated in GATT. Considering that many service industries are required to remain carefully regulated to protect public interest, GATS regulates trade barriers that distort competition or restrict access to markets on the one hand, and distinctively, requires legitimate policy objectives to be pursued and ensures the orderly functioning of markets on the other hand.

Thus, restrictions on service suppliers in specified fields or discrimination against foreign suppliers are considered as barriers to service trade, however, regulations requiring compliance with technical standards or qualification requirements to ensure the quality of service and the protection of public interest are considered as necessary. Multilateral negotiations have progressively liberalized GATS regulations by removing trade barriers in service markets, while not restricting the individual governments' authority to maintain and develop necessary regulations to pursue their national policy objectives."

Source: Eun Sup Lee, World Trade Regulation (Springer, 2012)

Protection of intellectual property rights at the international level was systematically restructured on the basis of existing conventions, the adoption of new disciplines on the availability, scope, coverage and use of intellectual property rights, and clear rules for their enforcement. It consists of the Agreement on Trade-Related Aspects of Intellectual Property Right (TRIPs). An important work program was also adopted on the relationship between international trade and the protection of the environment, and other issues such as investment and competition policies were clearly indicated as potential subjects for future negotiations.

1.2.2   Domestic Regulation

While international trade among states is internationally governed by multilateral regulation under the WTO mechanisms, international trade among private entities is domestically regulated by domestic laws covering export and import activities, customs duties and clearance, and exchange transactions. For practitioners to do their international trading business effectively, they are required to be familiar with the related trade regulations of the trade partner countries.

Before the WTO was launched in 1995, domestic trade-related laws were very different among the countries, rendering it difficult for practitioners to understand and apply the laws to real transactions. However, under the current WTO mechanisms, the main contents of the WTO member countries' domestic laws regulating trade are substantially similar to each other. This is because domestic laws to affect the member countries' interests in international trade are required to be in compliance with the regulations required by the WTO provisions.

Generally speaking, there have been only meager regulations imposed on exporters' activities, while simultaneous efforts have been made to encourage exporters to export their items and expand international markets. This is particularly true in developing countries with small and open economies.

Nevertheless, there are special cases where specified restrictions are imposed depending on the nature of the goods, the market to which the goods are to be transported, or some budgetary aspects including export tax, and remission of customs duties or domestic value added tax. Such regulations are usually imposed under the headings of export permissions or licenses.

An export permission or license is operated in parallel with the control of strategic goods, which is generally administered through specific regulations on their strategic goods. Basically, regulations on strategic goods constitute one kind of external control which is focused on specified classes of goods being imported from outside the exporting country and being exported/transited by the exporting country's resident entities to specifically listed countries. Strategic goods are transacted by way of official controls through which any transit or trade authorizations are required for the goods to cross the borders of different countries.

While exports are apt to be encouraged by the government, imports are generally regulated by the government, due to its interest in maintaining and improving the country's balance of payments.

Imports are regulated by tariff and non-tariff measures. Even though the average levels of tariff rates have fallen under GATT/WTO mechanisms, tariff measures have efficiently been used for the purpose of import restrictions and, sometimes, governments' own budgeting purposes. Recently, particularly, under the WTO mechanisms, many countries have positively operated non-tariff measures for their policy objectives, including protection of human health and life.

Importers are required to confirm that the imported goods are granted import permission or licenses before they make the import contract. In some countries, to regulate imports, all imported goods are grouped into: automatic-licensed goods; restrictive-licensed goods; and prohibited goods.

Automatic-licensed goods can be imported simply by registration with the domestic customs office, while restrictive-licensed goods can be imported only under specified conditions including, for example, receipt of an appropriate recommendation from the relevant traders' association or authorization from a specified government agency.

Importers are also required to confirm: the tariff rate before they import; if there are any kinds of non-tariff measures to be considered including sanitary and phytosanitary measures, technical regulations, technical conformity assessments, anti-dumping and subsidy-countervailing measures, etc.

Regarding customs regulation or customs entries, currently and particularly, in the case of countries with open and small economies being sustained by international trade, customs regulations: are basically designed to impose minimum necessary restrictions on the flow of trade; extend flexibility and convenience as far as possible when regulations are required for export and import; provide services and facilities for transshipment, warehousing, bonding, duties drawback, etc.

In some countries, exporters and importers avail themselves of the chance to claim kickbacks on import duties which they have paid on imported materials that have processed or transformed into final products and subsequently exported. In certain countries pursuing export-driven policies, potential exporters are permitted to import materials while claiming relief from customs duties on condition that they are to re-export final products.

Exporters and importers can use bonded warehouses when imported goods are perhaps not required immediately for domestic use or where there is a chance of re-exportation. A bonded warehouse is a designated warehouse which is licensed to accept imported goods for storage before paying customs duties or other related taxes.

In almost all countries, foreign exchange controls are imposed on international transactions, the purpose of which is to regulate the disposal and trade of the foreign currencies of their residents. Naturally countries facing difficulties in improving their balance of payments are apt to impose rather strict restrictions on the disposal of foreign currencies. Recently, foreign exchange control has been liberalized in many countries. However, the exporters and importers are required to verify if there are any obligations in the form of documentation or procedural practices in conducting their international business transactions.

1.3   Private Regulation on International Trade

International trade is a business transaction made across separate countries, and individual countries' regulations may conflict with each other. Countries have different economic and political systems and policy agendas, as well as different degrees of development, and accordingly, varying domestic private laws and commercial practices. These obvious discrepancies have led to a set of international private rules guiding inter-country business transactions, which has created a fair set of practices and regulations to securely facilitate business transactions internationally.

The United Nations Convention on Contract for the International Sale of Goods (1980),[3] as well as the CISG on the Law of Treaties,[4] has set the groundwork for international business relations by facilitating peaceful cooperation among individual countries in spite of constitutional and social differences. These are the most imperative international laws governing basic import and export contracts between parties. Closely correlated with the CISG, the International Rules for the Interpretation of Trade Terms, established in 2010 by the International Chamber of Commerce(or Incoterms®2010)was created to clarify international trade terms for matters such as dividing responsibilities and costs incurred between exporters and importers, while reflecting the most advanced transportation practices and methods. International trade contracts are replete with specified acronyms, such as FOB (free on board) and CIF (cost, insurance and freight), to expedite the trading process and insure clarity between trading partners.

---

[3] Adopted by a diplomatic conference on April 11, 1980, the Convention establishes a comprehensive code of legal rules governing the formation of contracts for the international sale of goods, the obligations of the buyer and seller, remedies for breach of contract and other aspects of the contract. The Convention entered into force on January 1, 1988.

[4] The Vienna Convention on the Law of Treaties (or VCLT) is a treaty concerning the customary international law on treaties between states. It was adopted on May 22, 1969 and opened for signature on May 23, 1969. The Convention entered into force on January 27, 1980. The VCLT has been ratified by 110 states as of October 2009; those that have not ratified it yet may still recognize it as binding upon them in as much as it is a restatement of customary law.

International Chamber of Commerce (ICC)

International Chamber of Commerce (ICC), founded in 1919, is the largest, most representative business organization in the world. Its hundreds of thousands of member companies in over 130 countries have interests spanning every sector of private enterprise.

ICC activities cover a broad spectrum, from arbitration and dispute resolution to making the case for open trade and the market economy system, business self-regulation, fighting corruption or combating commercial crime.

ICC has direct access to national governments all over the world through its national committees. The organization's Paris-based international secretariat feeds business views into intergovernmental organizations on issues that directly affect business operations.

ICC carries out following functions:

– **Setting rules and standards**
  - Arbitration under the rules of the ICC International Court of Arbitration is on the increase. Since 1999, the Court has received new cases at a rate of more than 500 a year.
  - ICC's Uniform Customs and Practice for Documentary Credits (UCP 500) are the rules that banks apply to finance billions of dollars worth of world trade every year.
  - ICC Incoterms are standard international trade definitions used every day in countless thousands of contracts. ICC model contracts make life easier for small companies that cannot afford big legal departments.
  - ICC is a pioneer in business self-regulation of e-commerce. ICC codes on advertising and marketing are frequently reflected in national legislation and the codes of professional associations.
– **Promoting growth and prosperity**
  - ICC supports government efforts to make a success of the Doha trade round. ICC provides world business recommendations to the World Trade Organization.
  - ICC speaks for world business when governments take up such issues as intellectual property rights, transport policy, trade law or the environment.
  - Signed articles by ICC leaders in major newspapers and radio and TV interviews reinforce the ICC stance on trade, investment and other business topics.
  - Every year, the ICC Presidency meets with the leader of the G8 host country to provide business input to the summit.
  - ICC is the main business partner of the United Nations and its agencies.
– **Spread business expertise**
  - At UN summits on sustainable development, financing for development and the information society, ICC spearheads the business contribution.

- Together with the United Nations Conference on Trade and Development (UNCTAD), ICC helps some of the world's poorest countries to attract foreign direct investment.
- In partnership with UNCTAD, ICC has set up an Investment Advisory Council for the least-developed countries.
- ICC mobilizes business support for the New Partnership for Africa's Development. At ICC World Congresses every two years, business executives tackle the most urgent international economic issues.
- The World Chambers Congress, also biennial, provides a global forum for chambers of commerce.
- Regular ICC regional conferences focus on the concerns of business in Africa, Asia, the Arab World and Latin America.

For more details, see http://www.iccwbo.org.

Further sets of regulations exist to clarify relations based on different transport methods. The Hague Conference on Private International Law, or HCCH, set forth The Hague Rules of 1924 as the first attempt by the international community to address the problem of ship-owners neglecting to take any responsibility for the loss or damage of cargo in transit. The rules specify that the carrier must take responsibility if the shipper suffering damage can prove that the vessel was not seaworthy, was improperly manned, or was not sufficiently adequate to safely transport and preserve the cargo.

HCCH

The Hague Conference on Private International Law (or HCCH, for Hague Conference/Conférence de la Hague) is the preeminent organization in the area of private international law.

HCCH was formed in 1893 to "work for the progressive unification of the rules of private international law". It has pursued this goal by creating and assisting in the implementation of multilateral conventions promoting the harmonization of conflict of laws principles in diverse subject matters within private international law. Sixty-eight nations are currently members of the Hague Conference, including China, Russia, the United States, and all member states of the European Union (the European Union itself is also a member of the Conference, so the total number of members is listed as 69 on the HCCH website).

The Hague Rules have occasionally been updated by protocols, the current form of which is deemed the Hague-Visby Rules established in 1968. The Rules are used by about 90 % of the international trading community. In the 1970s, pressure was building from developing nations and nations with insufficient competitive power in the transportation industry to require a reassessment of the liabilities and responsibilities between the carriers and shippers in freight contracts. This led to a renegotiation of international shipping policies under the UN Hamburg Rules of 1978. The rules were implemented in 1992, but their use has remained very limited in the global trade community, as the drafters may, arguably, have gone too far in allocating liabilities between shippers and carriers.

Hague-Visby Rules

The Hague-Visby Rules are a set of international rules for the carriage of goods by sea. The official title is "International Convention for the Unification of Certain Rules of Law relating to Bills of Lading" and was drafted in Brussels in 1924. After being amended by the Visby Amendments (officially the "Protocol to Amend the International Convention for the Unification of Certain Rules of Law Relating to Bills of Lading") in 1968, the Rules became known as the Hague-Visby Rules. A final amendment was made in the SDR Protocol in 1979.

Further sets of rules exist to regulate several aspects of trade. Liability in air transportation is covered by a separate agreement called the Uniform Rules for a Combined Transport Document of 1973. The most frequently adapted international regulations for insurance practices are outlined in the England Marine Insurance Act of 1906. International regulations for payment settlement by letter of credit are provided under the Uniform Customs and Practices for the Documentary Credits (UCP 600[5]), and the Uniform Rules for Collection 1995 is a supplemental set of rules to aid bankers, sellers and buyers in the payment-collecting process.

These international laws regarding trade contracts are grouped as follows.

1.3.1   Laws on International Sales Contracts

General laws to regulate international sales contracts include CISG 1980, UNIDROIT principles of 1994 and UNCITRAL Model Law on Electronic Commerce 1996.

The United Nations Convention on Contracts for the International Sale of Goods 1980 (CISG) is a uniform set of trade laws enacted by UNCITRAL in 1980, and which relates to the vast majority of international business transactions. The CISG

---

[5] The latest revision of UCP is the sixth revision of the rules since they were first promulgated in 1933. It is the fruit of more than three years of work by the ICC's Commission on Banking Technique and Practice.

1980 includes provisions concerning ① The formation of contracts ② general rules on sale of goods ③ The seller's obligations (delivery of goods and documents, conformity of contracts and third party's right of claim, remedies consequent on seller's breach) ④ buyer's obligations (payment, receipt, remedies consequent on buyer's breach) ⑤ transfer of risk ⑥ common regulations concerning the obligations of sellers and buyers (contract breaches before performance and installment contracts, damages, interest, exemption of obligations, the effect of contract cancellation, and storage of goods).

The International Institute for the Unification of Private Law (UNIDROIT) is an independent intergovernmental organization that works toward harmonizing private international law, specifically commercial law, between states. The UNIDROIT Principles on International Commercial Contracts enacted in 1994 applies to international business contracts for services, constituting complementary regulations in interpreting international laws, especially the CISG of 1980. In UNIDROIT, provisions are made on ① general rules ② formation of contracts ③ validity of contracts ④ interpretation ⑤ contents of contracts ⑥ performance of contracts ⑦ nonperformance of contracts.

UNIDROIT

"The International Institute for the Unification of Private Law (UNIDROIT) is an independent intergovernmental organization. Its purpose is to study needs and methods for modernizing, harmonizing, and coordinating private international law and in particular commercial law between states, and to draft international conventions to address the needs.

UNIDROIT is an independent intergovernmental organization with its seat in the Villa Aldobrandini in Rome. Its purpose is to study needs and methods for modernizing, harmonizing and coordinating private and, in particular, commercial law between states and groups of states.

O Technical approach to harmonization or unification favored by UNIDROIT

UNIDROIT's independent status amongst intergovernmental Organizations has enabled it to pursue working methods which have made it a particularly suitable forum for tackling more technical and correspondingly less political issues.

O Factors determining choice of instrument to be prepared

The uniform rules drawn up by UNIDROIT have, in keeping with its intergovernmental structure, traditionally tended to take the form of international conventions, designed to apply automatically in preference to a state's municipal law upon completion of all the formal requirements of that state's domestic law for their entry into force. However, the low priority which tends to be accorded by governments to the implementation of such conventions and the time it therefore tends to take for them to enter into force have led to the increasing popularity of alternative forms of unification in areas where a binding instrument is not felt to be essential. Such alternatives include model laws which states may take into consideration when drafting domestic

(continued)

legislation on the subject covered or general principles addressed directly to judges, arbitrators and contracting parties who are, however, left free to decide whether to use them or not. Where the subject is not judged ripe for the drawing up of uniform rules, another alternative consists in the preparation of legal guides, typically on new business techniques, types of transaction or on the framework for the organization of markets both at the domestic and the international level. Generally speaking "hard law" solutions (i.e. conventions) are needed where rules' scope transcends the bi-polar relationship underlying ordinary contract law and where third parties' or public interests are at stake as is the case in the law of property."

Source: http://www.unidroit.org/dynasite.cfm?dsmid=103284

The UNCITRAL Model Law on Electronic Commerce was enacted to assert common regulations to govern e-commerce practices, including e-trade, which is experiencing increased demand. The Model Law of Electronic Commerce consists of ① general rules ② legal application of rules to data messages ③ communication of data messages ④ product transport of e-commerce in certain areas.

UNCITRAL

The United Nations Commission on International Trade Law (UNCITRAL) was established in 1966 to promote the progressive harmonization and unification of international trade law.

The organization is established at three levels. The first level is UNCITRAL itself (The Commission), which holds an annual plenary session. The second level are the numerous intergovernmental working groups. Texts designed to simplify trade transactions and reduce associated costs are developed by these working groups participated in by all member nations of UNCITRAL, which meet once or twice per year. Non-member nations and interested international and regional organizations are also invited and can actively contribute to the work. The working groups' decisions are made by consensus, not by vote. Draft texts completed by these working groups are submitted to UNCITRAL for finalization and adoption at its annual session. The third level is the International Trade Law Division of the United Nations Office of Legal Affairs which provides substantive secretariat services to UNCITRAL, such as conducting research and preparing studies and drafts.

1.3.2 Laws on Typical Trade Terms

Defining and universalizing of trade terms is essential activities for maintaining clarity and simplicity in processing international trade contracts. Incoterms®2010 is a commonly referred to international piece of contract law, explaining buyers' and sellers' obligations by use of commonly used trade terms. Incoterms®2010 can be used in coordination with the American Foreign Trade Definitions of 1990 to sufficiently clarify terms and aid in drafting trade contracts.

The international commercial terms referred to as Incoterms consist of only thirteen commonly used trade terms: ① EXW (departure term) ② FCA, FAS and FOB (main carriage unpaid terms) ③ CFR, CIF, CPT and CIP (main carriage paid terms) ④ DAT, DAP and DDP (arrival terms). Each term is defined and states a buyer's and seller's obligations in the matter of the exchange.

Under the Revised American Foreign Trade Definitions, the set of revised definitions consists of trade terms, as well as six FOB terms that are specifically applicable in matters of trade with the United States. The initial law was ratified in 1919 when it was adopted by the US National Foreign Trade Council. Since then, the trade definitions have been revised twice – first in 1941, and then again in 1990. The definitions consist of a preface and eleven trade terms (including six FOBs) as follows.

① EXW: (named place)

② FOB: (named inland carrier at named inland point of departure)

③ FOB: (named inland carrier at named inland point of departure). Freight prepaid to: (named point of exportation)

④ FOB: (named inland carrier at named inland point of departure)

⑤ FOB: (named inland carrier at named inland point of departure)

⑥ FOB Vessel: ((named port of shipment) named inland point in country of importation)

⑦ FOB: (named inland point in country of importation)

⑧ FAS Vessel: (named port of destination)

⑨ CFR: (named point of destination)

⑩ CIF: (named point of destination)

⑪ DEQ: (duty paid)

The Warsaw-Oxford Rules for CIF Contract were implemented in 1928 after being enacted by the International Law Association (ILA), and revised in 1932, to properly outline the rights and obligations of each party in CIF contracts. The document consists of twenty-one rules covering sellers' obligations relating to shipment, dates, risks, property, type of vessel, freight collection rates, import tariffs and other charges, condition of goods, insurance, shipping notices, export and import permits, certificate of origin, quality certificate, references, required documents, destruction and damage after shipment, as well as buyers' obligations of payment and goods inspection. The Warsaw-Oxford Rules, however, have become obsolete in today's international world of commerce.

ILA

"The International Law Association (ILA) was founded in Brussels in 1873. Its objectives, under its Constitution, are "the study, clarification and development of international law, both public and private, and the furtherance of international understanding and respect for international law". The ILA has consultative status, as an international non-governmental organization, with a number of the United Nations specialized agencies.

The activities of the ILA are organized by the Executive Council, assisted by the Headquarters Secretariat in London. Membership of the Association, at present about 3700, is spread among Branches throughout the world. The ILA welcomes as members all those interested in its objectives. Its membership ranges from lawyers in private practice, academia, government and the judiciary, to non-lawyer experts from commercial, industrial and financial spheres, and representatives of bodies such as shipping and arbitration organizations and chambers of commerce.

The Association's objectives are pursued primarily through the work of its International Committees, and the focal point of its activities is the series of Biennial Conferences. The Conferences, of which 72 have so far been held in different locations throughout the world, provide a forum for the comprehensive discussion and endorsement of the work of the Committees."

Source: http://www.ila-hq.org/en/about_us/index.cfm

1.3.3   Laws on Trade Disputes

The New York Convention 1958 is shorthand for the United Nations Convention on the Recognition and Enforcement of Foreign Arbitral Awards enacted by UNCITRAL in 1958. It sets out guidelines for international arbitration in commercial matters. A "claim" is made by a contracting party when he believes that the other party did not fulfill his obligations as outlined in their contract.[6] The Convention describes the scope of coverage, arbitral agreement methods, recognition of

---

[6] In order to minimize litigation in the event of a dispute, a number of aspects must be borne in mind when drawing up a contract. An international contract should always contain either a jurisdiction and choice of law clause specifying the courts of which country are to have jurisdiction and the law of which country is to govern the contract, or alternatively, the parties may agree that disputes arising should be submitted to arbitration. To do this they would incorporate an arbitration clause specifying where the arbitration is to take place, the number of arbitrators and by whom they are to be appointed, and a choice of law clause. [See Chs 22 (Jurisdiction), 21 (English Law and Foreign Law) and 23 (Arbitration). Cited by (Murray et al. 2007) (1903)]. In English law, to be valid and binding a contract must be certain. An oral contract is normally equally as binding as a written one, although it is desirable that a commercial contract be in writing and signed [Murray et al. (2007, id.)]

awards and execution, recognition and application of execution, and recognition and cause to refuse, or delay execution.

There are other laws concerning conciliation and arbitration, including UNCITRAL Arbitration Rules 1976, UNCITRAL Model Law on International Commercial Arbitration 1985, and ICC Rules of Conciliation and Arbitration 1988, which stipulate provisions on arbitral awards and their enforcement.

New York Convention 1958

The Convention on the Recognition and Enforcement of Foreign Arbitral Awards, also named the New York Convention, was adopted by a United Nations diplomatic conference; it requires courts of contracting states to give effect to private agreements to arbitrate and to recognize and enforce arbitration awards made in other member countries. That is, countries which have adopted the New York Convention have agreed to recognize and enforce international arbitration awards. Widely considered the foundational instrument for international arbitration, it applies to arbitrations which are not considered as domestic awards in the state where recognition and enforcement is sought. Even though there are several international conventions applying to the cross-border enforcement of arbitration awards, the New York Convention has by far been considered the most important.

Public and Private Regulations on Process of International Trade

WTO Agreement / Public Regulations of Governments

Market Entry	Promotion	Formation of Contract	Delivery & Payment	Follow-up Management
Public Regulation on Customs Clearance/Tariffs; Public Regulations Including SPS and TBT Measures.	Public Regulation on Competition, etc.	Incoterms 2010; Revised American Foreign Trade Definitions; Uniform Commercial Code.	Uniform Customs and Practice for Documentary Credit; ICC Publication 600 (UCP600); International Standard Banking Practice (ISBP); Uniform Rules for Contract Guarantee.	New York Convention; UNCITRAL Arbitration Rules; UNCITRAL Model Law on International Commercial Arbitration; ICC Rules of Conciliation and Arbitration.

United Nations Convention on Contracts for the International Sale of Goods (CISG);

UNIDROIT Principle on International Commercial Contracts;

UNCITRAL Model Law on Electronic Commerce.

Assignment

『Guideline For Assignment』

For students to implement the assignments suggested in the following chapters, they are required to select an export item to be sold and determine the target market. When selecting their items, they are required to consider their individual or groups' comparative advantages when taking out their business transactions in the world market.

With the chosen items (hereinafter, selected goods), students are assumingly or actually going to take steps to participate in the international trade through the implementation of the assignments suggested in the following chapters.

When the students submit the report on their assignments, they are required to include the negotiating materials and communication records, such as e-mailed letters to support the business transactions.

1. Tariff and non-tariff barriers to be met for selected goods when they are marketed and distributed (for example, in EU countries), and make check-lists for such items to be efficiently marketed and distributed in the EU countries in compliance with public laws and regulations.

2. A comparative study of the sanitary and phytosanitary measures as between the United States and China in the case of trade in agricultural and live-stock products.

Reference

Carole Murray, David Holloway, Daren Timson-Hunt, Brian Kennelly, Giles Dixon, Schmitthoffs (2007) Schmitthoff Export Trade: The Law and Practice of International Trade, 11th edn, Sweet & Maxwell Ltd

Supplemental Reading

DiMatteo LA, Lucien J (2005) Dhooge, International Business Law – a Transaction Approach, 2nd edn. West, pp. 1–36
http://www.uktradeinvest.gov.uk
http://www.chamberonline.co.kr
http://www.edgd.gov.uk
http:///unece.org
http://www.export.org.uk

Overseas Market Research

2

1. Efficient ways to induce potential customers to be interested in the students' selected items based on their comparative advantages over competitive items in the target market;
2. Factors to be considered when attracting potential customers to the (assumed to be selected) items in the exporting market, compared with the factors to be considered in the domestic market where students' (assumed) companies are well recognized by the customers;
3. Functions and importance of established international business networks, based on mutual reliance in conducting international trade particularly with newly developed items;
4. Strategies for the cultivation of new markets abroad, with an item which is newly developed and not yet commercialized in the domestic market compared with the case of existing products which have been successfully commercialized in the domestic market;

The first step in any international trade negotiation, or any business venture, for that matter, is obtaining a good understanding of the market to assess viability and potential success. An exporter will then analyze the potential competitiveness of the exports, select a target market, conduct market research, find the best method to reach the target market overseas, and make a thorough credit inquiry to select the proper importer.

2.1 Overseas Market Research

Market research is defined as a "component of marketing research whereby a specific market is identified and its size and other characteristics are measured." Overseas market research is this process occurring outside of a firm's home country, which can face a new set of boundaries such as language, culture, data collection, networking, and differences in business laws and requirements. For

E.S. Lee, *Management of International Trade*, 25
DOI 10.1007/978-3-642-30403-3_2, © Springer-Verlag Berlin Heidelberg 2012

proper market research, an exporter needs to have a basic understanding of all aspects of the country that may affect the desirability and success of exporting, such as politics, economics, culture, history, scientific technology, climate, and language. An exporter who has done proper market research would know not to sell in-house heating systems in the Congo or pork in Syria. Based on this basic understanding about the target market, an assessment of the competitors, prices, customers and distribution structures should be made.

If, upon completing scientific research, results show that the product does not have any advantages over current competitors' products, or that product diversification is too slender to assure a high possibility of success, the exporter will have to reassess whether or not the export is viable in its current state. If the export is not assessed to be viable in the target market, changes will need to be made to the plan. One of the easiest ways to gain a basic understanding of a country's import and export situation is to look at statistical analyses of exports and imports. By analyzing the records of exports and imports at a country level, one can gain knowledge as to when items were exported and which countries they were exported to. Once the proper import countries have been determined, an exporter might be able to make lists of buyers of specific items, which can become the first procession for successful product marketing.

2.1.1 Contents

2.1.1.1 Target Market

The target market is the particular market segment on which a marketing activity is focused. Essentially, this is to whom the goods are intended to be sold. Particulars of the contents of the target market include: selection of target areas; understanding commercial practices of target countries; current situation of import and export of isolated products; climate and geographical conditions; import management systems (item management system, customs clearance, tariffs, foreign exchange, etc.); stability of currency and economic situation; transportation and communication (especially logistics facilities such as harbors and airports); etc.

2.1.1.2 Market Demand

Demand is a need or desire for a certain good or service supported by the capacity to purchase it. Demand analysis is an aspect of research that studies the sales generated by goods or service to determine the factors for its success or failure. Particulars of demand analysis are included: research into market potential; situation of supply and demand of the products (its own production, import quantity, and demand); estimate of market growth rates; research into market development; etc.

2.1.1.3 Consumer Research

Consumer research is conducted to assess the preferences, motivations, and buying behavior of the target market through observation, surveys, interviews, and pushcarts. A pushcart refers to the test-selling of one's intended product by tentatively exporting only a small amount of the item to be sold to verify the response. Considerations in consumer research include: population, its preferences and living standards; distribution of consumers by area and demographics such as age and income; purchasing motivation, place, means, time, quantity, and ability; satisfaction of goods and future change of consumers' tastes; etc.

2.1.1.4 Competitors

Any company that is in the same industry or offers like or competing products is a competitor. Thorough competitor analysis is one of the most important factors in success. Considerations in researching competitors include: competitors in countries designated as export targets, competitive products, prices, and price movements; marketing strategies of competitors; advantages and disadvantages of competitors; export prices of competitors, export quantity, and advantages of export competition; etc.

2.1.1.5 Products

To conduct a systematic research into products, the characteristics of a good or service must be examined to determine the qualities that make those goods or services desirable. Considerations in research into products include: kinds, quality, and size of demanded products; yield of local country, selling quantity, and ratio of exports and imports; quality comparison between local products and imported products; research of color, design, size, style, function, and packing of major local imports; etc.

2.1.1.6 Distribution Routes

The distribution route or channel is the path through which goods and services flow from the seller to the consumer, and the flow of money that accompanies it. The flow of a good in its simplest path is directly from a vendor to a consumer. More commonly, there are intermediaries along the way, such as wholesalers, distributors, agents, and retailers. At each stage in the transaction, the cost increases so that each player can receive a cut for his efforts. Considerations in researching distribution routes are as follows: distribution structure of the products (distribution type, market leader, margin rate by step); research into trade practices of the products; research into the distribution area; research into seasonality, that is, high-demand season and low-demand season of the products (some products are more susceptible to seasonality than others); etc.

2.1.1.7 Pricing

The market value or exchange value of products is largely determined by supply and demand. Considerations in researching price are as follows: research into the price of exports and imports within the area; price comparisons between local products and imports; trends in price fluctuation by season; price differences between the high-demand and low-demand season; etc.

2.1.1.8 Promotions

Promotion is the marketing activity of a product or service occurring through publicity or advertising. Considerations regarding promotion include the following: research into local advertisement, sales promotions, and P.R. (public relations); research into utilization of agencies and establishment of local subsidiaries; etc.

2.1.2   Reaching Potential Buyers

2.1.2.1 Market Segmentation

This is the process of defining and dividing a large market into clearly identifiable segments each having specified needs, wants, or demand characteristics. The objective is to design a marketing mix that precisely matches the expectations of customers in the targeted segment. Few firms are large enough to supply the needs of an entire market, and other smaller companies tend to break down the total market into segments and then choose the relevant parts of the market the firm is best equipped to handle.

2.1.2.2 Target Markets

After market segmentation has been decided, a firm needs to realize the best methods to reach its target market. The firm will develop specific marketing activities to create exposure and product awareness tailored to that specific market.

2.1.2.3 Finding Specific Customers

After target marketing, an exporting firm will hope to receive inquiries and responses from its promotion. The first line of customers consists of importers, and the second line consists of department stores, retailers, and vendors. Due to the Internet, it is easier to get products directly to the final customer than in the past, allowing for the exporter or producer to avoid the costs of the middlemen who often force them to sell their products at lower prices.

2.2   Overseas Exhibitions

One of the most effective ways to find buyers is to attend exhibitions (fairs, or expos), because an exporter can interact face-to-face with many potential buyers at once, and easily make public their companies and items based on general pamphlets, presentations, and a strong first impression. This is never enough to be considered as a thorough inquiry, but it can serve as a good starting point. By meeting potential buyers, exporters can also create interest about their products among similar importers or others networked with contacted potential buyers.

Oftentimes, an exhibition is a gathering of companies in an exhibition hall where each of them pays the hall for an allotted amount of space to set up a company display. Spots need to be reserved ahead of time, and can vary in size depending on the amount a company wants to pay for the space. Contracting a spot well ahead of time also allows firms to pick a location that they predict will see plenty of foot traffic, and therefore more visibility of their products, such as a spot close to the main entrance. Some displays of established companies are quite elaborate and require trucks to unload large props, while others are quite simple, consisting of a table, a couple of chairs, posters and pamphlets. Sufficient preparations are required for a meaningful exhibition to be staged.

Although setting up a booth at an exhibition is the most beneficial way to get exposure to contacts at exhibitions, doing this repetitively can be costly for small companies or individuals. Consequently making a comparative analysis between actual attendance at an exhibition and a simple visit to an exhibition is necessary.

On the one hand, when an exporter takes part in the exhibition, it can: save time in finding appropriate partners; save costs in sales promotions of exhibited items; induce interested companies to be potential buyers; provide opportunities to obtain information; and provide opportunities to learn trends in new technology, human networks, and advanced models.

When a firm's representative simply visits an exhibition, on the other hand, it can: help the firm to understand the transition of products; help the firm to learn about new products and new technology; help the firm learn changes in styles/fads; help the firm learn trends and marketing schemes of competitors; and help firms analyze the tastes of importers.

2.2.1   Preparation

It is important to note that all exhibitions are not the same and may not be relevant to a firm's products. For example, there might be a massive and globally recognized expo in Dubai on green technology and technological advancement, but if you are an exporter of sportswear, it is doubtful that you should be spending your time attending this particular expo because of a lack of potential interest. Another precursor to attending an exhibition is for a firm to determine its purpose in participating, whether it is to find potential buyers, to strengthen relationships with existing buyers, to undertake market research, to collect information, or to assess the response from consumers.

The target market should also be determined after understanding features of the firm's own products and researching market conditions to find the most profitable transactions. A target market determination will consist of multiple considerations, such as quality of the products, ability to pay for products, desire for products, political situation, trends, and fads.

After the target market is determined, proper transportation methods and means need to be considered. There are two main methods of transporting the display items to the exhibition: The first method is to pay the exhibition host or moving company to transport them for an exporter. The second method is for the exporter to transport the items personally. For the proper transportation of the exhibition items, it is generally required to prepare a carnet document, which is a specific customs document that allows exhibition items to be transported across borders for display at any sort of exhibition. The carnet document generally exempts the transportation tariff of items from normal import and export regulations imposed by governments. The items can then be sold during or after the exhibition, or imported back to their initial country free of import duties and approval. For the most part, the carnet currently in use for facilitating importing and exporting is termed "ATA Carnet."

The ATA Carnet is an international handbook issued for exemption from import duties and provide a rapid process of customs clearance for the temporary import or bonded transportation of working tools like movie cameras, sample items, and advertisement items, in accordance with the "tariff convention about extortion of temporary import clearance of goods" of the Customs Cooperation Council. If ATA Carnet holders try to clear items for temporary import to countries affiliated to the convention, the items are exempt from tariffs but must be taken out within a certain period of time. If the items are not taken out within a certain period of time, tariffs must be paid due to a breach of the convention agreements, and the institute extending guaranty to the temporary import and issuing the ATA Carnet in that country must pay instead.

2.2.2 Strategy

To ensure strong attendance at the exhibition, the proper exhibition should be screened and selected, the pre-marketing should be made to properly inform potential buyers of the exhibition, and the exhibition booth should be properly designed and installed.

With regard to exhibition selection, a lot of similar exhibitions are held around the world, so an exporter should thoroughly analyze various aspects of exhibition function to ensure that he is compensated with the best value for his money and efforts. There are sometimes more than several hundred exhibitions and several million visitors every year just in one country. The trend to aggressively visit famous foreign exhibitions to better understand the movement of newly developed technologies and marketing strategies of competitors is increasing. Particulars to consider include functions during the session, advertisements and sales plans of hosts, potential items to be displayed, and the estimated number and type of visitors.

With regard to pre-marketing, if potential buyers are not familiar with the exhibition, they will not just go ahead and visit any specific booth. In order to make the specific booth desirable enough for potential buyers to visit, extending personal invitations, making phone calls, and sending letters is needed to attract the appropriate visitors.

The aesthetic appeal of the display is another vital aspect to induce the number of high-quality customers to inquire about the exhibited products. Keep in mind here that bright lights and flashy props might attract attention, but, for example, if they take the focus away from the product they could prove to be counterproductive. An advertiser needs to find the right mix of flare and substance to attract customers' attention, and focus it on the products. Location is just as important as substance.

The entryway may be the best location, but, when it is unavailable, participating exporters should be sure to avoid corners and other low traffic areas.

2.2.3 Follow-Up Management

While consulting with a visitor about the products at an exhibition, an exporter should create a "counseling file" for that visitor, so that he can reference it when he negotiates with the potential buyer in the future. Files that an exporter gathers throughout the exhibition can provide great marketing leads if they are dealt with properly. Interested visitors should be re-contacted, sent thank-you notes for their inquiries, and receive answers to any specific questions that were not sufficiently answered at the exhibition. Keep in mind the fact that the collected information and potential customers are important assets in pursuing sales promotion of company's products.

2.3 Marketing Planning

2.3.1 Introduction

Once an exporting company has selected its target market and determined its basic direction and guidelines for trade, it can begin to form a marketing plan to insure the success of its exports.

First, an exact analysis of the exporter's company must be made. An unrealistic and unduly favorable assessment of its own company toward a more favorable aspect than reality will only hurt the company's venture. In assessing the exporter's company, relevant considerations include: advantages of the products; disadvantages of the products; opportunity factors of the company; threats to the company's business; financial factors, maximum production, and production capacity for the past few years; determined targets and marketing strategy; analysis of four basic factors including products, marketing, management, and information; etc.

Second, for an analysis of the external environment, external factors beyond the firm's control should be considered: world product trends; possibilities for exporting the products; other trends that may affect sales and profits, such as weather, the economy or the price of oil; etc.

Third, for an analysis of competitors, the following two factors should be considered: ① competitors' products compared against the exporter's own products, that is, examination of whether there is a difference between the two products in price, quality, or an innovation that will make the exporter's product succeed; ② market share in the targeted market, that is, examination of whether there is a monopoly making it difficult to crack the market, or whether there are many small companies competing for smaller slices of the market.

Fourth, research into local markets should be thoroughly made by visiting in person, inquiring to market research institutes, attending overseas exhibitions, speaking with customers, etc.

Fifth, in order to secure a trading partner in the target market, the following factors should be considered: a credit inquiry into the partner should be rigorously undertaken to assess its capacity to trade with; capacity of the partner's role and market share in terms of funds and marketing ability; the partner should be assessed in the importing market; the partner should be assessed in terms of its ability to become a sustainable business partner; the partner should be examined from the viewpoint of its ability to stay ahead of or keep abreast of changing market trends; its ability to be a leader in the market and give the exporting firm's product the greatest viability.

2.3.2 Method of Market Research

The most basic analysis of the means with which to reach overseas markets can be researched through online methods and off-line methods. Online research can be a great tool for saving time and money when the information is available and reliable, because browsing through websites might sometimes reap fruitful results. Government sites can also be useful in obtaining information about public regulation of trade including import restrictions, labeling requirements and tariffs.

At the very least, phone numbers and email addresses can be obtained for people or organizations who can answer questions. The most reliable method is hands-on and physical research conducted by travelling to the expected import country to assess the market in person. Business acquaintances, exhibitions and fairs, domestic organizations, embassies, chambers of commerce, trade-related media and traders' advice facilities can be valuable resources.

2.3.3 Verification of Regulations

2.3.3.1 Customs Regulations

In preparation for customs clearance, it is basically required for the exporter to verify the HS (Harmonized Commodity Description and Coding System) Code of the exported products, because public regulations on exported and imported products including customs clearance are imposed on the basis of the HS Code of the traded goods.

Developed by the World Customs Organization, the HS code is internationally standardized, and offers an all-encompassing method to classify traded products. An HS number has six digits but can have more digits depending on the country. More than 98 percent of world trade markets use the HS code to determine customs tariffs, rules of origin, transport tariffs and statistics, and to monitor controlled goods such as narcotics, chemicals, weapons, ozone layer depleting substances, and goods related to endangered species.

HS Code

The HS (Harmonized Commodity Description and Coding System) is an international system of names and numbers for classifying traded products established by the World Customs Organization and used in determining tariffs on goods moved internationally.

The HS is based on the fundamental principle that goods are classified by the existing status and not according to their stage of fabrication, use, "made in" status or any other such criteria.

The HS nomenclature is logically structured by economic activity or component material. The nomenclature is divided into 21 Sections, and each Section is comprised of one or more Chapters with the entire nomenclature being comprised of 97 Chapters.

World Customs Organization

"The World Customs Organization (WCO) is the only intergovernmental organization exclusively focused on customs matters. With its worldwide membership, the WCO is now recognized as the voice of the global customs community. It is particularly noted for its work in areas covering the development of global standards, the simplification and harmonization of customs procedures, trade supply chain security, the facilitation of international trade, the enhancement of customs enforcement and compliance activities, anti-counterfeiting and piracy initiatives, public-private partnerships, integrity promotion, and sustainable global customs capacity building programs. The WCO also maintains the international Harmonized System goods nomenclature, and administers the technical aspects of the WTO Agreements on Customs Valuation and Rules of Origin."

Source: http://www.wcoomd.org/home_about_us.htm

2.3.3.2 Export and Import

This refers to getting accurate information about tariffs, customs clearances, and other regulations and laws before proceeding with export activities. In the case of exporting to the United States, a valuable resource is the homepage of the ITA (International Trade Administration) – part of the United States Department of Commerce, from which firms can get useful information about current trading issues, the nation, specific industries, etc.

The ITA is an organization created largely to support US industries in their trading activities, but in doing so, it has created a valuable source of information for anyone with plans to trade with the US. Another source of valuable information is the ITC (International Trade Commission) which has compiled a database of US tariffs. The ITC website shows actual records of exports to, and imports from the US, rates of trade increase and decrease annually, and the latest accumulated records by HS, SIC and SITC. For example, you can find records of exports and imports of HS 6 in the US organized by price.

International Trade Commission

"The United States International Trade Commission (ITC) is an independent, quasijudicial Federal agency with broad investigative responsibilities on matters of trade. The agency investigates the effects of dumped and subsidized imports on domestic industries and conducts global safeguard investigations. The Commission also adjudicates cases involving imports that allegedly infringe intellectual property rights. Through such proceedings, the agency facilitates a rules-based international trading system. The Commission also serves as a federal resource where trade data and other trade policy-related information are gathered and analyzed. The information and analysis are provided to the President, the Office of the United States Trade Representative (USTR), and Congress to facilitate the development of sound and informed U.S. trade policy. The Commission makes most of its information and analysis available to the public to promote understanding of international trade issues.

The mission of the Commission is to ① administer U.S. trade remedy laws within its mandate in a fair and objective manner; ② provide the President, USTR, and Congress with independent analysis, information, and support on matters of tariffs, international trade, and U.S. competitiveness; and ③ maintain the Harmonized Tariff Schedule of the United States (HTS)."

Source: http://www.usitc.gov/

Standard Industrial Classification

The Standard Industrial Classification (SIC) was established in 1937, as the United States government system for classifying industries by a four-digit code, which was, in 1997, supplanted by the six-digit North American Industry Classification System.

Standard International Trade Classification (SITC) is a classification of goods maintained by the United Nations, which is used to classify the exports and imports of a country to compare with different countries and years.

Under SITC, goods are grouped reflecting factors: ① the materials used in production; ② the processing stage; ③ market practices and uses of the products; ④ the importance of the commodities in terms of world trade; and ⑤ technological changes.

2.3.4 Credit Inquiry

International trade comes with the added difficulties of differences in language, customs, culture and law, and therefore it is often difficult to determine whether a potential trade partner will be faithful in honoring the agreement. Realizing only too late the fact that a chosen trade partner is immoral can often cost the trader unredeemable amounts of time and money to recover from the difficult situation. One of the methods of determining whether the deal will go through as planned is to run a credit inquiry.

A credit inquiry is usually made focusing on three factors, namely the potential partner's character, capital and capacity:

The first aspect to review is the potential partner's character, the most difficult part of making an assessment of the partner's credit. If a firm fails to properly determine the partner's character, it can face detrimental results. Character refers to the sense of morality, faithfulness, reputation, and overall attitude of an individual or person representing the partnering firm. An exporter is recommended to review the partner's character from the viewpoint of whether this is a real person with whom you could maintain a long-term and serious business relationship.

The second aspect to review is the potential partner's capital ability, which verifies whether or not the trader has enough funds to make the contracted payments. The importer does not have to be rich himself, but his company needs to have the ability to make payments through capital on-hand, projected cash flows or borrowed money. If the importer has a poor credit rating, that is a sign that he has defaulted on payments before, and should raise a red flag.

The third aspect to review is the potential partner's capacity to activate the trade. This is a measure of the importer's ability to successfully sell an exporter's products. It is done by analyzing the company's history, annual sales, the type of corporation (private or publically traded), experience, marketing rights and abilities, and balance sheet. It is important to make sure that the importer has successfully been growing and developing, or is equipped with sufficient capacity, as indicated by factual evidence. Trading with a company that files liquidation, for example, would not be very advantageous to anyone's business.

In obtaining this information, the importer himself might be the worst source. To ensure getting reliable information, an exporter needs to research the importer, enquire to his relating banks, business partners, and other references that can give insight into the company's credibility or credit. Sometimes special agencies such as Dun & Bradstreet Information Service can be used. If the potential importer is a publically traded company, it will be subject to stricter transparency rules and it will be easier to find financial details.

Dun & Bradstreet Information Service

Dun & Bradstreet(DNB, D&B) is a public company which supplies information on businesses and corporations for use in credit decisions, B2B marketing and supply chain management, which is headquartered in New Jersey, USA

Credit inquiries can be obtained through banks by using the method of a bank reference or a trade-related organization, which is called a trade reference. Of course, these organizations only provide the actual credit standing, and therefore the other factors including capacity and character need to be measured separately.

Assignment

1. Selecting the target market through making the comparative assessments of different markets divided into EU countries, African countries, Far-east Arian countries, Middle-east Asian countries, Central Asian countries, and American countries. This should focus on the most efficient enforcement of concluded contracts depending on the particular characteristics of the specified markets, including the specific business customs and behaviors.
2. Finding out the appropriate buyers, send a circular letter, make an invitation to offer, and make an offer for the formation of contract.
3. Examination of the trade barriers that you have faced in pursuing international business transactions, or the potential trade barriers which are expected to be established in the export markets, making consideration of the specified characters of the potential export products.
4. Communications and negotiations with your counterpart to establish branch offices and subsidiaries abroad according to your plan to expand your selected items' market, beginning from the stage of market research. After the communications and negotiations, you are free to choose them as the branch offices or subsidiaries, or just as your general business partner, considering the cost and benefit from the market as well as the characters of the selected goods.

Supplemental Reading

Carr I (2007) International Trade Law, 3 rd edn. Cavendish Publishing, pp. 5–56
Fellmeth AX (2009) The Law of International Business Transaction. West, pp. 327–404
Fletcher I, Mistelis L, Cremona M (eds) (2001) Foundations and Perspectives of International Trade Law. Sweet & Maxwell, pp. 37–42
Honnold JO, Sales Transactions: Domestic and International Law, 3 rd end. Foundation Press, pp. 429–613

International Trade Contracts

3

Learning Objectives

1. Writing and formatting international trade contracts;
2. Defining and clarifying the relevant technical terms, including inquiries and invitations to contract, quotation, and offer, so as to give legal force to effective contract formation;
3. The importance and contractual function of unconditional and unqualified communication of acceptance;
4. The concept of contract by conduct compared with contract by expressed acceptance;
5. Newly established judicial trends reflecting the principle of "mirror image rule" in relation to the battle of forms;

3.1   Introduction

3.1.1   Concepts

3.1.1.1 Contracts for Sale of Goods

The sales contract for goods is a specific or general contract for sellers to transfer the ownership of goods to the specified buyer in return for a specified sum of money. The contract ensures the buyer his rights in securing the goods, and ensures the seller his rights in collecting payment for those goods. Stipulations should be made to clearly define the goods to be traded by quantity, quality and other aspects. If the details are not clearly defined, the importer could receive a shipment of goods very different from his expectations.

3.1.1.2 International Trade Contracts

Essentially, there is no difference between an international trade contract and a typical domestic sales contract, the only variance being that the international trade contract specifies the locations of the contracting parties in separate countries.

E.S. Lee, *Management of International Trade*,
DOI 10.1007/978-3-642-30403-3_3, © Springer-Verlag Berlin Heidelberg 2012

International business transactions are more complex in nature because they are subject to the laws of both contracting parties' countries, making the task of contract implementation more difficult and often calling for dispute settlements.

An "international sale of goods" is the prescribed term for such international business transactions dealing with goods, but trade in technology, services, finance, capital, and overseas construction also requires international transactions or license contracts. The international business contracts for such items other than physical goods are essentially similar to contracts for international sale of goods, and are sometimes accompanied by contracts of carriage, insurance, and foreign exchange (or settlement), which are supplemental to international sale of goods contracts.

3.1.2 Legal Characteristics

3.1.2.1 Remunerative Contracts
A trade contract is a remunerative contract (or compensatory contract) including economic considerations for the certain implementation of contractual obligations such as the delivery of goods. The specified means of payment is normally currency, but occasionally commodities or other goods could also be used to settle the transaction.

3.1.2.2 Bilateral Contracts
Bilateral contracts (where there is a trade of goods for something else, like commodities or money) are for the engagement of both parties concerned, and require obligations to implement the agreement. Specifically, sellers are obligated to make delivery of the contracted goods, and buyers are obligated to make payments under the contract stipulations. In this sense, they are different from unilateral contracts which include making donations or paying rent unilaterally without being compensated.

3.1.2.3 Consensual Contracts
The international sales contract is considered a "consensual contact," meaning that both parties agree upon the terms and pledge to go forth in faithfully executing their respective contractual obligations. The contract ultimately comes to its conclusion through offer and acceptance, although the proceeding and details could be substantially complex.

International business contracts may deal with very large sums of money, and each party will negotiate with the other party under consultation with its specialists in attempts to concede the least and gain the most from the deal. Some negotiations result in a contract to do business together, while many others end without agreement. All bilateral contracts that get signed are consensual contracts as well as remunerative.

3.1.2.4 Informal Contracts

International trade contracts are considered informal contracts because they do not require any form of documentation to be completed. "Informal" even goes so far as to mean that these contracts do not have to be in writing, but instead they can be orally binding agreements. In the SGA and CISG, it is stated that trade contracts are made by oral or written consent, or by partially oral and partially written consent. In business transactions, even in the case of contracting with a trusted member of one's supply chain, it is sensible to have proof of the concerned party's contracted agreements through written and signed proposals to safeguard against unforeseen disputes.

3.2   Conclusion of Contract

3.2.1   Offers

3.2.1.1 Concepts

The term "offer" is defined to be the statement intended by the offeror to induce a binding contract if it is duly accepted by the offeree.[1] For a proper offer to be made, it is necessary for the essential elements of the contract to be clearly expressed in the communications exchanged by the parties.[2] For example, in a contract for the sale of environmently-friendly products, the description of the products inducing the scientific effect on human health, selling price, terms of payment, and terms of delivery including instructions for packing and invoicing, transportation and insurance should be expressed without ambiguity.[3]

UCC

The Uniform Commercial Code (UCC or the Code), is one of a number of uniform acts that have been promulgated in conjunction with efforts to harmonize the law of sales and other commercial transactions in all states of the United States of America.

The Code, as the product of private organizations, is not itself the law, however, the substantive content of the Code has been similarly enacted in all of the 50 states except Louisiana, which has enacted most UCC provisions, with the exception of Article 2, preferring to maintain its own civil law tradition for governing the sale of goods.

---

[1] Murray et al. (2007, p. 62).
[2] *Id.*
[3] *Id.*

3.2.1.2 Invitation to Offer

An offer made to many unspecified potential partners is not generally and technically an offer, but just an invitation to offer. An offer to only a single party is considered an offer. Since the invitation to offer, meaning an action to invite the other party to make an offer,[4] is merely a proposal,[5] an acceptance of such an invitation to offer does not constitute a contract. For the invitation to an offer to be concluded as an effective contract, there needs to be confirmation on the part of the offeror.

The invitation to offer serves as an invitation for negotiations, and may ultimately produce a potential trade relationship that will be mutually beneficial. Parties often seek trade partners through mailing catalogues and other forms of advertisement. If specifications of the transactions are not sufficiently stipulated in the marketing material, they are assumed to be negotiable, and an interested partner will make a counter offer clarifying the specification.

In making an invitation to offer, it is sensible to induce the other party's interest in the negotiation by pointing out the distinguishing characteristics of the items to be offered. The other party is likely to respond positively to such an invitation when it can see the advantages of the potential transactions, which could be read from such invitations or other advertising materials. Considering these points, making the invitation to offer is an important step toward future potential transactions.

3.2.1.3 Firm Offer

Offers are divided into firm offers and free offers. In the case of a free offer, the offeror can make changes or cancel at any time. Therefore, one submitting a firm offer must be sure that he is satisfied with the terms, while one submitting a free offer can simply be "testing the waters."

In Traditional Anglo-American law, an offer can be revoked until such time as it is accepted, except in the case where the offeree has paid "to keep the offer open", which makes it an option. It can even be revoked if it is given as a "firm offer," that is, if it states that the offeror will consider himself bound by it for a specified period of time.[6]

Other legal systems adopt a different – and less dogmatic – attitude to the firm offer by considering it binding in certain circumstances.[7] For example, in the United States, a firm offer for the purchase or sale of goods given by a merchant in a signed and written statement is not revocable for lack of consideration.[8] In the

---

[4] Treitel (1983, p. 8).

[5] United Nations Convention on Contract for the International Sale of Goods, 1980, Art. 14.2 "A Proposal other than one addressed to one or more specific persons is to be considered merely as an invitation to make offers, unless the contrary is clearly indicated by the person making the proposal.".

[6] Murray et al. (2007, *supra* note 8, at 59).

[7] *Id.*

[8] Uniform Commercial Code (UCC) § 2–205.

case of CISG on Contracts for the International Sale of Goods, a firm offer shall be binding, however, unlike in the case of the United States, it does not require that it is made by a merchant and in a signed and written statement.[9]

3.2.2 Special Offers

3.2.2.1 Offer Without Engagement

This kind of offer maintains a "cancellation clause," meaning that the terms are completely changeable just like a free offer. However, an agreement can be reached when the acceptance from the offeree is finally confirmed by the offeror, in which it functions like a firm offer. In the case of offer without engagement, offered prices can change according to market fluctuations or other reasons. This offer is often used for the commercial transaction of commodities that are subject to severe price fluctuations such as natural resources.

3.2.2.2 Offer Subject to Being Unsold

When the offeror makes an offer subject to being unsold, even if the offer is accepted, the agreement can be reached only if stock unsold remains, which is called an "offer subject to prior sale." This offer can be used to sell leftover stock and serves as a safeguard against being stuck with unsellable stock.

3.2.2.3 Offer on Approval

An offer on approval is made when the offeror sends goods with an offer to the potential partner under the condition that if the offeree wants to buy the goods after reviewing the terms he may make payment to get the goods, and, on the other hand, if he does not want to engage in commerce, the goods may be returned to the offeror. This offer can be used if the offeror tries to sell newly developed products or poorly selling products directly to end consumers.

3.2.2.4 Offer on Sale or Return

An offer on sale or return is used when the offeror sends a certain amount of goods under an offer to the offeree to sell the goods, and allows him to return the unsold goods. Publishers in America use this offer often when they try to sell books to book stores. This offer can effectively be used if the offeror wants to sell newly developed products or poorly selling products directly to distributors.

3.2.2.5 Sub-counter Offer

This agreement is made with the offeror's final confirmation, not just with the offeree's acceptance. This is the same as a free offer in that it requires the offeror's

---

[9] Murray et al. (2007, *supra* note 8, at 59).

final confirmation, but is also the same as a firm offer in that it cannot be changed or cancelled at the offeror's discretion.

3.2.3   Counter Offers

If the offeree is interested in the trade terms presented by the offeror, he may return an offer of his own with modifications (if necessary) to fit his needs. These modifications to the initial offer are of effect, and the original offer is no longer effective. Essentially, the offeror and the offeree switch roles respectively through such modification. It is legally clear that the modifications to the original offer do not constitute acceptance, but merely constitute another newly made offer, and more serious attention should be paid to the counterpart's counter offer to proceed in doing business together. Counter offers (negotiations) continue until the two parties come to an agreement, or realize that they will not be able to reach a satisfactory agreement.

3.2.4   Withdrawal/Cancellation

3.2.4.1 Validity Period

An offeror is often indicated as "the master of the offer", which means that offerors have the power to determine the terms and conditions under which they are to be subject to the binding contract.[10] An offer should be as specific as possible in stating the period of time for which it is valid.[11] Offers that fail to provide a specific time for acceptance are essentially valid for a reasonable period of time, which should be clarified depending on the actual situation.[12] The "receipt theory" is generally adopted as the standard by which to determine an offer's validity.[13]

3.2.4.2 Withdrawal

An offer (even in the case of a firm offer) can be withdrawn if the declaration of withdrawal arrives with the offeree before acceptance.

3.2.4.3 Cancellation/Revocation

In the situation where the validity (response period) of the offer is not stipulated, the offer can be cancelled by making sure that the offeree receives the cancellation

---

[10] Mallor et al. (2003, p. 251).

[11] *Id.*

[12] *Id.* at 252.

[13] United Nations Convention on Contracts for the International Sale of Goods, (CISG), 1980, Art. 15.1.

letter before the initial offer is accepted.[14] On the other hand, if the offer states an expiration date on the offer, the offer cannot be cancelled before that date.[15]

3.2.5 Acceptance

3.2.5.1 Acceptance for Formation of Contract

(1) Acceptance

An acceptance is defined as "a manifestation of assent to the terms [of the offer] made by the offeree in the manner invited or required by the offer."[16] The acceptance is made unconditional and unqualified to the original terms of offer of the offeror. It will lose effect if it attempts to modify the terms of the offer or to add new terms, as in the case of conditional acceptance.[17] Conditional acceptance, contrary to acceptance, means that the offeree agrees with the essential part of the offer and agrees to do business with the offeror if certain changes are made or newly suggested requirements are satisfied. Acceptance accompanied by a request exemplifies conditional acceptance, which may be stipulated in the following terms: "We accepted your offer dated May. 10. 2012, subject to the condition of shipment to be made by the end of October, 2012."

If the original terms are modified or augmented by new terms as with the case of conditional acceptance, the resulting documented communication will be a counter offer and therefore a rejection of the original offer and a newly made offer.[18] If the original offeror receives a qualified acceptance and does not express consent, acceptance is considered as not having been made.[19] In judicially determining whether an offeree accepted an offer and created a contract or not, a court will look for evidence of three factors, namely the offeree's intention to enter into the contract, the offeree's acceptance on the original terms proposed by the offeror, and the offeree's communication of acceptance to the offeror.[20]

(2) Intention to Accept

In determining the effective acceptance of an offer, the offeree's actual intention to enter into a contract,[21] the terms of the original offer communicated to him from the offeror should be considered. However, it is sometimes difficult to clarify legitimate acceptance due to its ambiguous expression. For clarity in

---

[14] *Id.* Art. 16.1.

[15] *Id.*, Art. 16.2.

[16] Restatement (Second) of Contracts S.50(1)(1981), cited by Mallor et al. (2003, *supra* note 17, at 259).

[17] Lark v Outhwaie [1991] 2 Lloyd's Rep.132 at 39, *cited* by Murray et al. (2007, *supra* note 8, at 59).

[18] Murray et al. (2007, *supra* note 8, at 62).

[19] *Id.*

[20] *Id.*

[21] Mallor et al. (2003, *supra* note 17, at 259).

determining the legitimate acceptance in reaching an effective contract, it is
sensible for the offeror to specify the acceptance method for an effective contract
in his offer.[22] In indicating acceptance, the offeree must comply with the
specified method of acceptance for an effective contract to be concluded.[23]

(3) Acceptance on Original Terms

According to the traditionally established basic principles of contract law,
broadly known as the "mirror image" rule, an effective acceptance should be
made exactly according to the original terms of the offer made by the offeror.[24]
Any attempts made by offerees to modify the original terms of the offer or add
new terms to it are not considered an acceptance but a counter offer,[25] which is
interpreted to be a newly suggested offer rejecting the original offer. The strict
"mirror image" rule, however, has judicially changed in a more liberal direction
by being interpreted to allow only material modifications to be considered as an
implied rejection of the originally made offer.[26] However, for practical purposes
it is necessary for the offeree to be careful to remain in compliance with the
terms of the original offer in indicating acceptance for a binding contract.[27]

(4) Communication of Acceptance

An effective contract is generally made when acceptance is communicated to the
offeror. Silence, accordingly, cannot be treated as acceptance even where the
offer so stipulates unless there is "course of dealing" between the parties or
where circumstances give rise to an estoppels.[28]

ESTOPPEL

"1. A bar that prevents one from asserting a claim or right that contradicts
what one has said or done before or what has been legally established as true.
2. A bar that prevents the litigation of issues. 3. An affirmative defense
alleging good-faith reliance on a misleading representation and an injury or
detrimental change in position resulting from that reliance."

" 'Estoppel' says Lord Coke, 'cometh of the French word estoupe, from
whence the English word stopped; and it is called an estoppel or conclusion,
because a man's own act or acceptance stop or close up his mouth to allege or
plead the truth.' [Co. Litt. 352a.] Estoppel may also be defined to be a legal

---

[22] Id.

[23] Restatement (Second) of Contracts S.50(1)(1981), cited by Mallor et al. (2003, *supra* note 17,
at 259).

[24] Mallor et al. (2003, *supra* note 17, at 262).

[25] Id., at 262.

[26] Id.

[27] Id.

[28] For the detailed definition of estoppels. See further Chitty, Contracts, Vol. 1, para. 2–066, *cited*
by Lark v Outhwaie [1991] 2 Lloyd's Rep. 132 at 39, *cited* by Murray et al. (2007, *supra* note 8,
at 66).

result or 'conclusion' arising from an admission which has either been actually made, or which the law presumes to have been made, and which is binding on all persons whom it affects." Lancelot Feilding Everest, Everest and Strode's Law of Estoppel 1 (3 d ed. 1923).

"In using the term 'estoppel,' one is of course aware of its kaleidoscopic varieties. One reads of estoppel by conduct, by deed, by laches, by misrepresentation, by negligence, by silence, and so on. There is also an estoppel by judgment and by verdict; these, however, obviously involve procedure. The first-named varieties have certain aspects in common. But these aspects are not always interpreted by the same rules in all courts. The institution seems to be flexible." John H. Wigmore, "The Scientific Role of Consideration in Contract," in Legal Essays in Tribute to Orrin Kip McMurray 641, 643 (1935).

Source: Black's Law Dictionary (2009)

COURSE OF DEALING

"An established pattern of conduct between parties in a series of transactions (e.g., multiple sales of goods over a period of years). If a dispute arises, the parties' course of dealing can be used as evidence of how they intended to carry out the transaction."

"A course of dealing is distinguishable from a course of performance. As defined by the [UCC], 'course of dealing' relates to conduct under other transactions which occurred with regularity prior to the formation of the present contract, while 'course of performance' relates to the conduct of the parties under the contract in question subsequent to its formation. However, in meaning the two expressions are essentially equivalent." Ronald A. Anderson, Uniform Commercial Code § 1–205:86 (1997).

Source: Black's Law Dictionary (2009)

In determining where a contract is concluded, the place at which the acceptance is to be communicated is generally recognized as the place that the contract is made.[29] "Communication" is a term of art which means that the addressee must have been able to take notice of the statement at issue.[30] The statement is regarded to be duly communicated to the addressee if it has been received by the addressee,

---

[29] Murray et al. (2007, *supra* note 8, at 59).

[30] *Id.*

even if for certain reasons he has not read it, for example, because of a systematic problem in his internal office.[31]

3.2.5.2 Approval of Modification of Offer

There may be specific cases in which acceptance of the offer is actually intended by the offeree, but changes have been made to the offer to suit the party's needs.[32] In such a case, if the reply states that the party intends to accept the offer and there are very few minor changes that do not materially modify the originally made offer, it is practically considered acceptance according to the "modified mirror image rule". Major differences such as price, quality, quantity, delivery site and time, and major rights and obligations are too important to be considered trivial changes and are treated as counter offers required to be further negotiated.

(1) Delay of Acceptance

If acceptance is delayed, the acceptance is only valid if the offeror states that it is still valid,[33] because the delayed acceptance is essentially considered a new offer.

(2) Partial Acceptance

Since partial acceptance of the terms of the original offer, for example, the acceptance of only some parts of the quantities specified in the offer, would be inconsistent with the "mirror image rule," it would not be considered a valid form of acceptance under the common law system, but it would be considered a valid form of acceptance of the terms of offer which are commonly recognized by each party under the civil law system.[34]

(3) Acceptance of Sub-contract Offer

A sub-contract needs the offeror's final confirmation if it is to form a binding contract. Acceptance itself in such a case does not constitute a contract.

3.2.5.3 Cancellation

When dispatch theory is applied, if the cancellation notice arrives before or when an acceptance notice arrives with the offeror, the cancellation takes precedence and the contract is no longer valid.[35]

---

[31] Cf.The Brimnes [1975] Q.B. 929, *cited* by Lark v Outhwaie [1991] 2 Lloyd's Rep. 132 at 39, *cited* by Murray et al. (2007, *supra* note 8, at 59).

[32] CISG, 1980, Art. 19 *Formulation of Reservations.*

"A state may, when signing, ratifying, accepting, approving or acceding to a treaty, formulate a reservation unless: (a) the reservation is prohibited by the treaty; (b) the treaty provides that only specified reservations, which do not include the reservation in question, may be made; or (c) in cases not failing under subparagraphs (a) and (b), the reservation is incompatible with the object and purpose of the treaty."

[33] CISG, 1980, Art. 20.

[34] Mallor et al. (2003, *supra* note 17, at 259).

[35] CISG, 1980, Art. 22.

3.3   Performance of Contract

3.3.1   Delivery of Goods

If a specific site has been agreed upon for delivery, it must take place at that location unless both parties otherwise mutually agree to another location. If a specific delivery site had not been determined, the following rules apply:
① In case of delivery through multimodal transportation, goods should be delivered to the first carrier;
② If the parties know that the goods are in a specific site, or are manufactured or produced in a specific site while making a contract, delivery of the goods should be at the buyer's disposal. If a delivery site is not specified, it generally means that goods should be delivered at the choice of the buyer;
③ In other cases, goods should be delivered to the buyer's place of business.[36]

Meanwhile, INCOTERMS® 2010 provides delivery methods for goods differently according to the trade terms in use. For FOB, CFR and CIF, goods are delivered through the ship's rail at the port of shipment in the exporting country. For FCA, CPT, and CIP, goods are delivered to named carriers or a freight forwarder. For DAT, DAP and DDP, goods should be at the buyer's disposal at the named place in the importing country.

Regarding the delivery time of goods, the following apply:
① If the delivery time is specified to a particular month, day, and year, goods should be delivered on that designated date; ② If the delivery time is specified as a period of time, goods should be delivered within the allotted period; ③ If the date or period of delivery is not specified or cannot be confirmed, goods could be delivered within a "reasonable" period of time after the formation of the contract.[37]

If goods are not delivered on the date or within the period of time determined in the contract, the buyer can cancel the deal and force the seller to cover damages incurred in the process. On the other hand, if goods are delivered before the date agreed upon, the buyer may or may not accept the delivered goods at that time.[38] In some circumstances, it would make sense for the buyer to accept the goods early, but early delivery can also cause problems in terms of warehousing and other logistics if delivery is not prepared for.[39]

---

[36] *Id.* Art. 31–34.
[37] *Id.* Art. 33.
[38] *Id.*
[39] *Id.*

3.3.2 Payment

When "cash with order" (CWO) base, advanced remittance base (T/T base), packing Letter of Credit (red clause L/C), or extended Letter of Credit is used, payment in advance is required. In the case of "cash on delivery" (COD), "cash against delivery" (CAD), "document against payment" (D/P), usance base, open account base, current account base, or escrow account base (impound account base), a deferred payment is required within a certain period of time after the delivery of goods.

International Trade Contracts under CISG

O Outline

The "United Nations Convention on Contracts for the International Sale of Goods" drafted by UNITRAL, was adopted at the Vienna Diplomatic Conference in 1980. Sixty-two countries and eight international organizations were in attendance, and the laws took effect January 1, 1988, for the purpose of unifying laws of international trade sales. Its adoption was designed to remove legal barriers to international trade, and to improve the development of international trade by coding uniform practices about the international sale of goods.

The CISG 1980 provides guidelines for the formation of contracts, general rules for the sale of goods, obligations of the seller (delivery of goods and documents, the third party's right to claim, and remedies against a breach of contract by the seller), obligations of the buyer (payment of price, taking delivery, and remedies against a breach by the buyer), transfer of risk, common provisions about obligations of the seller and the buyer (breach of contract prior to a period of time for performance, damages, interests, exemptions, effect of avoidance of contract, and preservation of goods).

O Scope of Application

The Convention regulates rights and obligations of the seller and the buyer occurring in the formation of trade contracts. The Convention clearly outlines – except for any separate explicit provisions – that it is not associated with the effectiveness of contracts in any way, nor is it associated with the effect of property of goods sold in the contract. (Article 4)

O Application Requirements

Article 1 in the CISG (1980) provides that this Convention is to be applied to international trade contracts of goods transacted between parties whose place of business are in different countries. Article 6 provides that parties may exclude the application of this Convention, derogate from or vary the effect of any of its provisions in accordance with Article 12.

In short, the following four applicability requirements are outlined: the parties should have places of businesses or daily residence in different countries, the rules of private international law lead to the application of the law of a contracting state, the country which is the home of the transaction should be a member of the Convention, and there should be no agreements about the exclusion of application of the Convention between parties.

O Main Features

The existing Hague Convention was blamed for its extensive sphere of application while the CISG is applied only when parties' places of business are all in contracted states, or when the rules of private international law lead to the application of the law of a contracting state. (Article 1.1) The Hague Convention divides forms of breach of contract into time of delivery and place of delivery, and since it provides for different remedies, it has been blamed for causing complicated problems concerning other breaches of contract not contained in those two groups, while, on the other hand, the CISG does not divide forms of breach. Instead, it divides breaches into a seller's breach of contract and a buyer's breach of contract, and provides remedial methods for both. The Hague Convention allows avoidance of contract in a wider range of cases, while the CISG only allows for avoidance in cases of fundamental breaches of contract. Thus, the Convention emphasizes consideration to observe good faith and diligence by international traders, which is most unlike the Hague Convention.

O Interpretation

First, the CISG of 1980 needs to have a wider range of application within the realm of international trade, and traders are required to observe good faith and diligence in their commerce. (Article 7.1) Second, issues that are not explicitly settled in the Convention are settled in accordance with "general rules based on this Convention." If there are no such applicable rules, problems are settled by rules applied by the laws of international justice. Article 6 explains that individual contractual agreements between parties override the rules of the Convention. This allows parties to respond to new changes with agility.

3.4   Breach of Contract

3.4.1   Concepts

Common law defines a breach of contract as nonperformance of contract, when either party does not perform all contractually agreed upon factors, without any due reason after formation of the contract.

A fundamental breach of contract refers to instances which deprive a party of the rights it expects to have based on the contract. If a contract was violated from the start of performance of obligation and is a willful (not negligent) breach, it is considered a fundamental breach. If, however, the party in breach did not foresee the results as a consequence of its actions, it cannot be considered a fundamental breach.[40]

When the parties make the contract, it is advisable for them to specify in detail what qualifies as a fundamental breach. This can prevent any potential problems that might otherwise be caused due to a breach of contract. There is no standard period of time given for payment of damages resulting from a breach of contract, so this is another aspect that should be outlined clearly before any contract is signed.

The determination about whether certain acts or omissions constitute a breach of contract or not may generally depend on the stipulated governing law and jurisdictions and therefore the concerned parties to the contract should be diligent in determining the governing law and jurisdictions when making contracts.[41] In some cases, due to the huge expense and inconvenience of placing a legal action before a foreign court, the concerned parties to the contract fail to fully enforce a particular contract.[42]

3.4.2   Remedies

It has been the general rule of most legal systems to seek to avoid creating harsh remedies for minor breaches. However, some breaches are so serious or flagrant that the aggrieved party should have access to the full range of possible remedies including those of consequential damages.[43] If a party has performed the bulk of its obligations, that is, substantial performance, but has failed to perform only to a small degree or on unimportant matters, the aggrieved party may only be allowed to seek light remedy, for example, reducing a contracted price.[44]

---

[40] *Id*. Art. 25.
[41] Ramberg (2008, p. 50).
[42] *Id*.
[43] *Id*.
[44] *Id*.

On the contrary, if a breach is so serious that it deprived the aggrieved party of the intended benefits of the contract, constituting a fundamental breach, the aggrieved party may be allowed to terminate the contract.[45]

3.4.2.1 Remedies Available to Buyers

Types of remedy are determined according to the circumstances of a particular case.[46] According to the CISG, remedies will be different depending on the identity of the concerned party that initially breached the contract. If the seller breaches the contract and the buyer is taking action, the following remedies could be taken: ① claim for performance as measured against the contractual obligations agreed; ② fix an additional period of time for performance; ③ claim for repair; ④ claim for delivery of substitute goods; ⑤ claim for reduction of price; ⑥ avoid contract; ⑦ claim for damages. On the other hand, if the buyer has breaches the contract, the ensuing list should be followed by the seller: ① claim for performance of the contractual obligations as agreed; ② fix an additional period of time for performance; ③ avoid contract; ④ claim for damages; ⑤ confirm specification of goods.

O Right to Claim Delivery of Substitute Goods

If the goods do not conform to the contract, and that nonconformity is a fundamental breach of the contract, the buyer is allowed to order a delivery of substitute goods. This is only possible when the original goods can be returned to the seller in their original state. The notice that substitute goods are to be demanded must be made in conjunction with notices, (CISG Article 39) or at least within a "reasonable" period of time thereafter.

O Right to Claim for Repair

When the lack of conformity of the goods is not a fundamental breach, demanding substitute goods is likely unreasonable due to, for example, the high costs of transport. Minor nonconformity issues can be remediated by the buyer insisting that remedies be made to the goods, as long as it is not unfavorable to the buyer. (CISG Article 46.3) As with a claim to substitute goods, this claim must be made in conjunction with notices and within a reasonable time period. (CISG Article 39)

O Right to Fix Additional Time for Performance

The buyer is allowed to fix a reasonable period of time for performance of the seller's obligations. (CISG Article 47.1) If the requirements are not performed within this additional period of time, it is acceptable for the

(continued)

---

[45] *Id.*

[46] *Id.*

buyer to avoid contract. The buyer is allowed, but not required, to extend the period of time the seller has to fulfill his duties.

O **Right to Avoid Contract**

If the seller fails to perform any of his obligations, the first course of action is simply a notice from the buyer of his intentions if the obligations are not met. For example, if the seller did not deliver the goods within the allotted period of time, and if this is not a fundamental breach of contract, the buyer must notify the seller of his intention to avoid the contract. When the seller receives the notice, the intent of the declaration will take effect. (CISG Article 46.3)

O **Right to Reduce Price**

If the goods do not conform to the contract, irrespective of whether or not the goods have already been paid for, the buyer may reduce the price proportionally. However, if the seller remedies any failure to perform his obligations in accordance with article 37 or Article 48, or if the buyer refuses to accept performance by the seller in accordance with those articles, the buyer may not reduce the price.

O **Right to Claim Damages**

If the seller does not perform the obligations provided in the contract or stated by the applicable law, the buyer can claim damages for a breach of contract. (CISG Articles 74 and 78). This right to claim damages is not deprived by the right to reduce the price. Damages should be compensated to equate to the time that the contract was supposed to be completed, and the coverage should be as much as reasonably anticipated in making the contract. The party in breach may claim a reduction in the damages by the amount by which the loss should have been mitigated, and disciplinary damages cannot be added to the price tag.

3.4.2.2 Remedies Available to Sellers

The seller can, according to the CISG, require a buyer to make payment, take delivery, or perform other obligations.[47] As for the obligation of payment, the seller forces payment from the buyer even though the buyer did not take the delivery. If the seller requires performance, he should not exercise other remedies like the right to avoid incompatible contract. However, since the right to claim damages is

---

[47] CISG Art. 62.

compatible with the right to claim performance, the seller can claim damages and performance concurrently.

If the seller avoids contract (because the buyer rejects delivery or fails to make payment), he can resell the goods, receive the balance between the amount of the contract and the amount of disposal, and any additional damages should be compensated. The seller also retains the right to fix an additional time period for performance, the right to avoid the contract, the right to confirm specification and the right to claim damages.

O **Right to Fix Additional Time Period for Performance**

Unless the nonperformance of the buyer's obligations is not a fundamental breach of contract, an additional period of time of reasonable length for performance may be fixed instead of immediately avoiding contract. The seller can then claim for performance. (CISG Article 36.1) It is possible to avoid the contract if it is not executed within the additional period of time fixed by the buyer.

Unless the seller does not receive a notice that the buyer will not perform within the additional period of time, the seller is not warranted to use other remedies for the breach of contract. But, the seller can claim damages for the delay of performance separately. (CISG Article 36.2) The notice of additional period of time can be a premise to avoid a contract when it makes clear that this additional period of time will be the final extension. (Vienna Convention Art.63.1)

O **Right to Avoid Contract**

The right to avoid contract can be ascertained when either the seller or the buyer fails to perform his obligations as contractually outlined, as long as that breach qualifies as a fundamental breach of contract. (CISG Article 64)

O **Right to Confirm Specification**

The buyer should make specifications of the desired product clear in the description of the product on the contract as far as possible. If specifications which are to be made by the buyer are not made either on the date agreed upon or within a reasonable time after receipt of a request from the seller, the seller may make the specification. (CISG Article 65.1) This prevents the buyer from not providing specific details of the products and thus escaping from his obligations.

If the seller makes the specification himself, he should inform the buyer of the details thereof and must fix a reasonable time within which the buyer may make a different specification. If the buyer, after receipt of such a

(continued)

communication, fails to do so within the time so fixed, the specification made by the seller is binding. (Vienna Convention Art.65.2)

O **Right to Claim Damages**

The right to claim damages stays intact when other rights to remedies are used. The buyer can exercise rights to claim for damages when the seller fails to perform basic obligations as outlined in the contract.

3.4.3 Avoidance of Contract

Avoidance of a contract effectively terminates the agreement upon the party's declaration of cancellation. Avoidance is made when a party declares that the contract has been avoided by the other party, and it is irreversible. In this case, the contract is cancelled "retroactively," meaning that all evidence of a contract is erased, and in law, essentially never existed. The avoidance of contract has no effect on damage claims. Thus, avoidance and claim for damages cannot coexist.

Both the seller and the buyer have the right to avoid contracts. The buyer has the right to avoid contract in the following situations: ① If the seller does not conform to the contract agreed upon, for this is a fundamental breach of contract; ② If the seller fails to deliver the goods at the time or period of time outlined in the agreement. The seller has the right of avoidance in the following situations: ① If the buyer's nonperformance of obligations in accordance with the contract is a fundamental breach of contract; ② If the buyer does not pay within the additional period of time fixed by the seller, or declares that he will not make the payments in the designated period of time.

A party which has already performed all or part of a contract can claim to return what he already provided or paid for to the other party. If both parties have obligations to make returns to each other, this should occur concurrently. Meanwhile, it is certainly possible to declare avoidance of contract if either party anticipates a fundamental breach before the transactions take place.[48] As a matter of consideration, a party which tries to avoid contract should notify the other party so that it can provide proper compensation.

If a contract is avoided, the remainder of the contract becomes void, but actions that have already been taken must be restituted. For example, if a shipment was supposed to come in five separate installments and only one installment had been received before the avoidance of contract, only payment for the first installment would be required. If damage from avoidance of contract persists even after making restitution, parties can make claims for damages.

---

[48] CISG Art. 72.1

3.4.4 Partial Breach of Contract

3.4.4.1 Repairs After Period of Performance

The objective of extending the time period of requirements is to help facilitate the goals of the contract through mutual cooperation. When goods are not delivered on time, and an extra reasonable period of time has been allotted and once again missed, remedial action should then be taken.

In some contracts, the exact period of delivery is not a vital aspect to the deal. In these cases, if the seller is able to remedy the missed delivery within a considerable length of time after the fixed date, this should not be considered a breach of contract fundamental enough for the buyer to avoid the contract.

If a late delivery notice or offer to repair was sent and not responded to, it is still possible to repair. The seller then has an extended period of time in which to make delivery. During this time, the buyer is not allowed to seek remedies.[49] When the seller notifies the buyer of his plans to deliver, the buyer should respond to the notice – either confirming or denying its proposal.[50]

3.4.4.2 Partial Lack of Conformity

A proper balance of interests should be attempted in deference to the idea of contract maintenance, even if the seller delivers partial goods, or part of the received goods is not consistent with the contract's specifications. Also, the buyer can avoid a contract only if the partial nonperformance for delivery or nonconformity with contract is fundamental. In this case, it is acceptable to exercise the right to claim delivery of substitute goods, the right to claim for remedies, avoidance of contract for failure to conform to contract specifications, price reduction, etc.

When a partial breach of contract is fundamental enough to affect the entire contract and to cause damage, contract avoidance is allowed. When this occurs, the buyer must prove that the partial nonperformance of delivery is fundamental enough to affect the entire contract.[51]

3.4.4.3 Early/Late Delivery

Delivering goods before scheduled delivering time is not always a bad thing, but can often cause logistical issues for the buyer in terms of further transportation and storage. If goods are unexpectedly delivered early, the buyer has the right to accept or reject the delivery. If the goods are accepted, the buyer may need to take extra measures for housing and preserving the goods up to the expected time of arrival.

These costs can be passed on to the seller, whose haste was the cause of the inconvenience. If the goods are rejected, the seller must remedy the situation by redelivering during the scheduled period of time. If extra goods are delivered

---

[49] *Id.* Art. 48.3.

[50] *Id.*

[51] *Id.* Art. 51.2.

beyond the contracted quantity, the buyer once again has the discretion to accept or reject. Furthermore, the buyer may accept some or all of the excess goods, and pay the price in proportion to the initial agreement.[52]

3.5 Exemption

A party may in some cases be exempt from performing contractual obligations. While a buyer has supplied raw materials to the seller (producer) to make the products into finished goods that will be sold, if the producer is unable to produce the expected products due to the willful act of the third parties, or an act of God (force majeure), that party may be exempt from his contractual obligations.

If a contract cannot be fulfilled due to an impediment, the party must prove to the other that the nonperformance of obligations was due to an impediment beyond his control, and that the impediment was not reasonably foreseeable at the time of the conclusion of the contract or avoidable.[53] Any party failing to perform its contractual obligation due to the impediment beyond its control may be exempt from damages caused by that impediment for the period during which the impediment exists.[54] If it is possible to remove this impediment, the obligations of both parties will continue as planned. In the case of any partial nonperformance, if neither party can use the received goods, the contract can be avoided.

Once a party realizes that an impediment is beyond circumventing, it must notify the other party within a reasonable period of time. This period of time commences when the party knew, or reasonably should have known, that an impediment was going to prevent proper execution of the contract. If the other party is not notified within a reasonable period of time, the nonperforming party in breach must take responsibility for any damages that resulted from the other party's failure to notify quickly enough.

Assignment
1. Establishment of sales agreement with the students' (actual or assumed) counterparts with the selected items focusing on the avoidance of commercial disputes with them, based on the communications and negotiations made from the previous chapters.
2. Possible remedies which could be pursued under the sales contract concluded in this Chapter, assuming the various types of breach of the obligations, and principles of contracts and other statutes
3. Factors to be considered when concluding an international sales contract with a newly-developed and environment-friendly product which has not yet been commercialized in the domestic market and is not specially competitive in

---

[52] *Id.* Art. 52.

[53] *Id.* Art. 79.

[54] *Id.* Art. 79.3.

price; even though, it could be substantially attractive to high-level consumer groups, compared with the general products that the consumers are familiar with and view as competitive in price.

4. Importance of selection and establishment of the specific conditions in drafting sales contracts which would be suitable and specific to individual products based on their physical and commercial characteristics from the viewpoints of the sales promotion and avoidance of friction with the counterparts.

References

Mallor JP, Barnes AJ, Bowers T, Langvardt AW (2003) Business Law: the Ethical, Global, and E-commerce Environment, 12th edn. McGraw-Hill

Murray C, Holloway D, Timson-Hunt D, Kennelly B, Dixon G (2007) Schmitthoff export trade: the law and practice of international trade, 11th edn. Sweet & Maxwell, London

Ramberg J (2008) Guide to export-import basics, 3rd edn. ICC, Paris

Treitel GH (1983) The law of contract, 6th edn. Stevens, London

Supplemental Reading

Carr I (2007) International Trade Law, 3 rd edn. Cavendish Publishing, pp. 57–100

DiMatteo LA, Dhooge LJ (2005) International Business Law – Transactional Approach, 2nd edn. West, pp. 214–249

Fellmeth AX (2009) The Law of International Business Transactions. West, pp. 327–404

Fletcher I, Mistelis L, Cremona M (eds) (2001) Foundations and Perspectives of International Trade Law. Sweet & Maxwell, pp.37–42

Fletcher I, Mistelis L, Cremona M (eds) (2001) Foundations and Perspectives of International Trade Law. Sweet & Maxwell, pp. 28–36

Folsom RH, Gordon MW, Spanogle, Jr. JA, Fitzgerald PL (2009) International Business Transactions: Contracting Across Borders. West, pp. 52–289

Honnold JO (2006) Sales Transactions: Domestic and International Law, 3 rd edn. Foundation Press, pp. 429–613

Kouladis N (2006) Principles of Law Relating to International Trade. Springer, pp. 201–212

Kouladis N (2006) Principles of Law Relating to International Trade. Springer, pp. 151–178

Zeller B (2007) CISG and the Unification of International Trade Law. Routledge-Cavendish

Terms of International Trade

4

Learning Objectives

1. Responsibilities of the concerned parties to international trade under the special terms of international sale of goods;
2. Specific characteristics of the special terms of international trade from the viewpoints of both the seller and buyer;
3. Contractual relations between the exporter and importer under the special terms of international trade;
4. Basic conditions regulating foreign trade;
5. Passing of property between the seller and buyer under the specified terms of international trade;
6. Passing of the risk between the seller and buyer under the specified terms of international trade;
7. Contractual function and importance of the certification of quality and pre-shipment inspection under the international trade contracts;
8. Special problems relating to general conditions supplied by the trade associations in doing international trade;

4.1 Introduction

4.1.1 General

International trading companies are sometimes not so diligent in making specific and detailed written[1] contracts or are not familiar with the practical and legal aspects in making formal contracts.[2] Even though in a particular circumstance, informal and brief means of contract may actually be applicable, trading companies

---

[1] (Ramberg 2008), *supra* note 48, at 43).

[2] *Id.*

E.S. Lee, *Management of International Trade*,
DOI 10.1007/978-3-642-30403-3_4, © Springer-Verlag Berlin Heidelberg 2012

are recommended to detail a specific contract to minimize the risks that might result from improper contracts.[3]

The main contents of international trade contracts focus on exporters' and importers' obligations and rights under transactions, including, for example, the obligation to make payment under documentary letter of credit and to present the required documents in compliance with the terms of credit and clean bill.[4] Drafting a specific and clear contract is the first step to minimizing the uncertainty in international trade and to proceeding towards successful transactions.[5]

4.1.2   Law Sources of International Trade Contracts

4.1.2.1 Mutual Agreement

Trade contracts respect the principle of "free contract" or "parties-independent principle" which states that remediation through mutual agreement should be the first course of action. Even though traders can construct trade contracts according to mutual understanding under the principle of free contracts, parties are not allowed to violate mandatory trade laws such as foreign trade laws, customs laws, foreign exchange transaction acts, laws concerning foreign investments, or antitrust and fair trade laws. Therefore, all the provisions of the trade contract are required to be in compliance with such mandatory regulations.

4.1.2.2 International Practice/Customary Law

A "Custom" is a commonly recognized traditional pattern of behavior by a specific group of people over a long period of time. Mercantile customary law is a custom many people working in commerce recognize and observe as implied law. This law is applied just like the expressed statute among the merchants because it is highly customary and accepted in the mercantile world. Thus, any practice widely known to the contract parties in international commerce, without other agreement, is considered to be applied implicitly to the contract or the formation of contract because it is considered that parties know their terms.

4.1.3   Governing Law/Jurisdiction

4.1.3.1 Governing Law

When engaging in international business transactions, an agreement is required to be made between the trading partners as to which laws will apply, and those laws might need to be clarified to the contract parties. If the contract parties agree on a

---

[3] *Id.*

[4] *Id.*

[5] *Id.*

governing law in accordance with a mutual agreement, it is to be applied. However, if there is no nominated governing law or if the declaration of the parties' intentions is not clear, the governing law is determined according to the principle of the law of conflicts or private international law.

4.1.3.2 Jurisdiction

Disputes in international trade should be dealt with through discussion, compromise, mediation, or arbitration with the other party. If these methods do not produce a suitable resolution to the case, it is then important to specify which country has jurisdiction in enforcing the international sales contract.

4.2   Basic Terms

4.2.1   General

Clarification and understanding of proper terms are essential to the complete implementation of a concluded agreement. The basic conditions of foreign trade include major terms about product, shipment, quality, insurance, packaging, claims, etc.. The inclusion of Incoterms in clarifying the contract terms will help to comprehensively complement a contract.

In preparing the contract draft, it is recommended that traders focus on the agreement to be proceeded to finally be concluded, while at the same time protecting their rights from being damaged. Therefore, trade terms are surely required to be highly specific, and include arbitration and resolution clauses prepared in the case of the disagreements in the future.

4.2.2   Terms of Quality

Terms of quality refer to specific details about qualitative aspects of the products to be shipped, including but not limited to number, size, shape, color, production methods, origination, and age. Age and origin might be of particular interest when dealing with perishable items, like fruit or vegetable products. Also, quality and contents of the product you are looking to import should be in compliance with importing countries' regulations.

For example, products containing pollution-creating material are generally regulated very strictly in developed countries due to health concerns, but are sometimes not regulated in other developing countries. Buying orders for the industrial goods are normally specified through prior samples or brands, while agricultural, marine, forest, and mineral products are usually agreed upon by standards and product types instead of samples.

Thus, terms of quality are very important to contracting parties. Generally, three aspects are intrinsically related: ① methods of setting standards for qualities of products; ② time for inspecting quality of products; and ③ methods for inspecting quality of products.[6]

4.2.2.1 Setting Standards for Quality

(1) Sales by Sample

Sales by sample are the most widely-used methods for parties to set standards for quality of products. In the case of non-standardized goods such as clothing or shoes, using slightly more vague product descriptions like "as per" or "similar to" instead of "same as" or "up to" is reasonable in order to prevent disputes, especially those relating to market claims.[7]

Therefore, the phrase, "Quality to be considered as being about equal to sample" is better than the expression, "Quality to be fully equal to sample" or "Quality to be the same as sample" in seeking to avoid market claims: The latter pair of terms implies that the product must be exactly equal to the sample received by the buyer, while the former term implies that the shipped documents and the sample share only to close similarities. Sellers should always keep duplicate samples of the shipped product on hand, since this will allow for simpler remediation of product inquiries or disputes.

(2) Sales by Brand

In instances where the item to be shipped is of an internationally known and respectable brand, such as Montblanc, Rolex or Parker, it is normally unnecessary to send samples. Instead, the size and quality is stipulated with the brand name or trade mark, and that is considered as the sufficient description of the product.

(3) Sales by Specification/Description/Standard/Type

If dispatching actually a sample is too cumbersome, such as with the purchase of heavy machinery, the product could be outlined through industry-understood "specifications." One way to do this is to specify the sale by "grade," or quality measurements that are determined by the entity acknowledged to be in charge of standardization internationally organized or established in their respective countries. For some products, there are uniform international standards or national standards, as in the cases of ISO (International Organization for Standardization), BSS (British Standard Specification), KS (Korea Standard) and so on. Sales by types need to consider these stipulated standards as references when measuring quality of goods.

---

[6] Murray et al. (2007, *supra* note 8, at 87).

[7] Market claim means the claim raised against a very light breach of contract just for other purpose than enforcing the contract seriously.

In specified cases, certain abstract standard products are offered, and products similar to them in quality are delivered as follows:

(1) Fair Average Quality (FAQ)

Utilizing this term, parties insure that the supplier is promising to deliver average quality products among like products made in the same year and area. This term is usually adopted for commerce with regard to grain, cereal, or vegetables, and especially for transactions to be made at a future date.

(2) Goods Merchantable Quality (GMQ)

This term binds the seller to deliver products that, at the time of delivery, are in the best condition to be sold. Items that call for this term include timber, lumber, frozen fish, and other like products.

(3) Usual Standard Quality (USQ)

This term requires the supplier to deliver usual standard quality products, as assessed by publically recognized agencies in the exporting countries. This is applied to items like dry grass, ginseng, raw cotton, raw silk and other like products.

4.2.2.2 Standard Time for Quality Inspection

Shipping can be a slow and bumpy process, causing the quality of the shipped products to sometimes vary from the quality of the received products. Because of this potential change, it is essential to stipulate the actual time that the quality assessment will be made. An assessment before shipping is advantageous to the seller, while assessment after shipment is more beneficial to the buyer. Different inspection time has different obligations on buyers and sellers including shipped quality terms and landed quality terms.[8]

"Shipped quality terms" mean sellers are only responsible for the quality of goods before those goods are shipped, while "landed quality terms" put more obligations on sellers, because they bear responsibility for quality of goods until goods are landed.[9]

In international trade customs, there are special terms for transaction of cereals in respect to the time of inspection as follows.

(1) Tale Quale (TQ)

This quality term is a special kind of shipped terms which means that the product will be accepted "as is," at the time of shipment irrespective of its quality at the time of arrival.

(2) Rye Terms (RT)

This quality term is a variety of the landed terms. It means that the product will be accepted according to the quality at the time of arrival of the shipped goods.

---

[8] Murray et al. (2007, *supra* note 8, at 87).

[9] *Id.*

(3) Sea Damaged (SD)

This quality term is a mix of shipped quality and limited landed terms. Here, sellers take responsibility for products wet by sea water, fresh water, or rain water, vapor or moisture damage, or goods corrupted by mold or germs.

4.2.3 Terms of Quantity

Quantity specifications will either be stated in a weight range (such as for a delivery of agricultural products), with a specific weight (such as for the delivery of valuable materials) or a specific quantity (such as for the delivery of automobile). It is also important to specify the point at which the quantity measurement will be made.

4.2.3.1 Unit of Quantity

Fallows are the units and terms that are necessary to specify quantity options:

(1) "Ton"

- L/T = 1,016.1 kg (long ton, English ton, gross ton)
- S/T = 907.2 kg (short ton, American ton, net ton)
- M/T = 1,000 kg (metric ton, French ton, kilo ton)

(2) Measurement

- Liter, gallon, barrel, cubic meter, cubic foot, etc. are often used in liquid measurements.
- SF (super foot) is often used in lumber measurements.

(3) Gross

- Gross = 12 dozen = 12 × 12 (pcs)
- Small gross = 10 dozen = 10 × 12 (pcs)
- Great gross = 12 grosses = 12 × 12 × 12 (pcs)

4.2.3.2 Quantity Stipulation of Bulk Cargo

Certain items including bulk cargo are simply uncountable, and, for the purpose of identifying quantity, have to be dealt with differently from countable items. Some products including coal, ore, grain, petroleum, sand, cement, hay and crude petroleum fit into this uncountable category. For these items, a contract should be made permitting for minor quantity variations by setting forth a range.

(1) More or Less Clause (MOL)

The more or less clause allows for variations of the quantity specified in writing by a maximum of 3 percent. This means that the seller can be slightly carefree in measuring uncountable goods, or can intentionally measure to a point 3 percent higher or 3 percent lower than the quantity specified. Sending 3 percent less of some shipments can result in huge savings for the seller, and so this term in a contract should be used with discretion.

According to Uniform Rules of letter of credit,[10] as long as no statement exists in the letter of credit that declares that "more or less" will not be allowed, 5 percent plus or minus is considered acceptable. But, since there is no such provision in "document against payment" (D/P) and "document against acceptance" (D/A), it is advisable to include a "more or less" clause in the contract like "Quantity, unless otherwise arranged, shall be subject to a variation of 3 percent more or less at seller's option" or, "Seller shall have the option of shipment with a variation of more or less 3 percent of the quantity contracted, unless otherwise contracted."[11]

(2) Approximate Quantity Terms

"Approximate" quantity specifications are similar to a "more or less" clause, except that there are no specific parameters. Putting the word "approximately" or "about" in front of the quantity designated on a letter of credit,[12] allows practical discretion by the seller to make a 10 percent error either way. If the trade is not conducted using a letter of credit, using such vague terminology will likely lead to disputes, and should therefore be avoided.

4.2.3.3 Standard Time for Quantity Inspection

Quantity inspection is either made before the ordered goods are shipped, or once the ordered goods reach their destination. General terms are available to describe either method.

4.2.4   Terms of Price

It is important to clarify whether the buyer or seller is responsible for any given cost in the transaction. In clarifying these costs, it is important to keep in mind currency considerations. Different currencies, as well as constantly changing valuations in the strength of those currencies, need to be clearly explained in terms of which currency is being used, and what (by certain value or date) the exchange rate will be.

4.2.4.1 Price Terms in Incoterms® 2010

In Incoterms® 2010, 11 terms are divided into two groups, that is, the rules for any mode or modes of transport and the rules for sea and inland waterway transport as will be explained later in this chapter. The rules are grouped here as follows according to the allocation of cost between the concerned parties.

(1) EXW

The seller bears the cost required to deliver the goods out of the seller's premise (factory, plantation, warehouse, store etc).

---

[10] UCP600, Art.30(b).

[11] Murray et al. (2007, *supra* note 8, at 89).

[12] UCP600, Art. 30(a).

(2) FCA, FAS, FOB

The buyer bears the main carriage/freight fees required to deliver the goods to the destination port in the importing country.

(3) CFR, CIF, CPT, CIP

The seller bears the main carriage fees required to deliver the goods to the destination port of the importing country.

(4) DAT, DAP, DDP

The seller bears all costs required to deliver the goods from the designated port of the importing country to the buyer (consignee).

4.2.4.2 Other Price Terms

(1) At Station

The seller bears the cost required to deliver goods from the departure station in the exporting country.

(2) Loco

This term is synonymous with EX on spot (Canada), FOB origin and EX point of origin.

(3) In Lighter

The seller bears the cost required to deliver goods from the ship at the port of destination in the importing country to the lighter for unloading.

(4) Variation of CIF

Variation of CIF term includes CIF&C, CIF&I, CIF&C, CIF landed, CIF duty paid, CIF cleared, and etc.

(5) Franco

This term has the same meaning as DDP. The seller bears the cost required to deliver to the buyer after carrying goods to the specified destination in the importing country.

(6) Others

There are other price terms including FOR/FOT, FOA (FOB airport), etc.

4.2.5 Terms of Packaging

Beyond specifying shipment method and quantity, it is necessary to detail the packaging to meet the parties' desires. Packaging is an important trade term because improper packaging can lead to damaged items, which may eventually lead to a huge loss, while over-packaging is obviously a waste of money and at the same time may be in breach of the contract terms. In the case of a business that deals with many international shipments, proper packaging is imperative to insure the product safety at the lowest possible cost. Along with packaging, marking or labeling of packages should also be specified.

Packaging is one step in the supply chain. It is important to ensure proper packaging to save the handling costs of products. Traders, in turn, pass on these savings to customers leading to future profits for their firms. In shipments with varying products, labels will be more necessary to save time unloading, while homogeneous shipments will require less labeling.

4.2.5.1 Packing Unit/Material

The nature of the goods in shipment will determine how many of them will packed together, what material should be used for packing and how the goods should be packed. Specifications are once again vital to ensure proper descriptions of packaging for each individual item for both inner-packaging and outer-packaging.

4.2.5.2 Marking

The purpose of marking shipments with special symbols or letters is to easily and efficiently identify and handle cargo. The following is a list of typical marks

(1) Main Mark
  Abbreviations such as trade brands are in specific symbols so that they can be easily identified. This could be a consignee's mark.

(2) Counter Mark
  In case of potential problems associated with the use of only one main mark, abbreviations of producers or suppliers are added.

(3) Case Number
  This means the running number of the cargo.

(4) Port Mark
  A port of destination or other destination is often marked to avoid wrong delivery locations.

(5) Weight Mark
  Net weight and gross weight are marked to easily understand freight, clearance, unloading, and the level of loss or damage if any occurs.

(6) Origin Mark
  This states the origin of the product specified by the final country of production.

(7) Care Mark, Side Mark or Caution Mark
  These state the ways that the cargo should be carried. Common caution marks include "This Side Up", "Stand on End", "Do not Turn Over", "Keep Flat", "Keep Dry", "Keep Cool", "Perishable Goods", "Liquid", "Fragile", "Flammable" and "Explosive", "No Hooks".

None of the marks above are mandatory for international commerce, but a main mark, port mark, and case number are mandated. A shipment lacking a port mark which is very important for accurate delivery is known as "NM cargo," or "no-mark cargo," and can be an expensive mistake for the consignor to remedy.

4.2.6 Terms of Shipment

4.2.6.1 Shipping Time

Shipping, unlike what its name might suggest, includes all forms of transportation: ships, trains, airplanes, and trucks. Shipping time must be specific because it is not always a quick process, and many aspects of shipping activity might be pertinent.

All aspects of the shipping process are required to be stipulated on the letter of credit. For example, let us assume the task is to import coffee from Africa. First, the coffee must be loaded onto the vessel which will carry it to our country – a cargo ship. Once the ship reaches our domestic port, plans must be prepared for the coffee to be moved to trucks or trains in order to get it to our warehouse. Finally, the coffee would be delivered from the trains or trucks to its final destination (a retail storefront, for example).

4.2.6.2 Stipulation of Shipping Time
(1) Specific Conditions and Period Terms
  1) Time-Frame Terms
    Shipping times can be termed generally as follows: "May shipment" means that the shipment shall be made during May. "May/June shipment" means the shipment shall be made from May to June.
  2) Shipping Time before Specified Date
    "Latest shipping date: May 15, 2012" means that the shipment shall be made no later than May 15, 2012. In this case, "not later than" could be substituted with "until," or "to and by."
  3) Fixed Shipping Period before Specified Date
    The shipment should be made "within two months after seller's receipt of the letter of credit", or "Shipment: during May/June subject to seller's receipt of letter of credit".
(2) Period Terms Specified on UCP 600[13]
  1) From, To (Until)
    This designation includes the relevant date.
  2) After
    This designation includes the relevant date.
  3) On or About
    This includes a designated date, 5 days before and after the date. That is, 11 total days from the starting date to the ending date.[14] For example, "on or about May 25, 2012" means to ship goods from May 20th to May 30th, 2012.
  4) First Half and Second Half of Relevant Month
    This includes the former (1st ~ 15th) and the latter (16th ~ the end of the month).
  5) Beginning, Middle and End of Relevant Month
    This includes the first ten days of a month (1st ~ 10th), the second ten days of a month (11th ~ 20th) and the last ten days of a month (21st ~ the end of a month).

---

[13] UCP600, Art. 3.

[14] UCP600, Art. 3 provides that: "The expression "on or about" or similar will be interpreted as a stipulation that an event is to occur during a period of five calendar days before until five calendar days after the specified date, both start and end dates included."

(3) Expiry Date of Letter of Credit and Shipping Date

In a case in which the expiry date is fixed and the latest shipping date is not fixed on the letter of credit, the expiry date on the letter of credit is considered the latest shipping date. When the expiry date of the letter of credit falls on a bank holiday, such as Sunday, a national holiday, or during incidents that could require closings such as riots, civil commotions, insurrections, wars, strikes, or lockouts, the expiry date should be automatically delayed to the following first business day.[15] It is, however, required that the final shipping date should not be delayed.[16] Therefore, in this case, shipment should still be completed before the expiry date.

(4) General Terms

When the earliest shipping date available is desired from buyers, they usually include such terms as "as soon as possible," "immediately," "at once," or "without delay", which, however, are recommended not to be used as far as possible. This general expression of terms invites claims from the contracting parties. Where these general terms are used on the letter of credit, the bank dealing with the letter of credit can ignore the wording.[17]

4.2.6.3 Partial Shipment/Shipment by Installment

(1) Partial Shipment

Depending on the situation of the market and the buyer's intentions, shipments might be made all at once, or in separate installments over a period of time. When permitting partial shipments, it is advisable to stipulate the number of divisions desired, and the quantity and the shipping period of each division on the contract and letter of credit. Nonetheless, partial shipment is permitted as long as there is no statement of inhibition of partial shipment.[18]

Furthermore, when the same transportation methods are used and shipment is from the same export location and to the same destination, even if on different shipping dates, involving different shipping ports and receiving locations, it is provided that this is not considered partial shipment.[19] But, where the partial issue of bill of lading or draft (bill of exchange) is not permitted, it is evident that partial shipment is not be permitted.

---

[15] *Id.* Art. 29 (a): "If the expiry date of a credit or the last day for presentation falls on a day when the bank to which presentation is to be made is closed for reasons other than those referred to in Art. 36, the expiry date or the last day for presentation, as the case may be, will be extended to the first following banking day."

[16] *Id.* Art. 29 (c): "The latest date for shipment will not be extended as a result of sub-article 29 (a)."

[17] *Id.* Art. 38(b).

[18] *Id.* Art. 31(a): "Partial drawings or shipments are allowed".

[19] *Id.* Art. 31(b), stating that "presentation consisting of more than one set of transport documents evidencing shipment commencing on the same means of conveyance and for the same journey, provided they indicate the same destination, will not be regarded as covering a partial shipment, even if they indicate different dates of shipment or different ports of loading, places of taking in charge or dispatch."

(2) Shipment by Installment

If it is desired, a buyer can stipulate that the shipment should be separated into installments – a practice that is especially helpful when storage space is limited or costly. The letter of credit can stipulate that if one of the partial shipments is not shipped, the remainder of the letter of credit becomes invalid.

4.2.6.4 Transshipment

Transshipment means unloading from one means of transportation and reloading to another means of transportation (whether or not in different modes of transport) during the transportation from the place of dispatch, taking in charge of shipment to the place of final destination stated in the credit.[20]

A transport document can indicate that the goods will or may be transshipped provided that the entire carriage is covered by one and the same transport document.[21] A transport document indicating that transshipment will or may take place is acceptable by the bank, even if the credit prohibits transshipment.[22]

It is common practice to stipulate that trans-shipment is not allowed due to the increased chance of loss or damaged goods in transit. However, even when direct shipment such as "direct steamer by customary route" is stipulated, transshipment is allowed. That is, unless transshipment is not permitted on letter of credit, banks are mandated to accept any transportation documents stating that goods will indeed be transshipped.[23]

4.2.7   Terms of Insurance

The Institute Cargo Clauses (hereinafter ICC) established by the International Underwriting Association and the Lloyds Market Association is applied worldwide for marine cargo insurance. Basic clauses are found in the new policy which was implemented on January 2009, as well as the old policy of 1963. The modified documents as of 2009 are preferred by most developed countries, while developing countries sometimes use 1963 policies and sometimes use both policies interchangeably (as with Korea).

4.2.7.1 Institute Cargo Clauses 2009

The 2009 clauses consist of the ICC (C), ICC (B), and the ICC (A), as the principal policies. Each of these terms defines different levels of marine insurance coverage.

---

[20] *Id.* Art. 19(b).

[21] *Id.* Art. 19(c)(i).

[22] *Id.* Art. 19(c)(ii).

[23] *Id.* Art. 20(c)(ii), see also Art. 21(c)(ii).

The ICC (C) provides for the least amount of insurance coverage possible, ICC (B) is slightly less restrictive, and ICC (A) is the least restrictive, allowing for the widest range of insurance protections. Details are provided below of the specific risks covered by these clauses.

(1) Institute Cargo Clauses (C)

The following risks are covered by ICC (C) unless they are excluded by a general exclusion clause (making it a positive system):

① Loss of or damage to the subject-matter insured reasonably attributable to ⓐ fire or explosion; ⓑ stranding, grounding; ⓒ sinking or capsizing; ⓓ overturning or derailment of land conveyance; ⓔ collision or contact of vessel craft or conveyance with any external object other than water; ⓕ discharge of cargo at a port of distress;

② Loss or damage to the subject-matter insured caused by ⓐ general average sacrifice; ⓑ jettison;

③ General average and salvage charges;

④ Proportion of liability under the contract of affreightment "Both to Blame Collision" Clause.

(2) Institute Cargo Clauses (B)

ICC (B) is for compensating the following loss and damage, excluding the general exclusion clause:

① Loss of or damage to the subject-matter insured reasonably attributable to the following reasons: ⓐ fire or explosion; ⓑ stranding, grounding, sinking, or capsizing; ⓒ overturning or derailment of land conveyance; ⓓ collision or contact of ship, craft or conveyance with other external substance other than water; ⓔ discharge of cargo at the port of distress; ⓕ earthquake, eruption of volcanoes, and lightening.

② Loss of or damage to the cargo insured caused by the following reasons: ⓐ general average sacrifice; ⓑ jettison or washing overboard; ⓒ entry of sea, lake or river water into vessel, craft, hole, conveyance, container, lift van or place of storage;

③ Total loss of any package lost overboard or dropped whilst loading on to, or unloading from, vessel or craft.

④ General average and salvage charges.

⑤ Proportion of liability under the contract of affreightment "Both to Both Blame Collision" Clause.

(3) Institute Cargo Clauses (A)

ICC (A) is designed to cover all risks of loss and damage to the subject-matter insured due to all risks other than the risks included in the general exclusion clause, the unseaworthiness and unfitness exclusion clause, the war exclusion clause and the strike exclusion clause. This is the most commonly bought insurance in bulk deals.

An example for Insurance Terms: "all shipments shall be covered subject to ICC (A) for a sum equal to the amount of the invoice plus 10 (ten) percent. War risk and/or any other additional insurance required by the buyer shall be covered at his own expense. All policies shall be made out in U.S. Dollars and payable in Busan."

4.2.7.2 Institute Cargo Clauses 1963

Pertinent clauses here include ICC (FPA), ICC (WA) and ICC (A/R). FPA stands for "Free from Particular Average," WA stands for "With Average" and A/R for "All Risks". The ICC clause of 1963 calls for covering risks as follows:

(1) ICC (FPA)

The term of "Free from Particular Average" (FPA) means, in insurance terms, that of "free from partial loss." Here, the insurance company is not responsible for partial loss. FPA terms might be referred to as "Total Loss Only" terms because, in order for the insured to be compensated the damages from the insurer, a total loss of goods must be realized. Insurance, under the F.P.A terms, does cover perils of the sea, such as sinking or collision with an iceberg or another vessel, as well as circumstances that are generally out of human control. This coverage is often used for goods stored on the deck or as bulk cargo, and for scrap products like scrap metal or waste paper.

(2) ICC (WA)

"With Average" (WA) coverage is essentially the same as FPA coverage, but it is more inclusive in that it is extended to cover damage caused by heavy weather. Like FPA, this coverage can usually extend to cover damage incurred due to theft and non-delivery of the entire package insured.

(3) ICC (A/R)

"All risks" (A/R) coverage covers all risks excluding damage from the following: ① Loss from willful misconduct of the insured; ② Inherent vice or nature of the goods insured; ③ Loss from delay in transit; ④ Ordinary loss or damages not from maritime perils; ⑤ Risks from war, strike, riot, and civil commotion, and loss caused by capture.

4.2.7.3 Extraneous Clauses

(1) War, Strikes, Riots and Civil Commotion (W/SRCC)

This clause included in maritime insurance covers risks such as hostile actions and leftover mines. The possibility of war occurring in countries such as Iraq and Afghanistan will be noticeably higher than the global average, which would increase the chance of having this clause included in an insurance policy.

(2) Seizure and Capture (S&C)

Coverage is sometimes warranted to protect against pirates, who will operate in parts of the world.

(3) Contact with Oil or Other Cargoes (COOC)

This clause covers contact with oil or other cargoes.

(4) Theft, Pilferage and Non-delivery (TPND)

This clause covers theft, pilferage and non-delivery of the shipped cargo.

4.2.8 Terms of Payment

4.2.8.1 Means of Payment
When the parties determine and negotiate terms of payment, the means and date of the payment suitable for the purchase or sale should be indicated.

(1) Bill of Exchange (Draft)

General laws regulating international bills of exchange come from the Bills of Exchange Act 1882 (United Kingdom). A bill of exchange requires the person (drawee) to make payment as outlined in the form, which can be made immediately or at a specific date in the future.

(2) Other settlements

1) Cash or Check

In the cases of the terms such as "cash with order" (CWO), "cash on delivery" (COD), and "cash against document" (CAD), payments are made by cash or check without bills of exchange.

2) Exchange Settlement

This is used as advance payment or a down payment for deals that will be paid in separate installments over a period of time. Payment may be made through telegraphic transfer (T/T) or mail transfer (M/T).

3) Checks

Checks or traveler's checks are often used.

4) Goods

In a barter agreement, trade is made with goods, not actual money.

4.2.8.2 Settlement Terms

(1) Advance Payment

1) Cash with Order (CWO)

This term means that payment is settled immediately when making an order.

2) Remittance in Advance

This means that the goods are paid for before they have been exported and received.

(2) Concurrent Payment

1) At Sight

Payment is made against a documentary bill that is issued by a sight Letter of Credit.

2) Document against Acceptance (D/A)

Payment is made against acceptance of documents.

3) Cash on Delivery (COD)

Payment is made upon delivery of goods, delivery order (D/O) or warehouse warranty. Payment methods other than drafts are used for payments.

4) Cash against Document (CAD)

This is made upon delivery of transport documents including the bill of lading, and the payment means are the same as with cash on delivery.

(3) Deferred Payment

A deferred payment would be made when the merchant obtains authorization from the bank to defer the settlement process.

1) Usance Basis

Payment is made after the shipment against documentary bills under a usance letter of credit. "Days after sight" (D/S) base and "days after delivery" (D/D) base are most commonly used. In this context, "usance" refers to paying a bill over a period of time.

2) Document against Acceptance (D/A)

A deferred payment is made as the payment collection without issuing a letter of credit.

3) Escrow Account

Escrow means that money will be put aside, via a third party, and will be given to the grantee only after fulfillment of the terms of the agreement.

4) Open Account (Current Account)

If the two companies export to and import from each other frequently, they can balance their trade books after each transaction, and save the necessity of making full payments to each transaction over and over again.

(4) Mixed Payment

Progressive payments and long-term deferred payments are often made along with an advance payment, concurrent payment, and deferred payment, and are mostly made in installments according to agreement terms. For the long-term deferred payments used in major transactions of manufacturing plants, large machinery, railroads or trains, payments by installment are made by an advance payment (usually 10 percent), payment by working progress, and payment in delivery. The remainder of the payment is made through deferred payments normally over several years' duration.

4.3   Incoterms® 2010

4.3.1   Provisions of Incoterms

4.3.1.1 Jurisdiction of Risk

Incoterms clearly outlines the burden of risk for sellers and buyers in international commerce dealings.

4.3.1.2 Allocation of Cost

Among costs occurring in delivery of goods from production to final destination and consignee, Incoterms clearly states that the seller should bear costs occurring before a certain point, after which the buyer should bear the costs. Therefore, unless otherwise stipulated in the contract, jurisdiction will follow these mandates. Determination of cost-bearing obligations is directly connected to the price of the transaction, so it affects the profit or unit price of the exports.

4.3.1.3 Obligation

Incoterms states to whom the obligations belong and the manner of the obligations to be fulfilled. Obligations include making contract of carriage, making insurance contract, making export administrative formalities (export license, pre-shipment inspection, quarantine, export clearance), making import administrative formalities (import license, quarantine, import clearance), making different kinds of notices (goods delivery/shipment notice, carrier/ship designation notice, goods delivery place/point notice), requiring different kinds of cooperation (cooperation to offer documents, offering information of carriage/insurance), making goods delivery, taking goods, and making payments.

4.3.2 Trade Terms

Trade terms under Incoterms® 2010 are divided into two groups, that is, the rules for any mode or modes of transport and the rules for sea and inland waterway transport. The first class of the rules can be used irrespective of the mode of transport selected and irrespective of whether one or more than one mode of transport is employed, which include EXW, FCA, CPT, CIP, DAT, DAP and DDP. They can be used even when there is no maritime transport at all. These rules can conveniently be used where a ship is used for only a part of the carriage. In the second class of rules, the point of delivery and the place to which the goods are carried to the buyer are both ports, hence lading "sea and inland waterway" rules. FAS, FOB, CFR and CIF belong to this class.[24]

4.3.2.1 Ex Works (EXW)

This rule can be used irrespective of the mode of transport selected and may also be used where more than one mode of transport is employed. It is suitable for domestic trade, while FCA is usually more appropriate for international trade. "Ex Works" means that the seller delivers when it places the goods at the disposal of the buyer at the seller's premises or at another named place (i.e., "works", factory, warehouse, etc.). The seller does not need to load the goods on any collecting vehicle, nor does it need to clear the goods for export, where such clearance is applicable.

The parties are well advised to specify as clearly as possible the point within the named place of delivery, as the costs and risks to that point are for the account of the seller. The buyer bears all costs and risks involved in taking the goods from the agreed point, if any, at the named place of delivery.

EXW represents the minimum obligation for the seller. The rule should be used with care as:

① The seller has no obligation to the buyer to load the goods, even though in practice the seller may be in a better position to do so. If the seller does load the

---

[24] ICC, Incoterms® 2010, 7 (2010).

goods, it does so at the buyer's risk and expense. In cases where the seller is in a better position to load the goods, FCA basis, which obliges the seller to do so at its own risk and expense, is usually more appropriate.

② A buyer who buys from a seller on an EXW basis for export needs to be aware that the seller has an obligation to provide only such assistance as the buyer may require to effect that export: the seller is not bound to organize the export clearance. Buyers are therefore well advised not to use EXW if they cannot directly or indirectly obtain export clearance.

③ The buyer has limited obligations to provide to the seller any information regarding the export of the goods. However, the seller may need this information for, e.g., taxation or reporting purposes.[25]

If a seller wants a buyer to be responsible for loading the goods onto a particular vehicle upon delivery, this intention should be properly and explicitly stated in the agreement. If the buyer received goods at the seller's premises but cannot clear them for export, in order to change to FCA the seller agrees that he will load at his cost and risk. If any specific drop-off within the designated place for delivery is not agreed upon, or there are several viable places available, the seller can choose a proper point to unload at his convenience.

Obligations of Parties under Ex Works

The seller is required to:

① Supply conforming goods, which have been weighed, checked, measured and packed for delivery; ② Supply the invoice and any documents confirming conformity with terms that have been agreed by whatever method has been agreed, or by the agreed means including by electronic communication; ③ Deliver goods to buyer by placing them at the buyer's disposal or otherwise ensuring they may be collected, at the place agreed or at the usual place for such delivery, at the time agreed, and give the buyer sufficient notice of the fact without delay.

The buyer is required to:

① Accept delivery of and pay for the goods; ② Obtain appropriate licenses, authorizations for the export of the goods, and comply with customs formalities, whether in the country of delivery or in the exporting country or in a country of transit; ③ Pay any costs incidental to the exportation of the goods including reshipment inspection costs, any official charges and the seller's costs in rendering assistance requested by the buyer.

4.3.2.2 Free Carrier (FCA)

This rule may be used irrespective of the mode of transport selected and may also be used where more than one mode of transport is employed. "Free Carrier" means that

---

[25] *Id.*, at 15.

the seller delivers the goods to the carrier or another person nominated by the buyer at the seller's premises or another named place. The parties are well advised to specify as clearly as possible the point within the named place of delivery, as the risk passes to the buyer at that point.

If the parties intend to deliver the goods at the seller's premises, they should identify the address of those premises as the named place of delivery. If, on the other hand, the parties intend the goods to be delivered at another place, they must identify a different specific place of delivery. FCA requires the seller to clear the goods for export, where applicable. However, the seller has no obligation to clear the goods for import, pay any import duty or carry out any import customs formalities.[26]

Obligations of Parties under FCA

The seller is required to: ① Supply conforming goods, which have been weighed, checked, measured and packed for delivery; ② Supply the invoice and any documents confirming conformity with the terms that have been agreed by whatever method they have been agreed upon, or by the agreed means including by electronic communication. ③ Deliver the goods to the buyer by placing them in the charge of the carrier named by the buyer at the place agreed for delivery, in the manner agreed upon or which is customary for the place of delivery, or by loading them onto the carrier's vehicle if that has been agreed.

The buyer is required to: ① Accept delivery of and pay for the goods; ② obtain appropriate licenses, authorizations for the export of the goods, and comply with customs formalities, whether in the country of delivery or in the exporting country or in a country of transit; ③ Pay any costs incidental to the exportation of the goods and any costs incurred by the seller in giving any assistance which has been requested by the buyer including costs associated with the provision of documents or electronic messages.

4.3.2.3 Free Alongside Ship (Named Port of Shipment) (FAS)

This rule is to be used only for sea or inland waterway transport. "Free Alongside Ship" means that the seller delivers when the goods are placed alongside the vessel (e.g., on a quay or a barge) nominated by the buyer at the named port of shipment. The risk of loss of or damage to the goods passes when the goods are alongside the ship, and the buyer bears all costs from that moment onwards.

The parties are well advised to specify as clearly as possible the loading point at the named port of shipment, as the costs and risks to that point are for the account of the seller and these costs and associated handling charges may vary according to the practice of the port. The seller is required either to deliver the goods alongside the

---

[26] *Id.*, at 23.

ship or to procure goods already so delivered for shipment. The reference to "procure" here caters for multiple sales down a chain ("string sales"), particularly common in the commodity trades.

Where the goods are in containers, it is typical for the seller to hand the goods over to the carrier at a terminal and not alongside the vessel. In such situations, the FAS rule would be inappropriate, and the FCA rule should be used. FAS requires the seller to clear the goods for export, where applicable. However, the seller has no obligation to clear the goods for import, pay any import duty or carry out any import customs formalities. The FAS term is frequently used in circumstances where the buyer has a matching contract CIF terms.[27]

Obligations of Parties under FAS

The seller is required to: ① Supply conforming goods, packed appropriately or in accordance with the contract, and the commercial invoice or equivalent electronic message which has been agreed upon; ② Deliver the goods to the buyer by placing them alongside the vessel or the loading berth which has been notified by the buyer in the manner which is usual or customary at that port for such delivery, at the time agreed upon and without delay, giving the buyer sufficient notice of the fact; ③ Provide any assistance requested by the buyer in respect of obtaining documents facilitating export and providing information to enable the goods to be insured.

The buyer is required to: ① Give sufficient notice to the seller of the time and location of the delivery having, presumably, contracted for the carriage of the goods from the proof of shipment and bear any costs occasioned by his failure to do so; ② Obtain any appropriate licenses, authorizations for the export of the goods, and comply with customs formalities, whether in the country of delivery or in the exporting country or in a country of transit; ③ Pay any costs incidental to the exportation of the goods including pre-shipment inspection costs, any official charges and the seller's costs in rendering assistance request by the buyer;

4.3.2.4 Free on Board (Named Port of Shipment) (FOB)

This rule is to be used only for sea or inland waterway transport. "Free on Board" means that the seller delivers the goods on board the vessel nominated by the buyer at the named port of shipment or procures the goods already so delivered. The risk of loss of or damage to the goods passes when the goods are on board the vessel, and the buyer bears all costs from that moment onwards. The seller is required either to deliver the goods on board the vessel or to procure goods already so delivered for shipment. The reference to "procure" here caters for multiple sales down a chain ('string sales'), particularly common in the commodity trades.

---

[27] *Id.*, at 79.

FOB may not be appropriate where goods are handed over to the carrier before they are on board the vessel, for example goods in containers, which are typically delivered at a terminal. In such situations, the FCA rule should be used. FOB requires the seller to clear the goods for export, where applicable. However, the seller has no obligation to clear the goods for import, pay any import duty or carry out any import customs formalities.

Obligations of Parties under FOB

The seller is required to: ① Supply conforming goods, packed appropriately or in accordance with the contract, and any documents confirming conformity which have been agreed upon and supply a commercial invoice or its electronic equivalent; ② Deliver the goods to the buyer by placing them on board, that is over the rail of the vessel which has been notified by the buyer, in the manner which is usual or customary at that port for such delivery, at the time agreed upon and without delay, giving the buyer sufficient notice of the fact.

The buyer is required to: ① Give sufficient notice to the seller of the time and location of the delivery having, presumably, contracted for the carriage of the goods from the port of shipment, bear any costs occasioned by his failure to do so and bear the risk of loss or damage to the goods from the time they pass over the ship's rail; ② Obtain any appropriate licenses, authorizations for the import of the goods, and comply with customs formalities for importation whether in the country of destination or in a country of transit; ③ Pay any costs incidental to the importation of the goods, bear the risk in those goods from the time of their delivery and bear the costs of the provision of assistance by the seller at the request of the buyer.

4.3.2.5 Cost and Freight (CFR)

This rule is to be used only for sea or inland waterway transport. "Cost and Freight" means that the seller delivers the goods on board the vessel or procures the goods already so delivered. The risk of loss of or damage to the goods passes when the goods are on board the vessel. The seller must contract for and pay the costs and freight necessary to bring the goods to the named port of destination. When CPT, CIP, CFR or CIF are used, the seller fulfils its obligation to deliver when it hands the goods over to the carrier in the manner specified in the chosen rule and not when the goods reach the place of destination.

This rule has two critical points, because risk passes and costs are transferred at different places. While the contract will always specify a destination port, it might not specify the port of shipment, which is where risk passes to the buyer. If the shipment port is of particular interest to the buyer, the parties are well advised to identify it as precisely as possible in the contract.[28]

---

[28] *Id.*, at 95.

4.3.2.6 Cost, Insurance and Freight . . . (Named Port of Destination) (CIF)

This rule is to be used only for sea or inland waterway transport. "Cost, Insurance and Freight" means that the seller delivers the goods on board the vessel or procures the goods already so delivered. The risk of loss of or damage to the goods passes when the goods are on board the vessel. The seller must contract for and pay the costs and freight necessary to bring the goods to the named port of destination.

The seller also contracts for insurance cover against the buyer's risk of loss of or damage to the goods during the carriage. The buyer should note that under CIF the seller is required to obtain insurance only on minimum coverage. Should buyers wish to have more insurance protection, it will need either to agree as much expressly with the seller or to make their own additional insurance arrangements.

When CPT, CIP, CFR, or CIF are used, the seller fulfils its obligation to deliver when it hands the goods over to the carrier in the manner specified in the chosen rule and not when the goods reach the place of destination.

This rule has two critical points, because risk passes and costs are transferred at different places. While the contract will always specify a destination port, it might not specify the port of shipment, which is where the risk passes to the buyer. If the shipment port is of particular interest to the buyer, the parties are well advised to identify it as precisely as possible in the contract. This is the most recognizable term associated with the export trade from which the mercantile custom has evolved.[29]

Obligations of Parties under CIF

The seller is required: ① To ship goods of the description contained in the contract and clear the goods for export or to buy conforming goods afloat; ② If the goods are not bought afloat, to procure a contract of carriage by sea under which the goods will be delivered at the destination agreed by the contract and obtain the bill of lading as evidence of having done so; ③ To arrange, if this has not already been done, insurance on terms current in the trade which will be available for the benefit of the buyer and provide a policy or insurance document which entitles the buyer to make a claim against the insurer; ④ To make out an invoice which normally will debit the buyer with the agreed price, or the actual cost, commission charges, freight, and insurance premium, and credit him for the amount of the freight which he will have to pay to the ship-owner on delivery of the goods at the port of destination. ⑤ To tender these documents in the manner agreed upon whether by presentation directly, transmission by electronic means or otherwise; the bill of lading, insurance policy and invoice to the buyer, together with any other documents which may be agreed upon between the parties and/or might be required by the customs of the trade so that he may obtain delivery of the goods or coverage for their loss, if they are lost on the voyage, and know what freight he has to pay.

---

[29] *Id.*, at 105.

The buyer is required: ① To receive the goods at the agreed port of destination and bear, with the exception of the freight and marine insurance, all costs and charges incurred in respect of the goods in the course of their transit by sea until their arrival at the port of destination, as well as unloading costs, including lighterage and wharfage chares, unless such costs and charges have been included in the freight or collected by the carrying company at the time freight was paid; ② If war insurance is to be provided, to bear the cost; ③ To bear all risks to the goods from the time when they shall have effectively passed the ship's rail at the port of shipment; ④ If the buyer has reserved for himself the right to determine the period within which the goods are to be shipped and/or the right to choose the port of destination, and he fails to give instructions in time, he must bear the additional costs incurred as a result and all risks of the goods from the date of the expiry of the period fixed for shipment, provided always that the goods have been appropriated to the contract, that is to say, clearly set aside or otherwise identified as the contract goods; ⑤ To pay all customs duties as well as any other duties and taxes payable upon importation; ⑥ To obtain and provide at his own risk and expense any import license or permit or the like which he may require for the importation of the goods at the destination.

4.3.2.7 Carriage Paid to (Named Place of Destination) (CPT)

This rule may be used irrespective of the mode of transport selected and may also be used where more than one mode of transport is employed. "Carriage Paid to" means that the seller delivers the goods to the carrier or another person nominated by the seller at an agreed place (if any such place is agreed upon between the parties) and that the seller must contract for and pay the costs of carriage necessary to bring the goods to the named place of destination. When CPT, CIP, CFR or CIF are used, the seller fulfils its obligation to deliver when it hands the goods over to the carrier and not when the goods reach the place of destination.

This rule has two critical points, because risk passes and costs are transferred at different places. The parties are well advised to identify as precisely as possible in the contract both the place of delivery, where the risk passes to the buyer, and the named place of destination to which the seller must contract for the carriage. The parties are also well advised to identify as precisely as possible the point within the agreed place of destination, as the costs to that point are for the account of the seller. The seller is advised to procure contracts of carriage that match this choice precisely. If the seller incurs costs under its contract of carriage related to unloading at the named place of destination, the seller is not entitled to recover such costs from the buyer unless otherwise agreed upon between the parties.[30]

---

[30] *Id.*, at 33.

4.3.2.8 Carriage and Insurance Paid to (Named Place of Destination) (CIP)

This rule may be used irrespective of the mode of transport selected and may also be used where more than one mode of transport is employed. The rule is based on the model provided by the CIF contract. "Carriage and Insurance Paid to" means that the seller delivers the goods to the carrier or another person nominated by the seller at an agreed place (if any such place is agreed upon between the parties) and that the seller must contract for and pay the costs of carriage necessary to bring the goods to the named place of destination.

The seller also contracts for insurance coverage against the buyer's risk of loss of or damage to the goods during the carriage. The buyer should note that under CIP the seller is required to obtain insurance only on minimum coverage. Should the buyer wish to have more insurance protection, it will need to agree as much expressly with the seller or to make its own extra insurance arrangements. When CPT, CIP, CFR or CIF are used, the seller fulfils its obligation to deliver when it hands the goods over to the carrier and not when the goods reach the place of destination.[31]

4.3.2.9 Delivered at Terminal (Named Terminal at Port or Place of Destination) (DAT)

This rule may be used irrespective of the mode of transport selected and may also be used where more than one mode of transport is employed. "Delivered at Terminal" means that the seller delivers when goods, that have been unloaded from the arriving means of transport, are placed at the disposal of the buyer at a named terminal at the named port or place of destination. "Terminal" includes any place, whether covered or not, such as a quay, warehouse, container yard or road, rail or air cargo terminal. The seller bears all risks involved in bringing the goods to and unloading them at the terminal at the named port or place of destination.

The parties are well advised to specify as clearly as possible the terminal and, if possible, a specific point within the terminal at the agreed port or place of destination, as the risks to that point are for the account of the seller. The seller is advised to procure a contract of carriage that matcher this choice precisely. Moreover, if the parties intend the seller to bear the risks and costs involved in transporting and handling the goods from the terminal to another place, then the DAP or DDP rules should be used. DAT requires the seller to clear the goods for export, where applicable. However, the seller has no obligation to clear the goods for import, pay any import duty or carry out any import customs formalities.[32]

---

[31] *Id.*, at 41.

[32] *Id.*, at 53.

4.3.2.10 Delivered at Place (Named Place of Destination) (DAP)

This rule may be used irrespective of the mode of transport selected and may also be used where more than one mode of transport is employed. "Delivered at Place" means that the seller delivers when the goods are placed at the disposal of the buyer on the arriving means of transport ready for unloading at the named place of destination. The seller bears all risks involved in bringing the goods to the named place.

The parties are well advised to specify as clearly as possible the point within the agreed place of destination, as the risks to that point are for the account of the seller. The seller is advised to procure contracts of carriage that match this choice precisely. If the seller incurs costs under its contract of carriage related to unloading at the place of destination, the seller is not entitled to recover such costs from the buyer unless otherwise agreed between the parties. DAP requires the seller to clear the goods for export, where applicable. However, the seller has no obligation to clear the goods for import, pay any import duty or carry out any import customs formalities. If the parties wish the seller to clear the goods for import, pay any import duty and carry out any import customs formalities, the DDP term should be used.

4.3.2.11 Delivered Duty Paid (Named Place of Destination) (DDP)

This rule may be used irrespective of the mode of transport selected and may also be used where more than one mode of transport is employed. "Delivered Duty Paid" means that the seller delivers the goods when the goods are placed at the disposal of the buyer, cleared for import on the arriving means of transport ready for unloading at the named place of destination. The seller bears all the costs and risks involved in bringing the goods to the place of destination and has an obligation to clear the goods not only for export but also for import, to pay any duty for both export and import and to carry out all customs formalities.

DDP represents the maximum obligation for the seller. The parties are well advised to specify as clearly as possible the point within the agreed place of destination, as the costs and risks to that point are for the account of the seller. The seller is advised to procure contracts of carriage that match this choice precisely. If the seller incurs costs under its contract of carriage related to unloading at the place of destination, the seller is not entitled to recover such costs from the buyer unless otherwise agreed upon between the parties.[33]

4.4   Illustrated Forms of International Trade Contract

4.4.1   General International Contract

The international contract is required to be sufficiently detailed and workable so as to cope with all foreseeable and unforeseeable developments of events. Making a proper and sufficient contract is the basic step to legally managing risk in

---

[33] *Id.*, at 61.

international business transactions. Trade practitioners, even though they are familiar with international business transactions, are recommended to consult with a legal counselor when drafting international contracts. What follow are the basic and general formats of international contracts.

O **Title**

Headings in the agreement have been inserted for convenience and reference purposes only, and are not to be used in construing or interpreting the agreement.

O **Non operative Part**

① **Date (a)**

② **Concerned Parties**

THIS AGREEMENT made and entered into, in Seoul on the seventh day (a) of August, 1992, by and between ABC INTERNATIONAL CORP., a corporation (b) (c) duly organized and existing under the laws of the Republic of Korea and having (d) its principal office at 937, Namdaemun-ro 2-Ga, Jung-Gu, Seoul, Korea (e) (hereinafter referred to as "PRINCIPAL"), and Mr. Henry Smith Jr. residing (c) at 10 Broadway, New York 11037, U.S.A. (hereinafter referred to as "AGENT") (e) (f) WITNESSETH.

③ **Recitals, Whereas Clause**

WHEREAS PRINCIPAL is engaged in the business of manufacturing and exporting various Korea-made products (hereinafter referred to as "PRODUCTS") for sale of its majority in the world-wide markets including Indonesia; and WHEREAS, AGENT desires to be appointed an agent to solicit orders for PRODUCTS, and PRINCIPAL is willing to make such appointment, but only subject to the terms and conditions set forth below;

O **Operative Part**

① **Consideration**

NOW, THEREFORE, in consideration of mutual covenants and promises contained herein, both parties agree as follows ;

② **Definition**

Unless the context clearly requires otherwise, the following terms in this Agreement shall have the meanings attributed to them below;
(A) "KNOW-HOW" means
(a) rearrangement of machinery layout
(b) effective operation of machinery
(c) technical improvement of training process
(B) "TERRITORY" means the entire territory of Bangladesh

③ Period of Agreement

The term of this Agreement shall be three (3) years from the effective date of this Agreement and shall be automatically extended for a further three (3) years provided that PRINCIPAL shall give, at least three months prior to termination, a written notice to AGENT.

④ Termination of Contract

In the event of a breach of this Agreement not cured within ten (10) days from the receipt of notification when the breach consists of a failure to pay a sum due under this Agreement, or in the event of a different material breach of this Agreement not cured within thirty (30) days from the date of notification of such breach, this Agreement may be terminated by the aggrieved party.

Either party may terminate this Agreement immediately and without incurring thereby any liability to the other, by merely serving a notice of termination on the other in any of the following events:

(a) if the other party is declared in Court or notoriously becomes insolvent or bankrupt;
(b) if a Receiver is appointed to take possession of the business or assets of the other party and his appointment is not revoked within fifteen (15) days;
(c) if the other party closes or discontinues business operations relating to the Products for any reason, even beyond its control for more than ninety (90) days;

Termination of this agreement is without prejudice to any claim for any antecedent breach and to the right of the aggrieved party to recover damage, loss, compensation and all sums payable hereunder.

⑤ Force Majeure

Any delay or failure by either party hereto in the performance hereunder shall be excused if and to the extent caused by occurrences beyond such parties' control, including but not limited to, acts of God, strikes or other labor disturbances, war, sabotage and any other cause or causes, whether similar or dissimilar to those herein specified which cannot be controlled by such party.

(a) If the performance of this Agreement or of any obligation hereunder, except the making of payments under or in connection with this Agreement, is prevented, restricted or interfered with by reason of fire, storm, explosion, flood, earthquake, war, rebellion or other casualty or accident ; labor dispute, epidemics, quarantine restriction, transportation embargo, law, act, rule, regulation order, decision, or directive of any government of competent jurisdiction in matters relation to this Agreement or any agency

(continued)

thereof; or any other act or condition whatsoever beyond the reasonable control of the parties hereto, the party so affected, upon giving prompt notice to the other parties, shall be excused from such performance to the extent of such prevention, restriction or interference.

(b) The party so affected, however, shall use its best efforts to avoid or remove such causes of non-performance and to cure and complete performance hereunder with the utmost dispatch whenever such causes are removed.

(c) If due to any law, act, rule, regulation, order or decision of any government or competent jurisdiction or of currency as the debtor and the creditor shall mutually agree or in default of agreement between them in the currency of the country in which the creditor is incorporated.

If any agency or, for any other reason, a party hereto is unable to make payment of moneys due to another party hereto in a currency stipulated for the payment of those moneys hereunder, it may discharge the debt by making payment in such other.

⑥ Assignment

(a) None of the parties of this Agreement may directly or indirectly sell, assign or otherwise dispose of this Agreement to any third party unless it is assigned by the operation of law.

(b) This Agreement and any rights or obligations arising hereunder may not be assigned by either party without obtaining the prior written consent of the other party.

⑦ Arbitration

Any dispute arising out of or in connection with this contract shall be finally settled by arbitration in Seoul in accordance with the Arbitration Rules of the Korean Commercial Arbitration Board.

⑧ Jurisdiction

(a) Any Arbitration award rendered shall be final and binding upon the parties and may be enforced in any competent jurisdiction.

(b) Any and all disputes arising from this Agreement shall amicably be settled as promptly as possible upon consultation between the parties hereto.

The parties hereto agree that, should either party has been in a position to resort to a lawsuit, injunction, attachment, or any other acts of litigation, the Seoul District Court shall have Jurisdiction.

⑨ Governing Law

The formation validity, construction and the performance of this Agreement are governed by the laws of the Republic of Korea.

⑩ Integration, Entire Agreement

This Agreement sets forth the entire agreement and understanding between the parties as to the subject matter of this Agreement and merges and supersedes all prior discussions, agreements and understandings of any and every nature between them, and neither party shall be bound by any condition, definition, warranty or representation other than as expressly provided for in this Agreement or as may be on a subsequent date duly set out in writing and signed by a duly authorized officer of the party to be bound.

⑪ Modification of Agreement

This Agreement is not changed, modified or amended by the parties of this Agreement except as such change, modification or amendment is in writing and signed by both parties.

⑫ Notice

Any notice, request, consent, offer or demand required or permitted to be given in this Agreement, must be in writing and must be sufficiently given if delivered in person or sent by registered airmail or by cable confirmed by registered airmailed letter addressed as follows;
    To ; (address)
        Telex ;
        Answerback ;
    To ; (address)
        Telex ;
        Answerback ;
    Notice must be deemed to have been given on the date of mailing except the notice of change of address which must be deemed to have been given when received.

⑬ Waiver

The failure or delay of either party to require performance by the other party of any provision of this Agreement shall not constitute a waiver of, or shall not affect, its right to require performance of such provision.

⑭ Severability

If any provision of this Agreement or the application of any such provision to any person or circumstance shall be determined by any arbitration or court of competent jurisdiction to be invalid or unenforceable to any extent, S company may upon fifteen (15) days notice elect to (1) terminate this Agreement or (2) continue this Agreement, in which case the remainder of this Agreement or the application of such provision to such person or circumstance (other than those which it is so determined to be invalid and unenforceable), shall not be affected thereby and each provision of this Agreement shall be valid and shall be enforced to the fullest extent permitted by law.

⑮ Indemnification

In the event either party breaches an obligation under this Agreement or toward a third party, or delays or interferes with the other party in the performance of this Agreement, it shall be liable to the other party, but neither party shall be liable to the other party for any consequential damages or incidental damages, such as loss of profit.

Each party shall pay all reasonable expenses, including the costs of litigation and attorneys' fees, reasonably incurred by the other party in enforcing this Agreement. In the event a third party commences any proceeding for which a party hereto intends to claim indemnification against the other party, such party shall promptly notify thereof the other party and allow equitable participation in all stages of the proceeding and settlement thereof. Failure to promptly notify thereof or allow equitable participation by the other party shall reduce the right of indemnification to the extent of actual resultant prejudice.

⑯ Waiver of Sovereign Immunity

This Agreement constitutes a commercial act made by the Purchaser, and the Purchaser is therefore generally subject to set off, suit, judgment and execution and neither it nor its property has the right of immunity from setoff, judgment, attachment or execution on the grounds of sovereignty in regard to its obligations and liabilities under this Agreement. To the extent that the Purchaser or any of its property has or hereafter may acquire any such right of sovereign immunity, the Purchaser hereby irrevocably waives all such right to immunity from legal proceedings, attachment prior to judgment, other attachment, or execution of judgment on the grounds of sovereignty in any action arising hereunder on behalf of itself and all its present and future property.

Termination Clauses
① In Case of Contract without Seal

IN WITNESS WHEREOF, the parties have executed this Agreement in duplicate by their duly authorized representatives as of the date first above written.

② In Case of Contract with Seal

IN WITNESS WHEREOF, the parties have executed this Agreement by causing their corporate seals to be hereunto affixed and duly attested and these presents to be signed by their duly authorized representatives, this ____day of _____ 2012.

③ Signature

A & B Co., Ltd
   Fred Bialeh
   President

④ **Sealing**

(i) in the case of a person

Signed, Sealed and Delivered for and on behalf of Tom Jones
   by (Sign)
   .... L.S
   Mary Smith
   his duly authorized attorney in the presence of
   (Sign)
   ....

   Robert Blace

(ii) in the case of a company

The Common Seal of A & B Co., Ltd.
   was hereunto affixed in the presence of
   (Sign)
   ....
   Fred Bialck
   Common Director
   Seal (Sign)
   ....
   John Wheeler
   Secretary
   Source: The Korea Commercial Arbitration Board, http://www.kcab.or.kr

4.4.2   International Sales Agreement (Purchase Order Form)

Practically speaking, the short form of purchase order is accompanied by the general terms and conditions providing more detailed conditions for proper business transactions as follows. Enforcement of the contract should be made in accordance with the provisions stipulated in the short form of the contract as well as those stipulated in the general terms and conditions. Trade practitioners, therefore, should always be very careful to be in compliance with the trade contract itself as well as the terms and conditions under the letter of credit which is issued based on the trade contract. This means that trade practitioners should be very careful when making trade contracts.

MESSRS.   Date :

Contract No. :

ooo Corporation as Buyer hereby confirms having purchased from you as Seller, the following goods by contract of purchase made on the above date and on the terms and conditions hereinafter set forth. Seller is hereby requested to sign and return the original and if any discrepancy be found by Seller, Buyer should be informed immediately by FAX to be subsequently confirmed by registered airmail.

NO.	COMMODITY & SPECIFICATION	QUANTITY	UNIT PRICE	TOTAL AMOUNT

Time of Shipment :

Origin :

Port of Shipment :

Port of Destination :

Payment :

Insurance :

Packing :

Special Terms & Conditions :

This contract is subject to the general terms and conditions set forth on back hereof :

Accepted by :   [ooo Corporation]

on _____   _____

            (Seller)   (Buyer)

GENERAL TERMS AND CONDITIONS

The purchase specified on the face hereof shall be subject to the following terms and conditions :

Licenses

Seller at its own expense, shall obtain any and all necessary permits or licenses to export the Goods from the country of shipment and/or to import, sell, use or otherwise dispose of the Goods, including but not limited to the safety standard, in any countries where such Goods are imported, sold, used, or otherwise disposed of.

Shipment

Time of shipment is the essence of this Contract. Should Seller delay shipping the Goods for other reasons than those set forth in Clause Force Majeure hereof, Buyer may: (a) cancel this Contract in whole or in part, and/or (b) request to Seller, any Seller shall pay to Buyer, compensation for any and all damages incurred to Buyer and any special premium transportation or other costs required for the Goods to arrive at the destination as if the Goods be shipped as schedules.

Packing

Seller shall pack the Goods in strong wooden crate(s) or in carton(s), suitable for long distance ocean/parcel post/air freight transportation and for change of climate, well protected against moisture and shocks. Seller shall be liable for any damage of the Goods and expenses incident thereto on account of improper packing and/or improper protective measures taken by Seller in regard to the packing.

Price

Seller warrants that the prices sold to Buyer hereunder are no less favorable than the prices Seller currently extends to any other customer of the same Goods or similar goods and/or services in similar quantities. If Seller reduces its prices to others during the term of this Contract for such goods and/or services including but not limited to the Goods, Seller shall reduce the prices to Buyer for such Goods correspondingly.

Extra Expenses

Should the freight, insurance premium and other expenses at the time of shipment on this Contract be raised or changed owing to unexpected changes of circumstances after this Contract is executed, such differences and/or additional expenses shall be borne by Seller.

Insurance

In the event of CIF or CIP Contract, insurance contract shall be made by Seller. Such insurance will be bought at one hundred ten percent (110 %) of the invoice amount, and shall be issued by a first class underwriter and cover all risks.

Any insurance not set forth herein shall be arranged by Seller whenever requested by Buyer at the cost of Seller.

Adjustment

Buyer may at any time and without any notice deduct or set-off Seller's claims for money due or to become due from Buyer against any claims that Buyer has or may have arising out of this or any other transaction between the parties hereto.

Parts

Seller shall supply to Buyer the parts so long as Buyer continues to purchase the Goods pursuant to the terms and conditions of this Contract and for oo years after the last shipment of the Goods to Buyer.

Inspection

Inspection of the Goods shall be carried out at the place or port of unloading at Buyer's expense. Inspection may be done in the presence of Seller if Seller so desired. Provided, however, notwithstanding any inspection or payment made by Buyer, Buyer may without limiting its remedies reject, required corrections or refuse acceptance of the Goods which are not in conformity with the specifications or Seller's express or implied warranty. The Goods not accepted by Buyer shall be returned to Seller at Seller's account and risk or disposed of by Buyer at a time and price which Buyer deems reasonable and Seller shall reimburse Buyer any and all damage incurred to Buyer due to the Goods which are rejected.

Warranty

Seller represents and warrants that all Goods to be sold by Seller under this Contract shall conform in full to the specifications, analysis and other information furnished to Buyer and shall be merchantable, of good material and workmanship and free from any defects for at least [•] months from the date of unloading and further represents and warrants that the Goods shall be fit and sufficient for the purpose intended by Buyer and/or end users and that on delivery Buyer shall receive the title to the Goods, free and clear of all liens and encumbrances. Seller's warranty under this Contract as stated above shall be an essential condition of this Contract and any breach of the said warranty shall give Buyer the right (a) to reject the Goods so affected, without prejudice to any right to damages for such breach or to any other right arising from such breach of this Contract and/or (b) to terminate this Contract in whole or part.

Any and all warranty herein shall be in addition to any warranties express or implied by law or otherwise made by Seller and will survive acceptance and payment by Buyer.

Remedy

If Seller shall be in default of this Contract or shall fail to ship the Goods at the time scheduled, Buyer may by written notice to Seller exercise any of the following remedies: (a) terminate this Contract; or (b) terminate this contract as to portion of the Goods in default only and purchase an equal quantity of the Goods of same kind and grade and recover from Seller the excess of the price so paid over the purchase price set forth in this Contract, plus any incidental loss or expense; or (c) terminate this Contract as to any unshipped balance and recover from Seller as liquidated damages, a sum of five (5) percent of the price of the balance.

Further, it is agreed that the rights and remedies herein reserved to Buyer shall be cumulative and in addition to any other or further rights and remedies available at law.

Infringement

Seller shall be responsible for any infringement with regard to patent, utility model, trademark, design or copyright relating to the Goods in any country where the Goods are sold, used or otherwise disposed of. In the event of any dispute with regard to the said intellectual or industrial property right, Buyer may cancel this Contract. Seller shall be responsible for and shall defend, reimburse, indemnify and hold Buyer harmless from any and all liabilities, claims, expenses, losses and/or damages sustained thereby.

Force Majeure

In the event of any prohibition of import, refusal to issue an import license, act of Goods, war, blockade, embargo, insurrection, or any other action of governmental authorities, civil commotion, plague or other epidemic, fire, flood, or any other unforeseeable causes beyond the control of a party, the party shall not be liable for any default arising therefrom in performance of this Contract.

Arbitration

All disputes controversies, or differences which may arise between the parties hereto, out of or in relation to or in connection with this Contract, shall be finally settled by arbitration in [Name of Country] in accordance with the Commercial Arbitration Rules of The [Name of Country] Commercial Arbitration Board.

Trade Terms

All trade terms provided in this contract shall be interpreted in accordance with the latest Incoterms of the International Chamber of Commerce.

Source: Korea Eximbank, http://www.koreaexim.go.kr

4.4.3   International Sales Agreement (Selling Contract Form)

Practically speaking, the short form of a selling contract is accompanied by the general terms and conditions, providing more detailed conditions for proper business transactions, as in the case of a purchase order.

Ooo Company, as Seller, hereby confirms having sold to ooo as Buyer, the following goods by this sales contract made on the above date and on the terms and conditions hereinafter set forth.

ITEM NO.	COMMODITY & SPECIFICATION	QUANTITY	UNIT PRICE	AMOUNT

□ Time of Shipment :

□ Port of Shipment :

□ Port of Destination :

□ Payment

AT SIGHT L/C	By an irrevocable letter of credit payable at sight
USANCE	By an irrevocable, confirmed and unconditional letter of credit
DP	By documents against payment
DA	By bill(s) of exchange drawn on Buyer due ooo days from B/L date
DD	By D/D (Demand Draft) within ooo days after the date of B/L
TT	By T/T (Telegraph Transfer) within ooo days after the date of B/L
MT	By M/T (Mail Transfer) within ooo days after the date of B/L

□ Insurance : Seller to cover the CIF price plus ooo% against All Risk plus War and SRCC

Risks

□ Packing :

□ Marking :

□ Special Terms & Conditions :

□ This Contract is subject to the general terms and conditions set forth on back hereof :

Seller and Buyer

By ooo

Address ooo

Title ooo

Name ooo

Quantity

Quantity set forth in this Contract is subject to a variation of ten percent more or less at Seller's option.

Shipment

Date of bill of lading shall be accepted as a conclusive date of shipment. Ooo days grace in shipping shall be allowed. Partial shipment and/or transshipment shall be permitted unless otherwise stated in this Contract. Seller shall not be responsible for any delay of shipment, should Buyer fail to provide a timely letter of credit in conformity with this Contract or in case the

(continued)

sailing of the steamer designated by Buyer is deferred beyond the prearranged date of shipment.

Packing

Packing shall be at Seller's option. In case special instructions are necessary, Buyer should notify Seller thereof in time to enable Seller to comply with the same and all additional cost thereby incurred shall be borne by Buyer. Shipping Marks shall be made as shown in the oblong of the front page of this Contract.

Insurance

In case of CIF or CIP basis, ooo % of the invoice amount shall be insured, unless otherwise agreed; any additional insurance required by Buyer to be at his own expense; unless otherwise stated, insurance to be covered for marine insurance only FPA or ICC (C) Clause. Seller may, if he deems it necessary, insure against additional risks at Buyer's expense.

Increased Costs

If Seller's costs of performance are increased after the date of this Contract by reason of increased freight rates, taxes or other governmental charges or insurance rates, or if any variation in rates of exchange increases Seller's costs or reduces Seller's return, Buyer agrees to compensate Seller for such increased cost or loss of income. Further, if at any time Buyer requests shipment later than agreed and Seller agrees thereto, Seller may, upon completion of manufacture, store the Goods and charge all expenses thereby incurred to Buyer, plus reasonable storage charges when Seller stores the Goods in its own facilities.

Payment

O At Sight L/C

An irrevocable letter of credit, without recourse, available against Seller's sight drafts shall be established through a prime bank satisfactory to Seller within ooo days after the date of this Contract and be kept valid at least ooo days after the date of last shipment. The amount of such letter of credit shall be sufficient to cover the Contract amount and additional charges and/or expenses to be borne by Buyer.

O **Usance L/C**

For the payment of the Contract Price specified hereof the Buyer shall provide the Seller with the irrevocable, confirmed and unconditional letter of credit (hereinafter called "L/C") in the amount of USD ooo at ooo months usance basis (after the date of draft issued by the Seller or bill of lading) in favor of the Seller to be opened within ooo days from the signing date of the Contract under the agreed terms and conditions by the Seller and Buyer.

O **DP**

After shipment, the Seller shall deliver at sight bill(s) of exchange drawn on the Buyer together with the required documents to the Buyer through a bank. The Buyer shall effect the payment immediately upon the first presentation of the bill(s) of exchange and the required documents, i.e. D/P.

O **DA**

After shipment, the Seller shall deliver bill(s) of exchange drawn on the Buyer, payable ooo days after acceptance, together with the required documents to the Buyer through a bank for acceptance. The Buyer shall accept the bill(s) of exchange immediately upon the first presentation of the bill of exchange and the required documents and shall effect the payment on the maturity date of the bill(s) of exchange.

O **DD**

The Buyer shall pay the invoice value of the goods by means of D/D (Demand Draft) within ooo days after the receipt of the required documents; within ooo days after the date of the Bill of Lading.

O **TT**

The Buyer shall pay the invoice value of the goods to the Seller's account with the bank designated by the Seller by means of T/T (Telegraph Transfer) within ooo days after the receipt of the required documents; within ooo days after the date of the Bill of Lading.

O **MT**

The Buyer shall pay the invoice value of the goods by the Seller by means of M/T (Mail Transfer) within oo days after the receipt of the required documents; within ooo days after the date of the Bill of Lading.

Inspection

The inspection of the Goods shall be done according to the export regulation of the Republic of Korea and/or by the manufacturer(s) which shall be considered as final. Should any specific inspector be designated by Buyer,

(continued)

all additional charges incurred thereby shall be at Buyer's account and shall be added to the invoice amount, for which the letter of credit shall be amended accordingly.

Warranty

The Goods shall conform to the specification set forth in this contract and free from defects in material and workmanship for ooo months from the date of shipment. The extent of Seller's liability under this warranty shall be limited to the repair or replacement as herein provided of any defective Goods or parts thereof. Provided, however, this warranty does not extend to any of the said Goods which have been: (a) subjected to misuse, neglect, accident or abuse; (b) improperly repaired, installed, transported, altered or modified in any way by any other party than Seller; or (c) used in violation of instructions furnished by Seller. Except for the express limited warranties set forth in this article, seller makes no other warranty to buyer, express or implied, and herby expressly disclaims any warranty of merchantability or fitness for a particular purpose. In no event shall Seller be liable to Buyer under this Contract or otherwise for any lost profits or for indirect, incidental or consequential damages for any reason.

Claims

Any claim by Buyer of whatever nature arising under this Contract shall be made by facsimile or cable within ooo days after arrival of the Goods at the destination specified in the bills of lading. Full particulars of such claim shall be made in writing, and forwarded by registered mail to Seller within ooo days after such fax or cabling. Buyer must submit with particulars the inspection report sworn by a reputable surveyor acceptable to the Seller when the quality or quantity of the Goods delivered is in dispute. Failure to make such claim within such period shall constitute acceptance of shipment and agreement of Buyer that such shipment fully complies with applicable terms and conditions.

Remedy

Buyer shall, without limitation, be in default of this Contract, if Buyer shall become insolvent, bankrupt or fail to make any payment to Seller including the establishment of the letter of credit within the due period. In the event of Buyer's default, Seller may without prior notice thereof to Buyer exercise any of the following remedies among others:

(a) terminate this Contract;

(b) terminate this Contract as to the portion of the Goods in default only and resell them and recover from Buyer the difference between the price set forth in this Contract and the price obtained upon resale, plus any incidental loss or expense; or

(c) terminate the Contract as to any unshipped balance and recover from Buyer as liquidated damages, a sum of five (5) percent of the price of the unshipped balance. Further, it is agreed that the rights and remedies herein reserved to Seller shall be cumulative and in addition to any other or further rights and remedies available at law.

Force Majeure

Neither party shall be liable for its failure to perform its obligations hereunder if such failure is the direct result of circumstances beyond that party's reasonable control, including but not limited to, prohibition of exportation, suspension of issuance of export license or other government restriction, act of God, war, blockade, revolution, insurrection, mobilization, strike, lockout or any labor dispute, civil commotion, riot, plague or other epidemic, fire, typhoon, flood.

Patents, Trade Marks, Designs, etc.

Buyer is to hold Seller harmless from liability for any infringement with regard to patent, trade mark, copyright, design, pattern, etc., originated or chosen by Buyer.

Governing Law

This Contract shall be governed under the laws of Korea.

Arbitration

Any dispute arising out of or in connection with this contract shall be finally settled by arbitration in Seoul in accordance with the Arbitration Rules of the Korean Commercial Arbitration Board.

Language

This Agreement may be executed in English and in other languages (including Korean). In the event of any difference or inconsistency among different versions of this Agreement, the English version shall prevail in all respects.

Trade Terms

All trade terms provided in the Contract shall be interpreted in accordance with the latest Incoterms®2010 of International Chamber of Commerce.

Termination Clause

Between ooo Company as purchaser and ooo Company as supplier:
Dated: 2012
Source: Korea Eximbank, http://www.koreaexim.go.kr

4.4.4   Plant Supply Agreement

The following is an example of a plant supply agreement between the supplier and the purchaser.

This Plant Supply Agreement (the "Agreement"), made and entered into this ooo day of 2011 by and between ooo company, a corporation organized and existing under the laws of Korea having its registered office at Seoul ("Supplier") and ooo company, a corporation organized and existing under the laws of the United States having its registered office at New York ("Purchaser").

Witnesseth

WHEREAS, Supplier possesses technical information and manufacturing skills with respect to ooo; and
        WHEREAS, Purchaser desires to purchase from Supplier on a deferred payment basis and Supplier agrees to manufacture and supply on a deferred

payment basis to Purchaser, a certain quantity of ooo as more specifically described herein (the "Commodities") upon the terms and conditions set forth below.

NOW, THEREFORE, in consideration of the premises and mutual covenants hereinafter contained the parties hereby agree as follows:

(1) Definitions

In addition to the terms defined above, as used herein the following terms shall have the meanings set forth below:

"Bill of Lading" shall mean the bill of lading issued with respect to each shipment of the Commodities.

"Banking Day" shall mean a day on which banks are open for business in Seoul, London and New York.

"Certificate of Acceptance" shall have the meaning set forth in Article 6.2.

"Contract Price" shall mean the aggregate amount of the Installments and the Principal Amount to be paid by Purchaser to Supplier hereunder, which such amount is ooo United States Dollars (US$ ooo).

"Default Rate" shall mean ooo percent (ooo %) per annum.

"Dollars" and the sign "$" shall mean dollars in the lawful currency of the United States.

"Effective Date" shall have the meaning set forth in Article 16.

"Event of Default" shall have the meaning set forth in Article 9.1.

"Factory" shall have the meaning set forth in Article 2.2.

"First Installment" shall mean the first payment to be made by Purchaser hereunder which such payment shall be in the amount of ooo Dollars (US$ ooo).

["Guarantor" shall mean a first class international bank satisfactory to Supplier.] References to "Guarantor" and "Letter of Guarantee" or "Standby Letter of Credit" and "L/C Banks" should be included in this Agreement in accordance with the kind of security required by Supplier and Exim Bank.

"Installments Payable on or before the last Shipment" shall mean, collectively, the First Installment, the Second Installment and the Third Installment ooo. If necessary, there can be more Installments according to the nature of the Agreement.

"Interest Payment Date" shall mean the last day of each Interest Period.

"Interest Period" shall mean the period beginning on the last Shipment Date and having duration of six (6) months and each period thereafter commencing on the last day of the then current Interest Period and having duration of six (6) months.

"Interest Rate" shall mean ooo percent (ooo%) above CIRR (Commercial Interest Reference Rate) under the OECD Guidelines prevailing at the time of

(continued)

the Loan Commitment to the Supplier by the Export–import Bank of Korea (KEXIM).

"Last Shipment Date" shall mean the final Shipment Date set forth in Schedule III hereto.

["Letter of Guarantee" shall mean the irrevocable and unconditional guarantee to be issued by the Guarantor guaranteeing the payment of all sums due and payable under the Notes, substantially in the form of Exhibit ooo hereto and in any event in form and substance satisfactory to Supplier and its counsel.]

"Notes" shall mean the promissory notes of Purchaser evidencing the Principal Amount which such notes shall be substantially in the form of Exhibit A hereto and in any event in form and substance satisfactory to Supplier and its counsel.

"Payment Date" shall mean each of the ooo consecutive semi-annual dates occurring on ooo and ooo of each year, the first Payment Date being ooo, 2013 and the last Payment Date being ooo, 2014.

"Principal Amount" shall mean ooo Dollars (US$ ooo) and in any event, the amount equal to ooo percent (ooo %) of the Contract Price.

"Second Installment" shall mean the second payment to be made by Purchaser hereunder, which such payment shall be in the amount of ooo Dollars (US$ ooo).

"Shipment Date" shall mean the date entered on the Bill of Lading with respect to each shipment of the Commodities.

"Specifications" shall mean the specifications to be used for the manufacture of the Commodities as more specifically set forth in Schedule II.

"Third Installment" shall mean the third payment to be made by Purchaser hereunder, which such payment shall be in the amount of ooo Dollars (US$ ooo).

(2) Commodities
1) Description

The description, quantity and unit price of the Commodities to be supplied by Supplier to Purchaser hereunder shall be as set forth in Schedule Iattached hereto. All prices stated herein are CIF ooo.

2) Specification

The Commodities shall be manufactured in accordance with the Specifications set forth in Schedule II hereto. Manufacture of the Commodities shall occur at ooo (the "Factory"), or such other place as Supplier shall notify Purchaser. Supplier may at its own risk subcontract any part of the work undertaken hereunder without prior consent of Purchaser.

3) Samples

Supplier shall within ooo day after the Effective Date in accordance with Purchaser's written instructions produce such samples of the Commodities as Purchaser may reasonably require. The unit prices to be paid by Purchaser for the samples shall be determined by mutual agreement of the parties prior to the manufacture thereof. The samples may be altered, adapted or otherwise changed as Purchaser may reasonably demand to meet its requirements. Upon manufacture of the samples to the satisfaction of Purchaser, Purchaser shall notify Supplier in writing of its acceptance thereof, and thereafter full commercial production of the Commodities shall begin.

(3) Payment
1) Terms of Payment

The Contract Price shall be in an amount not exceeding ooo United States Dollars (US$ ooo) and shall be paid by Purchaser to Supplier in Dollars as follows:
(a) The Installments Payable on or before the last Shipment
   The First Installment of ooo United States Dollars (US$ ooo) shall be paid within ooo days after the Effective Date. The Second Installment of ooo Dollars ($ooo) shall be paid upon the ooo (ooo th) Shipment Date set forth in Schedule III hereto or on ooo whichever comes earlier. The Third Installment of ooo Dollars ($ooo) shall be paid on the ooo (ooo th) Shipment Date set forth in Schedule III hereto or on ooo whichever comes earlier. Purchaser shall remit the full amount of each of the Installments in immediately available funds by telegraphic transfer to the account of the Export–import Bank of Korea with [Name and Address of Bank] (Account Number ooo) in favor of the Supplier.
(b) Principal Amount
   The Principal Amount shall be paid in ooo equal (or as nearly equal as possible) to semi-annual installments one such installment being payable on each Payment Date. The last installment shall in any event be in the amount necessary to pay in full the Principal Amount outstanding. The

(continued)

Principal Amount and interest thereon shall be evidenced by and paid in accordance with the Notes which shall be executed and delivered by Purchaser to Supplier pursuant to Section 4.01 hereof.

(c) Interest

Purchaser agrees to pay interest on the Principal Amount outstanding from time to time on each Interest Payment Date for the Interest Period then ending at the Interest Rate. Interest shall accrue on the basis of the actual number of days elapsed and a year of 360 days. Interest shall accrue from and including the first day of an Interest Period to but not including the last day of such Interest Period.

2) Prepayment

Purchaser may prepay, in whole or in part, the Principal Amount together with all interests and other amounts then due hereunder on any due date of a Note, provided that the Purchaser shall have given not less than ooo days' prior written notice thereof to the Supplier, and shall pay to the Supplier a prepayment premium equal to the amount of the prepayment amount multiplied by the interest rate which means as in "the Article 1. Definitions" hereof and multiplied by ooo, if the remaining repayment period from the date of prepaying the said prepayment amount is three ooo years or less, or multiplied by ooo, if the remaining repayment period is between over ooo years and ooo years. Notwithstanding the foregoing, the Purchaser may prepay, without any prepayment premium, the Principal Amount if the remaining repayment period is ooo months or less. The amount of any prepayment shall be equal to the amount of an installment of repayment of Principal Amount or an integral multiple thereof. Any prepayment shall be applied to the installments of Principal Amount in inverse order of maturity.

(4) Security
1) Notes

Purchaser shall within ooo Banking Days before the Last Shipment Date, duly execute and deliver to the Supplier ooo Notes respectively numbered "1" to " ooo " inclusive, evidencing the Purchaser's obligation to pay to the Supplier the Principal Amount plus interest thereon.

2) Guarantee

Within ooo Banking Days before the Last Shipment Date, Purchaser shall furnish Supplier with the Guarantee duly executed by the Guarantor.

(5) Shipment
1) Shipment Schedule

Supplier shall cause shipment of the Commodities at any Korean port reasonably designated by Supplier not later than the end of each month commencing from ooo to ooo in accordance with Schedule III attached hereto. The Last Shipment Date shall be made not later than ooo, excluding delays due to such causes as defined in Article 7 hereof.

2) Shipping Advice

Shipping advice shall be given by Supplier to Purchaser promptly after the on-board date of the Bill of Lading and shall contain such information as the contract number, loading port, brief description of the Commodities shipped, name of vessel, expected time of arrival, invoice amount of shipment, and the name of the claim settling agent (if necessary) in Korea.

3) Title and Risk of Loss

Title to and risk of loss of the Commodities shall pass to Purchaser when the Commodities have effectively passed the ship's rail at the port of shipment.

4) Packing and Marking

Commodities shall be packed in accordance with standard export packing methods and shall be marked in accordance with the reasonable instruction of Purchaser.

5) Insurance, Freight, Export License

Supplier shall be responsible for insuring against all risks in maritime transportation from the time the Commodities effectively pass the ship's rail at the port of shipment and shall pay freight for the maritime transportation of the Commodities. Supplier at its own expense will obtain all necessary permits or licenses to export the Commodities prior to the relevant Shipment Date thereof.

(6) Inspection
1) Time and Place of Inspection

Prior to each Shipment Date, Purchaser of its agent or representative shall at its own expense inspect the Commodities at the Factory or such other place as may be notified by Supplier to Purchaser. Supplier shall provide Purchaser with all reasonable assistance in conducting the inspection. Supplier shall give Purchaser ooo days prior notice of the date on and the place at which the relevant Commodities will be ready for final inspection. If Purchaser fails to conduct inspection at such place within ooo days from the date stated in Supplier's notice, Supplier may conduct the final inspection without Purchaser being present, and in such case the Purchaser shall be obligated to accept such Commodities as are determined by Supplier to be in conformance with this Agreement.

2) Result of Inspection

Any Commodity or any accessory or part thereof failing to comply within ooo % of the Specification shall be deemed a defective Commodity and Supplier shall replace such Commodity, accessory or part with a conforming Commodity, accessory or part at its own expense. For inspected Commodities deemed to be conforming with the Specifications, Purchaser shall issue to Supplier a written certificate substantially in the form of Schedule IV to that effect (the "Certificate of Acceptance"), and such issuance shall constitute Purchaser's final and binding acceptance of the Commodities so inspected.

(7) Force Majeure
1) Causes of Delay

If the performance of this Agreement by any party, or of any obligation under this agreement, is prevented, restricted, or interfered with by reason of war, typhoon, revolution, civil commotion, acts of public enemies, blockade, embargo, strikes, lockouts, any law, order, proclamation, regulation, ordinance, demand or requirement having a legal effect of any government, or any other act whatsoever, whether similar or dissimilar to those referred to in this clause, which are beyond the reasonable control of the party affected or its sub-contractor, including weather, then the party so affected shall, upon giving prior written notice to the other party, be excused from such performance to the extent of such prevention, restriction or interference, provided that the party so affected shall use its best effort to avoid or remove such causes of nonperformance, and shall continue performance hereunder with the utmost dispatch whenever such causes are removed. Upon such circumstances arising, the parties shall meet forthwith to discuss what (if any) modification maybe required to the terms of this Agreement, in order to arrive at an equitable solution.

2) Excessive Delay

If the total accumulated time of all delays with respect to each shipment on account of the causes specified in Section (7–1) of this Article aggregates or can reasonably be expected to aggregate ooo calendar days or more, then in such event either party may terminate this Agreement in accordance with the provisions of Article 9 hereof.

(8) Warranty
1) Warranty Terms

Subject to the limitations set forth below, Supplier warrants that the Commodities will be free from defects in material and workmanship and undertakes to repair or replace free of charge any defective parts, including repaired or replaced parts, in the Commodities provided, however, that the parties expressly acknowledge and agree that this warranty is limited to only such defects in the commodities which are (i) due solely to defective material and/or poor workmanship on the part of Supplier and/or its sub-contractors, (ii) discovered within ooo months after the shipment date of the applicable commodity and (iii) for which notice thereof is duly given to Supplier as provided in Article 8.02 below.

2) Notice of Defects

Purchaser shall notify Supplier in writing, or by telex confirmed in writing, within ooo days after discovery of any defects for which claim is made hereunder. Purchaser's failure to give Supplier such notice within ooo days after discovery of the defect shall constitute an absolute, irrevocable and unconditional waiver of any and all claims arising out of or in any way connected with such defect.

3) Remedy of Defects

Upon receipt of notice, Supplier shall promptly deliver the replacement part (s) free of charge CIF ooo, or such other port as may be reasonably designated by Purchaser.

4) Disclaimer

Purchaser expressly acknowledges and agrees that the warranty contained herein shall not extend to material which ages or deteriorates due to ordinary wear and tear, or to defects or conditions caused, in whole or in part, by deficiencies in supplies, services or facilities furnished by Purchaser. in addition, this warranty does not extend to commodities that have been altered or repaired by personnel unauthorized by Supplier, or which have been subjected to misuse, neglect, improper maintenance, accident, or improper installation or storage by Purchaser, its customers or personnel acting at Purchaser's direction or behalf.

5) Purchaser's Responsibility

Purchaser shall indemnify and hold Supplier harmless against any and all claims, proceedings, losses, liabilities, suits, judgments, costs, expenses, penalties or fines for injury or damage to any property or person arising out of or in any way connected with the transportation, installation, use, or maintenance of the Commodities. For so long as this Agreement shall remain in force, Purchaser shall procure from a reputable insurance company a Comprehensive General Liability insurance policy (or its equivalent) in the minimum amount of US$ ooo, per occurrence, and shall at its own expense cause Supplier to be listed as a named insured in such policy.

6) Service Engineer

Upon Purchaser's request, Supplier shall dispatch a service engineer to a location reasonably designated by Purchaser to assist Purchaser in providing efficient service to its customers for the period of warranty hereunder. Purchaser shall pay to Supplier all costs associated with such service engineer including but not limited to, salary, transportation, communications, and housing.

(9) Default
1) Event of Default

Each of the following events and occurrences shall constitute an event of default ("Event of Default") :
  (a) Purchaser fails to pay on the due date any of the First Installment, Second Installment or Third Installment.
  (b) Purchaser rejects any shipment of the Commodities following the issuance of a Certificate of Acceptance with respect to such shipment.

(c) Purchaser fails to execute and deliver the Notes in accordance with Article 4.01 or the Guarantor fails to execute and deliver the Letter of Guarantee in accordance with Article 4 – 2.

(d) Purchaser fails to perform any of its obligations with respect to any of the security instruments provided by it under Article 4 hereof.

(e) Purchaser fails to pay on the relevant due date any payment of principal, interest, expenses or any other amount which it is obligated to pay under the terms of the Notes.

(f) Purchaser fails to perform or violates any provision of this Agreement or the Notes.

(g) Any governmental consent, filing, license or approval granted or required in connection with this Agreement or any Note expires or is terminated, revoked, withdrawn or modified in any way or any new law or decree is issued which in Supplier's opinion would prevent Purchaser from fulfilling its obligations hereunder or under any Note.

(h) The whole or a substantial part of the assets of Purchaser is confiscated or attached.

(i) Purchaser fails to pay when due any indebtedness or fails to observe or perform any term, covenant or agreement contained in any agreement by which it or its assets is bound evidencing or securing any indebtedness, and the effect of such failure is to accelerate, or to permit the acceleration of the maturity of such indebtedness.

(j) Any change occurs in the ownership or control of Purchaser or Guarantor which in the reasonable opinion of Supplier constitutes a material adverse change affecting the financial condition or operations of Purchaser or Guarantor, respectively.

(k) Purchaser or Guarantor suspends or discontinues its business operations, whether voluntarily or involuntarily, for a period of ooo or more days.

(l) Purchaser or the Guarantor becomes insolvent or unable to pay any money due under any agreement or document evidencing, securing, guaranteeing or otherwise relating to indebtedness in excess of $ ooo or its equivalent in any other currency when due or commits or permits any act of bankruptcy, which term shall include (i) the filing of a petition in any bankruptcy, reorganization, winding-up or liquidation proceeding or other proceeding analogous in purpose or effect, (ii) the failure by Purchaser or the Guarantor to have any such petition filed by another party discharged within ooo days, (iii) the application for or consent to the appointment of a receiver or trustee for the bankruptcy, reorganization, winding-up or liquidation of Purchaser or the Guarantor, (iv) the making by Purchaser or the Guarantor of an assignment for the benefit of its creditors, (v) the admission in writing by Purchaser or the Guarantor of its inability to pay its debts, (vi) the passing of a resolution by, or the entry of any court order or judgment confirming the bankruptcy or insolvency of, Purchaser or the

(continued)

Guarantor or approving any reorganization, winding-up or liquidation of Purchaser or the Guarantor or of a substantial portion of their respective properties or assets, or (vii) any creditor of the Guarantor exercises a contractual right to assume the financial management of the Guarantor.

(m) The Guarantor attempts to repudiate, rescind, limit or annul the Letter of Guarantee; or any legislation or regulation is proposed, enacted or promulgated the effect of which would be to repudiate, rescind, limit or annul the Letter of Guarantee; or the Guarantor fails to comply with any legislation or regulations concerning its organization or authority or any change is made in such legislation or regulations which failure or change, in the reasonable opinion of Supplier, has a material adverse effect on the ability of the Guarantor to meet its obligations under the Letter of Guarantee.

(n) It becomes unlawful for Purchaser to perform any obligation under this Agreement or the Notes, or for the Guarantor to perform any obligation under the Letter of Guarantee.

(o) Any competent governmental authority takes (i) any action to condemn, seize, requisition or otherwise appropriate any substantial portion of the properties or assets of Purchaser (either with or without payment of compensation), (ii) any action to dissolve, liquidate or terminate the existence of the Guarantor or to divest the Guarantor of any material portion of its properties or assets, or (iii) any action relating to Purchaser or the Guarantor which, in the opinion of Supplier, adversely affects Purchaser or the Guarantor's ability to pay its indebtedness under this Agreement, the Notes or the Letter of Guarantee.

(p) Any circumstances occur which in the opinion of Supplier give reasonable grounds for belief that Purchaser or the Guarantor may not (or may not be able to) perform its obligations under this Agreement, the Notes or the Letter of Guarantee.

(q) Supplier fails to manufacture the samples to the satisfaction of Purchaser in accordance with Article 2.03 hereof within ooo days after the Effective Date.

(r) Supplier fails to ship Commodities accepted by Purchaser within ooo days after Purchaser's issuance of a Certificate of Acceptance therefore.

(s) Supplier breaches any of its obligations hereunder and such breach is not cured or steps satisfactory to Purchaser have not been taken to effect cure within ooo days of Purchaser's written notice to Supplier.

2) Consequences of Default

(a) Upon the occurrence of any of the Events of Default specified in Article 9.01 (a) or (b), successive Shipment Dates shall be postponed until such Event of default is cured; provided, however, that if any such Event of

Default continues for a period of ooo days, Supplier may, at its option, rescind this Agreement by giving Purchaser notice to such effect. In the event of such rescission, Supplier shall be entitled to retain all or any part of the Installments paid by Purchaser hereunder.

(b) Upon the occurrence of any of the Events of Default specified in article 9.01 (c)–(p), and at the option of Supplier, the obligations of Supplier hereunder shall immediately cease ; Supplier may declare, by notice to Purchaser without presentment, demand, notice or protest, all of which are hereby expressly waived by Purchaser, the principal of any Install-ment and the principal and accrued interest on the Principal Amount payable hereunder and all other amounts payable hereunder immediately due and payable together with Default Interest accrued on all such sums from the date of such declaration.

(c) Upon occurrence of any of the Events specified in Article 9.01 (q)–(s), Purchaser may terminate this Agreement; provided, however, that all amounts then due and payable to Supplier hereunder shall have been paid in full. In the event of such termination, Supplier shall refund the Installments paid by Purchaser hereunder.

(d) All expenses incurred by either party in enforcing its rights hereunder, including the fees and expenses of counsel, shall be paid by the other party.

(10) Arbitration

All disputes arising between the parties in connection with this Agreement which cannot be settled by mutual agreement shall be finally settled by arbitration in accordance with the Rules of Conciliation and Arbitration of the International Chamber of Commerce before a board of three arbitrators, consisting of one member to be appointed by each of Purchaser and Supplier, respectively, and one third member to be selected by the two members so appointed. In the event the said two arbitrators fail to agree upon a third arbitrator within ooo days from the date of their appointment, the third arbitrator shall then be appointed by the president of the International Cham-ber of Commerce. The arbitration award may take the form of an order to pay a sum of money, to perform or refrain from an act, or any combination thereof. The award rendered shall be final and conclusive. No payment under this Agreement shall be delayed or withheld by Purchaser on account of any dispute of whatever nature arising between the parties hereto.

(11) Assignment

Neither of the parties hereto may assign this Agreement to a third party unless prior written consent of the other party has been obtained. In the event of any assignment by Purchaser, such assignment shall further be subject to the approval of Supplier's bank and/or the relevant Korean governmental authorities, and Purchaser shall at all times remain as the primary obligor for the due performance of all of its obligations under this Agreement. This Agreement shall inure to the benefit of and shall be binding upon the lawful successors, transferees and assigns of either of the parties hereto. Notwithstanding the foregoing, Supplier is entitled to assign to any other party its rights under the Notes and/or the Letter of Guarantee [Stand-by Letter of Credit] without Purchaser's prior consent.

(12) Taxes
1) Taxes in Korea

Supplier shall pay all taxes and duties imposed in the Republic of Korea in connection with the execution, delivery or performance of this Agreement.

2) Taxes outside Korea

Purchaser shall pay all taxes and duties imposed outside the Republic of Korea in connection with the execution, delivery or performance of this Agreement except for taxes and duties imposed upon those items to be procured by Supplier for the manufacture of the Commodities.

(13) Patents, Trademarks, and Copyrights

Nothing contained herein shall be construed as transferring any patent, trademark or copyright in the Commodities or any part thereof, all such rights being hereby expressly reserved to the true and lawful owners thereof.

(14) Confidentiality

Supplier shall retain all rights with respect to the Specifications, plans, working drawings, technical descriptions, calculations, test results and other data, information and documents concerning the design and manufacture of the Commodities, and Purchaser hereby agrees not to disclose the same or divulge any information contained therein to any third parties without the prior written consent of Supplier except to key employees involved in the usual operation or maintenance of the Commodities.

(15) Notice

Any and all notices and communications in connection with this Agreement shall be written in the English language and (i) personally delivered, (ii) transmitted by registered airmail postage prepaid, or (iii) transmitted by tested telex to the parties at the following addresses :
> To Purchaser :
> [Address]
> E-Mail Address: ooo
> To Supplier :
> [Address]
> E-Mail Address: ooo

Any notice given by registered airmail shall be deemed to have been received [•] days from the date of mailing, any notice personally delivered shall be deemed to have been received upon delivery and any notice sent by telex shall be deemed to have been received when sent. Any party may change its address for the purposes hereof by written notice to the other party.

(16) Effective Date

This Agreement shall become effective from the date (the "Effective Date") on which all of the following conditions have been met:
(a) This Agreement has been duly executed and delivered by the parties hereto.
(b) Supplier has obtained the relevant export license with respect to the Commodities from the government of the Republic of Korea.
Supplier shall promptly give notice to Purchaser upon the fulfillment of each of the above conditions. This Agreement shall terminate upon payment of all amounts due to Supplier under the terms of this Agreement.

(17) Miscellaneous
1) Applicable Law

The parties hereto agree that the validity, formation and interpretation of this Agreement, the Notes, and the Letter of Guarantee shall be governed by the laws of [Name of Country].

2) Discrepancies

In the event that any provision contained in the Specifications is inconsistent with any provisions of this Agreement, then in each and every such event the applicable provisions of this Agreement shall prevail.

3) Entire Agreement

This Agreement contains the entire agreement and understanding between the parties hereto and supersedes all prior negotiations, representations, understandings and agreements on any subject matter of this Agreement.

4) Severability

If any provision of this Agreement or any document executed in connection herewith shall be invalid, illegal or unenforceable, the validity, legality and enforceability of the remaining provisions contained herein shall not in any way be affected or impaired.

5) Waiver of Sovereign Immunity

Purchaser represents and warrants that this Agreement is a commercial rather than public or governmental act and that Purchaser is not entitled to claim immunity from legal proceedings with respect to itself or any of its properties or assets on the grounds of sovereignty or otherwise under any law or in any jurisdiction where an action may be brought for the enforcement of any of the obligations arising under or relating to this Agreement or the Notes. To the extent that Purchaser or any of its properties or assets has or hereafter may acquire any right to immunity from set-off, legal proceedings, attachment prior to judgment, other attachment or execution of judgment on the grounds of sovereignty or otherwise, Purchaser for itself and its properties and other assets hereby irrevocably waives such right to immunity in respect of its obligations arising under this Agreement, the Notes and all documents executed in connection herewith.

6) Amendment

No provision of this Agreement may be amended, modified, waived or rescinded except by a written agreement executed by the parties hereto.

7) Counterparts; Controlling Language

This Agreement may be executed in any number of counterparts. Any single counterpart or a set of counterparts executed, in either case, by both parties hereto shall constitute a full and original agreement for all purposes. This Agreement, all notices delivered hereunder and all documents to be delivered in connection with this transaction shall be in the English language and in the event of any conflict between the English-language version and the non-English-language version of any such notice or document, the English-language version shall prevail.

8) Independent Contractors

It is expressly understood and agreed that the relationship between the parties created by this Agreement is that of independent contractors. Nothing in this Agreement shall be construed to constitute either party as agent of the other for any purpose whatsoever, and neither party shall bind or attempt to bind the other party to any contract or the performance of any obligation, nor represent to third parties that it has any right to enter into any binding obligation on the other's behalf.

IN WITNESS WHEREOF, the parties hereto have caused this Agreement to be executed by their respective duly authorized signatories as of the day and year first written above.

[PURCHASER]   [SUPPLIER]

By : ooo Company   By : ooo Company

Name : ooo   Name : ooo

Title : ooo   Title : ooo

Source: Korea Eximbank, http://www.koreaexim.go.kr

1. Make an assessment of the sales contract made in Chapter 3, then modify and correct the previously made contract to produce a more complete contract which could be enforced without serious disputes with the concerned parties, and, at the same time, promote and facilitate processing of international trade contracts.
2. Communications and negotiations to make a mid-term (3 year) contract to construct a waste-water treatment plant in London with counterparts ranging from the stage of negotiation over tendering to the stage of concluding agreement. These communications and negotiations should be held under the scenario that students' own construction companies located in their home countries are trying to export a plant to London, based on their competitive power to treat waste water through an environmentally-friendly bio-organic system.
3. Quality-inspection issues including pre-shipment inspection particularly in the case of the students' newly-developed and environmentally-friendly products compared with other existing products which are comparatively easy to make quality inspection for, considering the fact that there have been numerous historical disputes among the concerned parties relating to the quality and function of environment-related products.

References

Carole Murray, David Holloway, Daren Timson-Hunt, Brian Kennelly, Giles Dixon, Schmitthoffs (2007) Schmitthoff Export Trade: The Law and Practice of International Trade, 11th edn, Sweet & Maxwell Ltd
Ramberg J (2008) Guide to Export-Import Basics, 3rd edn. ICC

Supplemental Reading

Honnold JO (2006) Sales Transactions: Domestic and International Law, 3 rd edn. Foundation Press, pp. 27–92
Folsom RH, Gordon MW, Spanogle, Jr. JA, Fitzgerald PL (2009) International Business Transactions: Contracting Across Borders. West, pp. 2–51
Fellmeth AX (2009) The Law of International Business Transactions. West, pp. 327–435
Fletcher I, Mistelis L, Cremona M (eds) (2001) Foundations and Perspectives of International Trade Law. Sweet & Maxwell, pp. 28–36
Kouladis N (2006) Principles of Law Relating to International Trade. Springer, pp. 201–212
Carr I (2007) International Trade Law, 3 rd edn. Cavendish Publishing, pp. 5–56
Zeller B (2007) CISG and the Unification of International Trade Law. Routledge-Cavendish

Payment Collection in International Trade

5

Learning Objectives

1. Importance of shipping documents which should accord with the terms of the letter of credit for the collection of payment through negotiation with the concerned banks and treatment of the shipping documents which are not in accordance with the terms of the letter of credit;
2. Function of the bill of lading and air way bill in negotiating with the bank;
3. Contractual function of commercial invoices in letter of credit transactions;
4. Nature of the bill of exchange from the viewpoint of facilitation of international trade;
5. Proceedings of transactions through bills of exchange under the documentary letter of credit;
6. Treatment of documents delivered contrary to instructions under the terms of letter of credit;
7. Characteristics of the letter of credit from the viewpoints of the exporter and importer.

There are a wide variety of payment methods available in international trade, each with having particular advantages and disadvantages.[1] In essence, if traders seek to assure a high level of security in payment, then more expensive payment methods are available. Conversely, if payment security is not an important issue, because the concerned parties trust each other, then considerably cheaper and simpler payment methods can be applied.[2]

---

[1] Ramberg (2008, *supra* note 48, at 147).
[2] *Id.*

E.S. Lee, *Management of International Trade*,
DOI 10.1007/978-3-642-30403-3_5, © Springer-Verlag Berlin Heidelberg 2012

5.1   Payment Collection Under Letter of Credit

5.1.1   Introduction

5.1.1.1 Payment Issue in International Trade

For a transaction in international trade to be carried out, an importer and an exporter are required to negotiate terms, agree to a contract, and perform their obligations to fulfill the contract. When conducting international trade, the importer needs to receive and secure the imported products, while the exporter must secure payment collection. Both parties want the deal to be executed flawlessly to obtain their goals, but they also have to compromise when it comes to the order of operations.

The buyer would prefer the goods to arrive in their entirety before making payment, in order to permit full inspection for quality and quantity. The Seller, conversely, would prefer for payment collection beforehand to cover the costs of the exportations, and to insure that the payment is made fully and punctually. Exporting is especially precarious because of the chance that an importer with unverified credit will default on his payment. This contrast of agendas leads to thorough negotiations in efforts to create an agreement that is suitable to both parties.

5.1.1.2 Intervention by Third Party

Generally speaking, one of the obstacles hindering international trade often results from uncertainties about collecting payment. Reconciling this issue is one of the most important aspects to insuring that the deal goes through. To overcome this issue, a third party may be involved in the transaction. The purpose of the third party is to facilitate the terms of price and payment for the two trading parties, avoiding potential problems and providing for an objective assessment and conclusion.

This third party is, more often than not, a bank. Large-scaled banks are often located internationally, and if not, are at least set up to do transactions overseas. Banks are equipped with the credit and financial power that the transaction might need. Banks are able to perform quick credit reviews on both parties, as well as determine their financial situations, which will help in constructing financing terms. On the other hand, banks tend to favor large scale international transactions, because of the large commissions they earn.

5.1.2   Letter of Credit

5.1.2.1 Introduction
Definition

A letter of credit is a crucial payment mechanism for international business. In particular, the documentary letter of credit facilitates international payments, providing the exporter with security of payment.[3] The exporter is assured of payment upon presenting documentary evidence of proper shipment of the contracted items made in accordance with the terms of the credit which was issued under the buyer's instructions.[4]

A letter of credit means any arrangement, however named or described, that is irrevocable and that constitutes a definite undertaking of the issuing bank to honor a duly made presentation, which is defined specifically as follows[5]:

"Any arrangement, however named or described, whereby a bank (issuing bank), acting at the request and on the instructions of a customer (applicant) or on its own behalf, ① is to make payment to or to the order of a third party (beneficiary), or is to accept and pay bills of exchange (draft(s)) drawn by the beneficiary; or ② authorizes another bank to effect such payment, or to accept such bills of exchange (drafts(s)); or ③ authorizes another bank to negotiate against stipulated document(s), provided the terms and conditions of the credit are complied with."[6]

When buyers and sellers are familiar with each other due to previous trade experience, letters of credit may not be needed. Without this familiarity, a buyer will be nervous of releasing the goods prior to payment. Worrying about the possibility that the buyer fails to pay, the seller will try to collect payment before the goods arrive. To remedy this situation, the buyer deposits the necessary funds to cover the goods with the issuing bank, and the issuing bank pays the seller or notifies the advising bank to pay the seller only when documents are presented within the time stipulated and in accordance with the terms stated under the letter of credit, through which the payment collection is completed.

The bank's decision to make payment has to be completely objective, and cannot evaluate whether the buyer has completely or substantially agreed to stipulations. The bank's job is really quite simple and straightforward, and it does not take on any risk.

Uniform Customs and Practice for Documentary Credits

The Uniform Customs and Practice for Documentary Credits, 2007 Revision, ICC Publication no. 600 (UCP 600) is a set of rules issued by the International Chamber of Commerce for the purpose of applying globally unified rules to transactions necessitating documentary letters of credit.[7] The intent of the rules to effect global unification has been highly successful and, through their progressive development

---

[3] *Id.*, at 165.

[4] *Id.*

[5] UCP 600, Art. 2.

[6] *Id.*

[7] Murray et al. (2007, *supra* note 8, at 186).

and revision over more than 70 years,[8] the UCP 600 is currently almost universally applied.[9]

UCP 600 rules may be applied to any kind of documentary credit (including, to the extent to which they may be applicable, any standby letter of credit) when it is expressly indicated in the credit that it is to be subject to these rules.[10] That is, the rules apply to letters of credit only when the parties have expressly incorporated them into their agreed letter of credit.[11] UCP, interpreted as a contractual term, shall naturally have precedence over the general domestic laws where any discrepancies between them exist, and such domestic laws might be applicable only to the extent that the letter of credit is not subject to the UCP.[12]

While in some domestic laws the UCP does not have the effect of law or the status of trade customs and may apply only if the parties have incorporated them into their contract,[13] in certain states of the United States, the provisions of the Uniform Commercial Code on letters of credit[14] are replaced by the UCP where the parties have agreed to apply them or where they are customarily applicable.[15] In many countries with national banking associations, the general standard conditions applied by the members of these associations often incorporate the UCP.[16] If the automated international transfer system (SWIFT)[17] is used by banks in letter of credit transactions, the UCP applies to the contractual relations between the banks and between them and SWIFT.[18] Even where the UCP is adopted specifically or generally, the parties are free to contract out of it, or to exclude application of specific parts.[19]

---

[8] UCP 600 is the seventh version of the rules. The first issue was published in 1933, the second appeared in 1951, the third in 1962, the fourth in 1974, the fifth in 1983 and the sixth-UCP 500 in 1993, *cited* by Murray et al. (2007, *supra* note 8, at 186).

[9] *Id.*

[10] *Id.*

[11] *Id.*

[12] Chuah (2009, p. 521)

[13] UCP 600, Art. 1.

[14] UCC Art. 5; for a discussion of the interaction between the UCP and the Uniform Commercial Code see Alaska Textile Co Inc V Chase Manhattan Bank [1992] 982 Fed. 2d. 813, *cited* by Murray et al. (2007, *supra* note 8, at 187).

[15] *Id.*

[16] *Id.*

[17] http://www.swift.com; SWIFT stand for Society for Worldwide Interbank Financial Telecommunications.

[18] Murray et al. (2007, *supra* note 8, at 187).

[19] *Id.*

5.1.2.2 Feature
Principle of Independence

The letter of credit is separate from and independent of the underlying actual contract of sale or other transaction.[20] A bank negotiating under the terms of credit considers whether the documents presented by the beneficiary are in compliance with the terms and conditions stipulated in the letter of credit.[21] The transaction under letter of credit is thus a documentary transaction. It is irrelevant to the bank relating to the letter of credit whether the underlying contract covers the purchase of specific products or whether it covers another transaction.[22]

Only when it is surely evident that the documents, although they are superficially in order, are actually fraudulent and that the beneficiary is involved in the fraud, the bank exceptionally should refuse to pay the price authorized by the letter of credit.[23] This is usually referred to as the "fraud exception".[24] Thus, banks must examine the documents presented with reasonable care to determine whether they comply completely with the requirements under the documentary credit.[25] Banks are only required to examine the contents of the documents, and not to investigate whether the statements contained in them are in compliance with the actual transaction.

> ## Principle of Independence
>
> "a. A credit by its nature is a separate transaction from the sale or other contract on which it may be based. Banks are in no way concerned with or bound by such contract, even if any reference whatsoever to it is included in the credit. Consequently, the undertaking of a bank to honor, to negotiate or to fulfill any other obligation under the credit is not subject to claims or defenses by the applicant resulting from its relationships with the issuing bank or the beneficiary. A beneficiary can in no case avail itself of the contractual relationships existing between banks or between the applicant and the issuing bank.
>
> b. An issuing bank should discourage any attempt by the applicant to include, as an integral part of the credit, copies of the underlying contract, proforma invoice and the like.[26]
>
> *(continued)*

---

[20] *Id.*, at 190.

[21] *Id.*

[22] *Id.*

[23] United City Merchants (Investments) Ltd v Royal Bank of Canada [1983] 1 A.C. 168; Tukan Timber Ltd v Barclays Bank Plc [1987] 1 Lloyd's Rep. 171 at 174. On fraud affecting letters of credit, *cited* by Murray et al. (2007, *supra* note 8, at 190).

[24] The paying bank's obligation is to consider the documents alone and not to take account of any other matters. The only established exception to this principle is the "fraud exception" and the so-called "nullity exception" forms no part of English law, Montrod Ltd v Grundkotter Flrischvertriebs GmbH [2002] 1 W.L.R. 1975, *cited* by Murray et al. (2007, *supra* note 8, at 190).

[25] UCP 600 Art. 14.

[26] Murray et al. (2007, *supra* note 8, at 192).

> Banks deal with documents and not with goods, services or performance to which the documents may relate." (Article 5 of UCP 600, Documents v. Goods, Services or Performance)

Principle of Strict Compliance

The legal principle that the documents presented for payment or negotiation to the bank under the letter of credit should strictly conform to the terms of the credit is generally referred to as the doctrine of strict compliance.[27] The reason underlying this rule that the bank is entitled to reject the documents not in strict compliance with the terms of credit – which can sometimes be burdensome to the beneficiary – is that the negotiation or paying bank acts only as a special agent of the issuing bank[28] that acts in turn as the special agent of the importer.[29] If an agent with limited authority acts beyond that conferred authority, the special agency should in principle be deprived and if he cannot recover the loss resulting from such unauthorized acts he has to bear such commercial risk of the transaction.[30]

In a falling market, a buyer is easily tempted to reject discrepant documents which the negotiating bank accepted even though they do not strictly conform to the terms and conditions stipulated in the letter of credit. Such things are likely to happen, because a commercial bank does not generally have expert knowledge or information on specific situations of actual business transactions.[31]

If the documents presented are not strictly in conformity with the terms of the credit and the bank refuses to accept them, the exporter should immediately contact his overseas customer (buyer) and request him/her to instruct the bank to accept the documents as presented.[32] Refusal of the bank to accept documents and pay against even a small and apparently insignificant discrepancy not sanctioned in the instructions of the credit has been legitimated by the courts in the overwhelming majority of litigated cases.[33] The doctrine of strict compliance was judicially interpreted in the following classic passage: "there is no room for documents which are almost the same, or which will do just as well".[34]

Practically speaking, however, the classic principle of strict compliance has been modified into a less strict rule. For example, banks are required to apply the International Standard Banking Practice (ISBP) in reviewing documents. The ISBP

---

[27] *Id.*

[28] Jack Malek and Quest, para. 6.4, *cited* by Murray et al. (2007, *supra* note 8, at 192).

[29] Murray et al. (2007, *supra* note 8, at 192).

[30] *Id.*

[31] *Id.*

[32] *Id.*

[33] *Id.*

[34] *Id.*

adopts the principle of "essential conformity" instead of that of "strict conformity" in reviewing documents, which rule is designed to prevent transactions from being unpaid due to minor documentary mistakes.

Notwithstanding such practical modifications, beneficiaries seeking to insure a guarantee of payment collection should keep in mind that documents not in strict conformity with a letter of credit can still be rejected. Due diligence should therefore be taken in the preparation of the required documents to ensure their strict compliance with the terms of the letter of credit. Many unpaid cases are intentionally tempted to be made due to unavoidable circumstances such as a rapidly deteriorating market. If any mistakes are found in the bank's investigation, the buyer can choose not to pay, henceforth avoiding the deal. When this occurs, the payment will only be made when the documents are presented faultlessly; any minor mistake can be the trigger to dismiss the payment.

5.1.3 Concerned Parties

5.1.3.1 Primary Concerned Parties
Applicant
The applicant is the party on whose request the credit is issued.[35] The applicant is the buyer of the goods, the final payer of the draft (indirect drawee), the accountee (payer), and the consignee of the shipped goods under the terms of the credit.

Beneficiary
Beneficiary means the party in whose favor a credit is issued.[36] The beneficiary is usually an exporter who collects payment once the required documents have been submitted with conformity, drawee, payee, and consignor or shipper under the terms of the credit.

Issuing Bank
Issuing bank means the bank that issues a credit at the request of an applicant or on its own behalf.[37] The issuing bank was formerly known as the opening bank, but has more recently been termed an issuing bank.

5.1.3.2 Other Concerned Parties
Advising Bank
Advising bank means the bank that advises the credit at the request of the issuing bank.[38] The Issuing bank of a letter of credit in most cases notifies a beneficiary of

---

[35] *Id.* Art. 2.

[36] *Id.*

[37] *Id.*

[38] *Id.*

its letter of credit through its main office, a branch, or a correspondent bank in the beneficiary's location. It should notify an exporter by request of the issuing bank, and should verify the authenticity of the letter of credit.

Negotiating Bank
Entering negotiations with the beneficiary upon the presentation of the draft accompanied by the transport documents, the negotiating bank acts to deduct interest and commissions until the final date of payment. Due to an obvious conflict of interest, the issuing bank and paying bank cannot be the same institution.

Confirming Bank (for Confirmed Letters of Credit)
Confirming bank means the bank that adds its confirmation to issued credit upon the issuing bank's authorization or request.[39] Essentially, a confirmation bank is just another layer of protection and security that payment will be made.

Nominated Bank
Nominated bank means the bank with which the credit is available or any bank in the case of a credit available with any bank.[40] It includes the paying bank when it is nominated separately by the issuing bank and the accepting bank when it is nominated separately by the issuing bank, to promptly make payment as soon as the documents are properly submitted in compliance with the stipulations set forth in the letter of credit. It also includes reimbursing bank which is to be instructed and authorized to provide reimbursement if the issuing bank makes reimbursement authorization, which is an instruction by an issuing bank to reimburse a claiming bank.

Transferring Bank
Transferring bank is the bank that acts to transfer the letter of credit in favor of a second beneficiary upon request of the first beneficiary. This can be performed under authorization of the issuing bank to pay, accept or buy the presented draft.

5.1.4   Kinds of Letter of Credit

5.1.4.1 Documentary Letter of Credit
There are four types of payment under the credit:payment at sight, deferred payment, by acceptance or by negotiation. The credit itself should state which of these four methods has been chosen by the parties and this issue should be settled beforehand in the contract under which the credit is issued.[41]

---

[39] *Id.*

[40] *Id.*

[41] Murray et al. (2007, *supra* note 8, at 216).

Sight Credit

If the parties have arranged a payment at sight credit, the advising bank is instructed to pay, or arrange for payment, to the seller on presentation of the draft accompanied by the transport documents. This is a case of payment against documents.[42] The authority to draw the sight bill of exchange for negotiation is vested as follows: "We hereby issue in your favor this documentary letter of credit which is available by negotiation of your drafts at sight for 100 % invoice amount drawn on OOO bank, Busan Branch".[43]

Deferred Payment Credit

If the parties have arranged a deferred payment credit, the advising bank is authorized to pay, or make arrangements for payment, at some future date determinable in accordance with the terms of the credit. The deferred payment credit may, for example, provide for payment 120 days from the date of the bill of lading.[44]

If the seller is to get the cash payment before the maturity date of the deferred payment credit, he can get paid through negotiating under the terms of the letter of credit. The negotiation under deferred payment credit is normally done at a discount, which reduces the payment amount of the credit conferred to the beneficiary.[45]

The undertaking of the issuing bank to make payment under the deferred payment letter of credit is made as follows: "We hereby engage that payment will be duly made at 60 days after bill of lading date against the documents presented in compliance with the terms of this credit".[46]

Acceptance Credit

The beneficiary under the acceptance letter of credit generally draws the bill of exchange as a usance draft on the negotiating bank in the specified manner.[47] By accepting the bill of exchange, the bank honors its commitment to pay the face value on maturity date to the party presenting it. The bill accepted by the negotiating bank provides the beneficiary, that is, the seller, with a considerable degree of guaranty to get paid at maturity.[48] If he does not want to hold the bill until the maturity date, he may turn it into cash through negotiation, e.g. by discounting it or selling it to the bank. Making negotiation, he is likely to get less than the face

---

[42] *Id.*

[43] *Id.*, at 217.

[44] *Id.*

[45] *Id.*

[46] *Id.*

[47] *Id.*

[48] *Id.*

value in the tenor of the bill of exchange because the negotiating bank deducts a discount, interest and commission.[49]

Another form of acceptance credit is credit which, according to the arrangement of the parties to the contract of sale, shall be accepted by the issuing bank or by the buyer (the applicant for the credit).[50] By issuing an irrevocable letter of credit, the issuing bank takes the liability to the bill of exchange to be duly accepted and paid by the buyer. By confirming the credit issued by the issuing bank, the confirming (advising) bank adds a similar guarantee additionally to the issuing bank's commitment that the buyer shall accept the bill.[51]

Negotiation Credit

Under the negotiation credit, the negotiating (advising) bank is only authorized to negotiate a bill of exchange drawn by the beneficiary on the buyer or the issuing bank.[52] The negotiating (advising) bank will indorse the bill of exchange and negotiate it, subject to deduction of discount or interest and commission. The bill of exchange may be drawn as a sight draft or a usance draft, according to the terms of the credit.[53]

The negotiation credit is subject to recourse against the beneficiary as drawer of the bill because the bank has only become an endorser of the bill of exchange. If, however, the negotiating bank is the confirming bank (and the tender of the document is in order), it does not have the recourse against the beneficiary since it takes liability to the beneficiary through the confirmation.[54]

The concerned parties to negotiations under the negotiation credit are advised as follows under the credit: "We hereby agree with the drawers, endorsers and bona-fide holders of draft drawn under and in compliance with the terms of this credits, that such drafts will be duly honored on due presentation and on delivery of documents as specified to the drawee bank".[55]

5.1.4.2 Revocable/Irrevocable Letter of Credit

The revocable letter of credit can be modified or cancelled without the beneficiary's consent. For that very reason, it is rarely used. The irrevocable letter of credit, however, can be modified or cancelled if the issuing bank, beneficiary and confirming bank (in case of the confirmed letter of credit) all agree that modification or cancellation should be made. Without this unanimous decision among the concerned parties to do so, the letter of credit is irrevocable.

---

[49] *Id.*

[50] *Id.*

[51] *Id.*

[52] *Id.*

[53] UCP 600 Art. 7.

[54] Murray et al. (2007, *supra* note 8, at 217).

[55] *Id.*

5.1.4.3 Confirmed/Unconfirmed Letter of Credit

A confirmation of letter of credit is an added level of protection for the beneficiary that is made by the confirming bank by insuring that payment shall be made under the terms and conditions of the confirmed letter of credit. If the letter of credit is confirmed, in addition to the issuing bank, another bank (selected by the issuing bank) also promises payment under the terms of the letter of credit. The promise is made in that bank's own name. The description of confirmation of a confirmed letter of credit is as follows: "We confirm the credit and thereby undertake that all drafts drawn and presented as above specified will be duly honored by us."

The unconfirmed letter of credit is one in which only the issuing bank has confirmed payment of the letter of credit. This is often deemed acceptable because an issuing bank's guarantee to pay rarely goes awry when the issuing bank's credit standing has been well established. Practically speaking, when the beneficiary as the exporter could not be substantially sure about the issuing bank's credit situation, he is recommended to ask the irrevocable and confirmed letter of credit to be issued to the buyer in advance.

5.1.4.4 Transferable/Nontransferable Letter of Credit

When a letter of credit is designated as transferable, a beneficiary can transfer all or some of the amount of the letter of credit to a third party. The rights of the credit are passed to the transferee who must comply with the terms in order to insure payment collection. This kind of letter of credit is common when the exporter is not the manufacturer of the exported goods, but a middleperson between the buyer and seller.

Before a transfer can be made, the beneficiary must first send a written request to the transferring bank, which does not have to make the transfer until it has been paid for its services. Most letters of credit are nontransferable. Under these stipulations, a letter of credit cannot be transferred, even when situations become otherwise advantageous to such a transfer.

5.1.4.5 Special Letters of Credit

Revolving Letter of Credit

When goods are going to be shipped several times continuously over a certain period of time, it is practical to use a revolving letter of credit, instead of issuing an individual letter of credit for each transaction. This letter of credit may limit the frequency at which the shipments can be made, and allows for the beneficiary to designate amounts of money over a specified allotted shipment.

Counter Trade Letter of Credit (Compensation Trade Letter of Credit)

A counter trade letter of credit is used when cash payments are difficult because of foreign exchange problems with the importing country. The letter of credit is made to balance the transaction for the importer and exporter. A counter trade letter of credit is subdivided into barter trade credit, compensation trade credit, parallel purchase credit, buy back credit, switch trade credit, and offset trade credit.

(1) Back to Back Letter of Credit

This letter of credit is often used in compensation trades in order to keep a balance between the importer and exporter. When an importer opens a letter of credit to import certain goods, this import letter of credit becomes valid only if an overseas exporter opens a letter of credit to import from the original importer's country, which makes it a conditional letter of credit. The description of such condition is similar to the following: "This letter of credit is valid if an exporter issues a counter letter of credit in favor of an importer within a certain period of time from the date of receipt of this letter of credit."

The term "back to back letter of credit" is sometimes used when the secondary letter of credit is issued, in triangular trades, to the supplier based on the terms and conditions of the beneficiary's original letter of credit (called the master letter of credit). This is done with the intention of helping the supplier, trader, and final buyer to complete the triangular trade smoothly.

(2) Escrow Letter of Credit

This letter of credit specifies that when an importer opens a letter of credit, he deposits funds in an escrow account in the name of the beneficiary without paying the beneficiary the negotiation amount of the draft issued by the letter of credit, which is one of the conditions of the letter of credit. Escrow accounts can be set up or operated through any negotiating bank, issuing bank, or any exchange transaction bank by agreement.

(3) Stand-by Letter of Credit

This type of letter of credit is a guarantee to the beneficiary against defaults of the other party in performing his commitments, and is often used instead of a performance guarantee. If a party does not pay his debt, the issuing bank assumes the obligation and will make the payment to the beneficiary. With a typical letter of credit, an issuing bank's obligation to payment is conditional upon presentation of the proper documents, accompanied by a standby letter of credit. Payment by the bank will only be made when the debtor has defaulted on his payment. Therefore, bank payment is made very rarely under a standby letter of credit. The beneficiary receiving a standby letter of credit can claim payment to the issuing bank when a company financed by the letter of credit did not fulfill its obligations.

The main stipulations of the stand-by credit are as follows: "We hereby issue our irrevocable stand-by letter of credit up to an aggregate security for your loan plus its interests extended to OOO for purchasing OOO as per contract underlined." "This credit is available against your sight draft drawn on us accompanied by your signed statement certifying that the borrower has defaulted in the payment of your loan plus its interest and that in consequence the amount drawn hereunder represents their unpaid indebtedness due to you."

For practical purposes, it is critical to understand the difference between a standby letter of credit and letter of guarantee (L/G). Both of them are guarantees, but a beneficiary can make use of a standby letter of credit much more favorably than a letter of guarantee. The formation of a letter of guarantee is guided by "Publication 325, ICC," and "Uniform Rules for Contract Guarantee," but these regulations are not yet widely recognized or accepted. Many beneficiaries receiving letters of guarantee are apt to have trouble because there is no proper set of international uniform rules to regulate interpretation and application of their terms. A standby letter of credit on the other hand has adopted the UCP 600 as its governing set of rules, which is widely recognized. Given this, deciding whether the UCP rules are to be applied to a standby credit is not a matter for debate.

5.1.5   Interpretation of Letter of Credit

5.1.5.1 General Rules

Since mutual legal relations of parties to letter of credit and interpretation of terms concerning letter of credit are decided by terms specified in the letter of credit, every word in the document must be chosen carefully in order to accomplish its intended goal. The UCP addresses this and encourages drafters to refrain from using of ambiguous words and expressions. Because the UCP is not mandatory law, any wording in the letter of credit is given precedence over any conflicting clauses in the UCP.

The UCP has provided the guidelines to avoid ambiguity in the drafted contract, which will undoubtedly help avoiding conflicts in the future and save both parties' time and money. The ambiguous wording as follows, for example, should be avoided: ① Concerning insurance coverage: usual risks, customary risks, insurance against all risks[56]; ② Concerning shipping period: prompt, immediately, as soon as possible[57]; ③ Concerning transferable credit: divisible, fractionable, assignable.[58]

5.1.5.2 Increase and Decrease of Quantity

Interpretation of Terms "about", "circa", "approximately", etc.
If any such words are written before a unit price or quantity, their meaning must be interpreted in accordance with the following principles: ① The above wording is applied only to amount, unit price, and quantity, not to period of time; ② The above wording is only effective to the clauses in which they are present, and not to surrounding clauses.

The words "about" or "approximately" used in connection with the amount of the credit or the quantity or the unit price stated in the credit are to be construed as allowing a tolerance not to exceed 10 percent more or 10 percent less than the amount, the quantity or the unit price to which they refer.[59] For example, when the quantity is written as "about 1,000pcs," it means that the maximum allowed is

---

[56] UCP 600 Art. 28.

[57] *Id.* Art. 3.

[58] *Id.* Art. 38(b).

[59] *Id.* Art. 30(a).

1,100pcs, and the minimum is 900pcs. Either amount or an amount in between is deemed acceptable.

Limit to Allowance of Plus or Minus Written Amount When "about," "circa," or "approximately" Is Not Made Explicit

Even when dealing with bulk cargo in which the exact amount is hard to be determined, such as ore, grain or oil, a variation of 5 percent is acceptable, and this is accompanied by the following stipulations and additions[60]:

It can be applied to items countable by packing unit. Even if shipment was done in excess, the amount of the invoice cannot exceed that of letter of credit, and the payment of the excess delivery should be handled by another method of payment.

Interpretation of Terms "by" or "to"

When increasing or decreasing the amount of letter of credit based on a change of condition, its interpretation could be different based on whether "by" or "to" is used. "By" means there is a net increase, and "to" refers to the total amount including the increase. For example, when an amount of letter of credit is increased from US$10,000.00 to US$300,000.00, it is increased by US$20,000.00, and it increased to US$30,000.00.

5.1.5.3 Period of Delivery
Terms Not to Be Used

The use of "prompt," "immediately," or "as soon as possible" should be avoided, but if included anyway, the bank should consider the letter of credit as having no shipping time and disregard those expressions.[61] If "on or about" is used with a fixed date, it means that delivery should be made within five days of that date. If the issuing date of a bill of lading is not within that eleven-day period, payment can be rejected.[62]

Starting Date of Time Period

When a month is used, and not a specific date, the expiration date is interpreted as one month minus one day. For example, if an opening date is May 10th, and the expiration date is for one month, the deadline is June 9th. When the words "to," "until," "'til," "from," etc. are written along with a specific date, this should be interpreted to count the period including the specific date.[63]

---

[60] *Id.* Art.30(b).

[61] *Id.* Art. 2.

[62] *Id.* "The expression "on or about" or similar will be interpreted as a stipulation that an event is to occur during a period of five calendar days before until five calendar days after the specified date, both start and end dates included".

[63] *Id.* "The words "to", "until", "till", "from" and "between" when used to determine a period of shipment include the date or dates mentioned, and the words "before" and "after" exclude the date mentioned".

When "after" is used with a specific date, the specific date is excluded and the period is counted from the next day.[64] The early period and the latter period of a month are specified as "first half of a month," and "second half of a month." A month can also be specified as "beginning of a month," "middle of a month," and "end of a month".[65]

Time Period for Document Presentation

Separately from a fixed expiry date of the letter of credit, if it is specified that "transport documents must be presented within ooo days after shipment", the actual period to present the documents under the letter of credit begins from the date of actual shipment to ooo days after the shipment within the period of expiration. If the letter of credit allows for an installment shipment, and the document presentation period is not stipulated with a special contract, the importer could experience trouble due to the delay of document presentation by exporters. Because of this, almost all installment letters of credit allowing installment shipment contain supplemental stipulations concerning the period for presentation of the documents.

When presentation period of transport documents is not specified on a letter of credit and the documents are accepted by the negotiating bank after twenty-one days from the actual date of shipment, the presented bill of lading is considered stale, which leads to cause for rejection.[66]

If "this office" is specified in front of "not later than" or "on or before," documents must be presented to the issuing bank, not the negotiating bank. The beneficiary must send the documents to the issuing bank quickly so that shipping documents can arrive before the expiration.

Shipping/Issuing Date of Document

Three terms "loading on board," "dispatch," and "taking in charge" are used for shipment in the standard form of credit on the basis of UCP 600. These mean that maritime transport, air transport and mailing, and multimodal transport are to be accepted.

(1) Maritime Transport

If goods are shipped by a general cargo ship, an effective transport date is the date loaded onboard and it is considered the same as the issuing date of bill of lading. Therefore, if an exporter was given a received bill of lading from a

---

[64] *Id.* "The words "from" and "after" when used to determine a maturity date exclude the date mentioned."

[65] *Id.* "The terms "first half" and "second half" of a month shall be construed respectively as the 1st to the 15th and the 16th to the last day of the month, all dates inclusive.";

"The terms "beginning", "middle" and "end" of a month shall be construed respectively as the 1st to the 10th, the 11th to the 20th and the 21st to the last day of the month, all dates inclusive."

[66] *Id.* Art.14(c): "A presentation including one or more original transport documents subject to Arts. 19, 20, 21, 22, 23, 24 or 25 must be made by or on behalf of the beneficiary not later than 21 calendar days after the date of shipment as described in these rules, but in any event not later than the expiry date of the credit."

shipping company, he should get an "onboard notation" confirmed by the captain. The notation date is considered a valid shipping date.[67]

(2) Air Transport and Mailing

If the exporter receives an air waybill (a document made out by, or on behalf, of the shipper, delivered electronically or conventionally) on the day the exporter takes cargo to carriers (airline, post office, private delivery company), that day is considered an actual shipping date.[68] But, if both the loading date of cargo and flight date are stipulated on the air waybill, the latter is considered as the shipping date.[69]

For mailing, since receipts are issued by parcel, even if a pile of parcels are accepted in the post office at the same time, they will arrive by different aircraft at importing locations on different days. Nevertheless, since conformity with the shipping date is judged with respect to the dispatch date on the document regardless of arriving dates, the receipt date (stamped date) is considered as the valid shipping date of the received mail.[70]

(3) Multimodal Transport

When the final destination of cargo is inland and not an airport, then the trip will likely utilize more than one means of transportation. Transshipment is often more likely to cause damage to the goods being shipped, making packaging important. In transport by container, the bill of lading is issued on the date of loading into the containers, or on the date of receipt of cargo, and this date is considered as the date of transport. This constitutes a received bill of lading, and as long as the letter of credit does not require the "onboard" bill of lading, the received bill of lading is effective under the documentary letter of credit.

Holidays for Banks/Transporting Companies

(1) Bank Holidays

When the expiration date of the letter of credit falls on a holiday of an issuing bank, the deadline is automatically extended to the next working day of the bank. In this case, the bank indicates an extension of the deadline resulting from the holiday on the cover letter, and sends it to the issuing bank.[71] But, if the holiday results from a "force majeure" such as a strike, riot, or war, the deadline cannot be extended.[72]

---

[67] *Id.* Art. 20(a)(ii).

[68] *Id.* Art. 23 & 25.

[69] *Id.* Art. 23(a)(iii).

[70] *Id.* Art. 23(a)(iii) & (25).

[71] *Id.* Art. 29.

[72] *Id.* Art. 36.

(2) Transporting Company Holidays

In the case that the final shipping date falls on a holiday in the exporting country, an extension of the deadline is not permitted. Because of this rule,[73] it is common for shipping companies to work on public holidays. If a shipping date is indicated on the letter of credit without an expiry date, the shipping and the expiry dates are assumed to be the same. If an expiry date is indicated on a letter of credit without a shipping date, that date is also assumed to be the dates of expiration and shipment.

5.1.5.4 Issuing or Expiring Date of Credit

The contract of sale usually makes explicit provision as regards the date at which the credit has to be issued. It is sometimes stated that the credit shall be issued by a specified date, and it is also sometimes provided that it shall be issued immediately, or the issuing time of the credit sometimes depends on an act by the seller relating to the delivery of the goods, e.g. the sending of a provisional invoice[74] or of an advice that the goods are, or will soon be, ready for shipment.[75] The issuing time of the credit may also depend on the seller's providing of a performance guarantee.[76]

When the contract does not provide the time of the credit to be issued, it is not normally assumed that the validity of the sales contract depends on issuing of the credit by the buyer. Where the sales contract is unconditional but does not provide a date on which the credit shall be issued, the credit has to be issued within a reasonable time.[77]

The letter of credit must stipulate a date on or before which documents must be presented by the beneficiary (at the stipulated place of presentation). An expiry date designated for honor or negotiation is deemed to be an expiry date for presentation.[78]

The expiry date of the credit is conceptually different from the latest shipment date. The latest shipment date is the date stipulated in the bill of lading as the latest date to load the goods on the board which is usually to be earlier than the expiry date of the credit.[79] The credit sometimes stipulates, in addition to its expiry date, that the bills of lading should be presented to the bank within a certain period of time

---

[73] *Id.* Art. 29(c).

[74] Knotz v Fairchough, Dodd & Jones Ltd [1952] 1 Lloyd's Rep. 226, *cited* by Murray et al. (2007, *supra* note 8, at 208).

[75] Plasticmoda SpA v Davidsons (Manchester) [1952] 1 Lloyd's Rep. 527. See also Establishments Chaombaux SARL v Harbormaster Ltd [1955] 1 Lloyd's Rep. 303, *cited* by Murray et al. (2007, *supra* note 8, at 208).

[76] Cf. State Trading Corporation of India Ltd v M Golodetz Ltd; The Sara D [1989] 2 Lloyd's Rep. 277; see below, para. 14–005, *cited* by Murray et al. (2007, *supra* note 8, at 208).

[77] Sinaision-Teicher Inter-American Grain Corporation v Oilcakes and Oilseeds Trading Co Ltd [1954] 1 W.L.R. 935, *cited* by Murray et al. (2007, *supra* note 8, at 209).

[78] UCP 600 Art. 6(d)(i).

[79] Murray et al. (2007, *supra* note 8, at 211).

after a date of shipment.[80] In addition to stipulating an expiry date for presentation of documents, where the credit calls for the tender of transport documents, presentation must be made not later than 21 days after the date of shipment, and in any event not later than the expiry date of the credit.[81]

5.1.6   Required Document

5.1.6.1 Document Under Letter of Credit
Significance of Document

Transport documents include the bill of lading, combined transport document, other shipping documents such as airway bill, postal receipt, rail bill of lading, commercial invoice, insurance document, certificate of origin, packing list, inspection certificate, beneficiary's certificate.

Since the transaction under the documentary letter of credit is a transaction by documents on the basis of the independence principle, a negotiating bank and an issuing bank make a decision about whether to pay the amount of a letter of credit based solely on the documents presented by a beneficiary. The beneficiary under the letter of credit should be careful to prepare for the required documents by the letter of credit for the negotiation with the bank after the shipment of the contracted goods in accordance with the terms of the letter of credit.

When the concerned parties face a question of sufficiency of documents under a letter of credit and this question cannot be resolved by reference to the instructions to the bank under the credit, they are required to turn to the UCP. It sets out in considerable detail the documents, in particular, the transport documentation which is normally acceptable to the bank.[82]

Document as Security

The documents as the securities against the shipped products (transport documents, insurance documents, drafts, etc.) out of multiple documents should be prepared and submitted to the bank in their original state. The documents without securities (commercial invoice, packing list, inspection certificate, etc.) should also be submitted as required under the letter of credit. Out of this batch of documents, one set of documents must be original, and the remaining documents can be duplicates.

The buyer is generally entitled to receive original documents.[83] A document bearing an apparently original signature, mark, stamp, or label of the issuer of the document, unless the document itself indicates that it is not an original, will be

---

[80] Id.
[81] Id.
[82] Id., at 200.
[83] Id.

considered as an original document.[84] And banks, unless otherwise indicated, will also accept a document as original if it: ①appears to be written, typed, perforated or stamped by the document issuer's hand; or ②appears to be on the document issuer's original stationery; or ③states that it is original, unless the statement appears not to apply to the document presented.[85]

Securities

"1. Collateral given or pledged to guarantee the fulfillment of an obligation; esp., the assurance that a creditor will be repaid (usu. with interest) any money or credit extended to a debtor. **2.** A person who is bound by some type of guaranty; SURETY. **3.** The state of being secure, esp. from danger or attack. **4.** An instrument that evidences the holder's ownership rights in a firm (e.g., a stock), the holder's creditor relationship with a firm or government (e.g., a bond), or the holder's other rights (e.g., an option). A security indicates an interest based on an investment in a common enterprise rather than direct participation in the enterprise. Under an important statutory definition, a security is any interest or instrument relating to finances, including a note, stock, treasury stock, bond, debenture, evidence of indebtedness, certificate of interest or participation in a profit-sharing agreement, collateral trust certificate, pre-organization certificate or subscription, transferable share, investment contract, voting trust certificate, certificate of deposit for a security, fractional undivided interest in oil, gas, or other mineral rights, or certificate of interest or participation in, temporary or interim certificate for, receipt for, guarantee of, or warrant or right to subscribe to or purchase any of these things. A security also includes any put, call, straddle, option, or privilege on any security, certificate of deposit, group or index of securities, or any such device entered into on a national securities exchange, relating to foreign currency." 15 USCA § 77b(1). – Also termed (in sense 4) evidence of indebtedness; evidence of debt. Cf. share (2); stock (4).

"Securities differ from most other commodities in which people deal. They have no intrinsic value in themselves – they represent rights in something else. The value of a bond, note or other promise to pay depends on the financial condition of the promisor. The value of a share of stock depends on the profitability or future prospects of the corporation or other entity which issued it; its market price depends on how much other people are willing to pay for it, based on their evaluation of those prospects." David L. Ratner, Securities Regulation in a Nutshell 1 (4th ed. 1992).

"What do the following have in common: scotch whisky, self-improvement courses, cosmetics, earthworms, beavers, muskrats, rabbits, chinchillas, fishing boats, vacuum cleaners, cemetery lots, cattle embryos,

(continued)

---

[84] UCP 600. Art. 17(b).

[85] *Id.* Art. 17(c).

> master recording contracts, animal feeding programs, pooled litigation funds, and fruit trees? The answer is that they have all been held to be securities within the meaning of federal or state securities statutes. The vast range of such unconventional investments that have fallen within the ambit of the securities laws' coverage is due to the broad statutory definition of a 'security'.... " 1 Thomas Lee Hazen, Treatise on the Law of Securities Regulation § 1.5, at 28–29 (3d ed. 1995).
>
> Source: Black's Law Dictionary (2009)

Documents Review

The negotiating and issuing banks must determine, according to the principle of independence, on the basis of the submitted documents alone whether or not the documents are in compliance with the terms of the credit. According to the doctrine of strict compliance the negotiating and issuing banks have the rights to refuse documents presented by the beneficiary when the particulars stipulated in the documents are not in compliance with the terms of the credit.[86] Beyond this restricted authorization, the bank is not obliged to do anything more and should not do anything more.[87] Even if their legal and practical effectiveness and value appear to be insignificant, particular form of documents required by the credit might have commercial value for the buyer and it is not the bank's job to reason why.[88] Thus, the bank is recommended to reject such discrepant documents unless it is instructed to accept them from the buyer.[89]

Time Period for Examination

The bank shall have a fixed maximum number of days-five banking days following the day of presentation-within which it is required to examine the documents, to determine whether or not the presentation is complying[90] and to decide whether to refuse to honor or negotiate, and shall give notice of refusing "no later than the close of the fifth banking day following the day of presentation".[91]

Discrepancy of Documents

Regarding the procedure for refusal of documents, if the bank decides to refuse to honor or negotiate the presentation, it must make notice of rejection to the

---

[86] Murray et al. (2007, *supra* note 8, at 196).

[87] *Id.*

[88] *Id.*

[89] *Id.*

[90] *Id.*, at 197.

[91] *Id.*

beneficiary specifying all the discrepancies.[92] The required rejection notice must be given by telecommunication or , if that is not possible, by other expeditious means[93] not later than the five day period prescribed and should be given to the party who has presented the documents to the bank.[94]

An issuing bank determining the documents to be discrepant may, however, exercise discretion to contact the applicant to see whether the application of a waiver of the discrepancies may be required.[95] This is usually done before a notice of rejection is sent.[96] If the applicant for the credit determines to waive the discrepancy, then documents will usually be taken up.[97] Rejection of non-conforming documents does not preclude the beneficiary from correcting the defects and re-presenting conforming documents provided that this is done within the period of validity of the credit.[98]

5.1.6.2 Transport Document

The most commonly required transport document under the documentary letter of credit is a bill of lading or a combined transport document. Transport documents may be issued by "any party other than a carrier, owner, master or charterer" provided that the transport document complies with the requirements for multi-modal transport documents,[99] bills of lading,[100] sea waybills,[101] air transport documents,[102] road transport documents,[103] rail transport documents[104] or inland waterway transport documents,[105] courier and post receipts, certificate of posting[106] and charter party bill of lading.[107]

---

[92] UCP 600 Art. 16(c)(ii).

[93] *Id*. Art. 16(d): "The notice required in sub-article 16 (c) must be given by telecommunication or, if that is not possible, by other expeditious means no later than the close of the fifth banking day following the day of presentation."

[94] *Id*. Art. 16(c).

[95] Murray et al. (2007, *supra* note 8, at 200).

[96] *Id*.

[97] UCP 600 Art. 16(b).

[98] Murray et al. (2007, *supra* note 8, at 200).

[99] *Id*. pp. 201,

[100] UCP 600 Art. 19.

[101] *Id*. Art. 20.

[102] *Id*. Art. 21.

[103] *Id*. Art. 22.

[104] *Id*. Art. 23.

[105] *Id*. Art. 24.

[106] *Id*. Art. 25.

[107] *Id*. Art. 22.

Combined Transport Document

When transport documents cover at least two different modes of transport (multi-modal or combined transport document), the documents must expressly indicate the name of the carrier and be signed by the carrier or his agent, or master or his agent.[108] Even though the credit may prohibit transshipment,[109] the bank will accept a transport documents indicating that transshipment will or may take place, provided the entire carriage is covered by one and the same transport documents.[110]

Transport Document Covering Different Modes of Transport

"a. A transport document covering at least two different modes of transport (multimodal or combined transport document), however named, must appear to:

i. Indicate the name of the carrier and be signed by:
  • the carrier or a named agent for or on behalf of the carrier, or
  • the master or a named agent for or on behalf of the master.

Any signature by the carrier, master or agent must be identified as that of the carrier, master or agent.

Any signature by an agent must indicate whether the agent has signed for or on behalf of the carrier or for or on behalf of the master.

ii. indicate that the goods have been dispatched, taken in charge or shipped on board at the place stated in the credit, by:
  • pre-printed wording, or
  • a stamp or notation indicating the date on which the goods have been dispatched, taken in charge or shipped on board.

The date of issuance of the transport document will be deemed to be the date of dispatch, taking in charge or shipped on board, and the date of shipment. However, if the transport document indicates, by stamp or notation, a date of dispatch, taking in charge or shipped on board, this date will be deemed to be the date of shipment.

iii. indicate the place of dispatch, taking in charge or shipment and the place of final destination stated in the credit, even if:
  a. the transport document states, in addition, a different place of dispatch, taking in charge or shipment or place of final destination, or
  b. the transport document contains the indication "intended" or similar qualification in relation to the vessel, port of loading or port of discharge.

---

[108] *Id.* Art. 19(a)(i).

[109] *Id.* Art. 19(b) : "unloading from one means of conveyance and reloading to another means of conveyance (whether or not in different modes of transport) during the carriage from the place of dispatch...".

[110] *Id.* Art. 19(c)(i).

iv. be the sole original transport document or, if issued in more than one original, be the full set as indicated on the transport document.

v. transportation contains terms and conditions of carriage or make reference to another source containing the terms and conditions of carriage (short form or blank back transport document). Contents of terms and conditions of carriage will not be examined.

vi. contains no indication that it is subject to a charter party.

b. For the purpose of this article, transhipment means unloading from one means of conveyance and reloading to another means of conveyance (whether or not in different modes of transport) during the carriage from the place of dispatch, taking in charge or shipment to the place of final destination stated in the credit.

c. i. A transport document may indicate that the goods will or may be transhipped provided that the entire carriage is covered by one and the same transport document.

ii. A transport document indicating that transhipment will or may take place is acceptable, even if the credit prohibits transhipment."(UCP 600 Article 19)

Bill of Lading

Under the general domestic laws, a bill of lading is recognized as a negotiable document of title.[111] Where a credit calls for a bill of lading covering a port-to-port shipment, the following are required to be applied[112]: The bill of lading must expressly indicate the name of the carrier and be signed by the carrier, master or a named agent of either.[113] It must also indicate that the goods have been shipped on board a named vessel at the port of loading stipulated in the credit which may be evidenced by pre-printed wording or an "on board notation" to this effect.[114] Further, the bill of lading must indicate shipment from the port of loading to the port of discharge stipulated in the letter of credit.[115]

Bill of Lading

"a. A bill of lading, however named, must appear to:
i. indicate the name of the carrier and be signed by:
  • the carrier or a named agent for or on behalf of the carrier, or
  • the master or a named agent for or on behalf of the master.

(continued)

---

[111] Murray et al. (2007, *supra* note 8, at 202).

[112] *Id.*

[113] UCP 600 Art. 20.

[114] *Id.*

[115] Murray et al. (2007, *supra* note 8, at 202).

Any signature by the carrier, master or agent must be identified as that of the carrier, master or agent.

Any signature by an agent must indicate whether the agent has signed for or on behalf of the carrier or for or on behalf of the master.

ii. indicate that the goods have been shipped on board a named vessel at the port of loading stated in the credit by:
   • pre-printed wording, or
   • an on board notation indicating the date on which the goods have been shipped on board.

The date of issuance of the bill of lading will be deemed to be the date of shipment unless the bill of lading contains an on board notation indicating the date of shipment, in which case the date stated in the on board notation will be deemed to be the date of shipment.

If the bill of lading contains the indication "intended vessel" or similar qualification in relation to the name of the vessel, an on board notation indicating the date of shipment and the name of the actual vessel is required.

iii. indicate shipment from the port of loading to the port of discharge stated in the credit.

If the bill of lading does not indicate the port of loading stated in the credit as the port of loading, or if it contains the indication "intended" or similar qualification in relation to the port of loading, an on board notation indicating the port of loading as stated in the credit, the date of shipment and the name of the vessel is required. This provision applies even when loading on board or shipment on a named vessel is indicated by pre-printed wording on the bill of lading.

iv. be the sole original bill of lading or, if issued in more than one original, be the full set as indicated on the bill of lading.

v. contain terms and conditions of carriage or make reference to another source containing the terms and conditions of carriage (short form or blank back bill of lading). Contents of terms and conditions of carriage will not be examined.

vi. contain no indication that it is subject to a charter party.

b. For the purpose of this article, transhipment means unloading from one vessel and reloading to another vessel during the carriage from the port of loading to the port of discharge stated in the credit.

c. i. A bill of lading may indicate that the goods will or may be transhipped provided that the entire carriage is covered by one and the same bill of lading.

ii. A bill of lading indicating that transhipment will or may take place is acceptable, even if the credit prohibits transhipment, if the goods have been shipped in a container, trailer or LASH barge as evidenced by the bill of lading.

d. Clauses in a bill of lading stating that the carrier reserves the right to tranship will be disregarded."(UCP 600 Article 20)

Non-negotiable Sea Waybill

Unlike bills of lading, sea waybills are not negotiable documents of title.[116] They provide evidence of the shippers' receipt of the goods to be loaded on the conveyance and the contract of carriage to a nominated consignee.[117] The provisions for non-negotiable sea waybills are substantially similar to those for bills of lading and permit a bank to accept such documents if the stipulated conditions are in compliance with the terms of letters of credit.[118]

Non-Negotiable Sea Waybill

"a. A non-negotiable sea waybill, however named, must appear to:

i. indicate the name of the carrier and be signed by:
- the carrier or a named agent for or on behalf of the carrier, or
- the master or a named agent for or on behalf of the master.

Any signature by the carrier, master or agent must be identified as that of the carrier, master or agent.

Any signature by an agent must indicate whether the agent has signed for or on behalf of the carrier or for or on behalf of the master.

ii. indicate that the goods have been shipped on board a named vessel at the port of loading stated in the credit by:
- pre-printed wording, or
- an on board notation indicating the date on which the goods have been shipped on board.

The date of issuance of the non-negotiable sea waybill will be deemed to be the date of shipment unless the non-negotiable sea waybill contains an on board notation indicating the date of shipment, in which case the date stated in the on board notation will be deemed to be the date of shipment. If the non-negotiable sea waybill contains the indication "intended vessel" or similar qualification in relation to the name of the vessel, an on board notation indicating the date of shipment and the name of the actual vessel is required.

iii. indicate shipment from the port of loading to the port of discharge stated in the credit.

If the non-negotiable sea waybill does not indicate the port of loading stated in the credit as the port of loading, or if it contains the indication "intended" or similar qualification in relation to the port of loading, an on board notation indicating the port of loading as stated in the credit, the date of shipment and the name of the vessel is required. This provision applies even when loading on board or shipment on a named vessel is indicated by pre-printed wording on the non-negotiable sea waybill.

(continued)

---

[116] UCP 600 Art. 21(a).

[117] Murray et al. (2007, *supra* note 8, at 202).

[118] *Id.*

   iv. be the sole original non-negotiable sea waybill or, if issued in more than one original, be the full set as indicated on the non-negotiable sea waybill.

   v. contain terms and conditions of carriage or make reference to another source containing the terms and conditions of carriage (short form or blank back non-negotiable sea waybill). Contents of terms and conditions of carriage will not be examined.

   vi. contain no indication that it is subject to a charter party.

  b. For the purpose of this article, transhipment means unloading from one vessel and reloading to another vessel during the carriage from the port of loading to the port of discharge stated in the credit.

  c. i. A non-negotiable sea waybill may indicate that the goods will or may be transhipped provided that the entire carriage is covered by one and the same non-negotiable sea waybill.

   ii. A non-negotiable sea waybill indicating that transhipment will or may take place is acceptable, even if the credit prohibits transhipment, if the goods have been shipped in a container, trailer or LASH barge as evidenced by the non-negotiable sea waybill.

  d. Clauses in a non-negotiable sea waybill stating that the carrier reserves the right to tranship will be disregarded." (UCP 600 Article 21)

Charter Party Bill of Lading

The requirements for charter party bills of lading are essentially similar to those for standard bills of lading. A charter party bill of lading can be signed by the master, owner or charter, or by an agent of either.[119] A bank may accept a charter party bill of lading instead of the charter party contract itself even if a charter party contract is required to be presented by the terms of the credit.[120]

Charter Party Bill of Lading

"a. A bill of lading, however named, containing an indication that it is subject to a charter party (charter party bill of lading), must appear to:

i. be signed by:

- the master or a named agent for or on behalf of the master, or
- the owner or a named agent for or on behalf of the owner, or
- the charterer or a named agent for or on behalf of the charterer.

Any signature by the master, owner, charterer or agent must be identified as that of the master, owner, charterer or agent.

Any signature by an agent must indicate whether the agent has signed for or on behalf of the master, owner or charterer.

---

[119] UCP 600 Art. 22(a)(i).

[120] *Id.* Art. 22, *cited* by Murray et al. (2007, *supra* note 8, at 202).

An agent signing for or on behalf of the owner or charterer must indicate
the name of the owner or charterer.
ii. indicate that the goods have been shipped on board a named vessel at the
port of loading stated in the credit by:
- pre-printed wording, or
- an on board notation indicating the date on which the goods have been
shipped on board.

The date of issuance of the charter party bill of lading will be deemed to be
the date of shipment unless the charter party bill of lading contains an on
board notation indicating the date of shipment, in which case the date
stated in the on board notation will be deemed to be the date of shipment.
iii. indicate shipment from the port of loading to the port of discharge stated in
the credit. The port of discharge may also be shown as a range of ports or a
geographical area, as stated in the credit.
iv. be the sole original charter party bill of lading or, if issued in more than
one original, be the full set as indicated on the charter party bill of lading.
b. A bank will not examine charter party contracts, even if they are required to
be presented by the terms of the credit." (UCP 600 Article 22)

Air Transport Document

Air transport documents are required to be signed by the carrier or a named agent
acting on his behalf.[121] The document must show that the goods have been accepted
for carriage[122] and should also show the airport of departure and destination as
being stipulated in the credit.[123] The date of issuance of the air transport documents
is deemed to be the date of shipment unless there is a specific notation indicating the
actual date of shipment in which case that date will be deemed to be the date of
shipment.[124]

Air Transport Document

"a. An air transport document, however named, must appear to:
i. indicate the name of the carrier and be signed by:
- the carrier, or
- a named agent for or on behalf of the carrier.

Any signature by the carrier or agent must be identified as that of the
carrier or agent.

(continued)

---

[121] *Id.* Art. 23(a)(i).

[122] *Id.* Art. 23(a)(ii);

[123] Murray et al. (2007, *supra* note 8, at 202).

[124] UCP 600 Art. 23(a)(iii), *cited* by Murray et al. (2007, *supra* note 8, at 202).

Any signature by an agent must indicate that the agent has signed for or on behalf of the carrier.

ii. indicate that the goods have been accepted for carriage.

iii. indicate the date of issuance. This date will be deemed to be the date of shipment unless the air transport document contains a specific notation of the actual date of shipment, in which case the date stated in the notation will be deemed to be the date of shipment.

Any other information appearing on the air transport document relative to the flight number and date will not be considered in determining the date of shipment.

iv. indicate the airport of departure and the airport of destination stated in the credit.

v. be the original for consignor or shipper, even if the credit stipulates a full set of originals.

vi. contain terms and conditions of carriage or make reference to another source containing the terms and conditions of carriage. Contents of terms and conditions of carriage will not be examined.

b. For the purpose of this article, transhipment means unloading from one aircraft and reloading to another aircraft during the carriage from the airport of departure to the airport of destination stated in the credit.

c. i. An air transport document may indicate that the goods will or may be transhipped, provided that the entire carriage is covered by one and the same air transport document.

ii. An air transport document indicating that transhipment will or may take place is acceptable, even if the credit prohibits transhipment."(UCP 600 Article 23)

Road, Rail/Inland Waterway Transport Documents

The road, rail and inland waterway transport documents govern the carriage by road, rail or inland waterways and similar principles to marine transport documents are applied to these documents.[125] In the absence of any indication on the rail, road or inland waterway transport documents as to the numbers issued, banks will accept the transport documents presented as constituting a full set. Banks will also accept such transport documents as originals, whether or not they are marked as originals.[126]

---

[125] Murray et al. (2007, *supra* note 8, at 202).

[126] UCP 600 Art. 24(c).

Road, Rail or Inland Waterway Transport Documents

"**a.** A road, rail or inland waterway transport document, however named, must appear to:

i. indicate the name of the carrier and:

- be signed by the carrier or a named agent for or on behalf of the carrier, or

- indicate receipt of the goods by signature, stamp or notation by the carrier or a named agent for or on behalf of the carrier.

Any signature, stamp or notation of receipt of the goods by the carrier or agent must be identified as that of the carrier or agent.

Any signature, stamp or notation of receipt of the goods by the agent must indicate that the agent has signed or acted for or on behalf of the carrier.

If a rail transport document does not identify the carrier, any signature or stamp of the railway company will be accepted as evidence of the document being signed by the carrier.

ii. indicate the date of shipment or the date the goods have been received for shipment, dispatch or carriage at the place stated in the credit. Unless the transport document contains a dated reception, stamp, an indication of the date of receipt or a date of shipment, the date of issuance of the transport document will be deemed to be the date of shipment.

iii. indicate the place of shipment and the place of destination stated in the credit.

b. i. A road transport document must appear to be the original for consignor or shipper or bear no marking indicating for whom the document has been prepared.

ii. A rail transport document marked "duplicate" will be accepted as an original.

iii. A rail or inland waterway transport document will be accepted as an original whether marked as an original or not.

c. In the absence of an indication on the transport document as to the number of originals issued, the number presented will be deemed to constitute a full set.

d. For the purpose of this article, transhipment means unloading from one means of conveyance and reloading to another means of conveyance, within the same mode of transport, during the carriage from the place of shipment, dispatch or carriage to the place of destination stated in the credit.

e. i. A road, rail or inland waterway transport document may indicate that the goods will or may be transhipped provided that the entire carriage is covered by one and the same transport document.

ii. A road, rail or inland waterway transport document indicating that transhipment will or may take place is acceptable, even if the credit prohibits transshipment."(UCP 600 Article 24)

Partial Shipment/Transshipment

(1) Case without Indication on Letter of Credit

In most cases, it is expressly indicated on the letter of credit whether or not to allow partial shipment and/or transshipment. If there is no indication on the letter of credit, it is acceptable to make partial shipments. Since there is no indication on the letter of credit concerning transshipment, discussions about the interpretation of its omission could ensue. More often than not, an absence of "transshipment" allowance stipulated expressly on the letter of credit would lead to the conclusion that it is not allowed.

(2) Partial Shipment on Same Ship and Voyage

Under the letter of credit does not cover for allowing partial shipment, for example, if the exporter shipped part of the cargo on the named ship to City A due to a manufacturing delay, and two days later he shipped the rest of the cargo to City B which was the next port, would the exporter be in breach of the provision of inhibition of partial shipment?

The shipping company may issue two copies of the bill of lading, and the shipping port and shipping date may both be different, seemingly breaking the provision of inhibition of partial shipment. But, it is clear that this does not constitute partial shipment despite the different shipping date and shipping port because it is "a couple of shipments done by the same ship and the same voyage."[127] Maintaining the same ship on the same voyage is not considered partial shipment. If a shipping port is indicated on the letter of credit (in the above example, City A or City B), the problem about inhibition of partial shipment is solved, but it breaks the obligatory provision of departure from the named port, which may lead to a claim from the importing party.

In terms of mailing, if several packages were sent by a post office on the same day, but delivered on different days because the packages may have been sent by different carriers, the delivery is not considered partial as long as the post office stamps indicate the same date.[128]

(3) Special Provision of Combined Transport and Container

Transshipment occurs when cargo is transferred from one transport means to another one on the way to its destination, frequently resulting in damage, loss of cargo, and additional costs. Obviously, importers prefer direct shipment to insure their imported goods to arrive safely. Debate can arise about transshipment if it is not explicitly included in the letter of credit.

If the letter of credit does not specify that the shipment will be direct, goods arguably can be transshipped. When the transport means are a trailer or containers, transshipment is allowed with a special provision.[129] When transshipment is not explicitly prohibited under the letter of credit,

---

[127] *Id.* Art. 32.

[128] *Id.* Art. 25(a).

[129] *Id.* Art. 20 & 21(a).

transshipment is allowed when transport documents indicate that transshipment is possible if those documents cover all aspects of the voyage.[130] In the case that transshipment is explicitly disallowed on the letter of credit, the following documents should be accepted: ① When "reservation of transshipment rights of shipping companies" among bill of lading clauses is included in "printed clauses"[131]; ② When the letter of credit allows for combined transports[132]; ③ When indicating that goods should be carried to the final destination loaded in a container, trailer or "lighter aboard ship (LASH)"[133] which is a smaller barge on a larger vessel; ④ When a shipping port and a destination port are indicated to container freight station(CFS) or container yard(CY) in the port concerned.

5.1.6.3 Invoice

The commercial invoice for the shipped goods must expressively indicate that it has been issued by the beneficiary nominated in the credit.[134] It should be made out to the applicant for the credit[135] and the description of the transacted items must be in compliance with the stipulations including the currency in the credit, though other documents are allowed to contain a description in general terms not inconsistent with the terms of the credit.[136] A bank has discretion to reject a set of documents containing an invoice issued for an amount in excess of the amount authorized to be negotiated or honored under the credit.[137]

Commercial Invoice

"a. A commercial invoice:
   i. must appear to have been issued by the beneficiary (except as provided in article 38);
   ii. must be made out in the name of the applicant (except as provided in sub-article 38 (g));
   iii. must be made out in the same currency as the credit; and
   iv. needs not be signed.
b. A nominated bank acting on its nomination, a confirming bank, if any, or the issuing bank may accept a commercial invoice issued for an amount in excess of the amount permitted by the credit, and its decision will be binding upon all parties, provided the bank in question has not honored or negotiated for an amount in excess of that permitted by the credit.

(continued)

---

[130] *Id.* Art. 20(b), (c) & 21(b).

[131] *Id.* Art. 20.

[132] *Id.* Art. 19(b).

[133] *Id.* Art. 20(c)(ii) & 21(c)(ii).

[134] *Id.* Art. 18(a)(i) & (iv).

[135] *Id.* Art. 18(a)(ii).

[136] *Id.* Art. 14(e).

[137] *Id.* Art. 18(b), *cited* by Murray et al. (2007, *supra* note 8, at 203).

c. The description of the goods, services or performance in a commercial
   invoice must correspond with that appearing in the credit." (UCP 600
   Article 18)

5.1.6.4 Insurance Document

Insurance documents must be in compliance with the stipulations in the credit and
issued and signed by the insurance company, or underwriters or their agents or
proxies.[138] Agents or proxies must provide an indication of the capacity in which
any signature is executed. If the insurance document indicates that it has been
issued in more than one original, all of the original sets must be presented.[139] Unless
specifically allowed under the credit, broker's cover notes are not acceptable,[140]
though (unless otherwise stipulated) banks will accept an insurance policy in lieu of
an insurance certificate or a declaration under an open cover.[141] Cover under the
insurance policy must be effective at the latest from the date of shipment and the
insurance documents must be expressed in the same currency to the currency
stipulated in the credit.[142]

The goods are required to be insured for at least their CIF or CIP value plus 10
percent. Should the bank be unable to determine the CIF or CIP value from the
documents, it will accept an insurance document stating that the minimum amount
of cover is 110 percent of the amount authorized to be negotiated or honored under
the credit, or the gross value of the goods as shown on the invoice, whichever is
greater.[143]

The credit should stipulate the required terms of insurance contract and any
additional risks to be covered. In the absence of such stipulation, the bank will
accept the insurance documents as presented by the seller and bears no responsibility for any risks not covered therein.[144] If the credit stipulates "all risks" terms, the
insurance document need not bear such a heading provided. It contains a clear "all
risks" clause or notation.[145]The bank is obligated to check for inconsistencies in
such additional documentation.[146]

---

[138] Murray et al. (2007, *supra* note 8, at 203).

[139] UCP 600 Art. 28(b)

[140] *Id.* Art. 28(c).

[141] *Id.* Art. 28(d).

[142] *Id.* Art. 28(f)(i), *cited* by Murray et al. (2007, *supra* note 8, at 203).

[143] *Id.* Art. 28(f)(ii), *cited* by Murray et al. (2007, *supra* note 8, at 203).

[144] *Id.* Art. 28(g).

[145] *Id.* Art. 28(h).

[146] *Id.* Art. 14, *cited* by Murray et al. (2007, *supra* note 8, at 203).

Insurance Document and Coverage

"a. An insurance document, such as an insurance policy, an insurance certificate or a declaration under an open cover, must appear to be issued and signed by an insurance company, an underwriter or their agents or their proxies.

Any signature by an agent or proxy must indicate whether the agent or proxy has signed for or on behalf of the insurance company or underwriter.

b. When the insurance document indicates that it has been issued in more than one original, all originals must be presented.

c. Cover notes will not be accepted.

d. An insurance policy is acceptable in lieu of an insurance certificate or a declaration under an open cover.

e. The date of the insurance document must be no later than the date of shipment, unless it appears from the insurance document that the cover is effective from a date not later than the date of shipment.

f. (i) The insurance document must indicate the amount of insurance coverage and be in the same currency as the credit.

(ii) A requirement in the credit for insurance coverage to be for a percentage of the value of the goods, of the invoice value or similar is deemed to be the minimum amount of coverage required.

If there is no indication in the credit of the insurance coverage required, the amount of insurance coverage must be at least 110 % of the CIF or CIP value of the goods.

When the CIF or CIP value cannot be determined from the documents, the amount of insurance coverage must be calculated on the basis of the amount for which honour or negotiation is requested or the gross value of the goods as shown on the invoice, whichever is greater.

(iii) The insurance document must indicate that risks are covered at least between the place of taking in charge or shipment and the place of discharge or final destination as stated in the credit.

g. A credit should state the type of insurance required and, if any, the additional risks to be covered. An insurance document will be accepted without regard to any risks that are not covered if the credit uses imprecise terms such as 'usual risks' or 'customary risks'.

h. When a credit requires insurance against 'all risks' and an insurance document is presented containing any 'all risks' notation or clause, whether or not bearing the heading 'all risks', the insurance document will be accepted without regard to any risks stated to be excluded.

i. An insurance document may contain reference to any exclusion clause.

j. An insurance document may indicate that the cover is subject to a franchise or excess (deductible). " (UCP Article 28)

5.1.6.5 Documents to Be Read Together

The bank is usually authorized to make finance available upon presentation of several documents in a set, and as stated, these would normally include the transport document, e.g. a bill of lading, the invoice and the insurance policy or certificate.[147] In such situations, without contrary instructions, it is sufficient if all the documents in the set, when taken together, contain the particulars required under the credit and every document in the set is not required to contain all of them.[148] For example, the goods must be fully described in the invoice in accordance with the credit instructions, but in the other documents they may be described in general terms.[149]

> ## Standards for Examination of Documents
>
> (a) "A nominated bank acting on its nomination, a confirming bank, if any, and the issuing bank must examine a presentation to determine, on the basis of the documents alone, whether or not the documents appear on their face to constitute a complying presentation.
>
> (b) A nominated bank acting on its nomination, a confirming bank, if any, and the issuing bank shall each have a maximum of five banking days following the day of presentation to determine if a presentation is complying. This period is not curtailed or otherwise affected by the occurrence on or after the date of presentation of any expiry date or last day for presentation.
>
> (c) A presentation including one or more original transport documents subject to articles 19, 20, 21, 22, 23, 24 or 25 must be made by or on behalf of the beneficiary not later than 21 calendar days after the date of shipment as described in these rules, but in any event not later than the expiry date of the credit.
>
> (d) Data in a document, when read in context with the credit, the document itself and international standard banking practice, need not be identical to, but must not conflict with, data in that document, any other stipulated document or the credit.
>
> (e) In documents other than the commercial invoice, the description of the goods, services or performance, if stated, may be in general terms not conflicting with their description in the credit.
>
> (f) If a credit requires presentation of a document other than a transport document, insurance document or commercial invoice, without stipulating by whom the document is to be issued or its data content, banks will accept the document as presented if its content appears to fulfill the function of the required document and otherwise complies with sub-article 14 (d).

---

[147] Murray et al. (2007, *supra* note 8), at 204.

[148] *Id.*

[149] UCP 600 Art. 14(e), cited by Murray et al. (2007, *supra* note 8), at 204.

(g) A document presented but not required by the credit will be disregarded and may be returned to the presenter.

(h) If a credit contains a condition without stipulating the document to indicate compliance with the condition, banks will deem such condition as not stated and will disregard it.

(i) A document may be dated prior to the issuance date of the credit, but must not be dated later than its date of presentation.

(j) When the addresses of the beneficiary and the applicant appear in any stipulated document, they need not be the same as those stated in the credit or in any other stipulated document, but must be within the same country as the respective addresses mentioned in the credit. Contact details (telefax, telephone, email and the like) stated as part of the beneficiary's and the applicant's address will be disregarded. However, when the address and contact details of the applicant appear as part of the consignee or notify party details on a transport document subject to articles 19, 20, 21, 22, 23, 24 or 25, they must be as stated in the credit.

(k) The shipper or consignor of the goods indicated on any document need not be the beneficiary of the credit.

(l) A transport document may be issued by any party other than a carrier, owner, master or charterer provided that the transport document meets the requirements of articles 19, 20, 21, 22, 23 or 24 of these rules." (UCP 600 Article 14)

Even though some latitude is allowed in the description of the goods in the documents other than the invoice, all documents tendered to the bank must clearly and unequivocally relate to the same goods. This question of identification of the goods is different from that of their description in the documents.[150] If the documents are not linked by an unambiguous reference to the same goods, the presentation is not properly made. But it is not necessary that the documents themselves be linked by mutual reference.[151]

5.1.7   Bill of Exchange

5.1.7.1 Concepts

A draft (bill of exchange) is defined as a formal instrument and negotiation tool which commits a creditor to give a certain sum to the payee or party the creditor appoints within a specified period of time at a designated place.

---

[150] Murray et al. (2007, *supra* note 8), at 204.

[151] *Id.*

The parties concerned to the draft as follows:

① Drawer: Party that issues and signs the drafts. Generally the drawer is the exporter and the beneficiary under the letter of credit; ② Drawee: A debtor who is trusted to repay in the future (to a paying bank), and an issuing bank of the letter of credit undertakes to make payments for the importer; ③ Payee: Party that makes the payment, which is usually a paying or negotiating bank; ④ Acceptor: If a draft is issued in usance (payment can immediately be made upon document presentation), it must be accepted by the drawee. "Acceptance" is completed by a drawee once the party becomes a drawee by officially declaring his intention.

5.1.7.2 Bill of Exchange Under Letter of Credit

Letters of credit are divided into letters of credit that require drafts, and letters of credit that do not require drafts, when the beneficiary under the letter of credit presents the required documents for payment collection under the letter of credit. Negotiation letter of credit, acceptance letter of credit, and reimbursement letter of credit require presenting the bill of exchange accompanied by the shipping documents, but payment letter of credit and deferred payment letter of credit do not require any such bill of exchange.

In case of the letter of credit that requires a bill of exchange accompanied by documents, drafts, that is, the bills of exchange, are required to be issued for presentation because they are expected to serve as a facilitator to negotiation and create convenience of payment. Letters of credit, sometimes, do not require a bill of exchange to be drawn because drafts are not expected to be advantageous to the transactions, where a bill of exchange would only slow down the transaction and increase the transaction cost. This is especially true in European countries where high stamp duties are commonly charged for issuing drafts.

"Order" Bill of Exchange:

1 May 2013

90 days after date pay to our order the sum of ten thousand USDOLLARS, value received,

US$10,000

KeumSam Na Ra Co. Ltd

To: Chinese Marine Trading Co. Ltd,

YangFu Economic Development Zone, YangFu

Hainan, P.R. China

> **"Bearer" Bill of Exchange:**
>
> 1 May 2013
>
> 90 days after date pay to our order the sum of ten thousand USDOLLARS, value received,
>
> US$10,000
>
> KeumSam Na Ra Co. Ltd
>
> To: Chinese Marine Trading Co. Ltd,
>
> YangFu Economic Development Zone, YangFu
>
> Hainan, P.R. China

5.1.8   Negotiation for Payment Collection

5.1.8.1 Negotiation of Documents
Introduction
The beneficiary should prepare all required documents to insure they are fully consistent with the terms of the letter of credit, and it is advisable to make sure all documents are in accordance with the doctrine of "strict compliance" to prevent future disputes over trivial errors.

Since the UCP 600 does not mention proper remedial actions to be taken when inconsistencies are found in documents, and because each country has different laws and practices, it would be difficult to settle disputes if they occur. Therefore, unnecessary descriptions in the documents should be avoided if they in no way affect the terms of the transaction. However, if there are mistakes or discrepancies in a document, it is advisable to reissue the document if circumstances allow this to be easily done. In any case, when corrections are needed, a signature or seal of the applicant is needed to approve the modification.

When a bank is designated for negotiation, the negotiations must essentially be carried out through the designated bank. If negotiations are done in a bank other than the designated negotiating bank, the negotiations must be redone with the designated bank properly. Negotiations must be done within the designated time limit so that documents can be presented before the expiry date:

① When the time limit to submit documents has expired, but the expiry date of the letter of credit has not passed, the deadline to submit the documents is seven days after the shipping date. Even though the expiry date could have initially been longer than seven days beyond the shipping date, documents must arrive within seven days of the shipping date. For example, if the shipping date is May 1st and the expiry date is May 10th, documents must be submitted by May 8th; ② When the time limit to submit documents exceeds the expiry date, the deadline to submit documents is ten days after the shipping date.

Required Documents for Negotiation
Documents are required for negotiation as follows:

Agreement of documentary draft or official seal, which is required to be submitted once in the first stage of transaction, and the exporter should sign his name on the document in accordance with the bank's instruction; draft, which is required in case of payment letters of credit and deferred payment letters of credit, but in the case of clean letters of credit it is normally not required; transport documents, which include the bill of lading, airway bill or post receipt; insurance documents which are always required in the contract in which the seller is responsible for making an insurance contract with an insurer; commercial invoice; a packing list and certificate of origin, among other documents, are often required; negotiation application; original letter of credit.

Negotiation Procedure
Banks receiving a negotiation application from the beneficiary under the letter of credit do their business generally through the following procedural processes:

① Review conformity of documentation with the terms of the letter of credit and any nonconformity among documents;

② Make suggestions for nonconformity remediation when small mistakes are found in documents that can be corrected within the permissible period of time;

③ Deposits remaining balance to the exporter's account after deducting the incurring fees, charges and interests from the value of the letter of credit, at which time the original letter of credit is returned to the exporter after writing proof of the negotiation on its back;

④ Dispatch documents: Commonly two sets of documents will be made and mailed by air to safeguard against possible lost documents;

⑤ Dispatch a reimbursement request to a reimbursing bank which is actually required to pay for the value of the letter of credit. When the reimbursing bank is specified on the letter of credit, shipping documents should be sent to the issuing bank. When it is specified that telegraphic transfer (T/T) reimbursement is acceptable, reimbursement by T/T to a reimbursing bank is requested, but when it is not accepted, drafts are required to be conventionally mailed. If this bank is not the designated bank under a restricted letter of credit, all documents should be sent to a restricted bank, and renegotiation should be applied for.

Practice of Negotiating Bank under Documentary Letter of Credit

○ Reviewing Documents

① The result of reviewing by negotiating bank leads to one of two conclusions: The first is to find a lack of conformity with the documents and specifications on the letter of credit, and the second is to find prefect conformity. When a lack of conformity is found, the letter of credit is handled accordingly. When the documents are perfectly in order, the bank would generally make payment to the exporter in advance, which is called a clean negotiation.

② A negotiating bank does not have to assess the particulars in the packing lists, invoice or a contract of sale in accordance with the "independence of the letter of credit" (UCP 600 Art. 4(a)). Herewith, independence of the letter of credit means that its terms are viewed independent of sale contracts. (UCP 600 Art.4(a))

③ A negotiating bank and an issuing bank do not have to review the quantity and unit price in an invoice, but if a bank overlooked evident errors due to negligence, that bank can be tried in court (ICC, UCP 600, p. 74). It is necessary for banks to use proper prudence in their reviews to avoid this costly mistake. (UCP 600 Art.34)

④ A negotiating bank must review the documents with reasonable care.[152] If no evident errors are found, the bank does not have to review detailed calculations of items such as quantity, unit price, and total amount in the invoice (ICC Pub.434, Opinion Banking Commission, p.22). Nevertheless, since there is always the possibility of being involved in unnecessary disputes with customers, it is advisable to review all calculations in detail. (UCP 600 Art.14(d))

⑤ If the bank is given any documents that the letter of credit did not require, it does not have to review them, and it may return them to the party or forward them to the next party without any further responsibilities. (UCP 600 Art.14(g))

⑥ The bank bears no responsibilities for satisfaction, exactness, authenticity, forgery, or legal effects of the documents. If the bank judges the documents to be legal forms, and reviews them with reasonable care, the bank has no responsibility if later the documents prove to be forged. However, even if the documents are perfect in form, if the bank recognized they were forged the bank is then to take responsibility for the forgery. This is particularly important with B/Ls because they are more frequently forged. If the bank is located in the country in which the document was issued, it must review the documents to insure they follow the legal form mandated by that country. If the

(continued)

---

[152] UCP 600 Art. 14(a).

bank accepts them despite their legally imperfect form, it cannot avoid this responsibility. (UCP 600 Art. 34)

⑦ Issuing banks, confirming banks, or designating banks review documents, decide to accept or reject, and are allowed a reasonable length of time within seven working days from the next working day after the acceptance of documents to be made for their examination. The banks are required to inform the party submitting documents of the decision. (UCP 600 Art. 14(b)).

○ **Handling Negotiation Documents**

① When a negotiating bank is designated, if the bank is not a designated bank, the documents can be sent to an issuing bank only through a designated bank to take proper procedures of renegotiation

② If a negotiating bank finds any lack of conformity within the documents, it will return the documents to the beneficiary to allow for corrections to be made and the documents to be resubmitted if possible.

③ When a negotiating bank sends documents on "approval basis" to an issuing bank, it must state "These documents are in accordance with UCP 600" on the cover letter. If this is not done, the forward is considered to be on a "collection basis," which means they are not protected on the basis of the UCP 600.

④ Although a negotiating bank finds conformity and there is a clean negotiation, if an issuing bank delays payment intentionally without a convincing reason, the negotiating bank should complain to the issuing bank requesting reimbursement of payment and urge payment of collection. (UCP 600 Art.13)

⑤ A negotiating bank must review the documents thoroughly in making negotiation. Generally speaking, when a negotiating bank receives a notice of "unpaid" from an issuing bank, the negotiating bank sends the "unpaid" notice to the beneficiary and requires him to handle it in person with the applicant rather than directly solving the problem with the issuing bank. The beneficiary must contact the applicant and settle the problem as soon as possible. (UCP 600 Art.16(e))

5.1.8.2 Right of Recourse by Negotiating Bank

With a payment letter of credit or deferred payment letter of credit, if a designating bank is any bank other than the issuing bank, the paying bank reimburses debts directly to an exporter (creditor). If a designating bank makes a payment, it cannot exercise recourse to an exporter even if it is unpaid from an issuing bank in the future. The payment made by the issuing bank or its designating bank is final.

On the other hand, a negotiating bank may have the right of recourse in the amount of the negotiated payment plus interest from the negotiation date to the reimbursement date, because the negotiating bank including the reimbursement or issuing bank made finance available to the exporter in advance by discounting drafts before another bank made the final payment. If the negotiating bank is not reimbursed for this amount, it has the right to claim for the "dishonored amount" from the exporter.

5.1.8.3 Discrepant Documents

A clean negotiation is always preferred because those discrepancies in documents can cause various difficulties to the concerned parties. If a lack of conformity in documents is easily correctable, a negotiating bank must point out the error and request an exporter to resubmit the documents with the proper amendments. Despite the initial inconsistency, if the documents are resubmitted they can still constitute a clean negotiation.

If a discrepancy in the exporter's documents is, however, too substantial to be easily corrected, the negotiating bank must handle the situation accordingly. Major discrepancies require consultation with the importer to clarify the agreement. If an importer decides that the discrepancies will not prevent the payment of the transaction, he can demand the bank to disregard the error, and payments will go through as planned. In the case of unchangeable discrepancy in the submitted documents, the negotiating bank can choose one of the follows:

Negotiation Under Letter of Indemnity

Indemnity means "protection or security against damage or loss" and a letter of indemnity is a letter guaranteeing that the person to whom the letter is written will not suffer a financial loss. Banks usually accept this letter because it is evident that recourse is possible in the future if the issuing bank makes a notice of "unpaid."

Cable Negotiation

If a negotiating bank finds a lack of conformity in the documents that is not easily fixed, the negotiating bank keeping the documents reports the inconsistency, asks an issuing bank whether to accept by cable, receives a reply of acceptance from the issuing bank, and negotiates the documents to pay the beneficiary the export price requested by the beneficiary under the letter of credit.

Negotiation on Approval Basis

If a negotiating bank considers the inconsistency in the documents too substantial to be modified, and is uncertain whether reimbursement by the issuing bank is to be made to the beneficiary, it will discuss the problem with the beneficiary, and send the documents "on approval basis or payment basis" to an issuing bank. In this case, a negotiating bank has no risk, but the beneficiary can have trouble in getting payment collection until the issuing bank receives the payment from the applicant.

Negotiation on Collection Basis

Collection basis means that a negotiating bank does not directly negotiate the documents made inconsistently with the terms of letter of credit, but instead sends the documents to an issuing bank, waits for approval from that bank, and, if it gets paid by the issuing bank, then makes payment to the exporter. If the lack of conformity is substantial, or if a letter of credit cannot be confirmed for its authenticity, collection basis will be used. An issuing bank bears no obligation to the negotiating bank under collection basis, and the beneficiary is in the position where he cannot exercise the right to claim payment. But, if an issuing bank makes the payment to the negotiating bank satisfactorily to the beneficiary's expectations, he can then exercise the right to claim payment to the negotiating bank.

Works of Issuing Bank Regarding Negotiation
O How to Review Documents

① An issuing bank reviews documents and then decides whether to accept or reject those documents. The bank has a reasonable length of time within seven working days from the next working day after acceptance of documents to inform the party that submitted the documents of its decision (UCP 600 Art. 14(b)).

② If the documents prove to be clean, the bank should deliver the documents to the importer upon payment from the importer. Under the usance letter of credit, the bank should do so upon receiving the documents. (UCP 600 Art. 15)

③ If an issuing bank notifies a negotiating bank of document inconsistencies after reviewing the documents, it should do so within seven working days from the next working day after receiving the documents. Furthermore, the issuing bank should notify the importer as soon as possible if the documents presented a lack of consistency. These inconsistencies are often disregarded by the importer if he is positive that the deal can still go through as planned. (UCP 600 Art.16(c))

O Handling Documents

An issuing bank should try to restrain any attempts of an applicant to insert too many statements in an issuing letter of credit. (UCP 600 Art. 9) The issuing bank is recommended to disallow the applicant from adding a pro forma invoice or sale contract to the issuing letter of credit. However, if it is necessary to include a pro forma invoice or sales contract, the beneficiary must review them closely and correct any differences to prevent future disputes. (Herewith, a proforma invoice is a document made by the exporter on behalf of the importer containing minimal information such as name, quantity, and cost of goods to be traded.) (ISBP 57)

② In case of bankruptcy, the issuing bank is required to keep the documents and wait for the beneficiary's directions to return them.

O Obligation to Make Payment

If the documents are clean, or when an importer allows them even if they are not clean, an issuing bank must make payment immediately. Under an "at sight letters of credit" (payment can be made once documents have been submitted, even before the applicant receives the goods), if an importer makes payment within three days from the date the documents arrived, the bank should pay the net of letter of credit price. But, if the bank delays the payment, the bank should pay the price plus interest accrued until the date of payment. Particularly, if payment is not made seven days after the documents arrived, there is an "overdue interest" fee, which further increases the transaction cost. (UCP 600 Art. 16(g))

② The terms of letter of credit are similar to those of a sales contract, and even if letter of credit includes a clause related to the sales contracts, it is not directly connected to them. An issuing bank must make payment to a beneficiary if the documents are consistent with the terms of the letter of credit. When a buyer brings forth questions about fraud to an issuing bank, unless the questions are settled, the bank must make payment. If it is later revealed that forgery did take place, as long as the beneficiary did not get the notice but instead a third party is noticed, the bank must make payment. The issuing bank does not have to perform obligations under the letter of credit only in case that a beneficiary recognizes the fraud or gross negligence in advance and has solid evidence to prove it. (UCP 600 Art.34)

Gross Negligence

"Negligence is gross if the precautions to be taken against harm are very simple, such as persons who are but poorly endowed with physical and mental capacities can easily take." H.L.A. Hart, "Negligence, Mens Rea and Criminal Responsibility," in Punishment and Responsibility 136, 149 (1968).

"Gross Negligence, as it originally appeared, means very great negligence, or the want of even slight or scant care. It has been described as a failure to exercise even that care which a careless person would use. Several courts, however, dissatisfied with a term so nebulous ... have construed gross negligence as requiring willful, wanton, or reckless misconduct, or such utter lack of all care as will be evidence thereof ... But it is still true that most courts consider that 'gross negligence' falls short of a reckless disregard of the consequences, and differs from ordinary negligence only in degree, and not in kind." Prosser and Keeton on the Law of Torts § 34, at 211–12 (W. Page Keeton ed., 5th ed. 1984).

5.1.8.4 Claim by Issuing Bank

If an issuing bank finds any lack of conformity from reviewing documents, a claim procedure will ensue. This process is as follows:

Consultation with Importer

If any discrepancy is found, it is commonly recommended to decide in consultation with an importer whether the issuing bank should make a claim to the negotiating bank. Even if the importer considers the discrepancy to be disregarded, a bank may still make a claim because it doubts the importer's financial ability to make payment. If the issuing bank does make a claim without discussions with the importer, the claim is valid.[153] An issuing bank or confirming bank can make a claim to the negotiating bank to get returned the paid amount plus the interest incurred from the date of the first payment to the date the documents were rejected.

Modification of Document

On the basis of "notice of discrepancies," an issuing bank that has received a notice of discrepancy returns the documents after correctly modifying them within the expiry date of letter of credit or document submitting date (shipping documents are usually required to be submitted within twenty-one days from the issuing date). In this case, the discrepancy has been fixed and the issuing bank can no longer make a claim based on that inconsistency.

Notice of Claim

If an issuing bank judges that it has all the requirements necessary to make a claim, it will do so with a written notice through mail or cable sent to a negotiating bank. The notice should specify in detail all discrepancies in the documents that are a cause to reject the documents. Any discrepancies that are not submitted in the first instance cannot be submitted later. The notice should reveal the location of the documents (whether an issuing bank has kept them or returned them),[154] indicating, for example, "holding document at your disposal."

5.1.9 Receipt of Goods by Buyer

In normal cases, reimbursement should be made when the issuing bank has received the documents and given them to the importer. The importer then receives an arrival notice from the shipping company, submits the received bill of lading to the shipping company, and finally receives the cargo. If something does not go as

---

[153] *Id.* Art. 16(b)
[154] *Id.* Art. 14(c)(ii).

planned, special measures might be required to resolve problems. The following section will analyze such special circumstances.

5.1.9.1 Trust Receipt

A trust receipt is required when an issuing bank has received the documents, notifies the importer that the documents have arrived, and requests the importer to take the documents against payment or acceptance, but the bank realizes that the importer is not able to make the payment. The bank cannot deliver the documents to the importer without getting paid, but it also cannot keep the documents because the bank will have to bear the responsibilities and costs of storage and risk of the cargo.

This kind of problem can be solved by a special type of international financing. If an importer accepts a trust receipt (T/R) agreement, the bank can then transfer the possession of the cargo to the importer along with the shipping documents, and make payment to the issuing or paying bank after the cargo is delivered to the importer or sold.

5.1.9.2 Letter of Guarantee

Normally, the documents will arrive at the issuing bank before the cargo arrives at the port. But, if a bank is notified by a shipping company that the cargo has arrived and the documents still have not arrived at the bank, the importer cannot receive the cargo. This is because the shipping company usually delivers the cargo in exchange for transport documents like a bill of lading. In such cases, if the letter of guarantee (L/G) is issued by the issuing bank, the shipping company can accept the letter of guarantee in place of a bill of lading, and the shipping company can deliver the cargo to the importer.

Herewith the letter of guarantee is a kind of a payment warranty or note that an issuing bank issues in favor of a shipping company with promissory statements to provide a shipping company with the bill of lading upon arrival and to take all responsibilities in respect of cargo delivery without the bill of lading. In the case of air transport, cargo normally arrives before documents, and a letter of guarantee can be issued with air transport just as in the case of marine transportation.

5.1.10 Illustration of Letter of Credit by Kind

5.1.10.1 Irrevocable Letter of Credit at Sight with Reimbursement

This credit is unconfirmed (see code 49) irrevocable (see code 40A) documentary (see code 46A) credit, under which the beneficiary draws the sight (see code 42 C) draft on the drawee bank that acts as the reimbursement bank (see code 42A). During negotiations, the negotiating bank which is not restricted by the issuing bank (see code 41D) is required to send the draft to the drawee bank (see code 78) and the documents to the issuing bank directly (see code 78).

```
---------------------------------------------- TRANSMISSION ----------------------------------------------
SEND TO                      : SWIFT
MESSAGE ID                   : 20101222M0000117
MESSAGE STATUS               : SEC
MESSAGE INPUT REFERENCE
                             : 14:31:39-2010/12/22-NACFKRSEXXX-6383-612184


---------------------------------------------- MESSAGE HEADER ----------------------------------------------


SENDER         : NACFKRSEXXX NATIONAL AGRICULTURAL COOPERATIVE
                 FEDERATION(NH BANK)
RECEIVER       : WPACAU2SXXX WESTPAC BANKING CORPORATION
                 (FOR ALL NEW SOUTH WALES BRANCHES)
MESSAGE TYPE   : MT700   [ ISSUE OF A DOCUMENTARY CREDIT ]


---------------------------------------------- MESSAGE TEXT ----------------------------------------------


SEQUENCE OF TOTAL                  27 : 1/1
FORM OF DOCUMENTARY CREDIT         40A: IRREVOCABLE
DOCUMENTARY CREDIT NUMBER          20 : M0301012NS00484
DATE OF ISSUE                      31C: 2010-12-22
APPLICABLE RULES                   40E: UCPURR LATEST VERSION


                                       *Date    *Place
DATE AND PLACE OF EXPIRY           31D: 2011-01-25 Australia
APPLICANT                          50 : ABC CORPORATION
                                       CHUNG-KU, SEOUL, KOREA
BENEFICIARY                        59 : BBC PTY LIMITED

1. LOCK WAY RIVERVIEW QUEENSLAND 4303 AUSTRALIA


                                       *Currency  *Amount
CURRENCY CODE AMOUNT               32B: USD     79,650.00
PERCENTAGE CRDT AMT TOLERANCE      39A: 05/05
AVAILABLE WITH..BY..-NAME/ADDR     41D: ANY BANK BY NEGOTIATION
DRAFTS AT...                       42C: AT SIGHT
DRAWEE                             42A: PNBPUS3NNYC WELLS FARGO BANK,
                                   N.A.(FORMERLY KNOWN AS WACHOVIA)
                                   (NEW YORK INTERNATIONAL BRANCH)
PARTIAL SHIPMENTS                        43P: ALLOWED
```

TRANSSHIPMENT   43T: ALLOWED

PORT OF LOADING/AIRPORT OF DEPARTURE   44E: BRISBANE

PORT OF DISCHARGE/AIRPORT OF DESTINATION   44F: PUSAN PORT, KOREA

Place of Final Destination/ For Transportation/Place of Delivery

PLACE OF FINAL DESTINATION/ FOR TRANSPOR   44B: ICHEON WAREHOUSE

LATEST DATE OF SHIPMENT   44C: 2011-01-10

DESCP OF GOODS AND/OR SERVICES   45A:

   +CHILLED BEEF OFFALYPS CHUCK RIB G/F MW/VACYPS SHORT

   RIB DEN 3 RIB G/F MW/VA

   +CHILLED BONELESS BEEFYPS TOPSIDE G/F IW/VACYPS EYE ROUND

   G/F IW/VACYPS CHUCK EYE ROLL G/F IW/VACYPS PE BRISKET

   D/OFF G/F IW/VACYPS SHIN SHANK G/F MW/VACYPS BOLAR BLADE

   G/FYPS OYSTER BLADE G/F

   TOTAL QUANTITY : 15MT TOTAL AMOUNT: 79,650.0

   +TERMS OF PRICE : CFR

   +PLACE OF TERMS OF PRICE : ICHEON WAREHOUSE

   +COUNTRY OF ORIGIN : AUSTRALIA

DOCUMENTS REQUIRED   46A:

   +SIGNED COMMERCIAL INVOICE IN 3 COPIES

   +FULL SET OF CLEAN ON BOARD OCEAN BILLS OF LADING MADE OUT

   TO THE ORDER OF NATIONAL AGRICULTURAL COOPERATIVE

   FEDERATION MARKED FREIGHT PREPAID AND NOTIFY APPLICANT

   +PACKING LIST IN 3 COPIES

   +CERTIFICATE OF ORIGIN 2 FOLD ISSUED BY CHAMBER OF

   COMMERCE OR GOVERNMENTAL AUTHORITY WHERE

   SHIPMENT IS MADE.

   +PHOTO COPY OF OFFICIAL CERTIFICATE WITH RESPECT TO MEAT,

   MEAT PRODUCTS AND EDIBLE OFFAL.

ADDITIONAL CONDITIONS   47A:

   +MULTI-MODAL BILLS OF LADING ARE ACCEPTABLE

   +T/T REIMBURSEMENT IS ALLOWED.

   +ORDER NO : L183637/1

   +DISCREPANCY FEE OF USD 60.00 OR EQUIVALENT WILL BE

   DEDUCTED FROM THE PROCEEDS OF EACH PRESENTATION OF

   DOCUMENTS WITH DISCREPANCY(IES) FOR

   PAYMENT/REIMBURSEMENT UNDER THIS LETTER OF CREDIT.

```
          +INSURANCE WILL BE COVERED BY THE APPLICANT
          +5 PCT MORE OR LESS IN QUANTITY AND AMOUNT ARE ACCEPTABLE


CHARGES                          71B: +ALL BANKING CHARGES OUTSIDE OF
                                 AUSTRALIA, INCLUDING REIMBURSING FEES,
                                 ARE FOR THE ACCOUNT OF APPLICANT.
                                 DISCREPANCY CHARGES, IF ANY, ARE FOR THE
                                 ACCOUNT OF THE BENEFICIARY


PERIOD FOR PRESENTATION   48 : +DOCUMENTS TO BE PRESENTED
                                 WITHIN 10 DAYS AFTER THE DATE OF
                                 SHIPMENT BUT IN ANY EVENT WITHIN THE
                                 VALIDITY OF THE CREDIT.


CONFIRMATION INSTRUCTIONS     49 : WITHOUT
REIMBURSING BANK              53A: PNBPUS3NNYC
                              WELLS FARGO BANK,
                              N.A.(FORMERLY KNOWN AS WACHOVIA)
                              (NEW YORK INTERNATIONAL BRANCH)


INSTRUC TO PAY/ACCPT/NEGOT BNK       78 :
        +ALL DOCUMENTS SHOULD BE FORWARDED TO THE NATIONAL
        AGRICULTURAL COOPERATIVE FEDERATION INTERNATIONAL
        BANKING SERVICE CENTER, IMPORT DEPARTMENT, NONGHYUP
        SINCHON COMPLEX B/D 6F, 49-31 NOGOSAN-DONG, MAPO-GU, SEOUL,
        KOREA IN ONE LOT BY REGISTERED AIRMAIL OR AIR-COURIER.

        +PLEASE CLAIM REIMBURSEMENT BY FORWARDING BENEFICIARYS'
        SIGHT DRAFT OR T/T (ONLY IN CASE REIM. CLAIM IS ALLOWED UNDER
        THIS CREDIT) TO THE REIMBURSING BANK.
--------------------------------------- END OF MESSAGE-----------------------------------------
```

Source: National Agricultural Cooperative Federation

5.1.10.2 Irrevocable Letter of Credit at Sight with Remittance

This credit is the same as in the case of form "irrevocable letter of credit at sight with reimbursement" except for the fact that, in making negotiations, negotiating bank, which is not restricted by the issuing bank (see code 41D), is required to send both the draft and the documents to the issuing bank (see code 78).

```
------------------------------------- TRANSMISSION -------------------------------------

 SEND TO                    : SWIFT
  MESSAGE ID                : 20101229M0000075
 MESSAGE STATUS             : SEC
 MESSAGE INPUT REFERENCE
                            : 16:45:59-2010/12/29-NACFKRSEXXX-6388-623215


------------------------------------- MESSAGE HEADER-------------------------------------

 SENDER          : NACFKRSEXXX NATIONAL AGRICULTURAL COOPERATIVE
                   FEDERATION(NH BANK)
 RECEIVER        : ICBKCNBJTSN INDUSTRIAL AND COMMERCIAL BANK OF
                   CHINA
                   (TANGSHAN CITY BRANCH)
 MESSAGE TYPE    : MT700  [ ISSUE OF A DOCUMENTARY CREDIT ]


------------------------------------- MESSAGE TEXT-------------------------------------

 SEQUENCE OF TOTAL                  27 : 1/1
 FORM OF DOCUMENTARY CREDIT         40A: IRREVOCABLE
 DOCUMENTARY CREDIT NUMBER          20 : M0301012NS00712
 DATE OF ISSUE                      31C: 2010-12-29
 APPLICABLE RULES                   40E: UCP LATEST VERSION


                                    *Date    *Place
 DATE AND PLACE OF EXPIRY           31D: 2011-04-25 China
 APPLICANT                          50 : ABC CORPORATION
                                    CHUNG-KU, SEOUL, KOREA
 BENEFICIARY                        59: BBC METALLURGICAL ROLL CO. LTD.
                                    TANGSHAN CITY, HEBEI PROVINCE,CHINA


                                    *Currency *Amount
 CURRENCY CODE AMOUNT               32B: USD      98,390.00
 AVAILABLE WITH..BY..-NAME/ADDR     41D: ANY BANK BY NEGOTIATION
 DRAFTS AT...                       42C: SIGHT
 DRAWEE                             42A: NACFKRSEXXX NATIONAL

                                    AGRICULTURAL COOPERATIVE
                                    FEDERATION(NH BANK)
```

PARTIAL SHIPMENTS	43P: ALLOWED
TRANSSHIPMENT	43T: PROHIBITED
PORT OF LOADING/AIRPORT OF DEPARTURE	44E: Tianjin
PORT OF DISCHARGE/AIRPORT OF DESTINATION	44F: Busan
LATEST DATE OF SHIPMENT	44C: 2011-04-15
DESCP OF GOODS AND/OR SERVICES	45A:

    +HS CODE : 8455.30.1000

    ROLL FOR ROLLING MILL DETAILS ARE AS PER P/O GBT010-002-E

    DATED DEC. 26, 2010 CFR BUSAN

    +TERMS OF PRICE : CFR

    +COUNTRY OF ORIGIN : CHINA

DOCUMENTS REQUIRED   46A:

    +SIGNED COMMERCIAL INVOICE IN 3 COPIES

    +FULL SET OF CLEAN ON BOARD OCEAN BILLS OF LADING MADE OUT

    TO THE ORDER OF NATIONAL AGRICULTURAL COOPERATIVE

    FEDERATION MARKED FREIGHT PREPAID AND NOTIFY APPLICANT

    +PACKING LIST IN 3 COPIES

ADDITIONAL CONDITIONS   47A:

    +DISCREPANCY FEE OF USD 60.00 OR EQUIVALENT WILL BE

    DEDUCTED FROM THE PROCEEDS OF EACH PRESENTATION OF

    DOCUMENTS WITH DISCREPANCY(IES) FOR

    PAYMENT/REIMBURSEMENT UNDER THIS LETTER OF CREDIT.

    +INSURANCE WILL BE COVERED BY THE APPLICANT

    +T/T REIM. CLAIM PROHIBITED

CHARGES   71B: +ALL BANKING CHARGES INCLUDING

                REIMBURSEMENT CHARGES AND POSTAGE

                UTSIDE KOREA ARE FOR ACCOUNT OF BENEFICIARY

PERIOD FOR PRESENTATION   48 : +DOCUMENTS TO BE PRESENTED

                            WITHIN 21 DAYS AFTER THE DATE OF

                            SHIPMENT BUT IN ANY EVENT WITHIN THE

                            VALIDITY OF THE CREDIT.

| CONFIRMATION INSTRUCTIONS | 49 : WITHOUT |
| INSTRUC TO PAY/ACCPT/NEGOT BNK | 78 : |

    +ALL DOCUMENTS SHOULD BE FORWARDED TO THE NATIONAL

    AGRICULTURAL COOPERATIVE FEDERATION INTERNATIONAL

    BANKING SERVICE CENTER, IMPORT DEPARTMENT, NONGHYUP

    SINCHON COMPLEX B/D 6F, 49-31 NOGOSAN-DONG, MAPO-GU, SEOUL,

    KOREA IN ONE LOT BY REGISTERED AIRMAIL OR AIR-COURIER.

```
+UPON RECEIPT OF DOCUMENTS IN COMPLIANCE WITH THE TERMS
AND CONDITIONS OF THE CREDIT, WE WILL REMIT THE PROCEEDS AS
PER YOUR INSTRUCTIONS.
+REMITTANCE COMM. AND CABLE CHARGE ARE FOR ACCOUNT OF
BENEFICIARY
ADVISE THROUGH BANK-BRANCH/OFF          57B: YR. TANGSHAN BRANCH

-------------------------------------- END OF MESSAGE --------------------------------------

Source: National Agricultural Cooperative Federation
```

5.1.10.3 Banker's Usance Credit

For the banker's usance credit, the beneficiary draws drafts payable at 120 days after sight (see code 42 C) on the drawee bank (see code 42A). The negotiating bank, which is not restricted by the issuing bank (see code 41D), begins the negotiation, sends the usance draft to the drawee bank (see code 78) and sends the documents to the issuing bank (see code 78). This credit is the banker's usance credit under which interest for the period of 120 days will be charged to the buyer, so the draft is to be negotiated with the beneficiary on an at sight basis (see code 78). With regard to the negotiated amount, from the viewpoint of the beneficiary, usance credit is the same as sight credit.

--- TRANSMISSION ---

SEND TO   : SWIFT
MESSAGE ID   : 20101215M0000188
MESSAGE STATUS   : SEC
MESSAGE INPUT REFERENCE
                           : 15:30:27-2010/12/15-NACFKRSEXXX-6378-601829

--- MESSAGE HEADER ---

SENDER   : NACFKRSEXXX NATIONAL AGRICULTURAL COOPERATIVE
                  FEDERATION(NH BANK)
RECEIVER   : MHCBJPJTXXX MIZUHO CORPORATE BANK, LTD.
MESSAGE TYPE   : MT700 [ISSUE OF A DOCUMENTARY CREDIT]

--- MESSAGE TEXT---

SEQUENCE OF TOTAL   27 : 1/1
FORM OF DOCUMENTARY CREDIT   40A: IRREVOCABLE
DOCUMENTARY CREDIT NUMBER   20 : M0301012NU00299
DATE OF ISSUE   31C: 2010-12-15
APPLICABLE RULES   40E: UCPURR LATEST VERSION

                                     *Date   *Place
DATE AND PLACE OF EXPIRY   31D: 2011-02-28 JAPAN
APPLICANT   50 : ABC CORPORATION
                                     CHUNG-KU, SEOUL, KOREA
BENEFICIARY   59 : BBC CORPORATION 103-0027,JAPAN

                                     *Currency *Amount
CURRENCY CODE AMOUNT   32B: USD   284,700.00
PERCENTAGE CRDT AMT TOLERANCE   39A: 10/10
AVAILABLE WITH..BY..-NAME/ADDR   41D: ANY BANK BY NEGOTIATION
DRAFTS AT...   42C: 120 DAYS AFTER SIGHT
DRAWEE   42A: SCBLHKHHXXX

                                     STANDARD CHARTERED BANK
                                     (HONG KONG) LIMITED
PARTIAL SHIPMENTS   43P: ALLOWED
TRANSSHIPMENT   43T: ALLOWED

PORT OF LOADING/AIRPORT OF DEPARTURE   44E: JAPANESE PORT
PORT OF DISCHARGE/AIRPORT OF DESTINATION   44F: KOREAN ANY PORT
LATEST DATE OF SHIPMENT   44C: 2011-02-20
DESCP OF GOODS AND/OR SERVICES   45A:
   +DESCRIPTION
    1.HOKUETSU 2-SIDES COATED PAPER
    HI ALPHA
    QUANTITY: 30MT
    AMOUNT: USD 24,300
    2.HOKUETSU 2-SIDES COATED PAPER
    ALPHA MATT
    QUANTITY: 330MT
    AMOUNT: USD 260,400
   +TERMS OF PRICE : CIF (COST, INSURANCE AND FREIGHT)
   +COUNTRY OF ORIGIN : JAPAN
DOCUMENTS REQUIRED   46A:
   +SIGNED COMMERCIAL INVOICE IN 3 COPIES
   +FULL SET OF CLEAN ON BOARD OCEAN BILLS OF LADING MADE OUT
   TO THE ORDER OF NATIONAL AGRICULTURAL COOPERATIVE
   FEDERATION MARKED FREIGHT PREPAID AND NOTIFY APPLICANT
   +FULL SET OF INSURANCE POLICY OR CERTIFICATE, ENDORSED IN
   BLANK FOR 110PCT OF THE INVOICE VALUE. INSURANCE POLICY OR
   CERTIFICATE MUST EXPRESSLY STIPULATE THAT CLAIMS ARE
   PAYABLE IN THE CURRENCY OF THE DRAFT AND MUST ALSO
   INDICATE A CLAIMS SETTLING AGENT IN KOREA.
    INSURANCE MUST INCLUDE : INSTITUTE CARGO CLAUSE : ALL RISK
   +PACKING LIST IN 3 COPIES
ADDITIONAL CONDITIONS   47A:
   +10 PCT OF TOLERANCE ON AMOUNT AND TONNAGE TO BE ALLOWED
   +THIRD PARTY B/L ACCEPTABLE
   +NO COMMERCIAL VALUE IS ACCEPTABLE
   +T/T REIM. CLAIM ALLOWED
   +DISCREPANCY FEE OF USD 60.00 OR EQUIVALENT WILL BE
     DEDUCTED FROM THE PROCEEDS OF EACH PRESENTATION OF
     DOCUMENTS WITH DISCREPANCY(IES) FOR
     PAYMENT/REIMBURSEMENT UNDER THIS LETTER OF CREDIT.
CHARGES   71B: +ALL BANKING CHARGES INCLUDING
     REIMBURSEMENT CHARGES AND POSTAGE
     OUTSIDE KOREA ARE FOR ACCOUNT OF BENEFICIARY

PERIOD FOR PRESENTATION	48 : +DOCUMENTS TO BE PRESENTED
	WITHIN 21 DAYS AFTER THE DATE OF
	SHIPMENT BUT IN ANY EVENT WITHIN
	THE VALIDITY OF THE CREDIT.
CONFIRMATION INSTRUCTIONS	49 : WITHOUT
REIMBURSING BANK	53A: SCBLHKHHXXX
	STANDARD CHARTERED BANK
	(HONG KONG) LIMITED
INSTRUC TO PAY/ACCPT/NEGOT BNK	78 :

+ALL DOCUMENTS SHOULD BE FORWARDED TO THE NATIONAL
AGRICULTURAL COOPERATIVE FEDERATION INTERNATIONAL
BANKING SERVICE CENTER, IMPORT DEPARTMENT, NONGHYUP
SINCHON COMPLEX B/D 6F, 49-31 NOGOSAN-DONG, MAPO-GU, SEOUL,
KOREA IN ONE LOT BY REGISTERED AIRMAIL OR AIR-COURIER.
+DRAFT IS TO BE NEGOTIATED AT SIGHT BASIS.
ACCEPTANCE COMM. AND DISCOUNT CHARGES FOR BUYER'S ACCT.
NEGOTIATING BANK SHALL OBTAIN REIMBURSEMENT BY SENDING
BENF'S TIME DRAFT TO DRAWEE OR T/T (ONLY IN CASE T/T REIM.
CLAIM IS ALLOWED UNDER THIS CREDIT) WITH INFORMATION
ABOUT B/L DATE, COMMODITY, LOADING PORT AND DESTINATION,
NAME OF THE APPLICANT, NAME OF THE BENEFICIARY, VESSEL NAME.
-- END OF MESSAGE --

Source: National Agricultural Cooperative Federation

5.1.10.4 Shipper's Usance Credit

Shipper's usance credit is the same essentially in form as "banker's usance credit", except for the fact that the issuing bank and the drawee bank are one and the same (see code 42A), and under this credit interest for a period of 60 days will be charged to the beneficiary (see code 78).The drafted amount is therefore to be discounted through negotiations. With regard to the negotiated amount, from the viewpoint of the beneficiary, shipper's usance credit is different from the case of a banker's usance credit.

```
-------------------------------------- TRANSMISSION ----------------------------------------------

SEND TO                   : SWIFT
MESSAGE ID                : 20101217M0000301
MESSAGE STATUS            : SEC
MESSAGE INPUT REFERENCE
                          : 16:59:08-2010/12/17-NACFKRSEXXX-6380-606660


------------------------------------- MESSAGE HEADER----------------------------------------------

SENDER          : NACFKRSEXXX NATIONAL AGRICULTURAL CO OPERATIVE
                  FEDERATION(NH BANK)
RECEIVER        : LUMIILITTLV BANK LEUMI LE ISRAEL B.M.
                  (TEL-AVIV MAIN BRANCH)
MESSAGE TYPE    : MT700  [ ISSUE OF A DOCUMENTARY CREDIT ]


---------------------------------------- MESSAGE TEXT -------------------------------------------

SEQUENCE OF TOTAL                   27 : 1/1
FORM OF DOCUMENTARY CREDIT          40A: IRREVOCABLE
DOCUMENTARY CREDIT NUMBER           20 : M0397012NU00025
DATE OF ISSUE                       31C: 2010-12-17
APPLICABLE RULES                    40E: UCP LATEST VERSION


                                    *Date    *Place
DATE AND PLACE OF EXPIRY            31D: 2011-02-16 IN THE BENEFICIARY
                                         COUNTRY
APPLICANT                           50: ABC. CO.,LTD KIMHAE-CITY,
                                        KYONGNAM, KOREA
                                        82 55 342 9058 (82 54 973 1021)
BENEFICIARY                         59: BBC LTD.


                                    *Currency *Amount
CURRENCY CODE AMOUNT                32B: USD      74,277.00
AVAILABLE WITH..BY...-NAME/ADDR     41D: ANY BANK BY NEGOTIATION


DRAFTS AT...                        42C: 60 DAYS AFTER B/L DATE
DRAWEE                              42A: NACFKRSEXXX
                                         NATIONAL AGRICULTURAL
```

COOPERATIVE FEDERATION

(NH BANK)

PARTIAL SHIPMENTS   43P: ALLOWED

TRANSSHIPMENT   43T: ALLOWED

PORT OF LOADING/AIRPORT OF DEPARTURE   44E: ISRAELI PORT, ISRAEL

PORT OF DISCHARGE/AIRPORT OF DESTINATION 44F: BUSAN PORT, KOREA

LATEST DATE OF SHIPMENT   44C: 2011-02-01

DESCP OF GOODS AND/OR SERVICES   45A:

   +HS-CODE: 3105901000

   COMMODITY DESCRIPTION

   QUANTITY UNIT PRICE AMOUNT

   ....

   POTASSIUM NITRATE GREENHOUSE

   GRADE 56.70 975.00 55,282.50

   POTASSIUM NITRATE GG PHAST

   18.90 1,005.00 18,994.50

   ....

   TOTAL   75.60MT   USD74,277

   +PRICE TERM : CIF BUSAN PORT, KOREA

   +COUNTRY OF ORIGIN : ISRAEL

DOCUMENTS REQUIRED   46A:

   +SIGNED COMMERCIAL INVOICE IN 3 FOLD(S)

   +FULL SET OF CLEAN ON BOARD OCEAN BILLS OF LADING MADE OUT

   TO THE ORDER OF NATIONAL AGRICULTURAL COOPERATIVE

   FEDERATION MARKED 'FREIGHT PREPAID' AND 'NOTIFY APPLICANT'

   +FULL SET OF INSURANCE POLICY OR CERTIFICATE, ENDORSED IN

   BLANK FOR 110PCT OF THE INVOICE VALUE. INSURANCE POLICY OR

   CERTIFICATE MUST EXPRESSLY STIPULATE THAT CLAIMS ARE

   PAYABLE IN THE CURRENCY OF THE DRAFT AND MUST ALSO

   INDICATE A CLAIMS SETTLING AGENT IN KOREA.

   INSURANCE MUST INCLUDE : INSTITUTE CARGO CLAUSE : ICC(A)

   +PACKING LIST IN 3 FOLD(S)

ADDITIONAL CONDITIONS   47A:

   +T/T REIM. CLAIM PROHIBITED

   +DISCREPANCY FEE OF USD 60.00 OR EQUIVALENT WILL BE

   DEDUCTED FROM THE PROCEEDS OF EACH PRESENTATION

   OF DOCUMENTS WITH DISCREPANCY(IES)

   FOR PAYMENT/REIMBURSEMENT UNDER THIS LETTER OF CREDIT.

CHARGES   71B: +ALL BANKING CHARGES INCLUDING
                                REIMBURSEMENT CHARGES AND POSTAGE OUTSIDE
                                KOREA ARE FOR ACCOUNT OF BENEFICIARY
PERIOD FOR PRESENTATION   48 : +DOCUMENTS TO BE PRESENTED
                                WITHIN 21 DAYS AFTER THE DATE OF
                                SHIPMENT BUT IN ANY EVENT WITHIN THE
                                VALIDITY OF THE CREDIT.
CONFIRMATION INSTRUCTIONS   49 : WITHOUT
INSTRUC TO PAY/ACCPT/NEGOT BNK   78 :
    +ALL DOCUMENTS SHOULD BE FORWARDED TO THE NATIONAL
    AGRICULTURAL COOPERATIVE FEDERATION INTERNATIONAL
    BANKING SERVICE CENTER, IMPORT DEPARTMENT, NONGHYUP
    SINCHON COMPLEX B/D 6F, 49-31 NOGOSAN-DONG, MAPO-GU, SEOUL,
    KOREA IN ONE LOT BY REGISTERED AIRMAIL OR AIR -COURIER.
    +INTEREST IS FOR ACCOUNT OF BENEFICIARY.
    +UPON RECEIPT OF DOCUMENTS IN CO MPLIANCE WITH THE TERMS
    AND CONDITIONS OF THE CREDIT, WE WILL REMIT THE PROCEEDS AS
    PER YOUR INSTRUCTIONS AT MATURITY.
    +REMITTANCE COMM. AND CABLE CHARGE ARE FOR ACCOUNT OF
    BENEFICIARY.

-- END OF MESSAGE --

Source: National Agricultural Cooperative Federation

5.1.10.5 Guarantee

A guarantee is similar to a stand-by letter of credit, under which the beneficiary is guaranteed by the issuing bank that he gets payment on demand of up to US $42,023.00 in the event of the applicant failing to fulfill the terms and conditions of the contract (NO. 93528156).

```
------------------------------------------ TRANSMISSION ----------------------------------------------

 MESSAGE ID                        : 20110110G0000001
 MESSAGE STATUS                    : SEC

-------------------------------------------- MESSAGE HEADER --------------------------------------------


 SENDER        : NACFKRSEXXX NATIONAL AGRICULTURAL COOPERATIVE
               FEDERATION(NH BANK)
 RECEIVER      : NACFKRSEXXX NATIONAL AGRICULTURAL COOPERATIVE
               FEDERATION(NH BANK)
 MESSAGE TYPE : MT760  [ GUARANTEE ]

--------------------------------------------- MESSAGE TEXT ---------------------------------------------

 SEQUENCE OF TOTAL                 27 : 1/1
 TRANSACTION REFERENCE NUMBER      20 : G03Y7101XD00018
 FURTHER IDENTIFICATION            23 : ISSUE
 DATE                              30 : 110110
 APPLICABLE RULES                  40C: OTHR/THE LAWS OF TOKYO, JAPAN
 DETAILS OF GUARANTEE              77C:       .
      TO: BBC LTD
      IBARAKI 300-0013.
      DATE: 2011.01.10.
      OUR GUARANTEE G03Y7101XD00018.
```

WE UNDERSTAND THAT YOU HAVE ENTERED INTO A CONTRACT NO 93528156 WITH ABC OF 502-1, OSIKDO-DONG, GUNSAN, JEONBUK, KOREA 573-540 FOR THE SUPPLY OF AIR COOLER HEAT EXCHANGERS AND THAT UNDER THE CONTRACT THE APPLICANT MUST PROVIDE A BANK WARRANTY GUARANTEE FOR AN AMOUNT OF USD 42,023.00, BEING 10PCT OF THE VALUE OF THE CONTRACT.

WE, NATIONAL AGRICULTURAL COOPERATIVE FEDERATION (NH BANK) HEREBY GUARANTEE PAYMENT TO YOU ON DEMAND OF UP TO USD 42,023.00(SAY, IN WORDS USD FORTY TWO THOUSAND TWENTY THREE DOLLARS) IN THE EVENT OF THE APPLICANT FAILING TO FULFIL THE TERMS AND CONDITIONS OF THE CONTRACT.

THIS GUARANTEE SHALL EXPIRE ON MAY 5TH 2013. ANY CLAIM HEREUNDER MUST BE RECEIVED IN WRITING AT THIS OFFICE BY HAND, BY REGISTERED POST OR BY COURIER BEFORE EXPIRY ACCOMPANIED BY THIS ORIGINAL GUARANTEE AND YOUR STATEMENT (BEARING YOUR ORIGINAL HANDWRITTEN SIGNATURE) THAT THE APPLICANT HAS FAILED TO FULFIL THE CONTRACT. SUCH CLAIM AND STATEMENT SHALL BE ACCEPTED AS CONCLUSIVE EVIDENCE (AND ADMISSIBLE AS SUCH) THAT THE AMOUNT CLAIMED IS DUE TO YOU UNDER THIS GUARANTEE.

CLAIMS, DOCUMENTS AND STATEMENTS AS AFORESAID MUST BEAR THE DATED CONFIRMATION OF YOUR BANKERS THAT THE SIGNATORIES THEREON ARE AUTHORISED SO TO SIGN.

ANY CLAIM AND STATEMENT HEREUNDER ACCOMPANIED BY THE ORIGINAL OF THIS GUARANTEE DOCUMENT MUST BE RECEIVED AT THIS OFFICE BEFORE EXPIRY. AFTER EXPIRY THIS GUARANTEE SHALL BECOME NULL AND VOID WHETHER RETURNED TO US FOR CANCELLATION OR NOT AND ANY CLAIM OR STATEMENT RECEIVED AFTER EXPIRY SHALL BE INEFFECTIVE.

THIS GUARANTEE IS PERSONAL TO YOURSELVES AND IS NOT TRANSFERABLE OR ASSIGNABLE.

THIS GUARANTEE SHALL BE GOVERNED BY AND CONSTRUED IN ACCORDANCE WITH THE LAWS OF TOKYO, JAPAN AND SHALL BE SUBJECT TO THE EXCLUSIVE JURISDICTION OF THE TOKYO, JAPAN COURTS.

FOR AND ON BEHALF OF NATIONAL AGRICULTURAL COOPERATIVE FEDERATION (NH BANK)

(Source: National Agricultural Cooperative Federation)

5.1.10.6 Performance Bond

Performance bonds are popularly used in international construction contracts, under which the beneficiary is guaranteed to get payment of US$79,000 (in the example set out below) against the sight draft accompanied by the beneficiary's statement when the applicant fails to fulfill his obligation under the contract (NO. THFSC 12–030)

```
-------------------------------------- TRANSMISSION--------------------------------------------

SEND TO                     : SWIFT
MESSAGE ID                  : 20101229G0000007
MESSAGE STATUS              : SEC
MESSAGE INPUT REFERENCE
                            : 16:51:50-2010/12/29-NACFKRSEXXX-6388-623220

-------------------------------------- MESSAGE HEADER ------------------------------------------
SENDER          : NACFKRSEXXX NATIONAL AGRICULTURAL COOPERATIVE
                  FEDERATION(NH BANK)
RECEIVER        : NACFKRSEXXX NATIONAL AGRICULTURAL COOPERATIVE
                  FEDERATION(NH BANK)
MESSAGE TYPE    : MT760  [ GUARANTEE ]

---------------------------------------- MESSAGE TEXT------------------------------------------

SEQUENCE OF TOTAL                       27 : 1/1
TRANSACTION REFERENCE NUMBER            20 : G03NR012XD00032
FURTHER IDENTIFICATION                  23 : ISSUE
DATE                                    30 : 101229
APPLICABLE RULES                        40C: OTHR/UCP 600
DETAILS OF GUARANTEE                    77C:
```

WE ISSUE OUR IRREVOCABLE LETTER OF CREDIT FAVORING FOREIGN TRADE DEPARTMENT OF ABC, SEOUL, KOREA FOR ACCOUNT OF BBC AND FEED CO., LTD. IN AN AGGREGATE AMOUNT OF USD 79,000.00 (U.S. DOLLARS SEVENTY NINE THOUSAND ONLY) REPRESENTING PERFORMANCE BOND.

THIS LETTER OF CREDIT IS AVAILABLE BY BENEFICIARY'S SIGHT DRAFT DRAWN ON US ACCOMPANIED BY THE BENEFICIARY'S STATEMENT STATING THAT THE BBC AND FEED CO., LTD. HAS FAILED TO FULFILL ITS OBLIGATION UNDER THE CONTRACTS NO. THFSC12-030 FOR 4,000M/T 5PCT MORE OR LESS OF CHINESE CORN GLUTEN FEED TO BE SHIPPED AT C AND F FREE-OUT AT SOUTH KOREAN PORT(S).

THIS CREDIT EXPIRES ON MAY 14, 2011 IN BORAME TOWN BRANCH, NATIONAL AGRICULTURAL COOPERATIVE FEDERATION (NH BANK), SEOUL, KOREA AND SUBJECT TO U.C.P FOR DOCUMENTARY CREDIT (2007 REVISION) ICC PUB 600.

```
-------------------------------------- END OF MESSAGE --------------------------------------
```
(Source: National Agricultural Cooperative Federation)

5.2   Payment Collection Without Letter of Credit

5.2.1   Document Against Payment

"Document against payment" (D/P) means that when presenting shipping documents to the bank, the bank can hand over documents to the importer after the bank gets paid by the importer. It allows for simultaneous exchange of documents and payment collection, so the collecting bank cannot release the cargo unless the importer has made payment. For the document against payment transaction, the exporter makes and submits a collection-requesting form (in a fixed form) to a bank specified in the contract to send documents for payment collection. The bank then requesting payment on behalf of the exporter confirms whether the documents submitted with the collection-requesting form are consistent with the submitted document lists, and then sends the documents to a collecting bank in the importing country. If the importer confirms his acceptance of the document and pays for the exported goods, the bank hands over the documents to the importer.

The collecting bank transfers the payment from the importer to the bank requesting payment, and the bank requesting payment makes payment to the exporter.

Special D/P

O D/P Usance

Irrespective of "D/P at sight" or "D/P usance", when the documents arrive at the collecting bank of the importing country, the bank must collect the payment from the importer and deliver the documents. In case of "D/P usance," even though the documents are delivered after getting paid by the importer, the payment to the exporter is to be made within a specified length of dates after the document is presented for payment collection.

O D/P negotiation

Since the bank requesting collection on behalf of the exporter has no obligation to negotiate documents under the terms of payment by collection, the bank transfers the documents from an exporter to the collecting bank for payment collection without reviewing them and does not have to pay the exporter in advance. In this case, the exporter bears the burden of funds for a certain period of time until the collecting bank gets paid from the importer and sends it to the exporter. At this time, the exporter can request financing in advance, as in the case of an L/C, to the bank requesting collection on behalf of the exporter, which may or may not accept such request.

5.2.2   Remittance

5.2.2.1 Outline

In the case of the terms of remittance, the exporter sends the goods directly to the importer, and the importer makes payment directly to the exporter. Therefore, the exporters or importers should assume the credit risk by themselves. If remittance is made before the goods are delivered, the risk is on the importer due to the possibility that the goods are never shipped, or are damaged during transportation. Conversely, if the remittance is made after shipping the goods under the condition of "cash or collect on delivery" (COD) or "cash after delivery" or "cash after documents" (CAD), the exporter must hope that the importer is faithful to his promises.

Payment means are usually determined under the contract, which includes demand drafts (D/D) or demand transfer (D/T), mail draft (M/D) or mail transfer (M/T), and telegraphic transfer (T/T). A demand draft is payable upon demand by the presenter. A telegraphic transfer is also called a wire transfer. Telegraphic transfers are mainly completed through the "Society for Worldwide Inter-bank Financial Telecommunication" (SWIFT). A SWIFT transaction is only possible when both banks have access to the system, and it is often used for remittance, collection, letter of credit issuing, and other financial services because of its cheap and speedy service.

5.2.2.2 Remittance in Advance

This method means that the payment collection is made, under the term "cash with order" (COW), before the exporter ships goods after conclusion of a contract. This is safe for exporters but very risky for importers because importers assume the risk that goods will not be shipped after making payment to exporters overseas in advance.

5.2.2.3 Remittance upon Performance of Contract

This term means that payment will come from the foreign exchange bank upon delivery of goods, or within a certain period of time after delivery of goods. This remittance method is divided into "cash on delivery" (COD) and "cash against documents" (CAD). With CAD, payment is made within a certain period of time after the shipping date, or a certain period of time after the arrival date. This method can usually be used when an exporter ships goods and presents shipping documents to an importer's branch or agent in the exporting country, at which point the importer takes the shipping documents and makes payment. Typically, the importer's agent in the exporting country will inspect the manufacturing process and make a pre-shipment inspection.

This method can usually be used when an exporter's company has branches or agents in the importing country. The exporter sends his goods to this branch, and the importer makes payment promptly after inspecting the goods for conformity with the agreement. In this case, it is possible for the importer to write in the contract that he has the right to renegotiate the price if the goods are not up to his expectations, adding safety for the importer, and at the same time adding risk for the exporter.

5.2.3   Open Account

An open account is used when the parties involved continue business transactions, and should only be used when the parties are familiar with each other and have built a solid business relationship based on trust. An open account means that parties do not have to calculate the price with every deal, and, instead, the books are balanced after each transaction. This is more efficient for partners who frequently engage in commerce because it allows them to cut down on fees relating to making payments.

The exporter sends shipping documents to the importer without issuing a bill of exchange. When the importer notifies the exporter of shipment, the amount on the commercial invoice is written in credits for the exporter. This is a kind of sale on credit, and since it solely depends on an importer's credit, it is commonly used when both parties are related to each other through a main office and its branch.

5.2.4   Factoring

5.2.4.1 Outline
Factoring is used where the exporter wants a letter of credit to insure a safe collection of payment, but the importer does not want to use a letter of credit because of concerns about the quality of the traded goods, and when the exporter wants "at sight" payment, but the importer wants to buy on credit. Factoring is a combination of letter of credit and non-letter of credit transactions.

Factoring is "the business of purchasing and collecting accounts receivable or of advancing cash on the basis of accounts receivable." To make factoring plausible, international organizations of factors were created, the most notable of which is Factors Chain International (FCI). Based in the Netherlands, FCI created international rules for factoring called the "Code of International Factoring Customs" and "Rules of Arbitration." Essentially, these "factors" replace banks in international negotiations. Instead of the importer, it is the export factor that buys at sight account receivables, lessening the risk to the importer. The import factor lends credit to the importer.

Factoring companies offer further assistance to help facilitate trade, such as researching a company's credit standing. They also accept the credit risk, serve as a collection agency, deal with accounting, and so on. These services reduce concerns about the payment collection followed by credit-based export when the exporter needs to be financed in exporting before collecting. In the case of importing, the importer can reduce transaction costs by making usance payment available backed by the guarantee of the factoring company instead of issuing a letter of credit. International factoring can utilize open account credit terms, open account, "document against acceptance" and "document against payment", but cannot use letters of credit or cash.

By using international factoring, exporters can capitalize on export account receivables upon shipment while performing a trade on credit, and importers can conveniently purchase goods on credit. Depending on the recourse, factoring may be grouped into factoring with recourse and factoring without recourse. The export factor can also make a payment in advance discounting account receivables according to requests and the credit of the exporter, or make payment after payment collection made by the import factor.

5.2.4.2 Features

Exporters and importers can, through the use of factoring, get finance only by credit without security. When the export factor buys account receivables from the exporter, it does not require security. Instead, the notice of credit approval for the importer serves as security. Furthermore, the import factor does not require any security when the importer gets goods on credit, and compensates for it if the importer goes bankrupt. Thus, the most important aspect in factoring transactions is the credit standing of the exporters and importers. Inquiring into receiving proof of credit is categorically required before entering a trade agreement with another party. Factoring can make the negotiation much more favorable to exporters and importers than is the situation with a letter of credit, "document against payment", or "document against acceptance."

This financing method is, particularly, advantageous to small and medium-sized companies to expand their export markets with their newly developed products, because their credit standings do not have to be revalued with every transaction.

Procedures of Factoring Transactions

The factoring service is usually carried out as follows:

① Consultation with export factoring and conclusion of an export factoring contract;

② Applying credit approval: After consultation with the potential exporter, a Credit Approval Request (CAR) is dispatched to the import factor;

③ Determining credit line after credit inquiry → An import factoring contract is concluded after consultation concerning a credit line and terms between the importer and the import factor;

④ Notification of credit approval → The import factor forwards an answer in the form of the CAR to the exporter through the export factor after reviewing the credit line or individual credit approval (ICAR), approved amount, and settlement period;

⑤ Issuing a credit approval notice → The export factor issues a credit approval notice to the exporter upon accepting the notice;

⑥ Formation of sale contract by factoring → Specifications on the export contract concerning settlement conditions between the exporter and the importer must be made under the credit approval condition. If necessary, export approval should be given by a relevant organization;

⑦ Shipment of goods by exporter;

⑧ Requesting negotiation of shipping documents and offering advancement → The exporter can get an advancement within the export bond amount after presenting the proper documents; inducing a negotiation form of export bonds, export permit, commercial invoice, copy of B/L, etc.;

⑨ Dispatching shipping documents and transferring export bonds;

⑩ Delivering shipping documents to the importer;

⑪ Settlement of import price → The importer must deposit payment to the import factor upon maturity of the contract. If the importer delays the payment, the exporter bears the interest for the delay. The importer then remits the price with the interest rate in accordance with the terms of the exporter's contract;

⑫ Remitting import price;

⑬ Balancing after calculating the export price and advancement.

5.2.5   Forfaiting

Forfaiting has many similarities to factoring, but is distinctively different in the dealing amount, recourse, interest rate, and the method of payment involved. Factoring is a firm-based operation, while forfaiting is a transaction-based operation, meaning that it is merely a debt instrument: note, bond, promissory note, or draft. Forfaiting is made when an exporter's accounts receivable, which is the amount the importer owes to the exporter, are purchased by a third party at a discount because the payment is made in cash.

The forfaiter, that is, the entity that purchased the account receivables, then becomes the entity to whom the importer must make payments. By purchasing account receivables, the forfaiter relieves the exporter of the burden of credit, and eliminates the risk that payment might not be realized. On the other side of the transaction, the importer has been given up the ability to purchase goods that it cannot immediately pay for.

Forfaiting was first introduced in 1950s to the world when Credit Suisse in Switzerland started doing business with companies throughout Western Europe. For extremely costly imports such as of machinery, plants and ships, the importer will naturally want to pay on a deferred payment system. But, if the credit of the importing party, his country, or the letter of credit opening bank is not stable, it is likely that the exporter will require payment immediately to avoid the risk of taking a huge loss. There is also the risk of foreign exchange fluctuations. The forfaiter eliminates such risks of the buyer, the issuing bank and foreign exchange fluctuations.

Since the forfaiter's payment is being discounted on the condition that recourse to long-term accounts receivable (usually 1–5 years, sometimes 10 years or more) will not occur, the forfeiter is able to set a reasonable discount rate by evaluating the importer's credit risk, the issuing bank's credit, and the reliability of business relations with that country. If credit history is not obtainable, the forfaiter will likely require an aval from the importer's bank or a third bank. An aval is a guarantee made by a third party who insures that the payment will be made in the case that the nominated entire defaults on his payments.

Under the terms of forfeiting, the seller does not take responsibility if the buyer (or issuing bank) goes insolvent or is delayed on maturity, because the forfaiter does not exercise recourse, and the seller does not assume the fluctuations of exchange rates or interest rates because payment is made upon shipment.

Procedures of Forfaiting Transaction

Forfeiting procedures are generally as follows:

① The seller, under the terms of forfeiting, ships and delivers goods to the buyer in accordance with the contract;

② The buyer requires to submit a draft that the seller issued in favor of himself, or the promissory note that the buyer issued to the bank so it can be guaranteed;

③ The importer's bank (payment guaranteeing bank) sends the draft or the payment guarantee after it marks "Aval" on the back of the draft or makes another payment guarantee;

④ The seller makes a forfaiting contract with a forfeiter;

⑤ The seller hands over the payment guarantee or aval from the bank in contract to the forfeiter;

⑥ The forfaiter pays a discounted price to the seller after receiving the drafts;

⑦ On maturity, the forfaiter presents an aval from the seller or the payment guarantee from the bank to the guaranteeing bank;

⑧ When the guaranteeing bank pays the price to the forfaiter, the deal is closed.

Assignment

1. Create a confirmed irrevocable letter of credit in accordance with the final sales contract made by students in Chap. 4, and indicate the reasons why the letter of credit is to be issued as an irrevocable letter of credit from the viewpoints of risk management of the exportation.

2. Comparative study between bank guarantees procured by the buyer and bank guarantees procured by the seller from the viewpoints of ensuring security in international business transactions.

Reference

Chuah JCT (2009) Law of International Trade: Cross-Border Commercial Transactions. Sweet & Maxwell

Supplemental Reading

Kouladis N (2006) Principles of Law Relating to International Trade. Springer, pp. 213–236

Carr I (2007) International Trade Law, 3rd edn. Cavendish Publishing, pp. 57–100

Wilson JF (2008) Carriage of Goods by Sea, 6th edn. Pearson Longman, pp. 113–172

Folsom RH, Gordon MW, Spanogle Jr. JA, Fitzgerald PL (2009) International Business Transactions: Contracting Across Borders. West, pp. 52–110

Honnold JO (2006) Sales Transactions: Domestic and International Law, 3rd edn. Foundation Press, pp. 502–607

Fellmeth AX (2009) The Law of International Business Transactions. West, pp. 405–435

DiMatteo LA, Dhooge LJ (2005) International Business Law – Transactional Approach, 2nd edn. West, pp. 290–323

International Transportation

6

Learning Objectives
1. Importance of carriage of goods in export transactions;
2. Course of business in the carriage of goods by sea;
3. Contractual and statutory effect of bills of lading and other transportation documents in international maritime transportation;

6.1 Introduction

6.1.1 Concepts

Transport in international business transactions has a direct impact on such key sales contract elements as price, speed of delivery and risk of loss or damage.[1] Transport means "to carry, move or convey from one place to another." In international business transactions, the purpose of transport is to improve the effective value of the goods being moved, and in turn, create advantageous situations and profits for both the buyer and seller.

Under the circumstances that the world market is becoming smaller and closer, internationally high competition has forced companies to streamline their operations and supply-chains to insure that the products can be sold at competitive prices through the reduction of operating costs. Global integration that has been accelerated provides companies with availability to one country's cheap natural resources, another's cheap labor, and another's advanced technology, through which the international enterprise may establish a comprehensive global supply-claim system.

International transport involved in international business transactions often utilizes international marine and aircraft navigation, but can also use railroads and trucks when the countries are connected to each other as in the case of Europe.

---

[1] Ramberg (2008, *supra* note 48, at 225).

E.S. Lee, *Management of International Trade*,
DOI 10.1007/978-3-642-30403-3_6, © Springer-Verlag Berlin Heidelberg 2012

Combined transport is often utilized for the international commerce because it can improve transport logistics.

6.1.2 Transportation in International Trade

Punctual delivery according to the trade terms and conditions through proper transportation means is essential for the successful business transactions. If the goods are not delivered on time due to poor selection of transport means, or if a claim for transported cargo occurs due to improper packing or unloading, the results can be fatal to the exporter. Proper transportation planning can create notable competitive advantage for a company over others in the industry by finding the fastest and cheapest method of delivery, and reducing costs due to prompt and precise planning and actions.

The shipper, under the transactions with letter of credit, usually the exporter, seeking proper transportation, is to obtain shipping documents required by the letter of credit for the preparation of negotiation with the negotiating bank, and the consignee, usually the importer, is to take the shipping documents through the issuing bank and receive the imported goods when they arrive at the final destination. Even though transportation is under the charge of professional carrying companies under transport contract, the shipper as the user of the transport services is recommended to have a sufficient understanding of the transport documents, including bill of lading, in use, the responsibilities of the carrier, and proper actions to take if the carrier breaches the contract.

Procedures of International Transport under Documentary Letter of Credit

The following details are the steps under the transactions with documentary letter of credit needed to begin and finalize an international transport:

① The letter of credit based on the sales contract needs to be issued by the importer;

② Under the letter of credit terms, after processing the export actives before transportation, the exporter looks into shipping companies (or forwarders) to find a liner that will satisfy his needs of exporting location and destination port. The exporter is always to reserve ship space with a shipping company in advance;

③ Customs clearance → the exporter reports the export directly or by EDI (Electronic Data Interchange) to customs office in jurisdiction for the legitimately recognized export;

④ The exporter transports goods to the shipping vessel or other bonded area including container yard designated by the shipping company;

⑤ After cargo is shipped overseas, the exporter receives the issued bill of lading from the shipping company or forwarder. After getting the issued bill of lading from the shipping company, the exporter collects payment from the relevant bank. At this time, transport document including bill of lading and other shipping documents required under the letter of credit must be presented to the bank;

⑥ If the importer who paid the import price to the issuing bank in exchange for shipping documents including transport document, he submits the transport document to the shipping company, receives an arrival notice from a port in the importing country or a bonded area including container yard and gets import permission or license from the customs house.

⑦ If the importer submits the original bill of lading to the shipping company that transported the cargo, the shipping company issues the importer delivery order (D/O). The importer takes the cargo from the bonded area where the cargo was stored.

6.2   Means of Transportation

There are three kinds of transport including land transport, maritime transport and air transport. Recently, transport markets are complicated and competitive, which means shippers find it sometimes difficult to seek out the proper transporting companies for the shipping of their goods. Under such circumstances, freight forwarders, specialists in shipping, have served for the shippers. The freight forwarder is generally an entity carrying out transport logistics or transporting actions for a shipper without possession of his own transporting means. The forwarder is a middleman who provides service of a carrier to a shipper, and service of a shipper to a carrier.

The "freight forwarder" is commonly associated with an ocean freight forwarder, but air freight forwarders also exist. The freight forwarder's responsibility is to provide door-to-door transportation between the exporter and importer. The forwarder gives one quoted price to the exporter which includes shipping, handling, import and customs duties, and other transport expenses that may be applicable. A combined transport bill of lading is issued under the forwarder's liability.

Freight Forwarders

"As an indispensable member of the international trade community, the freight forwarder generally acts as an agent for the exporter or importer in transporting traded cargo internationally. Like travel agents-but dealing with cargo rather than passengers-freight forwarders use their knowledge of varying freight rates to offer the customer the best "package deal". Amongst the many additional services offered by freight forwarders are the handling of export and customs documentation, insurance, and port and terminal charges. Small-sized or individual exporters without rich experience in internal business will, therefore, often consult with their freight forwarder before quoting a price in making offers for certain international business transactions."

Source: Jan Ramberg, Guide to Export–import Basics, (2008) at 233.

6.2.1   Maritime Transportation

Since maritime transport allows for shipping of large volumes of cargo at one time, which is more economical than other methods, most international transport depends on marine transportation. It is not only cheaper, but also an internationally competitive and important strategic industry because ships can set sail freely from any port in any country.

The safety in marine transportation has improved dramatically since its initiation through continuous technical innovations, such as development of shipbuilding, and development of electronics and information networks. The utilization of containers in shipping goods has expedited multimodal transport and reduced transportation costs.

6.2.1.1 Ships

The ships used in international trade are naturally gargantuan vessels designed specifically for carrying cargo. One of these ships is either a tanker designed for liquids like oil or a dry cargo ship designed more for solid cargo.

Ships are measured by their weight and volume. Weight can be measured by displacement ton, which is a measure of the water displaced by the ship, and is therefore effected by the cargo onboard. Another means to measure weight is by "deadweight ton" (DWT), which is the maximum weight of cargo that can be loaded on the ship. Volume can be measured by gross ton (G/T) which is known as a long ton, or net ton(N/T) which is the measure of the parts of the ship that are directly used for carrying cargo. Either measurement will be subject to port charges, canal tolls and tariffs.

6.2.1.2 Ports

Ports were previously considered just a place to load or unload cargo, however, as they have emerged as outposts for exporting and importing, and as logistics bases, their significance in international trade has vastly increased. Ports are mainly divided into two groups, that is, exclusive ports for contained cargo and conventional ports which handle general cargo not in containers.

Ports need to be equipped with the proper transportation methods to quickly, easily and safely move, load, unload, and store cargo. Besides this, facilities must be available for inspection, weighing, appraising, employing safety measures, cleaning, oiling, and repairing containers. Ports have evolved into a one-stop shop to ease the burdens of transport.

6.2.1.3 Container Terminals

These are short-term storage facilities where cargo containers can be transshipped between different transport vehicles. This transshipment may occur between ships and land vehicles, or two land vehicles. Inland container terminals are often located in or near major cities, with easy access to trains, trucking routes, etc..

One of the main objectives of container terminals is to standardize cargo completely in order to save the transporting time by handling it by mechanical facilities, not by people. These terminals often supply other services, such as container installation, collection, repair and cleaning.

The attached facilities to the container terminal are as follows:

Berth
This is a docking place equipped with facilities located inside a port, which usually has a facility to dock one average-sized ship.

Apron
This place is a part of the yard alongside the pier and the nearest point to the ocean, normally 30–50 m wide, and equipped with gantry crane, where containers are loaded and unloaded.

Marshalling Yard
Usually located near to the apron, this is a large place to arrange containers that were unloaded or prepared for loading. It occupies much of the container yard and is an important part in operating any container terminal.

Container Yard
This is a place to accept, deliver and store containers. The container yard often encompasses the marshalling yard, apron, and cargo freight station as well. It usually occupies about 65 percent of the entire area.

Cargo Freight Station
This is a place to accept, deliver, and store cargo that is not large enough to fill an entire container, that is, "less than container load cargo (LCL cargo)".

Control Tower
This is a control center positioned at a high place to oversee the entire container yard. It is responsible for planning, directions, and supervision of operations.

6.2.1.4 Containers
Today, containers are a major transportation means in international trade due to the convenience of standardization that they provide, and are fastly growing to be used at ports worldwide. They enable the fast and easy packing, storing, loading, and transport of goods because their standardization allows the cargo to be moved efficiently.

Containers reduce packing costs, marine transport fees, land transport fees, and cargo-working costs. Other costs that decrease with the use of containers are insurance premiums, labor costs, and office costs. Besides a huge potential for cost savings, containers also provide high productivity that lessens the transport time due to easy handling and simple shipping documents. A further advantage that shippers may enjoy is that it prevents the loss and damage of goods, which means that they are less likely to be charged with mishandling goods.

6.2.2   Liners/Trampers

6.2.2.1 Liners

Regular liners sail in accordance with fixed schedules, and usually carry general cargo including finished products or half-finished products. A company running regular liners is often referred to as a "line shipping company." A liner can be a container ship, conventional ship, multi-purpose ship, or "roll on/roll off" including a car ferry ship (RO/RO) which is designed specifically to load and unload cargo using ramps so that cargo does not have to be lifted.

Container ships are divided into full containers and semi-containers which accommodate smaller cargo loads. Full container ships have no equipment to load or unload containers, but semi-container ships should come with a crane to load and unload cargo. A conventional ship, on the other hand, is not made to carry containers. A multi-purpose ship is made with the functions of both a general cargo ship and a bulk ship. Thus, it is available to both regular and irregular voyages.

A shipping conference means that more than two regular liner companies make agreement for the purpose of standardizing different aspects of their businesses such as freight, piling capacity, wiring, and the bunker adjustment factor. The purpose of standardizing these items is to avoid unnecessary competition that will cause all of the companies to get less profit.

The conferences may create flexible rates but in a way were initially intended to impose or keep high rates. Most companies adopt these rate agreements, sailing agreements and pooling agreements domestically, and conduct various contract systems to bind shippers in the conference. By doing this, the shipping companies of a particular country can strengthen their businesses and be more competitive against outside carriers.

As intermodal transport is becoming active due to a rapid progress in containerization and shipping companies are more commonly offering door-to-door service, shipping conferences that are serving port-to-port needs would lose their market share. From the mid-1980s, around the routes like the Pacific route, the Europe route and the Atlantic route, they have increased their "around the world services" and "pendulum services" more positively, making it difficult of the shipping companies to participate in those particular conference specialized in a certain routes, which caused those conferences to lose much of their power. Pendulum routes are routes that consist of a set of ports that are structured as a continuous loop and designed for container transport.

Pendulum Services

"Pendulum services involve a set of sequential port calls along a maritime range, commonly including a transoceanic service from ports in another range and structured as a continuous loop. They are almost exclusively used for container transportation with the purpose of servicing a market by balancing the number of port calls and the frequency of services. For instance, pendulum services between Asia and Europe have on average 8 to 10 containerships assigned and involve 8 to 12 port calls. Most transatlantic pendulum services have 6 to 8 containerships and involve 6 to 8 port calls. A pendulum service is fairly flexible in terms of the selection of port calls, particularly on maritime ranges that have nearby and competing ports grouped as regional clusters (e.g. North American East Coast, Western Europe). This implies that a maritime company may opt to bypass one port to the advantage of another if its efficiency is not satisfactory and if its hinterland access is problematic. The shipping network consequently adapts to reflect changes in market conditions. The structure of pendulum service networks can take many shapes depending on factors such as the markets being serviced, trade imbalances and regulations:

O **Symmetrical.** Pendulum routes that involve a relatively similar number of port calls on the maritime facades serviced. Such a structure offers a good level of market coverage if the number of allocated vessels is sufficient, but with the drawback of longer cycle times.

O **Asymmetrical.** Involves fewer port calls along one of the maritime facades serviced. This can reflect several situations, including trade imbalances, cabotage constraints or export-oriented strategies. For instance, a maritime shipping company would be reluctant to offer several port calls along a facade within the same country (such as the United States) if cabotage regulations are present. It won't be able to ship containers between ports of the same facade, only pick or drop them. Trade imbalances are also reflective of asymmetrical pendulum services as traffic is collected along one facade and unloaded at a few major gateways accessing inland corridors of the other facade.

O **Inter-hub.** These services are almost similar to charter services as they directly connect major hubs or gateways. Their advantages are high capacity and frequency as well as lower cycle time, which can be offered when there is a substantial demand between the few ports serviced. They tend to involve the largest containerships available."

Source: http://people.hofstra.edu/geotrans/eng/ch3en/conc3en/pendulumservices.html

6.2.2.2 Trampers

The term "tramper" means to walk aimlessly. A tramp steamer, naturally, is a ship that is not confined to certain ports of call, or even has a fixed schedule, but instead, a tramp steamer, also known as a tramp freighter or tramper, trades on the spot market and can ship at the time and route that the shipper desires. Early in the maritime industry, trampers were highly common, but their use has decreased as regular liners have increased due to shipbuilding development.

Typically, a tramper's cargo is in bulk such as oil, iron ore, coal, grain, and cement. Since these ships can change their routes according to demand, trampers have a global market. Any tanker's individual market share is, therefore, understandably small because of which shipping conferences are difficult to be established for trampers.

Unlike contracts of carriage for a regular liner, a shipper makes a charter contract with a ship he wants by making charter party considering the shipping place, unloading place, transporting time and terms of voyage. The charter party means the contract for the lease of the vessel. Charter party contracts are formed as a time charter party, voyage charter party, and a bare boat charter (demise charter), out of which the voyage charter is largely used by shippers.

Trip/Voyage Charter Party

A charter party is a legal instrument to specify a contract between a ship-owner and a merchant, for which a ship is hired to transport goods on a particular voyage. A charter party is generally contracted for transportation of goods, sometimes a ship is hired to transport passengers. Route, cargo, period of contract, etc., are determined by the agreement of parties. In this case, a ship-owner bears all responsibilities and costs for equipment for the ship and voyage, and its freight is determined by quantity of cargo.

Time Charter Party

Under a time charter party, the ship is rented for a certain period of time, not for a certain voyage. The owner still manages the vessel, but takes orders from the charter until the expiry date. Shippers use this contract when they need to transport bulk cargoes during a certain period of time.

Bare Boat Charter (Demise Charter)

This is a subtype of a time charter under which the vessel is not under the guidance of the ship-owner, but instead the charter takes all responsibilities of sailors, port duties, repair costs, voyage costs, hull premium and etc. The personnel and materials needed for the voyage are all responsible to the charterer. The charterer assumes all legal responsibilities with relation to the vessel operation.

6.2.2.3 Freight

The measurement of freight is by the weight of shipped cargo, not by container as it is with regular container ships. The amount of freight is not stable as with regular liners because of extreme fluctuations according to market conditions. Generally speaking, freight under the charter party is grouped into lump sum freight, dead freight and long-term contract freight:

Lump sum freight is calculated on the basis of trip or voyage, or a ship's space regardless of number, weight or measurement of cargo. What is actually boarded upon the ship is irrelevant; Under the terms of dead freight, when the actual shipping quantity is less than agreed upon by contract, a shipper who is a charterer pays for the shortage; When concluding a long term contract of carriage to carry materials or goods repeatedly, they can make contract under the terms of long term contract freight.

6.2.2.4 Bill of Lading
Concepts
A bill of lading (B/L) is defined as "a written receipt given by a carrier for goods accepted for transportation." The bill is issued by a carrier, acknowledging that cargo has been received onboard, and that a certain place is named for delivery. In today's international commerce world, settlement of payment is often made with a documentary bill of exchange accompanied by shipping documents including bill of lading, commercial invoice, insurance policy, etc. The bill of lading, in general cases, contains the particulars including the leading marks necessary for identification of the shipped goods, the number of packages or pieces, the quantity or weight of the goods, the apparent order and condition of the goods.[2]

Bills of lading are usually issued in sets by an agent of the ship owner (or a ship master). Each bill of lading in the set is sufficient and valid to induce delivery of the goods[3]: one is kept on board the vessel whilst the others will be remitted to consignees of goods or issuing banks of documentary credit for the goods.[4] The bill of lading contains usually a clause to the effect that once one in the set have been presented to demand delivery of the goods, the others are to "stand void".[5]

Types
(1) Shipped or Shipped on Board Bill of Lading and Received for Shipment Bill of Laing
Shipped or shipped on board bill of lading is issued after a shipping company ships on board the received cargo from a shipper. "Shipped" or "Shipped on Board" is indicated on the bill of lading. Received for shipment bill of lading is issued before shipment is made after a shipping company receives cargo when a designated ship is waiting on the berth, or when a ship is designated even though it is not yet in the port. If a shipping company writes a date and signs after shipment, and thereby the "on board notation" is written on the bill, it is valid as shipped or shipped on board bill of lading. Currently, according to UCP 600, unless the letter of credit specifically requires a shipped on board bill of lading, banks will accept a received bill of lading.
(2) Clean Bill of Lading and Foul or Dirty Bill of Lading
A clean bill of lading is issued when there are not mistakes indicated in the remarks column of the bill of lading in relation to the status of cargo shipped on board. "Shipped on board in apparent good order and condition" may be

---

[2] Hague-Visby Rules, Art. III(3).

[3] Chuah (2009, p. 169).

[4] *Id.*

[5] *Id.*

indicated on the policy. The effect of a clean bill of lading, as far as the carrier is concerned, would be that the carrier is estopped from claiming that the goods were damaged at the time of shipment unless the damage was such that it would not have been apparent on reasonable examination at that time.[6] A foul or dirty bill of lading is issued when a bill of lading indicates something wrong with the status of the goods for shipping at the time of shipment.

The bank will refuse to negotiate on this type of imperfect bill of lading.[7] Thus, as soon as the exporter discovers something wrong with the cargo, it must replace or repack it immediately to resolve the problem. If this is impossible due to time restraints, the exporter submits a letter of indemnity and can then be given a clean bill of lading.

Indemnity:

"1. A duty to make good any loss, damage, or liability incurred by another. 2. The right of an injured party to claim reimbursement for its loss, damage, or liability from a person who has such a duty. 3. Reimbursement or compensation for loss, damage, or liability in tort; esp., the right of a party who is secondarily liable to recover from the party who is primarily liable for reimbursement of expenditures paid to a third party for injuries resulting from a violation of a common-law duty."

(Source: Black's Law Dictionary, 2000)

The shipping company can be exempt from the responsibilities for the improper cargo if the letter of indemnity is received by the exporter in exchange for issuing a clean bill of lading for the improper cargo shipped.

---

[6] *Id.*, at 188.
[7] UCP 600 Art. 14(b).

Letter of Indemnity

L.O.I. for Non-Presentation of Bill of Lading
LETTER OF INDEMNITY
(FOR CARGO DELIVERY WITHOUT ORIGNAL BS/L)
TO:
THE OWNERS OF THE MV ....
DATE............
DEAR SIRS,
SHIP:
LOADING PORT :
DISCHARGING PORT :
CARGO:
BILL OF LADING:
The above goods were shipped on the above vessel by ..... and consigned to..... for
delivery at the port of ...., but the bill of lading has not arrived and we, ..., hereby
request you to give delivery the said cargo to .... without production of the original bills of
lading.

In consideration of your complying with our above request, we hereby agree as follows:

1. To indemnify you, your servants and agents and to hold all of you harmless in
respect of any liability, loss, damage or expenses of whatsoever nature which you may
sustain by reason of delivering the cargo in accordance with our request.

2. In the event of any proceedings being commenced against you or any of your
servants or agents in connection with the delivery of the cargo as aforesaid, to provide you or
them on demand with sufficient funds to defend the same.

3. If, in connection with the delivery of the cargo as aforesaid, the ship, or any
other ship or property in the same or associated ownership, management or control,, should
be arrested or detained or should the arrest or detention thereof should be threatened, or
should there be any interference in the use or trading of the vessel (whether by virtue of a
caveat being entered on the ship's registry or otherwise howsoever), to provide on demand
such bail or other security as may be required to prevent such arrest or detention or to secure
the release of such ship or property or to remove such interference and to indemnify you in
respect of any liability, loss, damage or expense caused by such arrest or detention or
threatened arrest or detention or such interference, whether or not such arrest or detention or
threatened arrest or detention or such interference may be justified..

4. If the place at which we have asked you to make delivery is a bulk liquid or gas
terminal or facility, or another ship, lighter or barge, then delivery to such terminal, facility,
ship, lighter or barge shall be deemed to be delivery to the party to whom we have requested
you to make such delivery.

5. As soon as all original bills of lading for the above cargo shall have come into our
possession, to deliver the same to you, whenever our liability hereunder shall cease.

6. The liability of each and every person under this indemnity shall be joint and several
and shall not be conditional upon your proceeding first against any person, whether or not
such person is party to or liable under this indemnity.

7. This indemnity shall be governed by and construed in accordance with English Law
and each and every person liable under this indemnity shall at your request submit to the
jurisdiction of the High Court of justice of England.

YOURS FAITHFULLY   YOURS FAITHFULLY
Charterers   Receivers
(insert name of requestor)   (insert name of requestor)

-----------------------------------   -----------------------------------
(insert name /title)   (insert name /title)

(3) Straight Bill of Lading and Order Bill of Lading

A straight bill of lading is a bill of lading indicating a certain consignee on the bill, which is meaningless to others in relation with the document of title unless the indicated consignee transfers it to them, in which case it is unable to be negotiated. An order bill of lading indicates "to order," "order of shipper," or "order of 'OOO' Bank" without indicating any specified consignee.

(4) Third Party Bill of Lading

Generally, a shipper on a bill of lading is the beneficiary of the letter of credit, but a third party can be the beneficiary with the use of a third party bill of lading, also known as a neutral party bill of lading. It is usually used as a transit trade, and, unless otherwise specified on the letter of credit, it is accepted by banks.

(5) Through Bill of Lading

This bill of lading means that in carrying cargo to its final destination multiple carriers and multiple modes of transport may be used. The former carrier is responsible for connection to the next carrier.

(6) Multimodal Transport Bill of Lading

This bill of lading is a single contract used when at least two separate modes of transport will be used. The multimodal transport operator (MTO) is the person who is named on the face, concludes the contract, and acts as carrier.

(7) Short Form Bill of Lading

This is a bill of lading with all of the necessary schedules, but it omits the terms and conditions on the back of the bill of lading. Instead, the bill of lading will reference other documents where the details are contained. It is used in several areas, including the U.S.A.

Shipper:		**SHORT FORM** UK Customs B/L No.
		BILL OF LADING Assigned No.
		Shipper's Reference
		F/agent's Reference
Consignee(if "Order state Notify Party and Address)		Name of Carrier:
Notify Party and Address (leave blank if stated above)		The contract evidenced by this Short Form Bill of Lading is subject to the exceptions, limitations, conditions and liberties (including those relating to pre-carriage and on-carriage) set out in the Carrier's Standard Conditions applicable to the voyage covered
Pre-Carriage by*	Place of Receipt by Pre-Carrier*	by this Short Form Bill of Lading and operative on its date of issue.
		If the carriage is one where the provisions of the
Vessel	Port of Loading	Hague Rules contained in the International Convention
		for unification of certain rules relating to Bills of Lading
Port of Discharge	Place of Delivery by On-Carrier*	dated Brussels on 25th August, 1924, as amended by the Protocol signed at Brussels on 23rd February, 1968 (the Hague Visby Rules) are compulsorily applicable under Article X, the said Standard Conditions contain or shall be deemed to contain a Clause giving effect to the Hague Visby Rules Otherwise except as provided

below the said Standard Conditions contain or shall be deemed to contain a Clause giving effect to the provisions of the Hague Rules.

The Carrier hereby agrees that to the extent of any inconsistency the said Clause shall prevail over the exception, limitations, conditions and liberties set out in the Standard Conditions in respect of any period to which the Hague Rules or the Hague Visby Rules by their terms apply Unless the Standard Conditions expressly provide other wise neither the Hague Rules nor the Hague Visby Rules shall apply to this contract where the goods carried hereunder consist of live animals or cargo which by this contract is stated as being carried on deck and is so carried.

Notwithstanding anything contained in the said Standard Conditions the term Carrier in this Short Form Bill of Lading shall mean the Carrier named on the front thereof.

A copy of the Carrier's said Standard Conditions applicable hereto may be inspected or will be supplied on request at the office of the Carrier or the Carriers' Principal Agents.

Marks and No.:	Container No.	Number and kind of packages:	Description of Goods	Gross Weight:	Measurement:

Freight Details; Charges etc. GCBS CSF BL ·1979	**RECEIVED FOR CARRIAGE** as above in apparent good order and condition, unless otherwise stated hereon, the goods described in the above particulars. **IN WITNESS** whereof the number of original Bills of Lading stated below have been signed, all of this tenor and date, one of which being accomplished the others to stand void.
Ocean Freight Payable at	Place and Date of Issue
Number of Original Bs/L	Signature for Carrier; Carrier's Principal Place of Business
Printed by The Cariton Berry Co. Ltd. Authorized and licensed by the General Council of British Shipping.	

(8) Stale Bill of Lading

This is not a particular kind of bill of lading, but any bill of lading can turn stale if it is presented to the bank for negotiation when the letter of credit has already expired, or if it reaches the consignee after the arrival of cargo. If this occurs, the buyer may be involved in legal or administrative complications as well as being liable for additional costs resulting from the delay. When it is not specified to be acceptable on the letter of credit, if bill of lading or other shipping documents are presented to a negotiating bank for negotiation after a period of time that a bank allows from an issuing date, the bank refuses to accept the document unless the notation "stale bill of lading acceptable" is indicated on the letter of credit.

(9) Transshipment Bill of Lading

This is a bill of lading showing that when there is no direct service between ports, the cargo will be transferred to another ship during transporting on its route.

(10) Master Bill of Lading and House Bill of Lading

A master bill of lading is issued by the operator (a shipping company), while a house bill of lading is issued by a non-vessel operating common carrier (NVOCC).

Main Clauses

(1) Negligence Clause

With respect to faults in navigation and management of the vessel, the carrier is generally free from damages resulting from "any faults about technical actions of a ship necessary for control of ship and safe voyage" by captain, sailor, coast pilot, or employees of a shipping company. With respect to the commercial fault, however, the carrier is generally liable for any damage resulting from shipping, preparing, storing, discharging, or delivering caused by the commercial fault.

(2) Potential Repair Clause

Warranty of seaworthiness of a ship is imposed on the carriers by the laws of each country, however, if the seaworthiness of the ship is evidenced to be secured through the pre-departure inspection, ensuing unavoidable damage or technical defects to the hull, engine and other areas are free from the liability of the carrier.

(3) Off-Route Clause

Deviations from the routine course of navigation for the reasons of rescue of life and property, refuge, etc. are free from the carrier's liability.

(4) Unknown Clause

In making shipment, a shipping company does not have to inspect the details of its cargo and can indicate "we ship cargo in good condition by appearance and deliver it in a similar way as it was received" on the bill of lading. This shows that the shipping company is not responsible for the cargo's weight, measurements, quantity, quality, type, or price.

Unknown Clause

Any reference on the face hereof to marks, numbers, description, quality, quantity, gauge, weight, measure, nature, kind, value and any other particulars of the Goods is as furnished by the Merchant, and the Carrier shall not be responsible for the accuracy thereof. The Merchant warrants to the Carrier that the particulars furnished by him are correct and shall indemnify the Carrier against all loss, damage, expenses, liability, penalties and fines arising or resulting from inaccuracy thereof.

(5) Breakage and Leakage (Cargo's Inherent Nature)

Breakage, leakage, decomposition, death of live animals, fish and shellfish, fruit, perishable cargo and etc. are free from the carriers' liability.

(6) Valuables

When a consignor ships the cargo, if he does not state the type of cargo, quality, price, and other details, or if freight is not calculated, due to the specific characters of the goods, by closing rate, a shipping company is just responsible for compensating a minimum amount for probable damage.

Clause on Valuables

The Carrier shall not be responsible for valuable goods, such as specie (coins), bullion (paper money), precious stones, bonds or other negotiable documents, until such goods are delivered to and receipted for by the Master or the officer on duty personally.

(7) Dangerous Goods

If a consignor fails to report the dangerous character of goods in shipping, a captain can create a special contract to dispose of them as he deems worthy, such as discharging or jettisoning when the cargo could become dangerous. This rule applies for any goods that are illegal to export or import.

Clause on Dangerous Goods

Goods known to be of a dangerous or hazardous nature must not be tendered for shipment unless written notice of their nature and the name and address of the Merchant have been previously given to the Carrier and the nature is distinctly marked on the outside of the package. A special stowage order giving consent to shipment must also be obtained from the Carrier.

Any goods that are in fact or may be considered by any civil or military authorities or the Carrier inflammable, explosive, noxious, hazardous, or dangerous, shipped without such full disclosure, or if shipped with the knowledge and consent of the Carrier as to their nature and character, shall become a danger to the Vessel or those aboard, the goods or other property, or any part thereof, may at any time or place be landed, thrown overboard, destroyed or rendered innocuous without compensation to the Merchant, and

(continued)

extra charges and expenses if any, for returning, discharging, lightering, handling, caring for, disposing of or otherwise occasioned by such goods shall be borne by the Merchant.

If at any time the goods, whether ashore or afloat, are, in the judgment of the Carrier or of the health or other authorities, spoiling, decayed, injurious, offensive, unfit for further carriage or storage, or dangerous to health or other property, of if the goods are condemned or ordered to be destroyed by any such authorities, or if the goods are contraband or prohibited by any laws or regulations of the port of shipment, discharge, call or any place during transit, the goods may, forthwith and without notice, be thrown overboard, destroyed, discharged, returned, stored, put ashore at any place or aboard lighters or craft or otherwise disposed of by the Carrier, at the sole risk and expense of the Merchant, when the Carrier's responsibility shall cease, and the Carrier shall not be liable for any loss or damage whatsoever.

In any event, the Merchant shall be liable for and fully indemnify the Carrier and to hold it harmless in respect to any injury or death of any person and loss of or damage to the Vessel, cargo or other property which may arise from the dangerous or hazardous nature of the goods carried hereunder.

(8) General Average Clause

It is agreed that each country follows the York-Antwerp Rule of 1950, excluding their domestic laws and customs concerning general average clause. The General Average Clause states that, concerning maritime insurance, the insurers of different interests should voluntarily share the portion of losses incurred to save the voyage.

General Average Clause

General Average shall be adjusted, stated and settled in Tokyo or any other port or place at the Carrier's discretion according to York Antwerp Rules, 1974, and as to matters not provided for by the Rules, according to the laws and usages of the port or place of adjustment, and in the currency selected by the Carrier. The General Average Statement shall be prepared by the adjusters, if necessary, appointed by the Carrier.

In the event of accident, danger, damage or disaster, before or after commencement of the voyage resulting from any cause whatsoever, whether due to negligence or not, for which, or for the consequence of which the Carrier is not responsible by statute, contract or otherwise, the goods and the Merchant, jointly and severally shall contribute with the Carrier in General Average to the payment of any sacrifices, losses or expenses of General Average nature that may be made or incurred and shall pay salvage and special charges incurred in respect of the goods.

If a salving ship is owned or operated by the Carrier, salvage shall be paid for in full and in the same manner as if such salving ship or ships belonged to strangers.

Legal Characteristics
(1) Bill of Lading as Receipt

The bill of lading as a receipt is an acknowledgement made by the carrier that the goods have been shipped or received for shipment as the case may be.[8] This acknowledgement will also contain statements as to the apparent condition of the goods, the quantity, markings and other relevant information known to the carrier.[9] In practice, the shipper or his freight forwarders would usually fill in the particulars in the bill of lading, and the shipmaster (the carrier's agent) makes signature on it.[10] The shipmaster should indicate on the bill of lading whether the goods have been merely received for shipment or have been actually loaded on board the vessel. In case of the former, only a "received for shipment" bill of lading may be issued.[11]

From the viewpoint of the shipper, the bill of lading as a receipt is prima facie evidence that the shipper has performed his obligation under the contract to the extent that the goods have been duly shipped.[12] For the consignee or endorsee of the bill of lading, it functions as conclusive evidence that the goods have been shipped as per contractual conditions reflecting the accuracy of documents in documentary transactions.[13]

(2) Bill of Lading as Evidence of Contract

The bill of lading through the usage and customs of the international trade community has long been recognized as not only being evidence of contract of carriage but as being that contract itself.[14] The terms contained in the bill of lading may therefore in some situations be effectively the terms of the contract or in others, merely evidence of the actual terms.[15] The distinction is significant to the extent that as a primary and negotiable document, it is treated by law as the actual contract once it has been indorsed by a third party.[16]

---

[8] Chuah (2009, *supra* note 252, at 179).

[9] *Id.*, at 179–180.

[10] *Id.*, at 180.

[11] *Id.*

[12] *Id.*

[13] *Id.*

[14] *Id.*

[15] *Id.*

[16] *Id.*

That is, while the bill of lading is kept in the hands of the shipper, the bill of lading functions merely as the evidence of the contract, and the parties to the contract are free to modify and amend the contract as they so desire, however, once it has been transferred or indorsed to a third party, the bill of lading should not be treated as simply the evidence of the contract of carriage, but should be treated as the contract itself to bind the concerned parties.[17]

(3) Bill of Lading as Document of Title

The bill of lading can only be treated as a document of title when it is made clear on its face that it is negotiable, that is, it must be issued as an "order" bill of lading which is in contrast with a "straight" bill of lading. The former is made out to a named consignee or to his "order or assigns".[18] This means that, in case of the "order" bill of lading, the named consignee could transfer or assign the bill of lading to any third party simply by delivery or endorsement, which, in case of the "straight" bill of lading, the bill of lading is impossible to be transferred to the third party once it has been delivered to the designated party.[19]

Bill of Lading

"a. A bill of lading, however named, must appear to:

i. indicate the name of the carrier and be signed by:

- the carrier or a named agent for or on behalf of the carrier, or
- the master or a named agent for or on behalf of the master.

Any signature by the carrier, master or agent must be identified as that of the carrier, master or agent.

Any signature by an agent must indicate whether the agent has signed for or on behalf of the carrier or for or on behalf of the master.

ii. indicate that the goods have been shipped on board a named vessel at the port of loading stated in the credit by:

- pre-printed wording, or
- an on board notation indicating the date on which the goods have been shipped on board.

The date of issuance of the bill of lading will be deemed to be the date of shipment unless the bill of lading contains an on board notation indicating the date of shipment, in which case the date stated in the on board notation will be deemed to be the date of shipment.

If the bill of lading contains the indication "intended vessel" or similar qualification in relation to the name of the vessel, an on board notation indicating the date of shipment and the name of the actual vessel is required.

---

[17] *Id.*, at 189.

[18] *Id.*, at 196.

[19] *Id.*, at 196–197.

iii. indicate shipment from the port of loading to the port of discharge stated in the credit.

If the bill of lading does not indicate the port of loading stated in the credit as the port of loading, or if it contains the indication "intended" or similar qualification in relation to the port of loading, an on board notation indicating the port of loading as stated in the credit, the date of shipment and the name of the vessel is required. This provision applies even when loading on board or shipment on a named vessel is indicated by pre-printed wording on the bill of lading.

iv. be the sole original bill of lading or, if issued in more than one original, be the full set as indicated on the bill of lading.

v. contain terms and conditions of carriage or make reference to another source containing the terms and conditions of carriage (short form or blank back bill of lading). Contents of terms and conditions of carriage will not be examined.

vi. contain no indication that it is subject to a charter party.

b. For the purpose of this article, transhipment means unloading from one vessel and reloading to another vessel during the carriage from the port of loading to the port of discharge stated in the credit.

c. i. A bill of lading may indicate that the goods will or may be transhipped provided that the entire carriage is covered by one and the same bill of lading.

ii. A bill of lading indicating that transhipment will or may take place is acceptable, even if the credit prohibits transhipment, if the goods have been shipped in a container, trailer or LASH barge as evidenced by the bill of lading.

d. Clauses in a bill of lading stating that the carrier reserves the right to transship will be disregarded."(UCP 600 Article 20)

Illustration of Bill of Lading Form

Straight Bill of Lading

⑲ Date: ⑤ B/L No.:

① **Shipper** Name: Street Address: City. ST ZIP Code: FAX: TEL:	③ **Destination:** ④ **Agent's No.:**
② **Consignee** Name: Street Address: City. ST ZIP Code: FAX: TEL:	⑥ **Notify Party** Name: Address:
⑦ **Port of Loading:**	⑧ **Port of Discharge:**
⑨ **Route:**	⑩ **Vehicle Car No.**

⑪No. Packages	⑫ Description of Articles, Special Marks and Exceptions	⑬ Weight Subj. to Correction	⑭ Class or Rate	⑮ Charges
	Total:			

Hazardous Material Emergency Contact:	⑯ **C.O.D. Shipment:** ▫ Prepaid ▫ Collect ▫ Third Party	⑰ **Shipment Declared Value:**
DECLARED VALUE Where the rate is dependent on value, shippers are required to state specifically in writing the agreed or declared value of the property as follows: The agreed or declared value of the property is specifically stated by the shipper to be not exceeding _____per _____		The carrier shall not make delivery of this shipment without payment of freight and all other lawful charges. _____ Shipper Signature

NOTE Liability Limitation for loss or damage in this shipment may be applicable. See 49 U.S.C. – 14706(c)(1)(A) and (B).

RECEIVED, subject to individually determined rates or contracts that have been agreed upon in writing between the carrier and shipper, if applicable, otherwise to the rates, classifications and rules that have been established by the carrier and are available to the shipper on request. The property described above, in apparent good order, except as noted (contents and condition of contents of packages unknown), marked, consigned and destined as shown above, which said carrier agrees to carry to destination, if on its route, or otherwise deliver to another carrier on the route to destination. Every service to be performed hereunder shall be subject to all bill of lading terms and conditions in the governing classification on the date of the shipment. Shipper hereby certifies that he is hereby familiar with all the bill of lading terms and conditions in the governing classification and the said terms and conditions are hereby agreed to by the shipper and accepted for himself and his assigns.

This is to certify that the above named materials are properly classified, described, packaged, marked, labeled and in proper condition for transportation according to the applicable regulations of the Department of Transportation.

⑱ Shipper Company Name:	Carrier:	Trailer Loaded	Freight Counted
		□ By Shipper	□ By Shipper
Shipper Signature/Date:	Driver:	□ By Driver	□ By Driver/pallets
		said to contain	
			□ By Driver/pieces

The contents to fill in the above bill of lading are explained below:

① **Shipper**: Enter the company name and address of the shipper (consignor).

② **Consignee**: Enter the full of the final recipient of the shipment, the ultimate consignee, if different than destination, for carrier notification purposes.

③ **Destination**: Enter the street address, city, and zip code where the carrier will make delivery to the consignee in Field 2.

④ **Agent's Number**: Enter carrier's control number, if known or required.

⑤ **B/L No.**: Enter the bill of lading issuing number made by the shipping company.

⑥ **Notify Party**: Enter the name of the company which will take initial control of the shipment and oversee its delivery to the consignee.

⑦ **Port of Loading**: Enter the name of port where the shipment is made.

⑧ **Port of Discharge**: Enter the name of port where the shipped cargo is discharged.

⑨ **Route**: If applicable, enter the route the Carrier will take to the consignee. This field may also be used to specify docks, warehouses, etc., and to specify any intermediate Carriers.

⑩ **Vehicle/Car No.**: Enter any vehicle identifying numbers or initials, if applicable.

⑪ **No. Packages**: Enter the total number of packages per line item; if the packages are consolidated on a pallet or in an outer container, note this information on a second line. Ex: 112 PKGS 3 Pall.

(12) **Description of Shipment**: Enter the description of each line item, noting the type of package (carton, barrel, etc.) and the quantity per package. Since the correct freight classification is essential in describing an item, there must be a separate line item for each different freight classification description. If more than one type of packaging is used per freight classification, a separate entry must be used for each type of package. Enter any special package markings, special handling requirements, and delivery instructions. For hazardous material items, special provisions must be met in completing this field.

(13) **Weight**: Enter the total gross weight, in pounds, for each line item. For bulk shipments, the tare (weight of packaging) and net weights should also be referenced in the description field. For package shipments, include the weights of pallets and skids. The total weight of the merchandise should be shown after the last line item, with pallet and dunnage weights shown separately.

(14) **Class or Rate**: Enter the 5-digit class (per the Uniform Freight Classification or the National Motor Freight Classification) or a two digit class rate (a percentage of the First class 100 rate) per line item. This information may be determined with the Carrier.

(15) **Charges**: Enter the freight amount by packages.

(16) **C.O.D. Shipment**: First, check whether the freight charges are prepaid (the carrier bills the shipper) or collect (the carrier deducts the freight charges from the amount collected from the consignee). Second, enter the amount to be collected for the merchandise itself – be sure to include the freight charges. Third, enter any collection fees, if applicable. Enter total charges to be collected by the carrier.

(17) **Shipment Declared Value**: When the weight charged by the carrier is dependent upon the value of the shipment, the dollar value per unit of measure (ex: $100/pound) must be stated by the Shipper – enter this information in field 14.

(18) **Shipper Company Name**: Enter the company name of the shipper.

(19) **Date**: Enter the date of the shipment; that is, the date the Carrier took control of the merchandise.

6.2.3   Air Transportation

6.2.3.1 Introduction

Air cargo is either shipped: along with luggage in passenger planes; in hybrid aircraft with special compartments for cargo, or in cargo aircraft.[20] Technological innovations have recently allowed the size and weight of most mechanical goods to shrink considerably, under which light-weight products could be transported via air transport, which has proven to be particularly advantageous for high-value emergency goods to be delivered fast in comparison with marine transport.

---

[20] Ramberg (2008, *supra* note 48, at 246).

Air transport offers advantages over marine transport in the shipping of certain items. Air transport is both faster and safer than maritime or land transportation, and it makes it is possible to reduce inventory costs and cost of capital through just-in-time delivery of cargo. Just-in-time delivery means that goods are ordered promptly before they are needed, and only by an amount that will be quickly demanded. By utilizing this method, the need for storage facilities may be minimized and buyers can make smaller purchases that require less financing. Finally, aircraft are rarely if ever subject to damage or burglary, but with ships such complications are not so uncommon.

6.2.3.2 Preparation for Transportation
Packing
Packing is extremely important due to the fact that aircraft has a minimal amount of space for cargo, and because extra weight will cause fuel costs to be increased. Because of this, packing must be done like a puzzle, leaving no extra unused air space, and appropriate, light-weight materials must be used.

Transport Inquiry
It is just to ask a consignor if he carries cargo to an airline agent directly. If so, there is no need to make a formal document besides a signed air waybill, which can be done immediately. This airway bill can then be presented along with the shipper's other mandated documents which may include a declaration for dangerous goods, shipper's certification for live animals, a commercial invoice, or other documents required by the customs authority of the concerned country.

Restricted Items
With air transport, it is necessary to provide a precise description of the cargo, and to specify that consignors are required to submit documents accompanied with the cargo. This allows authorities to make the proper decisions concerning whether the cargo is legal for transport. Restricted items include live animals, arms (weapons), ammunition, other war paraphernalia, human remains, alcohol and other flammable goods such as canned air, and machinery.

Gross Weight
The weight of cargo must be calculated exactly when being accepted and calculated under the supervision of employees of the airline or agent appointed by the airline. If the weight of cargo is uncertain in flight, the exact rate to charge will not be accurate, and the shipper cannot claim appropriately when items have been missed.

Prepaid Freight
A consignor should designate whether the payment of freight is prepaid or collected by a consignee. With prepayment there is not a problem, but if the payment should be later collected from a consignee, complicated problems could potentially arise:

Declared Value for Carriage

The term "declared value for carriage" is defined as the "value of a shipment as declared by its shipper to serve as the basis for computing freight charges, and for limiting the carrier's liability for damage, loss, or delay." A consignor must give an accurate price for the cargo, or write "no value declared" (NVD) in the column of declared value for carriage. If it exceeds a certain price (set by the airline) per airway bill, the consignor must discuss it with the airline before carrying.

Declared Value for Customs

The term "declared value for customs" is defined as the "value of a shipment as declared by its shipper to serve as the basis for computation of duties and taxes. It usually reflects the selling price of the shipment, and is equal to or higher than the declared value for carriage." A tariff is imposed on the declared value that is marked in the price column. If it is not mandatory to write down the declared value according to the laws of the importing country, it is acceptable to be indicated "no customs declared" (NCD).

6.2.3.3 Air Waybill

Concepts

An air waybill is a type of bill of lading used specifically when goods are transported via airplanes. It serves both as a receipt of goods by an airline (carrier), and as a contract of carriage between the shipper and carrier. The airline industry has adopted a formal standardized air waybill for simplicity, which is accepted domestically and internationally. Air waybills are not negotiable, but only function as a means of receipt. Also unlike a bill of lading, an air waybill does not specify when the goods will reach their final destination, or on what airplane goods will be transported. It does specify a carrier's limits of liability, description of goods, and accompanying charges. The contract of carriage is valid from the time that the air waybill is issued, and it expires when the cargo is delivered to the consignee.

Function

The air waybill is the most basic shipping document guaranteeing the distribution of cargo. The bill guarantees transport from departure to destination, regardless of distance, number of airlines engaged in the transport, and even local transport. Its various functions include: a receipt that cargo is entrusted for transport; written evidence of a conclusion of contract of carriage; a freight bill; proof of insurance when a consignor takes out a shipper's insurance; a customs declaration; and a guideline of cargo transport (handling, transit and delivery, etc).

The air waybill or the cargo receipt is prima facie evidence of the conclusion of the contract, of the acceptance of the cargo and the contents of the contract but it is not a document of title.[21] The statements in the waybill relating to the weight,

---

[21] Chuah (2009, *supra* note 252, at 371).

dimensions and packaging of the cargo, and to the number of packages, are prima facie evidence of the facts stated.[22] Those relating to the quantity, volume and condition of the cargo, however, do not constitute evidence against the carrier unless the waybill or cargo receipt states that the carrier had actually examined the goods in respect of these issues at the presence of consignor or relates to the apparent condition of the goods.[23]

---

[22] *Id.*

[23] *Id.*

Airway Bill

MAERSK LINE

NON-NEGOTIABLE	SCAC
WAYBILL	B/L NO.

Shipper	Booking No.
	Export references

Consignee	

This contract is subject to the terms and conditions, including the law & jurisdiction clause and limitation of liability & declared value clauses, of the current Maersk Line Bill of Lading (available from the carrier, its agents and at www.maerskline.com), which are applicable with logical amendments (mutatis mutandis). To the extent necessary to enable the Consignee to sue and to be sued under this contract, the Shipper on entering into this contract does so on his own behalf and as agent for and on behalf of the Consignee and warrants the he has the authority to do so. The shipper shall be entitled to change the Consignee at any time before delivery of the goods provided he gives the Carrier reasonable notice in writing.

Notify Party

Delivery will be made to the Consignee or his authorized agent on production of reasonable proof of identity (and, in the case of an agent, reasonable proof of authority) without production of this waybill. The Carrier shall be under no liability whatsoever for misdelivery unless caused by the Carrier's negligence.

Onward inland routing (Not part of Carriage as defined in clause 1. For account and risk of Merchant)

Vessel	Voyage	Place of Receipt. Applicable only when document used as Multimodal Waybill
Port of Loading	Port of Discharge	Place of Delivery. Applicable only when document used as Multimodal Waybill

PARTICULARS FURNISHED BY SHIPPER		

Kind of Packages; Description of goods; Marks and Numbers; Container No. /Seal No.	Gross Weight	Measurement
Above particulars as declared by Shipper, but without responsibility of or representation by Carrier.		

Freight & Charges	Rate	Unit	Currency	Prepaid	Collect
Carrier's Receipt. Total number of containers or packages received by Carrier.	Place of Issue of Waybill	Shipped, as far as ascertained by reasonable means of checking, in apparent good order and condition unless otherwise stated herein the total number of quantity of Containers or other packages or units indicated in the box opposite entitled "Carrier's Receipt"			
Shipped on Board Date	Date Issue of Waybill				
Declared Value Charges (see clause 7.3 of the Maersk Line Bill of Lading) for Declared Value of US$					
		Signed for the Carrier A.P. Moller-Maersk trading as Maersk Line			
		As Agent(s) for the Carrier			

6.2.4 Tariff

A tariff is a list of fares, freight charges and rates applied to goods that cross international borders. A rate means that the fee is calculated by unit weight and unit container of freight collected, and it is usually calculated in kilograms. Charges refer to extra costs such as transport facilities, handling costs, pick-up service expenses, costs for handling dangerous goods, settlement fees, etc.

The rate had traditionally been determined through different methods and procedures outlined by the country's government, not by airlines, but, recently, following some deregulation in the air freight field, airlines increasingly decide their own tariffs and rates, creating a more liberalized market for international shipment. International tariffs take effect by approval of both countries, but since a lot of air routes are connected through various airlines and different cities and countries, an international forum called IATA Cargo Tariff Coordinating Conference was created to discuss the tariff issues and prevent excess tariff competition.

6.2.5 Combined Transport

6.2.5.1 Concepts

Combined transport is made when cargo is transported door to door through at least two different transportation means, but on the basis of a single contract of carriage. Combined transport has the following advantages compared with the single transport:

First, reduction of operation costs occurs at a point of contract such as the inspection of transshipment and allows for a smoother operation and improvement of discharging productivity.

Second, transportation formalities are simplified due to containerization such as a simple confirmation of cargo and documents.

Third, unification is made because the task is being completed via a team effort, and therefore, claims can be applied and settled jointly as well.

Fourth, the cargo tracking system is easy because cargo is handled by a single carrier.

The combined transportation has also the following distinguished characters compared with other single transportation:

First, since a combined carrier is in position to plan the entire transport, to properly connect transport sections, to adjust the transport smoothly by supervision, as well as acting as a party to contract to a consignor with his name and property, and to take responsibility for the whole transpiration.

Second, the combined transport bill of lading is issued as a combined carrier's document to cover all transporting segments of the trade.

Third, the combined carrier sets the "through rate" as a reward of service for the entire service, not in installments, and offers it to the shipper.

6.2.5.2 Combined Transport Bill of Lading

The combined transport bill of lading is a bill stating that cargo was accepted through combined transport, and is to be delivered in accordance with the contract. The bill of lading was designed specifically only for marine transport, and is not suitable for combined transport by land, sea, and air.

The combined transport bill of lading was made to address the following needs: The combined transport bill of lading covers all transporting sections with liability for the loss or damage of cargo. Unlike a basic bill of lading, it can be issued by forwarders as well as carriers. It is issued when cargo is entrusted or taken by the combined carrier before shipment is made on board. Its security functions are the same as with a normal bill of lading.

The special forms of combined transport bill of lading are as follows:

Combined transport bill of lading with bill of lading includes combined transport bill of lading which is a "multimodal transport bill of lading" and "intermodal transport bill of lading" comprised of the existing bill of lading along with the name of combined transporters. A FIATA bill of lading established by FIATA is normally used just like a normal bill of lading; other types are issued by name of actual carriers such as marine carrier, air carrier, ground carrier, and by freight forwarder – a combined carrier.

Assignment

1. Communications and discussions with the concerned parties for the efficient transportation contract from the factory or warehouse of the items previously screened for export to the final destination in the importing country.
2. Special factors to be considered to make transportation contracts with the environmentally-friendly products which are particularly easy to be damaged or open to depreciation in value during the international transportation, for example, due to heavy weather conditions.

Reference

Chuah JCT (2009) Law of International Trade: Cross-Border Commercial Transactions, 4th edn. Sweet & Maxwell

Supplemental Reading

Folsom RH, Gordon MW, Spanogle Jr. JA, Fitzgerald PL (2009) International Business Transactions: Contracting Across Borders. West, pp. 52–110

Fellmeth AX (2009) The Law of International Business Transactions. West, pp. 327–404

DiMatteo LA, Dhooge LJ (2005) International Business Law – Transactional Approach, 2nd edn. West, pp. 251–289

Kouladis N, Fellmeth AX (2009) The Law of International Business Transactions. West, 2009, Springer, 2006, pp. 75–128

Marine Cargo Insurance

7

Learning Objectives

1. Function and importance of marine insurance contracts in doing international trade;
2. Risks covered and risks not covered ("or excluded") under the variable marine insurance terms made by ICC;
3. Comparative analysis between the terms under Lloyd's Marine Policy and the Institute Cargo Clauses A, B and C;
4. Process to make claims under the marine cargo insurance;

7.1 Marine Cargo Insurance Contract

7.1.1 Concepts

7.1.1.1 Definition

The term "marine cargo insurance contract" means a "contract whereby, for a consideration, that is, premium, stipulated to be paid by one party, that is, the policy holder or insured, interested in shipped cargo that is subject to the risks from or incidental to the maritime navigation, another party, that is, the insurer or insurance company, undertakes to indemnify him against some or all of loss or damage caused by those risks during a certain period of time or voyage." Briefly speaking, obtaining marine insurance policy means that you are paying a fee to someone that will in turn make payments to cover any accidents if they occur during transportation. The insurance company is to bet that there will be far much more transports without damage than transports with damage and to cover the few transports that will have to enforce its insurance contract.

Even though it is termed "marine insurance", the contract of marine insurance can, by agreement of the parties or international trade customs, be extended so as to protect the assured against losses on inland waters or land which are incidental to the maritime transportation.[1] In international business transactions covered by marine insurance policies are made frequently in order to cover not only the maritime transportation but also the transportation of goods from the warehouse of the seller located in inland to that of the overseas buyer.[2]

The contract of marine insurance must relate to marine losses, that is to say, losses are to be "from or incidental to" maritime navigation.[3] Maritime perils, that is, the perils consequent on or incidental to the navigation of the sea include: "perils of the seas, fire, war, war perils, pirates, rovers, thieves, captures, seizures, restrains and detainments of princes and peoples, jettisons, barratry and any other like perils".[4]

7.1.1.2 Concerned Parties

In marine cargo insurance contracts, there are parties concerned including: insurer, assurer, underwriter or insurance company, who promise to pay the claim amount to an insured, who is given a premium for the risks taken by him/her; the policy holder, who buys insurance contracts and promises to pay a premium according to a conclusion of insurance contract with an insurer; the insured or assured, who files a claim and is compensated for damage by the insurer in case of the loss caused by the risks covered under the insurance contract; insurance agent whose job is to conclude insurance contracts on behalf of the insurer or to mediate the insurance contracts between the policy holder and the insurer as an independent merchant; and insurance broker whose job is to mediate an insurance contract between insurer and policy holder on behalf of the policy holder and at the same time the unspecified insurer, as an independent merchant.

In an international business transaction, the terms of the sale's contract normally provide whether the costs to effect insurance contract shall be assumed by the seller or by the buyer.[5] If the products are sold on FOB terms, these costs have to be paid by the buyer, and this is true even when seller, by request of the buyer, has made an insurance contract.[6] If the products are sold on CIF terms, it is the duty of the seller to make the insurance contract and pay the costs of insurance.[7] In CFR terms the seller is not obliged to insure, and the buyer is not obliged to do so either, unless the CFR contract contains a clause "insurance to be effected by the buyer" or a clause in similar terms.[8] Under the CFR terms, if the clause is indicated "insurance to be effected by the buyer", the obligation to insure is thereby put into reverse, and the

---

[1] Marine Insurance Act 1906, §.2(1), *cited* by Murray et al. (2007, *supra* note 8, at 393).

[2] *Id.*

[3] Chuah (2009, *supra* note 252, at 404).

[4] *Id.*

[5] Murray et al. (2007, *supra* note 8, at 394).

[6] *Id.*

[7] *Id.*

[8] *Id.*

buyer is required to make the insurance contract which the seller would have been obliged to do so if it had been a CIF contract.[9]

7.1.2 Insurance Brokers in Marine Insurance

In the ordinary course of international business transactions, the exporter, who wishes to have his products insured, sometimes, does not approach the insurer directly but instructs an insurance broker to effect insurance on his behalf.[10] Where the exporter is the regular client of an insurance broker, he forwards his instructions on a form supplied by the broker and gives the required particulars.[11] The broker, who is usually authorized to place the insurance within certain limits as to the rates of premium, writes the essentials of the proposed insurance in customary abbreviations on a document called "the slip", which he takes to a marine insurance company.[12]

An insurer, who is prepared to accept part or all of the risk, writes on the slip the amount for which he is willing to insure and adds his initials; this is known as "writing a line", and the insurer who insures goods and adds his initials is called as underwriter.[13] The act of "writing a line" constitutes a marine insurance contract between the parties. That is, writing each line on a slip gives rise to an immediately binding contract between the underwriter and the assured.[14]

The broker then takes the slip to other insurers who successively write lines until the whole risk is accepted and underwritten by the underwriters.[15] The broker then sends the assured a memorandum of the insurance bought, that is, the cover note, which is usually executed on a duplicate form of the instructions.[16] Herewith the cover note means a written statement by an insurance agent confirming that coverage is in effect, and is distinguished from a binder, which is prepared by the insurance company.[17]

The memorandum assumes the form of a closed or open cover note. A closed cover note contains full particulars as to cargo and shipment and the insurance has thus been made definite.[18] An open cover note contains just general and indefinite terms and further particulars defining the cargo, voyage or interest shipped under

---

[9] Id.

[10] Id.

[11] Id.

[12] Id.

[13] Id., at 395.

[14] Id.

[15] Id.

[16] Id.

[17] Id., at 396.

[18] Id.

the insurance are to be declared before each shipment.[19] The open cover note is issued where the assured requires an "open cover" or a "floating policy".[20]

7.1.3 Insurable Interests

7.1.3.1 Definition

With relation to the term "insurable interest", every person has an insurable interest who is interested in maritime transportation: for the object to be insurable interest, it should have legality, economic efficiency, determinacy of the loss or accident and possibility of loss.

In particular, a person is interested in marine navigation where he stands in any legal or contractual relation to the navigation or to any insurable property at risk therein, in consequence of which he may benefit by the safety or due arrival of insurable property, or may be prejudiced by its loss or by damage thereto, or by the detention thereof, or may incur liability in respect thereof. It should be noted that with regard to the insurable interest, the marine insurance contract covers not the actually shipped products but a relationship to those products.

7.1.3.2 Insurable Value

Insurance value is an amount rated by economic value of the insurable interest. In marine insurance contract on goods or merchandise, the insurable value is the prime cost of the insured property, plus the expense of and incidental to shipping and the charges of insurance as a whole. It is customary to insure for an agreed value as a fixed insurable value which is about 110 percent of the CIF value of the property insured in order to cover incidental loss and out-of-pocket expenses as well as the CIF value of the goods when the loss occurs.

7.1.3.3 Insured Amount

Insured amount is the amount actually insured in conclusion of insurance contract on the basis of insurable value. In respect of the relation between the insurable value and insured amount, following relations are established: Full Insurance means the case where the insured amount is equal to the insurable value; Under Insurance means the case where insured amount is more than the insurable value; Over Insurance means the case where insured amount is more than the insurable value; Co-Insurance means the case where several insurers buy parts of an insurance policy so that the total amount insured does not exceed the insurable value; Double Insurance means the case where more than two insurance contracts are concluded with the same period of insurance for the same insurable interests, the total of which exceeds the insurable value.

---

[19] *Id.*

[20] *Id.*

7.2   Maritime Loss

7.2.1   Concepts

Loss in a marine insurance contract is realized when the insurable interest of an insured is lost or injured due to any of the perils of the sea commonly ensured for, or perils that are specifically covered by the insurance contract. When goods are not lost but merely damaged, the assessment of the claim amount to be paid is generally determined by the cost of restoring the damaged cargo. If the cargo is lost, the claim payment would be the amount that costs to recover or replace the cargo. The insured's entitlement to the claim amount is dependent on the type of loss he has suffered. The type of loss could be grouped as follows:

Loss is divided into direct loss and indirect loss according to whether the loss relates to the insurable interest directly or indirectly. A direct loss comes from actual damage to the insurable interest. This type of loss is normally the object of the insurance contract. An indirect loss is a financial loss incurred incidentally to a direct loss. In terms of cargo insurance, an indirect loss can be incurred, for example, when the delivery is delayed and therefore sales and profits are lost. Indirect losses are not typically included in insurance policy, but can be insured if they are specifically requested and covered by the general or specific terms of insurance policy. When the indirect loss is covered under the marine insurance, the insurance premium will be adjusted to a higher rate to cover their additional risk.

Losses are grouped into physical or property loss and expenditure loss according to whether the actual loss or the expenditure loss occurred to the subject-matter insured. A physical loss is an actual loss incurred to the subject-matter insured which is physically damaged or lost. A cost loss is incurred to the insured being resulted by the covered risk that the insurer takes, which is same to the indirect loss.

Losses could also be grouped into total loss and partial loss according to the degree of occurred loss. Total loss could further be divided into actual total loss and constructive total loss, and partial loss is further divided into general average and particular average.

7.2.1.1 Actual Total Loss
Actual total loss occurs where the subject-matter insured is actually lost, the original nature of the subject matter insured altered or lost and the insured ship or cargo is missing for a substantial period of time.

7.2.1.2 Constructive Total Loss
Constructive total loss occurs when a total loss of subject-matter insured is highly likely to be inevitable but not definite. For example, ① the control of the insured subject-matter is lost and is not likely to be restored, or when even though it can be restored, the resorting cost is expected to exceed the price of cargo, or ② the cost to be spent for repairing and carrying to the destination exceeds the value of cargo in arrival. Constructive total loss is contractually constituted by duly abandoning the subject-matter insured to an insurer, but if it is not abandoned, it is only treated as a

partial loss. Abandonment occurs when, although it is not a total loss caused by to a certain accident, the total loss is likely to be inevitable, the insured transfers all rights to the subject-matter insured to the insurer, and then make a claim for total loss under the insurance contract.

7.2.1.3 Particular Average

Particular average occurs when the partial loss is incurred fortuitously to the insured himself. This includes direct harm to the ship or cargo, and the insured has to assume all of it. Thus, particular average is a partial loss caused by a peril insured against which rests on the insured himself/herself and is, not distributed over the whole of the interests at risk in the common adventure, which is different from general average. The common form of particular average is maritime loss not amounting to total loss. For example, the partial loss caused by the perils insured against, e.g., collision or fire, is the particular average. It does not necessarily follow that all particular average caused by a peril insured against is recoverable from insures. The insurance policy may be expressed not to cover partial loss under the terms of e.g., "against total loss of vessel only".

7.2.1.4 General Average

Regarding the definition of general average, there is a general average act, when, and only when any extraordinary sacrifice or expenditure is internationally and reasonably made or incurred to secure the common safety for the purpose of preserving from imminent risks upon the property involved in a common maritime adventure.

Herewith the term "general average" is quite separate from the marine cargo insurance, that is, the general average is based upon a relationship between the ship owner and all the shippers who have cargo shipped on the ship. At the moment when a particular shipper's cargo has to be sacrificed for the common safety against imminent risks to the navigation parties, the act of general average is declared by the master and then the ship owners and the other shippers whose cargoes have arrived safely, are called upon to contribute towards the sacrificed cargo in proportion to the value of the ship and the shipped cargo. Herewith, the particular interest which has suffered the loss due to the general average act is entitled to a contribution from the other interest, which is called a general average contribution.[21]

General average is divided into two types, that is, "general average expenditure" and "general average sacrifice," General Average expenditure can occur when a ship runs aground and needs to pay a tug to refloat the vessel in order to deliver the cargo to the destination. General average sacrifice is a sacrifice of cargo by jettisoning cargo overboard to ensure that the ship can float and to reduce draught. Where the assured assumes a general average expenditure, according to the cargo insurance contract, he may be indemnified by the insurer in respect of the

---

[21] Chuah (2009, *supra* note 252, at 487).

proportion of the loss attributing to him.[22] When the assured has faced a general average sacrifice, he may recover from the insurer in respect of the whole loss without having enforced his right of contribution from the other party who is liable to contribute.[23] Where the assured has paid or liable to pay a general average contribution in respect of the subject matter insured, he may be indemnified that amount from the insurer.[24]

7.2.1.5 Expenditure Loss

Expenditure losses that might be incurred include salvage charges, particular charges, sue and labor charges, and survey fees.

Sue and Labor Charges

Sue and Labor charges are costs incurred by the insured or his agent to prevent damages or relieve cargo from damage occurring due to an insured risk, in accordance with his obligation to avert or minimize the loss. Also, this charge must be incurred only to insure the profits of the relevant subject-matter insured. Thus, costs spent for common profits of the interested parties belong to general average, not to sue and labor charges. All sue and labor charges are particular charges, but the former must be incurred by the insured or his agents and, in the case of goods, must be incurred before they are arrived at destination, while no such restriction applies to the particular charges.

Thus, the term "particular charges" is more comprehensive, embracing certain disbursements which are not, strictly speaking, included in sue and labor charges. Warehousing costs of the insured cargo incurred at the refuge port before the cargo arrives at the destination would be sue and labor charges and the reconditioning charges at destination would be the particular charges. The nature of sue and labor charges differs from salvage charges in that whilst the former is incurred by the insured and/or his agents, for example, the master of the ship, the latter occurs out of the efforts of independent parties in minimizing loss to the subject-matter insured.[25]

Salvage Charges

A salvage charge is a fee paid by the owner of the ship whose ship was at risk. The fee covers the costs of securing the vessel from an impending peril. The cost of a salvage fee is set before the vessel is rescued.

Particular Charges

A particular charge is a fee incurred by or for the insured party to insure the safety or preservation of the subject matter insured. It is a separate cost to general average

---

[22] Id.

[23] Id.

[24] Id.

[25] Dover (1982, pp. 435–454).

and salvage costs. This is not included in a particular charge in the particular average; it needs to meet certain requirements. That is, the reason for the cost must be from insured risks, and it must be fortuitous charge, that is, it must not be an ordinarily incurred expense.

Survey Fee
When damage does occur, the reason of the damage and its extent are thoroughly investigated. In order to make the investigation, a fee called a survey fee will be charged.

7.2.2   Insurer's Compensation

The insurer takes on the responsibility of compensating for any direct loss that is incurred during the period of risk, but does not have to compensate for indirect losses unless otherwise specifically described on the governing insurance contract. The insurer takes also on the responsibility of compensating for property loss, but not for expenditure losses other than salvage charges, particular charges, sue and labor charges, and survey fees, which are provided for in insurance contract clauses and laws.

The insurer compensates the insured with the amount covering the property loss and expenditure loss, and, in principle, within the insured amount. Therefore, after salvage or general average has occurred, if cargo is totally lost, the maximum amount compensated from the insurer is limited to the insured amount. For sue and labor charge, however, if the total physical loss and sue and labor charges exceeds the insured amount, it is additionally compensated by the insurer.

7.3   Insurance Policies

7.3.1   Types of Insurance Contract

7.3.1.1 Valued Policies
A valued policy is a policy which specifies the agreed value of the subject-matter insured, while an unvalued policy[26] states merely the maximum limit of the amount insured and leaves the insurable value to be ascertained subsequently.[27] In practice, valued policies are usually used and unvalued policies are rarely used.[28] The main difference between these two types of policy is that in the case of a valued policy the value fixed by the policy is, in the absence of fraud and gross negligence, conclusive as the insurable value of the insurable interest, while in the case of an

---

[26] Unvalued policies are sometimes called open policies. This term should not be confused with the open cover.

[27] Murray et al. (2007, *supra* note 8, at 398).

[28] *Id.*

unvalued policy, the value of the insurable interest has to be ascertained by production of invoices, vouchers, estimates and other evidence.[29]

The difference between valued and unvalued policies is of great practical importance. In a valued policy, the buyer's expected profits are normally included in the declared value, that is, insurable value, by adding a percentage of 10 or 15 percent to the invoice value and the incidental shipping and insurance charges of the goods. In an unvalued policy, the buyer's expected profits are not included in the insurable value.[30]

The "insured value" is the agreed value (if any) specified in the policy; the "shipping value" is defined in identical terms with the definition of insurable value for unvalued policies. If there is the possibility of rising market prices during the transit of the goods, the assured who has covered the goods under an ordinary policy can obtain a so-called "increased value" policy.[31]

7.3.1.2 Voyage Policies

Policies are also classified as voyage, time and mixed policies. Under a voyage policy, the subject-matter is insured in transit from one place to another.[32] It is usual for the traded goods to be insured for a particular maritime voyage, but considering the combined transport and convenience, traders can take a mixed land and marine policy to cover the land or inland water parts of the carriage.[33] In practice of international trade, under the Institute Cargo Clauses A, B and C, insurance coverage is provided from warehouse to warehouse and, hence, the transit clause extends marine insurance to land risks incidental to the sea voyage.[34]

Under a time policy the subject-matter is insured for a fixed period of time. The policy will specify the period of time to cover the insurance.[35] Under a mixed policy, the subject-matter is insured both for a particular voyage and, at the same time, a certain period of time.[36] In the past, time policies were rarely used in international business transactions but are recently found more frequently.[37] These policies may cover a period exceeding 12 months, and they often contain the "continuation clause" under which the parties agree that: "should the vessel at the expiration of this policy be at sea, or in distress, or at port of refuge or of call, she shall, provided previous notice be given to the underwriters, be held covered at a pro rata monthly premium to her port of destination."[38]

---

[29] *Id.*

[30] *Id.*

[31] *Id.*

[32] *Id.*, at 399.

[33] Chuah (2009, *supra* note 252, at 437).

[34] Murray et al. (2007, *supra* note 8, at 399).

[35] Chuah (2009, *supra* note 252, at 440).

[36] *Id.*

[37] *Id.*

[38] *Id.*

7.3.1.3 Floating Policies

The floating policy lays down the general conditions of insurance, but not the particulars of the individual consignments intended to be covered. Floating policies operate in a very similar way to open coverage, except that an actual policy is in existence.[39] These particulars are usually unknown to the assured when obtaining insurance. Notwithstanding this element of uncertainty, the floating policy covers automatically all shipments made thereunder and the assured is obliged to "declare" the individual shipments to the insurer promptly.[40] Under a floating policy, the insured amount of each voyage is deducted from the total value of the insurance contract and the insured amount is automatically renewed after the each voyage is completed.

Form of Declaration		
Please insure the following under the open policy in the name of		
Messers		
Vessel		
From	To	Via
Marks	Description of Goods	CIF Value
		Insured Value
Please send cover note to us.		

7.3.2 Insurance Policies

7.3.2.1 Outline

The mother of insurance policies now used in the marine insurance market is Lloyd's S.G. Policy, which is provided in the first appendix of the Marine Insurance Act 1906 of England. The S.G policy as such was first adopted in 1779. It would appear that at the time of the policy form as adopted by Lloyd's in 1779, separate forms were used for ship and goods respectively, the former bearing the cipher "S" and the latter the cipher "G", but after a short lapse of time a common form (S.G.) was prescribed.[41]

---

[39] *Id.*, at 441.
[40] *Id.*
[41] Dover (1982, *supra* note 297, at 33).

HULL

No

The Institute of London Underwriters
SPECIMEN FOR INFORMATION ONLY / POUR INFORMATION UNIQUEMENT

Companies Combined Policy

Be it known that

as well in their own Name, as for and in the Name and Names of all every other Person or Persons to whom the same doth, may, or shall appertain, in part or in all, doth make Assurance, and cause themselves and them and every of them, to be insured lost or not lost at and from

upon the body, Tackle, Apparel, Ordnance, Munition, Artillery, Boat and other Furniture, of and in the good Ship or Vessel called the

whereof is Master, under God, for this present Voyage,

or whosoever else shall go for master in the said Ship, or by whatsoever other Name or Names the same Ship, or the Master thereof, is or shall be named or called, beginning the Adventure upon the said Ship, upon the said Ship, &c, as above,

and shall so continue and endure, during her Abode there, upon the said Ship, &c ; and further until the said Ship, with all her Ordnance, Tackle, Apparel, &c, and shall be arrived at as above,

and until she hath moored at Anchor in good Safety : and it shall be lawful for the said Ship, &c, in this voyage to proceed and sail to and touch and stay at any Ports or Places whatsoever without Prejudice to this insurance. The said Ship, &c, for so much as concerns the Assured, by agreement between the Assured and Assurers in this policy are and shall be valued at

TOUCHING the adventures and Perils which we the Assurers are consented to bear and to take upon themselves in this Voyage, they are, of the Seas, Men-of-War, Fire, Enemies, Pirates, Rovers, Thieves, Jettisons, Letters of Mart and Countermart, Surprisals, Takings at Sea, Arrests, Restraints and Detainments of all Kings, Princes and People, of what Nation, Condition or Quality soever, Barratry of the Master and Mariners, and all other Perils, Losses and Misfortunes, that have or shall come to the Hurt, Detriment or Damage of the subject matter of this Assurance : and in case of any Loss or Misfortune, it shall be lawful to the Assured, their Factors, Servants and Assigns, to sue, labor, and travel for, in and about the Defense, Safeguard and Recovery of the said subject matter of Assurance, without Prejudice to this Insurance ; to the Charges whereof the Assurers will contribute, each company proportionally according to the amount of their respective subscriptions hereto. And it is especially declared and agreed that no acts of the Assurer or Assured in recovering, saving, or preserving the property Assured, shall be considered as a waiver of acceptance of abandonment. And it is agreed by us, the Assurers, that this Writing or Policy of Assurance shall be of as much Force and Effect as the surest Writing or Policy of Assurance heretofore made in Lombard Street, or in the Royal Exchange, or elsewhere in London.

Warranted free of capture, seizure, arrest or detainment, and the consequences thereof or of any attempt thereat : also from the consequences of hostilities or warlike operations, whether there be a declaration of war or not : but this warranty shall not exclude collision contact with any fixed or floating object (other than a mine or torpedo), stranding, heavy weather or fire unless caused directly (and independently of the nature of the voyage or service which the vessel concerned or, in the case of a collision, any other vessel involved therein, is performing) by a hostile act by or against a belligerent power and for the purpose of this warranty "power" includes any authority maintaining naval, military or air forces in association with a power. Further warranted free from the consequences of civil war, revolution, rebellion, insurrection, or civil strife arising therefrom or piracy.

NOW THIS POLICY WITNESSETH that we, the Assurers, the Companies whose names are set out overleaf, take open ourselves the burden of this Assurance each of us to the extent of the amount underwritten by us respectively and promise and bind ourselves, each Company for itself only and not the one for the other and in respect only of the due proportion of each Company, to the Assured, their executors, Administrators and assigns for the true performance and fulfillment of the Contract contained in this Policy in consideration of the person or persons effecting this Policy promising to pay a premium at and after the rate of

IN WITNESS whereof, the assurers, have subscribed our Names and Sums Assured in London
As hereinafter appears, and the Manager and Secretary of the Institute of London Underwriters has subscribed his name on behalf of each of us.
N.B: The Ship and Freight are warranted free from Average under three pounds per cent, unless general, or the Ship is stranded, sunk or burnt.

Signed..

General Manager and Secretary
The Institute of London Underwriters

Note: This policy must bear the seal of the Institute of London Underwriters Policy Department.

Since the S.G. Policy was officially adopted in 1779, as marine trade has developed, covered risks and clauses of the SG Policy have become insufficient. To address this problem, the Technical & Clauses Committee representing Lloyd's Underwriters' Association and the insurance company's market in London formed the special cargo insurance clauses in 1912, which has been used among the insurance-related parties. Such clauses were generalized, standardized, and added to the SG Policy.

These clauses include Institute Cargo Clause "Free from Particular Average"(FPA), Institute Cargo Clause "With Average" (WA), and Institute Cargo Clause "All risks" (A/R). These clauses were revised multiple times, and finally revised in 1963 to a version that was world-widely used. Despite the amendments and modifications of these clauses, the rules were still not satisfactory to many parties concerned and public opinion was that it needed to be revised in order for general traders to easily understand the terms of the cargo insurance because the contents and expression of the clauses were quite difficult to understand even though the SG Policy had been in use over 200 years.

In 1979, a report about marine insurance was made by UNCTAD (United Nations Conference on Trade and Development), and on the basis of this, the Institute Cargo Clauses A, B, and C were enacted in 1982. These Institute Cargo Clauses were updated by the Joint Cargo Committee made up of members of the International Underwriting Association and the Lloyds Market Association in 2008 and implemented from 2009. Institute Cargo Clauses (A) provides coverage for all risks of loss or damage to cargo, except those excluded by a few specific standard exclusions, such as the willful misconduct of the insured or ordinary wear and tear. The words "all risks" should be understood in the context of the "A" clause to cover "fortuitous loss", but not "loss that occurs inevitably."

Institute Cargo Clauses (B) provides not only all of the cover that is available under Institute Cargo Clauses (C), but also covers loss of or damage to the subject matter insured if it can be "reasonably attributable to" earthquakes, lightening, washing overboard, etc. Institute Cargo Clauses (C) covers loss or damage to the subject matter insured when it can be "reasonably attributable to" fire or explosion, a stranded, grounded, or capsized vessel, collision, or a discharge of cargo at a port of distress. Essentially, ICC (C) provides major casualty coverage during land, air, or water transport.

7.3.2.2 Illustration of Insurance Policy Form

CENTRAL MARINE & FIRE INSURANCE CO., LTD		
MARINE CARGO INSURANCE POLICY		
② Assured.		③ Ref. No.
① Policy No.		
⑥ Claim, if any, payable at/in		④ Amount Insured
⑦ Survey should be approved by		
⑧ Local vessel	⑨ From (interior port or place of loading)	
⑩ Ship or Vessel called the	⑪ Sailing on about	⑤ Conditions and Warranties
⑫ at and from	⑬ Transshipped at	
⑭ Arrived at	⑮ Thence to	
⑯ Goods and Merchandise		
Marks and Numbers as per Invoice No. specified above.		
⑰ Place and date signed in		⑱ No. of Policies issued
㉑ (Marginal clauses, important matter)		⑳ (text clauses)
⑲ For CENTURY MARINE & FIRE INSURANCE CO., LTD.		
By (signature of insurer)		
AUTHORIZD REPRESENTATIVE		

The contents to fill in the above policy are explained as below:
① **Policy No.**: A serial number which the insurer specifies to the specified contracts.
② **Name of insured (policy holder)**: Normally the exporting/importing company. In CIF export, unless there is no agreement or direction about the assured, the exporter nominated as the insured transfer the status of the insured to the importer or bank through the blank endorsement.
③ **Reference No.**: Number insurer designates for his convenience in referring to the policy.
④ **Insured amount**: The amount of coverage the policy holder obtains, and the maximum amount the insurer pays as claim amount when covered accidents occur. The insured amount is fixed by the agreement of both parties but must not

be more than the insurable value. The currency used must be the same as that indicates on the letter of credit unless otherwise directed.

⑤ **Conditions and warranties**: The covering scope should be determined by the agreement of the parties to the insurance contract, which should be based on the insurance terms on the letter of credit.

⑥ **Place of payment of claim amount**: This is the place for the claim amount to be requested to the insurer. In export, the final destination port is generally indicated. In import, the relevant insurer is generally indicated.

⑦ **Notify party**: This is the party to be notified of the insured accident when the losses are incurred by the accident insured against. In export, the name or address of an agency of the insurer in the final destination port is indicated. In import, the insurer's name is indicated.

⑧ & ⑨ **Local vessel, From**: When the place of shipment is different from the loading location, that place is indicated here. "Local Vessel or Conveyance" is the local means of transporting.

⑩ **Ship or Vessel called the**: Name of the ship to load the cargo is indicated here.

⑪ **Arrived at**: Month, date and year loaded and departed, or is expected to be departed, are indicated here. Especially with export, indication herewith must be the same as specified on the bill of lading.

⑫ **Port of shipment**: The port to make the shipment of the cargo is indicated here.

⑬ **Port of transshipment, if any**: The port to make the transshipment, when the transshipment is required, is indicated here.

⑭ **Port of discharging**: The port to discharge the shipped cargoes is indicated here.

⑮ **Final destination and transporting means**: When the discharging port is different from the final destination because the final destination is inland, the final destination and transporting means are indicated according to transport clauses in insuring the cargo from the departing place to the final destination.

⑯ **Statement of cargo insured**: Name of cargo, quantity and brand, etc, are indicated as those indicated on the letter of credit or bill of lading.

⑰ **Place of issuance and date of insurance policy**: The issuance date of the insurance policy must be before that of bill of lading.

⑱ **Number of issuance of insurance**: Usually the original policy is issued by duplicate. If an insurer pays-off by the first policy, the second policy automatically becomes invalid.

⑲ **Signature of Insurer**: A marine insurance policy must be signed by an insurer or his agent. But, if the insurer is corporate, the seal of the corporation will suffice.

⑳ **Text clause**: It is about the governing law, other insurances, contract, and deposition.

An example of the "text clause" is given as follows:

"Notwithstanding anything contained herein or attached hereto to the contrary, this insurance is understood and agreed to be subject to English law and practice only as to liability for and settlement of any and all claims.

This insurance does not cover any loss of or damage to the property which at the time of the happening of such loss or damage is insured by or would but for the existence of this Policy be insured by any fire or other insurance policy or policies except in respect of any excess beyond the amount which would have been payable under the fire or other insurance policy or policies had this insurance not been effected.

We, hereby agree, in consideration of the payment to us by or on behalf of the Assured of the premium as arranged, to insure against loss damage liability or expense to the extent and in the manner herein provided.

Whereof, I, the Undersigned of
On behalf of the said Company have subscribed my name in the place specified as above, of the same tenor and date, one of which being accomplished, the others to be void, as of the date specified as above."

㉑ **Marginal clause**: It provides all the various actions and procedures that the insured must take, which is called an "important clause".

An example of an "important clause" is as follows:

"IMPORTANT PROCEDURE IN THE EVENT OF LOSS OR DAMAGE FOR WHICH UNDERWRITERS MAY BE LIABLE; LIABILITY OF CARRIERS, BAILEES OR OTHER THIRD PARTIES

It is the duty of the Assured and their agents, in all cases, to take such measures as may be reasonable for the purpose of averting or minimizing a loss and to ensure that all rights against Carriers, Bailers or other third parties are properly preserved and exercised. In particular, the Assured or other Agents are required:

1. To claim immediately on the Carriers, Port Authorities or other Bailees for any missing packages.
2. In circumstances, except under written protection, to give clean receipts where goods are in doubtful condition.
3. When delivery is made by Container, to ensure that the Container and its seals are examined immediately by their responsible official.
   If the Container is delivered damaged or with seals broken or missing or with seals other than as stated in the shipping documents, to clause the delivery receipt accordingly and retain all defective or irregular seals for subsequent identification.

4. To apply immediately for survey by Carriers' or other Bailees' Representatives if any loss or damage be apparent and claim on the Carriers or other Bailees for any actual loss of damage found at such survey.
5. To give notice in writing to the Carriers or other Bailees within 3 days of delivery if the loss of damage was not apparent at the time of taking delivery.

Notice: The Consignees or other Agents are recommended to make themselves familiar with the Regulation of the Port Authorities at the port of discharge.

INSTRUCTIONS FOR SURVEY

In the event of loss of damage which may involve a claim under this insurance, immediate notice of such loss or damage should be given to and a Survey Report obtained from the Company Office or Agents specified in this Policy of Certificate.

DOCUMENTATION OF CLAIMS

To enable claims to be dealt with promptly, the Assured or their Agents are advised to submit all available supporting documents without delay, including when applicable:

1. Original policy or certificate of insurance.
2. Original or certified copy of shipping invoices, together with shipping specification and/or weight notes.
3. Original or certified copy of Bill of Lading and/or other contract of carriage.
4. Survey report or other documentary evidence to show the extent of the loss or damage.
5. Landing account and weight notes at port of discharge and final destination.
6. Correspondence exchanged with the Carriers and other Parties regarding their liability for the loss of damage.

In the event of loss or damage arising under this Policy, no claims will be admitted unless a survey has been held with the approval of this Company's office or Agents specified in this policy."

7.3.3   Covered Risks

When choosing a marine cargo insurance policy, there are basically two options, that is, an insurance policy to cover the exhaustively illustrated risks by the terms of insurance contract only or to cover all risks. Under the policy to cover exhaustively illustrated risks, the insured is protected only against certain kinds of risks specifically indicated in the policy. These terms have been adopted by WA, FPA, ICC (B), and ICC (C). The burden of proof of casual relationship between the risk insured against and the caused loss goes to the insured and the insured must demonstrate the fact that the damage or loss of subject-matter insured was caused by the covered risks.

The policy with the terms of all risks covers all risks without specifying the risks in the policy, and may exclude only risks that are expressively excluded in the policy. It is also called a general risk policy, and has been adopted by the terms of A/R and ICC (A). The burden of proof of casual relationship, under the terms of "all risks" or ICC (A), goes to the insurer. As long as any loss or damage is not demonstrated to have happened by a reason under the exemption clauses, the insurer must compensate the insured for the loss resulted from fortuitous external risks. The charts below will further clarify the differences of covered risks and excluded risks under these clauses.

7.3.3.1 Covered/Excluded Risks Under Institute Cargo Clauses (FPA, WA and A/R)

ICC (A/R)	ICC (WA)	ICC (FPA)	
			① total loss of insured cargo (actual loss or constructive total loss)
			② particular average such as stranding, grounding, sinking, or fire of ship or barge (regardless of casual relationship)
			③ general average sacrifice, general average expenditure, general average contribution, salvage, sue and labor charge
			④ particular average due to loading, transshipment, or discharging.
			⑤ particular average due to fire, explosion, collision, contact
			⑥ particular average discharging at the port of disaster
			⑦ particular charges for discharging or storing at the port of call in transit, or at a place of refuge
			⑧ partial loss (particular loss) due to heavy weather
			⑨ any loss from incidental external reasons other than the following exemption clauses
Exemption Clauses			① a total loss due to intentional, wrongful acts of a policy holder or the insured
			② any loss due to insured cargo's own defect, nature, or late transport
			③ usual loss due to an ordinary action of the winds and waves.
			④ any loss due to war, riot, strike, etc.

Covered Risks Clause of ICC (A/R)

"This insurance is against all risks of loss of or damage to the subject-matter insured but shall in no case be deemed to extend to cover loss damage or expense proximately caused by delay or inherent vice or nature of the subject-matter insured. Claims recoverable hereunder shall be payable irrespective of percentage."

Covered Risks Clause of ICC (WA)

"Warranted free from average under the percentage specified in the policy, unless general, or the vessel or craft be stranded, sunk or burnt, but notwithstanding this warranty the Underwriters are to pay the insured value of any package which may be totally lost in loading, transshipment or discharge, also for any loss of or damage to the interest insured which may reasonably be attributed to fire, explosion, collision or contact of the vessel and/or craft and/or conveyance with any external substance (ice included) other than water, or to discharge of cargo at a port of distress. This clause shall operate during the whole period covered by the policy."

Covered Risks Clause of ICC (FPA)

"Warranted free from Particular Average unless the vessel or craft be stranded, sunk, or burnt, but notwithstanding this warranty the Underwriters are to pay the insured value of any package or packages which may be totally lost in loading, transshipment or discharge, also for any loss of or damage to the interest insured which may reasonably be attributed to fire, explosion, collision or contact of the vessel and/or craft and/or conveyance with any external substance (ice included) other than water, or to discharge of cargo at a port of distress, also to pay special charges for landing, warehousing and forwarding if incurred at an intermediate port of call or refuge for which Underwriters would be liable under the standard form of English Marine Policy with the Institute Cargo Clauses (WA) attached. This clause shall operate during the whole period covered by the policy."

7.3.3.2 Covered Risks Under Institute Cargo Clauses (A)(B)(C)

ICC (A)	ICC (B)	ICC (C)	
			① fire or explosion
			② stranding, grounding, sinking or capsizing of a vessel or craft barge
			③ overturning or derailment of ground transport vehicle
			④ collision or contact of the vessel craft, or conveyance with any external object other than water
			⑤ discharging of cargo at the port of disaster
			⑥ general average sacrifice
			⑦ jettison
			⑧ general average and salvage charges[42]
			⑨ such portion of liability under "both to both lame collision" clause in the contract of carriage[43]
			⑩ earthquake, volcanic, eruption, lightning
			⑪ washing overboard
			⑫ entry of sea water, lake water or river water into vessel, craft, hold, conveyance, container, or place of storage.
			⑬ total loss of any package lost overboard or dropped whilst loading on to or unloading from vessel or craft
			⑭ all risks of loss of or damage to the subject matter insured except exempted losses

Covered Risks under ICC (A)

1. Risks Clause

"This insurance covers all risks of loss of or damage to the subject-matter insured except as provided in Clauses 4, 5, 6 and 7 below."

---

[42] General Average Clause: "This insurance covers general average and salvage charges, adjusted or determined according to the contract of affreightment and/or the governing law and practice, incurred to avoid or in connection with the avoidance of loss from any cause except those excluded in Clauses 4, 5, 6 and 7 or elsewhere in this insurance."

[43] "Both to Blame Collision" Clause: "This insurance indemnifies the Assured, in respect of any risk insured herein, against liability incurred under any Both to Blame Collision Clause in the contract of carriage. In the event of any claim by carriers under the said Clause, the Assured agree to notify the insurers who shall have the right, at their own cost and expense, to defend the Assured against such claim."

Covered Risks under ICC (B)

1. Risks Clause

"This insurance covers, except as provided in Clauses 4, 5, 6 and 7 below,

1.1 loss of or damage to the subject-matter insured reasonably attributable to

    1.1.1 fire or explosion

    1.1.2 vessel or craft being stranded grounded sunk or capsized

    1.1.3 overturning or derailment of land conveyance

    1.1.4 collision or contact of vessel craft or conveyance with any external object other than water

    1.1.5 discharge of cargo at a port of distress

    1.1.6 earthquake volcanic eruption or lightning,

1.2 loss of or damage to the subject-matter insured caused by

    1.2.1 general average sacrifice

    1.2.2 jettison or washing overboard

    1.2.3 entry of sea lake or river water into vessel craft hold conveyance container or place of storage,

1.3 total loss of any package lost overboard or dropped whilst loading on to, or unloading from, vessel or craft."

Covered Risks under ICC (C)

1. Risks Clause

"This insurance covers, except as provided in Clauses 4, 5, 6 and 7 below,

1.1 loss of or damage to the subject-matter insured reasonably attributable to

    1.1.1 fire or explosion

    1.1.2 vessel or craft being stranded grounded sunk or capsized

    1.1.3 overturning or derailment of land conveyance

    1.1.4 collision or contact of vessel craft or conveyance with any external object other than water

    1.1.5 discharge of cargo at a port of distress,

1.2 loss of or damage to the subject-matter insured caused by

    1.2.1 general average sacrifice

    1.2.2 jettison."

7.3.3.3 Exemption Risks Under Institute Cargo Clauses

		Risks Excluded under Institute Cargo Clauses (A), (B) and (C)
ICC	ICC	① loss, damage, or expense attributable to willful misconduct of the assured
(B)	(A)	② ordinary leakage, ordinary loss in weight or volume, or ordinary wear and tear of the subject matter insured
(C)		③ loss, damage, or expense caused by insufficiency or unsuitability of packing or preparation of the subject-matter insured to withstand the ordinary incidents of the insured transit where such packing or preparation is carried out by the Assured or their employees or prior to the attachment of this insurance
		④ loss, damage, or expense, inherent vice or nature of insured subject matter
		⑤ loss, damage, or expense caused by delay, even where the delay is caused by a risk insured against
		⑥ loss, damage, or expense caused by insolvency or financial default of the owners managers charterers or operators of the vessel where, at the time of loading of the subject-matter insured on board the vessel, the Assured are aware, or in the ordinary course of business should be aware, that such insolvency or financial default could prevent the normal prosecution of the voyage
		⑦ loss, damage, or expense directly or indirectly caused by or arising from the use of any weapon or device employing atomic or nuclear fission and/or fusion or other like reaction or radioactive force or matter
		⑧ loss, damage, or expense arising from unseaworthiness of vessel or craft or unfitness of vessel or craft for the safe carriage of the subject-matter insured, where the Assured are privy to such unseaworthiness or unfitness, at the time the subject-matter insured is loaded therein
		⑨ loss, damage, or expense arising from unfitness of container or conveyance for the safe carriage of the subject-matter insured, where loading therein or thereon is carried out prior to attachment of this insurance or by the Assured or their employees and they are privy to such unfitness at the time of loading
		⑩ loss, damage, or expense caused by war, civil war, revolution, rebellion, insurrection, or civil strife arising therefrom, or any hostile act by or against a belligerent power
		⑪ loss, damage, or expense caused by capture, seizure, arrest, restraint or detainment, and consequences thereof or any attempt thereat
		⑫ loss, damage, or expense caused by derelict mines, torpedoes, bombs or other derelict weapons of war
		⑬ loss, damage, or expense caused by strikes, locked out workmen, or persons taking part in labor disturbances, riots or civil commotions
		⑭ loss, damage, or expense resulting from strikes, lockouts, labor disturbances, riots or civil commotions caused by any terrorist or any person acting from a political motive
		⑮ loss, damage, or expense caused by any act of terrorism being an act of any person acting on behalf of, or in connection with, any organization which carries out activities directed towards the overthrowing or influencing, by force or violence, of any government whether or not legally constituted
		⑯ loss, damage, or expense caused by any person acting from a political, ideological or religious motive
		⑰ deliberate damage to or deliberate destruction of the subject matter insured or any part thereof by the wrongful act of any person or persons

Excluded Risks under ICC (A)

4. General Exclusion Clause
"In no case shall this insurance cover
4.1 loss damage or expense attributable to willful misconduct of the Assured
4.2 ordinary leakage, ordinary loss in weight or volume, or ordinary wear and tear of the subject-matter insured
4.3 loss damage or expense caused by insufficiency or unsuitability of packing or preparation of the subject-matter insured to withstand the ordinary incidents of the insured transit where such packing or preparation is carried out by the Assured or their employees or prior to the attachment of this insurance (for the purpose of these Clauses "packing" shall be deemed to include stowage in a container and "employees" shall not include independent contractors)
4.4 loss damage or expense caused by inherent vice or nature of the subject-matter insured
4.5 loss damage or expense caused by delay, even though the delay be caused by a risk insured against (except expenses payable under Clause 2 above)
4.6 loss, damage, or expense caused by insolvency or financial default of the owners managers charterers or operators of the vessel where, at the time of loading of the subject-matter insured on board the vessel, the Assured are aware, or in the ordinary course of business should be aware, that such insolvency or financial default could prevent the normal prosecution of the voyage
4.7 loss, damage, or expense directly or indirectly caused by or arising from the use of any weapon or device employing atomic or nuclear fission and/or fusion or other like reaction or radioactive force or matter"

5. Unseaworthiness and Unfitness Exclusion Clause
"5.1 In no case shall this insurance cover loss, damage or expense arising from
5.1.1 unseaworthiness of vessel or craft or unfitness of vessel or craft for the safe carriage of the subject-matter insured, where the Assured are privy to such unseaworthiness or unfitness, at the time the subject-matter insured is loaded therein
5.1.2 unfitness of container or conveyance for the safe carriage of the subject-matter insured, where loading therein or thereon is carried out prior to attachment of this insurance or by the Assured or their employees and they are privy to such unfitness at the time of loading

(continued)

5.2 Exclusion 2.1.1 above shall not apply where the contract of insurance has been assigned to the party claiming hereunder who has bought or agreed to buy the subject-matter insured in good faith under a binding contract

5.3 The Insurers waive any breach of the implied warranties of seaworthiness of the ship and fitness of the ship to carry the subject-matter insured to destination. "

6. War Exclusion Clause

"In no case shall this insurance cover loss damage or expense caused by

6.1 war civil war revolution rebellion insurrection, or civil strife arising therefrom, or any hostile act by or against a belligerent power

6.2 capture seizure arrest restraint or detainment (piracy excepted), and the consequences thereof or any attempt thereat

6.3 derelict mines torpedoes bombs or other derelict weapons of war."

7. Strikes Exclusion Clause

"In no case shall this insurance cover loss damage or expense

7.1 caused by strikers, locked-out workmen, or persons taking part in labour disturbances, riots or civil commotions

7.2 resulting from strikes, lock-outs, labour disturbances, riots or civil commotions

7.3 caused by any act of terrorism being an act of any person acting on behalf of, or in connection with, any organization which carries out activities directed towards the overthrowing or influencing, by force or violence, of any government whether or not legally constituted

7.4 caused by any person acting from a political, ideological or religious motive."

Excluded Risks under ICC (B)

4. General Exclusion Clause

"In no case shall this insurance cover

4.1 loss damage or expense attributable to willful misconduct of the Assured

4.2 ordinary leakage, ordinary loss in weight or volume, or ordinary wear and tear of the subject-matter insured

4.3 loss damage or expense caused by insufficiency or unsuitability of packing or preparation of the subject-matter insured to withstand the ordinary incidents of the insured transit where such packing or preparation is carried out by the Assured or their employees or prior to the attachment of this insurance (for the purpose of these Clauses "packing" shall be deemed to include stowage in a container and "employees" shall not include independent contractors)

4.4 loss damage or expense caused by inherent vice or nature of the subject-matter insured

4.5 loss damage or expense caused by delay, even though the delay be caused by a risk insured against (except expenses payable under Clause 2 above)

4.6 loss, damage, or expense caused by insolvency or financial default of the owners managers charterers or operators of the vessel where, at the time of loading of the subject-matter insured on board the vessel, the Assured are aware, or in the ordinary course of business should be aware, that such insolvency or financial default could prevent the normal prosecution of the voyage

4.7 loss, damage, or expense directly or indirectly caused by or arising from the use of any weapon or device employing atomic or nuclear fission and/or fusion or other like reaction or radioactive force or matter

4.8 deliberate damage to or deliberate destruction of the subject-matter insured or any part thereof by the wrongful act of any person or persons."

5. Unseaworthiness and Unfitness Exclusion Clause

"5.1 In no case shall this insurance cover loss, damage or expense arising from

5.1.1 unseaworthiness of vessel or craft or unfitness of vessel or craft for the safe carriage of the subject-matter insured, where the Assured are privy to such unseaworthiness or unfitness, at the time the subject-matter insured is loaded therein

5.1.2 unfitness of container or conveyance for the safe carriage of the subject-matter insured, where loading therein or thereon is carried out prior to attachment of this insurance or by the Assured or their employees and they are privy to such unfitness at the time of loading

5.2 Exclusion 2.1.1 above shall not apply where the contract of insurance has been assigned to the party claiming hereunder who has bought or agreed to buy the subject-matter insured in good faith under a binding contract

5.3 The Insurers waive any breach of the implied warranties of seaworthiness of the ship and fitness of the ship to carry the subject-matter insured to destination. "

6. War Exclusion Clause

"In no case shall this insurance cover loss damage or expense caused by

6.1 war civil war revolution rebellion insurrection, or civil strife arising therefrom, or any hostile act by or against a belligerent power

6.2 capture seizure arrest restraint or detainment, and the consequences thereof or any attempt thereat

6.3 derelict mines torpedoes bombs or other derelict weapons of war."

(continued)

7. Strikes Exclusion Clause

"In no case shall this insurance cover loss damage or expense

7.1 caused by strikers, locked-out workmen, or persons taking part in labour disturbances, riots or civil commotions

7.2 resulting from strikes, lock-outs, labour disturbances, riots or civil commotions

7.3 caused by any act of terrorism being an act of any person acting on behalf of, or in connection with, any organization which carries out activities directed towards the overthrowing or influencing, by force or violence, of any government whether or not legally constituted

7.4 caused by any person acting from a political, ideological or religious motive."

Excluded Risks under ICC (C)

4. General Exclusion Clause

"In no case shall this insurance cover

4.1 loss damage or expense attributable to willful misconduct of the Assured

4.2 ordinary leakage, ordinary loss in weight or volume, or ordinary wear and tear of the subject-matter insured

4.3 loss damage or expense caused by insufficiency or unsuitability of packing or preparation of the subject-matter insured to withstand the ordinary incidents of the insured transit where such packing or preparation is carried out by the Assured or their employees or prior to the attachment of this insurance (for the purpose of these Clauses "packing" shall be deemed to include stowage in a container and "employees" shall not include independent contractors)

4.4 loss damage or expense caused by inherent vice or nature of the subject-matter insured

4.5 loss damage or expense caused by delay, even though the delay be caused by a risk insured against (except expenses payable under Clause 2 above)

4.6 loss, damage, or expense caused by insolvency or financial default of the owners managers charterers or operators of the vessel where, at the time of loading of the subject-matter insured on board the vessel, the Assured are aware, or in the ordinary course of business should be aware, that such insolvency or financial default could prevent the normal prosecution of the voyage

4.7 loss, damage, or expense directly or indirectly caused by or arising from the use of any weapon or device employing atomic or nuclear fission and/or fusion or other like reaction or radioactive force or matter

4.8 deliberate damage to or deliberate destruction of the subject-matter insured or any part thereof by the wrongful act of any person or persons."

5. Unseaworthiness and Unfitness Exclusion Clause

"5.1 In no case shall this insurance cover loss, damage or expense arising from

5.1.1 unseaworthiness of vessel or craft or unfitness of vessel or craft for the safe carriage of the subject-matter insured, where the Assured are privy to such unseaworthiness or unfitness, at the time the subject-matter insured is loaded therein

5.1.2 unfitness of container or conveyance for the safe carriage of the subject-matter insured, where loading therein or thereon is carried out prior to attachment of this insurance or by the Assured or their employees and they are privy to such unfitness at the time of loading

5.2 Exclusion 2.1.1 above shall not apply where the contract of insurance has been assigned to the party claiming hereunder who has bought or agreed to buy the subject-matter insured in good faith under a binding contract

5.3 The Insurers waive any breach of the implied warranties of seaworthiness of the ship and fitness of the ship to carry the subject-matter insured to destination. "

6. War Exclusion Clause

"In no case shall this insurance cover loss damage or expense caused by

6.1 war civil war revolution rebellion insurrection, or civil strife arising therefrom, or any hostile act by or against a belligerent power

6.2 capture seizure arrest restraint or detainment, and the consequences thereof or any attempt threat

6.3 derelict mines torpedoes bombs or other derelict weapons of war."

7. Strike Exclusion Clause

"In no case shall this insurance cover loss damage or expense

7.1 caused by strikers, locked-out workmen, or persons taking part in labour disturbances, riots or civil commotions

7.2 resulting from strikes, lock-outs, labour disturbances, riots or civil commotions

7.3 caused by any act of terrorism being an act of any person acting on behalf of, or in connection with, any organization which carries out activities directed towards the overthrowing or influencing, by force or violence, of any government whether or not legally constituted

7.4 caused by any person acting from a political, ideological or religious motive."

7.3.3.4 Covered/Excluded Risks Under Institute Cargo
Clauses (A)(B)(C) by Comparison

○ : Covered; △ : Not covered; X : Excluded

Risks Covered	Institute War Clauses (Cargo)	Institute Strikes Clauses (Cargo)	Institute Cargo Clauses		
			(A)	**(B)**	**(C)**
Cover	Risks Stipulated in Clause 1	Risks Stipulated in Clause 1	All Risks Except Excluded Risks	Risks Stipulated in Clause 1	Risks Stipulated in Clause 1
General Average	○ (clause 2)	○ (clause 2)	○ (clause 2)	○ (clause 2)	○ (clause 2)
Salvage Charges	○ (clause 2)	○ (clause 2)	○ (clause 2)	○ (clause 2)	○ (clause 2)
Both to Blame Collision	△	△	○ (clause 3)	○ (clause 3)	○ (clause 3)
Risks Excluded			**(A)**	**(B)**	**(C)**
Willful Misconduct	X (clause 3.1)	X (clause 3.1)	X (clause 4.1)	X (clause 4.1)	X (clause 4.1)
Ordinary Trade Losses	X (clause 3.2)	X (clause 3.2)	X (clause 4.2)	X (clause 4.2)	X (clause 4.2)
Insufficiency Unsuitability of Packing	X (clause 3.3)	X (clause 3.3)	X (clause 4.3)	X (clause 4.3)	X (clause 4.3)
Inherent Vice	X (clause 3.4)	X (clause 3.4)	X (clause 4.4)	X (clause 4.4)	X (clause 4.4)
Delay	X (clause 3.5)	X (clause 3.5)	X (clause 4.5)	X (clause 4.5)	X (clause 4.5)
Insolvency Financial Default of Carrier	X (clause 3.6)	X (clause 3.6)	X (clause 4.6)	X (clause 4.6)	X (clause 4.6)
Frustration	X (clause 3.7)	X (clause 3.8)	○	○	○
Deliberate Damage	○	○	○	X (clause 4.7)	X (clause 4.7)
Nuclear Weapons	X (clause 3.8)	X (clause 3.9)	X (clause 4.7)	X (clause 4.8)	X (clause 4.8)
Unseaworthiness	X (clause 4.1)	X (clause 4.1)	X (clause 5.1)	X (clause 5.1)	X (clause 5.1)
War	○	X (clause 3.10)	X (clause 6)	X (clause 6)	X (clause 6)
Terrorists	○	○	X (clause 7.3)	X (clause 7.3)	X (clause 7.3)
Strikes	○	○	X (clause 7)	X (clause 7)	X (clause 7)
Shortage of Labor	○	X (clause 3.7)	○	○	○

7.3.3.5 Additional Coverage

By buying an insurance policy with AR in ICC 1963 or ICC (A) in ICC 2009, the insured can get indemnification against the loss resulting from all risks under the insurance terms. The insured, however, can make use of additional coverage against additional insurance premiums to an insurer under the ICC (WA) and ICC (FPA) in ICC 1963, and ICC (B) and ICC (C) in the ICC 2009. The following additions can be made in insurance agreements to provide for more comprehensive coverage.

Theft, Pilferage & Non-Delivery (TPND)	In conditions other than ICC (A) and A/R, it can be compensated for if a TPND clause is added. Herewith, theft means general stealing, pilferage means partial loss by burglary, and non-delivery occurs when all of the cargo does not arrive at a destination
Rain and/ or Fresh Water Damage (RFWD)	Damage from fresh water and rain can be covered additionally with this coverage. ICC (B) only covers "damage caused by sea water, lake water and river water into storehouses in a ship, barge or hold". Rain must be insured against separately additionally to ICC (B) or ICC (C).
Breakage	Fragile cargo including glass must be insured separately
Sweating & Heating Damage	Damage caused by sweating of moisture in pier, or heating moisture of the products including grain due to poor ventilation could be insured against additionally.
Leakage/Shortage	Herewith, leakage means the damage caused due to liquid or gas leaking from its containers, and the shortage means reduction of weight or short quantity. However, ordinary linkage and shortage of the products including grain and liquid cargo are not usually covered, and thus leakage and storage must be extraordinary for being covered.
Jettison & Washing Overboard	Jettison and washing over deck can be insured against when the cargo is allowed to be shipped on the deck.
Denting / Bending	Dented or bent due to shock in transport can additionally be insured against
Spontaneous Combustion	It can additionally been insured against.
Mold & Mildew	It can be insured against in case of damage by mold and mildew.
Rust	Damage of rust due to seawater or fresh water can additionally be insured against.
Hook and Hole	Damage caused by any hook and hole in discharging can additionally be insured against.

7.4   Cargo Insurance Under Letter of Credit

7.4.1   Insurance Clauses on Letter of Credit

Insurance terms on letters of credit are as follows, for example:

> "INSURANCE POLICY/CERTIFICATE IN DUPLICATE COVERING INSTITUTE CARGO CLAUSES (A), INSTITUTE STRIKE CLAUSES, INSTITUTE WAR CLAUSES BLANK ENDORSED FOR 110 PCT OF CIF VALUE, CLAIMS PAYABLE AT DUBAI WAREHOUSE TO WAREHOUSE."

With regard to the term "certificate", the policy holder concludes an "open insurance" policy with an insurance company for a long-term period of time, and on the basis of this insurance contract a certificate is issued. It has the same validity as an actual insurance policy. In many cases of cargo insurance, shipments are not insured individually; instead, it is common for a merchant to arrange for his broker to implement a long term insurance contract (termed "open cover") against which all shipments can be declared and certificates of insurance are issued.

Usually in insurance terms on letters of credit, basic conditions, for example, ICC (A), should be specified, and additional conditions (for example, "Institute War Clauses" and "Institute Strike Clauses") that are usually excluded from insurer's liability should also be specified. The additional risks require an additional insurance premium to be insured against.

"Blank endorsed 110 % of CIF value" means that the insured amount is the invoice amount plus 10 %. The 10 % can be considered the expected profit resulting from the transaction at issue. The terms "to order of endorsee" or "blank endorsed" means that the right to make claim is not affixed to a specified person and the endorsed person can make claim for the compensation to the insurer when the loss occurs from the covered risks.

The term "claim payable at Dubai" means that if an occurred accident is covered under the insurance policy, the place of payment will be at Dubai. The term "warehouse to warehouse" means that the coverage of the policy should begin when cargo leaves the exporter's warehouse for ocean transportation, and continues until cargo arrives at the importer's warehouse. The insurance will also terminate if the cargo has been unloaded for sixty days, regardless of whether it is warehoused.

7.4.2   Insurance Documents Under Letter of Credit

Insurance documents are required as follows under documentary letter of credit:
① They must be issued and signed by an insurance company, underwriter or agent
② If it is specified that more than two sets of original documents were issued, all sets of originals must be presented unless the letter of credit authorizes otherwise
③ Unless the letter of credit authorizes, cover notes issued by the insurance broker are not accepted.
④ Certificates on the basis of blanket insurance are accepted

⑤ Unless there is another agreement on the letter of credit, the currency on insurance documents must be the same as specified in the letter of credit

⑥ Unless there is another agreement on the letter of credit, the minimum insured amount specified on the insurance documents must be CIF or CIP plus 10 percent

⑦ Unless there are other terms on letter of credit, the insurance policy is valid from loading onboard, dispatch or trust, and banks do not accept the insurance document specifying a later issuing date than the onboard date, dispatch or trust for shipment. In fact, in export cargo insurance, exporters sometimes obtain insurance after the shipping date. But, since this is a cause to reject to pay the claim amount, the insurance company should indicate a contract date not later than the shipping date on the policy, and indicate "warranted no loss reported as of... (actual date of contract)." If there was an accident before the date the insurance was enacted, and the insured was not aware of it, it should be compensated for by the coverage.

⑧ The letter of credit must provide the kinds of insurance required and, if necessary, additional risks to be insured against. An insurance document will be accepted without regard to any risks that are not covered if the credit uses imperfect terms such as "usual risks" and "customary risks".[44]

⑨ Unless there is another agreement on the letter of credit, banks accept the document indicating that it is subject to "franchises" or "excess" clauses. For example, for grain it is sometimes necessary to add specifications of "shortage". For example, in the cargo insurance premium table, a contract is allowed to specify "in excess of 1 %"or "in excess of 5 %." Despite such specification, the bank accepts the document as it is stated.[45]

⑩ If the letter of credit includes the term "all risks," the bank assumes any risk that is not specifically insured without liability, regardless of the "all risks" specification.[46]

7.5   Insurance Premium

An insurance premium is the cost of obtaining insurance coverage, paid as a lump sum, or in installments throughout the period of an insurance contract. If the premium fails to be paid, the coverage will automatically be cancelled, but can be restored if it is paid within a certain grace period after cancellation. Rate of premium means the proportion of the premium to the insured amount. Factors affecting the computation of a cargo insurance rate include features of cargo including kinds of cargo and condition, voyage including route, departure, and destination, insurance conditions, transporting means, level of ship, damage

---

[44] UCP600 Art. 28.

[45] *Id.*

[46] *Id.*

percentage, etc. Each insurance company has its own formula to determine premium rates, and because of this, it is recommended to the shipper to shop around for the best rates for the coverage desired.

7.6   Claims

Under certain terms of the trade contract including C.I.F. terms, the exporter arranges insurance, procures the appropriate policy or certificate and sends it to his customer with other relevant documents such as the bill of lading and the commercial invoice.

Typical actions that the insured is required to take before making claims to the insurer are all appropriate steps to minimize damage, and the sue and labor clause may entitle him to make payment for any expenses involved in carrying out such operations.

The insured, as soon as he becomes aware of loss or damage, should send written notice to the insurance company or their agent in order to arrange a survey and obtain the necessary survey report. The Corporation of Lloyd's for insurance has their agents in major cities throughout the world, and it is the usual practice for policies to state that, in the event of loss or damage, settlement of claims will be facilitated if Lloyd's Agents are called in to hold a survey.

The insured will be concerned with claiming for the loss under three basic headings, namely, partial loss, total loss or constructive total loss. The first two are self-explanatory. Constructive total loss applies, for example, when the consignment may not be completely damaged, but is in such a state that it would cost more than putting it back in its original form and it might therefore have to be sold for scrap.

For total loss of part of the cargo, the claim calculation would be simple, like the following example:

10-cartons of products, which should have A gross arrived value of	US$5,000.00
Actual consignment arrived has a value of (owing to total loss of 1 carton)	US$4,500.00
Amount of loss	US$500.00
Amount of loss = US$500 or 10 %	
Therefore claim based upon 10 % of insured value, say 10 % of US$5,000.00 = US$500.00	

An example of partial loss, if 1 carton was totally lost and 1 carton was not lost but was in fact damaged, might be as follows:

Gross arrival value should be	US$5,000.00
Totally damaged 1 carton	US$500.00
Actual arrival value of 8 cartons which is sound	US$4,000.00
Damaged amount of 1 carton (that is, damaged carton realizes US$50)	US$ 450.00
Actual consignment arrived has a value of (owing to total loss of 1 carton and partial loss of 1 carton out of 10 cartons)	US$4,050.00
Amount of partial loss of 1 carton = US$450.00 or 9 % of gross arrived value	
Total Amount of Loss (total loss of 1 carton + partial loss of 1 carton) = US$950.00 or 19 % of gross arrived value US$5,000.00	

Claims should be filed with the insurance company at its nearest agency as soon as possible. The insured should verify the terms of policy or certificate to see if any express instructions pertaining to claims are contained therein, but he would normally be expected to send the following documents:

① Insurance policy or certificate suitably endorsed
② Survey Report
③ Possibly and Outturn Report
④ Master's Protest-usually a formal statement commenting on the conditions and causes relating to the loss
⑤ Bill of Lading
⑥ Invoice
⑦ Accounts sales if there are proceeds of sales
⑧ Any correspondence with ship owner or other third parties
⑨ Letter of Subrogation which transfers any rights of claimant against carriers to the insurer.

Letter of Subrogation

Vessel: _____

Voyage: _____

Sum Insured: _____

In consideration of your paying us for a total loss on the under -mentioned goods insured with you (in virtue of which payment you will become subrogated to all our property, rights and interests in the said goods and in any monies payable or recoverable in respect thereof on account of general average, salvage, or otherwise howsoever) we hereby authorize you to make use of our name for the purpose of any proceedings or measures, legal or otherwise, which you may think fit to take in respect of the said goods, and we declare that we were the owners thereof at the time of the loss, and we undertake to furnish you with all the papers and correspondence in our possession or control relating t hereto, and to make any affidavits and to give any oral evidence which we can properly make or give, and generally to render to you any such assistance as you may from time to time reasonably require, in connection with any such proceedings or measure, you indemnifying us against all liability costs charges and expenses incurred in connection therewith and with the use of our name therein.

Dated _____ day of _____

Description of Goods _____

Assignment

1. Communications and negotiations with (assumed) marine insurance company, or its agent, to make a cargo insurance contract under the terms of the sales contract and the letter of credit made and issued in Chaps. 4 and 5 respectively.
2. Special factors to be considered to make the cargo insurance contracts with the environment-friendly made products which are particularly easy to be damaged or open to depreciation in value during the international transportation, for example, due to weather conditions.
3. Factors to be considered in making contract of insurance from the viewpoint of risk management in doing international trade.

Reference

Dover V (1982) A Handbook to Marine Insurance, 8th edn. Witherby & Co. Ltd.

Supplemental Reading

DiMatteo LA, Dhooge LJ (2005) International Business Law – Transactional Approach, 2nd edn. West, pp. 251–289.
Folsom RH, Gordon MW, Spanogle Jr. JA, Fitzgerald PL (2009) International Business Transactions: Contracting Across Borders. West, pp. 52–110
Fellmeth AX (2009) The Law of International Business Transactions. West, pp. 327–404
Kouladis N, Fellmeth AX (2009) The Law of International Business Transactions. West 2009, Springer 2006, pp. 75–128.

Foreign Exchange Risks

8

Learning Objectives
1. Function of foreign exchange transactions viewed from the international business transaction;
2. Importance of forward exchange transactions from the viewpoint of risk management of companies involved in international trade;
3. Necessity to do forward exchange transactions in international trade; particularly, in the case of long-term transaction contracts;
4. Foreign exchange position, and management of foreign exchange risks;

8.1   Foreign Exchange in International Trade

8.1.1   Foreign Exchange Risks

Almost all companies involved in international trade face exchange rate risk. Under the uncertainty of foreign exchange markets, companies failing to hedge exchange rate risk are inevitably exposed to financial difficulties.[1] Exchange rate risk is necessarily related to profit or loss possibilities: financial profits can be secured if changes in the exchange rate are in compliance with the trader's expectations, while losses can be realized if changes in the exchange rate are in contrast with expectations.[2] Thus, international trading companies have opportunities to make additional profits from exchange rate fluctuations, and, at the same time, they can face the possibility of losing money from these fluctuations.[3]

International trading companies without experience and industry know-how may prefer simply to avoid exchange rate risk altogether and thereby give up the

---

[1] Ramberg (*supra* note 48, at 189).

[2] *Id.*

[3] *Id.*

E.S. Lee, *Management of International Trade*,   255
DOI 10.1007/978-3-642-30403-3_8, © Springer-Verlag Berlin Heidelberg 2012

possibility of making supplemental profits from fluctuations, while experienced and well-established trading companies may prefer to take the deliberate assumption of exchange rate risk to shoot at making greater profits from fluctuations.[4] Foreign exchange risks are generally divided into three categories, that is, transaction risk, translation risk and economic risk.[5]

Transaction risk occurs when international business transactions involve parties from countries whose currencies' exchange rates fluctuate substantially, under which uncertainty exists.[6] Transaction risk is faced by each of the trading counterparts when the exchange rate has the chance of moving towards a disadvantageous direction between the time the price is contracted and the time payment is made or collected.[7]

Translation risk is incurred from the periodic nature of accounting report practices. A trade transaction will periodically need to be stated on its balance sheet, by a particular reporting currency, assets and liabilities that may be denominated in another currency.[8] In between two reporting periods, the relative values of the two currencies may have changed.[9] To some extent, the exposure to translation risk can be said to be a strategic risk factor, which should be considered when measuring the potential costs and benefits associated with foreign business transactions.[10]

The Yen's Lesson for the Yuan
By JOSEPH A. MASSEY and LEE M. SANDS

"AMONG the many points of tension between the United States and China, perhaps the single greatest one concerns exchange rates. For more than a decade, Beijing has kept the value of the renminbi, also known as the yuan, more or less constant to the dollar, a strategy that critics say increases the price of American exports to China and fuels the rapidly growing trade deficit with Beijing.

Despite its decision to let the yuan rise 21 percent against the dollar between 2005 and 2008, China has remained a favorite target of Congress. Democrats and Republicans have consistently called for punitive action against China, including sanctions on imports, unless it completely de-links the two currencies.

---

[4] Id.
[5] Id., at 191.
[6] Id.
[7] Id.
[8] Id.
[9] Id.
[10] Id.

Lost in the noise, however, is the question of whether de-linkage would actually have any effect on the trade deficit. On this, the United States' 40-year history of pressuring Japan to let the yen appreciate against the dollar is instructive. It indicates that de-linking the yuan would make barely a dent in America's trade deficit. Luckily, this history also points to a different, more effective way for the United States to benefit from China's economic growth.

The Japanese story began in August 1971 when, with the American economy under strong inflationary pressure, President Richard Nixon took the dollar off the gold standard, letting its value fall. At the same time, with our trade and current-account balances going from surplus to deficit because of rapid export growth in Germany and Japan, President Nixon began pushing the other industrialized countries to allow their currencies to appreciate. With Japan – whose yen was fixed at 360 to the dollar – Nixon played hardball, temporarily imposing a 10-percent surcharge on imports and banning soybean exports to the country. The strategy worked. That December Japan and nine other countries agreed to let their currencies fluctuate against the dollar within a narrow range of exchange rates. The yen shot up to 315 by the end of the month.

Still our trade deficit with Japan continued to grow. At the end of 1970 it stood at $1.2 billion; by the end of 1972, with the yen at 302 to the dollar, it was $4.1 billion. Thanks to changes in the global economy, the multilateral currency agreement soon failed, and this allowed the value of the yen to continue rising. By 2006 it stood at 119 to the dollar – more than three times as expensive as in 1971 – and yet the deficit hit an all-time high of $90 billion. What happened? Whatever effect yen revaluation might have had was outweighed by two far more potent forces: American consumers' insatiable demand for Japanese products and Japanese producers' ability to cut their costs and stay competitive. There is no reason to believe that things would be any different with Chinese goods today. So, might it work to instead use tariffs to make American goods more competitive in China? Probably not. The problem is that the United States lacks the domestic industry to make many of the things we currently buy from China. And China would retaliate with tariffs of its own, hurting our exports to the country, which have recently been growing faster than those to anywhere else.

Fortunately, there are other ways to deal with our trade deficit with Beijing. For one, America could substantially increase its exports, a goal embraced by the Obama administration's National Export Initiative, which calls for doubling American exports in five years. This initiative focuses on the 99 percent of American companies that do business exclusively within the domestic market. Many of them are in sectors where our technology leads the world – like biomedical and clean-tech products. Many of these companies are too small to move into the global market on their own, but with federal support they could significantly raise American exports. For maximum

(continued)

effectiveness, President Obama should pair his export initiative with a push for China and other countries to increase their direct investment in the United States. Here again, our history with Japan is instructive. As Japan's surplus with America ballooned during the 1970s and '80s, its companies began building factories and making other substantial investments in the United States as a hedge against protectionist measures – after all, tariffs wouldn't apply to products made by Japanese companies here. This was a boon for the American economy: through 2007, Japan had invested almost $260 billion, supporting more than 600,000 jobs.

Chinese companies should be persuaded to do the same today. American purchases of Chinese goods have helped create vast pools of Chinese capital, and we should do all we can to bring that money back home. Fighting China over the yuan is a losing battle. There are better ways to use the global economy, and China's rapid growth, to put money into the pockets of American workers."

Source: http://www.nytimes.com/2010/08/24/opinion/24massey.html?_r=1&ref=yen

Economic risk comes from the fluctuations of currencies' exchange rates over a certain length of time, and thus also comes from strategic selection, which originates from an international trader's commitment over a certain period of time to particular partner countries and their currencies.[11] Economic risk from international business transactions cannot be avoided through simple management of foreign exchange. For example, an exporter can transfer transaction risk to the importer by collecting payment in the exporter's currency.[12] However, over a certain period of time, if the exporter relies to a great deal on that particular market, he will inevitably be affected by substantial exchange rate fluctuations between the two base currencies.[13]

8.1.2 Foreign Exchange

Foreign exchange is succinctly defined as "any currency other than the local currency which is used in settling international business transactions." The exchange needs to facilitate a transfer of money from one currency to another, and therefore requires the intervention of a bank or financial institution. In foreign exchange transactions, there is no central paying institution like a central bank for the case of domestic transactions. Furthermore, because currencies of each country

---

[11] *Id.*

[12] *Id.*

[13] *Id.*

are different, the structure of these transactions becomes more complicated. Thus, to settle each transaction each bank has a respective exchange transaction practice and method.

Foreign exchange transactions are related to the balance of international payments, which is closely affected by the overall economic situation of a given country. To avoid a speculative and short-term movement and flight of foreign currency, most countries control the supply and demand of foreign currencies and transactions.

8.1.2.1 Foreign Exchange Transaction

Foreign exchange transactions are divided into remittance in advance and collection. The former is a way to transmit the funds, which is also called circular exchange, and the latter is a way to claim by collection and receive funds, which is also called adverse exchange. If foreign exchange is considered as a product, a bank functions as the buyer and seller of the foreign exchange. Foreign exchange is divided into selling exchanges and buying exchanges. With selling exchanges, there are both outward remittance and inward collection; with buying exchanges, there are both inward remittance and outward collection.

Remittance

Remittance is defined as "the transfer of funds, usually from a buyer to a distant seller." Inward remittance means that the creditor's or the beneficiary's bank accepts a certain amount of funds remitted by an overseas remitter through its corresponding bank, and transfers it to the domestic payee. Outward remittance refers to when a bank remits a certain amount of foreign exchange to the payee at the request of the customer. There are three ways to use remittance in exchange transactions: demand draft (D/D), mail transfer (M/T) and telegraphic transfer (T/T).

Payment Collection

Collection is an adverse exchange transaction in which a creditor claims payment collection, which is opposite to remittance. When the commercial bank is committed, the commercial bank buys checks or bills whose place of payment is overseas from the creditor, and then gets paid directly from the paying bank or through the correspondent bank. A creditor's commercial bank collects checks or bills through one of two methods, that is, bills purchased or bills sold. Bills purchased means to make payment to a customer in advance, and bills sold means to make payments after being required to make payment. A significant proportion of movement of international funds is made through collection by foreign exchange bills.

Bills purchased are made when an exporter is paid in advance by the bank before collecting checks or bills are presented from the oversea bank. The bank gets paid by requesting collection to the paying bank later. With this method, the commercial bank assumes a significant amount of risk due to the possibility of failure of payment. Because of this, payment in advance must be made when checks or bills are required to be paid from the paying bank, and the beneficiary must have ample collateral or a good credit standing.

8.1.2.2 Correspondent Arrangement

In order for a commercial bank to conduct foreign exchange services like remittance and collection and notice of letter of credit internationally, there must be a foreign-exchange brokering bank in the other country. If the bank has a branch in the other country, exchange transaction can be simplified and done through that branch. It is convenient and effective for banks to be internationally established, but if not, banks can make contracts to facilitate foreign exchange transactions with foreign countries' local banks, and serve customers with economic efficiencies. This arrangement is known as a "correspondent arrangement," and the counterpart bank is termed the correspondent bank. A bank that opens a deposit account with the correspondent bank in its name to make payments along with a foreign exchange transaction is called as a depositary correspondent bank.

8.2   Exchange Rates

8.2.1   Concepts

An exchange rate is a price at which one currency can be converted into another currency, that is, the exchange rate is the price that a bank charges to transfer the submitted currency into the currency requested by the customer who is to pay his foreign trading partner, i.e., the price of foreign exchange. Factors influencing exchange rates include interest rates, inflation rates, trade balance, political stability, transparency of a country's legal and administrative organizations, and the general state of the economy.

When you come into a bank, you might see a board that lists the exchange rates of major world currencies, and the rates often change minimally day-to-day and throughout the day. But, how exactly is this exchange rate decided? If you consider foreign currency as a product, the exchange rate is decided by its supply and demand. Since foreign currency is a means of international settlement, an international balance of payment reflects supply and demand of foreign currency, and thereby an exchange rate is decided.

If your exchange is done through a bank, the ratio from one currency to the other will not exactly be the price of exchanging the currency back to the original currency. The reason is that one is a bid rate, and the other one is an offer rate. The difference in the two rates is the bank's profit for the transaction. The bid rate (price) is the exchange rate at which the dealer is willing to buy a currency, and the offer (asking) rate (price) is the exchange rate at which the dealer is willing to sell the currency. The midpoint price is the overall of the bid and offer price. Suppose a dealer provides the following quotes:

Quote in the U.S.	Bid	Offer
Direct (US$/Euro€)	US$ 0.9836	US$ 0.9839
Indirect (Euro€/US$)	Euro€ 1.0164	Euro€ 1.0167

Offering a US$ 0.9839/ Euro€ (asking rate) is equivalent to a counter-party bidding $1/0.9839 =$ Euro€ 1.0167 per US dollar. Another way to describe exchange rates is that it is the purchasing power to buy foreign goods and services with domestic currency. For example, we might assume that the value of the Japanese Yen is quoted as 120 Yen per US Dollar. In other words, one dollar (US $) can be exchanged in the foreign exchange market for 120 Japanese Yen (JPY, ¥). Currently, the value of one Japanese Yen in terms of US dollars is given by the reciprocal of 120, which is worth one US dollar. Thus, it is defined as ¥/US$ as the number of Japanese Yen per US dollar and US$/Yen as the number of US dollars per Japanese Yen: ¥/US$ $= 120$ and US$/¥ $= 0.0833$. Quotations for the yen are usually indicated for 100 Yen rather than one Yen.

The difference between a bid rate and an offer rate is called the bid-offer spread, and it is the exchange profit the specified bank will make, that is why this spread can be slightly different among different banks. The width of the spread is determined according to the demand to convert the currency, that is, the spread rate will be higher when conversation is strongly or immediately demanded. For example, the spread in a bank located in the airport would be bigger than that of a bank located downtown.

8.2.2   Spot Rate/Forward Rate

A spot rate is the foreign exchange market price at which a currency is delivered on a spot date. The spot date is the date within two days from the date the transaction is concluded, and at that date that the currency sold must be delivered. The spot rate is the starting point for all foreign exchange transactions. A forward rate, on the other hand, is the exchange rate to be applied for a future's date. The forward rate is used for a transaction that will take place at some point set in the future (for example, 6 months).

8.2.3   Methods to Determine Forward Rate

Methods to determine the forward exchange rate include forward outright rate, premium rate or discount rate (by year), and forward differential.

8.2.3.1 Forward Outright Rate
This is the actual foreign exchange rate used in a forward contract. It is used to determine the outright price to be applied to forward exchange transaction as is done with spot rates. It exists exclusively for customers like trading companies, not for banks. A forward rate is decided by the spot rate plus a premium or discount of

forward exchange to the spot rate, and so the premium margin or discount margin is more important than forward rate itself. In practice, a premium margin or discount margin is fixed per one day while the spot rate changes constantly even during one day, and therefore, it is inconvenient to announce the newly determined forward outright rate whenever it changes.

8.2.3.2 Premium/Discount Rate

The premium rate or discount rate of forward exchange is determined annually. Since it can be used as a determining indicator of interest arbitrage transaction by contrasting the interest rate gap (annual rate) of both countries' currencies, companies and small banks prefer this method. It is not used in banks, but is a computing basis of the "forward differential."

8.2.3.3 Forward Differential

Forward differential or forward margin, indicates and determines the premium or discount of forward exchange to the spot rate by decimalization, and is used by dealers in foreign exchange markets and banks. The last decimal point of the forward differential is called the "point" or "pip". The euro is indicated down to four decimal places, and the yen down to two decimal places. The forward differential is indicated by units of this point (pip). Bids and offers of banks are generally announced at the same time, so it is sometimes indicated just as a premium or discount, or P (or +) or D (or −), but more generally a premium without discount or only forward differential is announced. When the spot rate and forward rate are the same, it is indicated as "flat."

8.2.4   Forward Exchange Transactions

8.2.4.1 Concepts

A foreign exchange transaction is a type of exchange transaction in which a certain amount in one currency will be swapped for the value of that amount in another currency at a fixed (forward) exchange rate within a certain period of time thereafter for forward exchange. The foreign exchange contract will state the currency being traded, the currency being bought, the amount, the value date, and the forward rate. The value date refers to the date that the transaction is made, and the accounts are settled. For a spot exchange, the value date will be within two working days after the agreement of the transaction, while for a forward exchange, the value date will be within a certain period of time, for example, 1 month or 3 months.

8.2.4.2 Object of Forward Transactions
Exchange Risk Coverage (Hedging)

The major objective in utilizing forward exchange is to avoid exchange risk caused by exchange rate fluctuations between the contract date and value date by agreeing on a certain exchange rate to be applied to the settlement of foreign exchange.

Hedging is a term that is used to describe the action of minimizing risk by taking a certain exchange position.

The importer, exporter, debt owner and asset owner can hedge through the forward exchange transaction as follows.

(1) Importer

Let us assume that the spot rate is US$/¥ 120, an import contract is concluded, and its value date is three months later. On the value date if the exchange rate has moved up, then a foreign exchange loss occurs. To avoid the risk, the importer can make a contract to buy the US dollars utilizing a forward rate with a maturity of three months. By doing this, the buyer knows exactly the rate that will be applied to buy the exchange, irrespective of the spot rate three months later from the dealing date.

For example, if the selling forward exchange rate of 3 months is US$/¥ 118, three months later, the importer makes a payment of the import price by buying US$ by the rate of US$/¥ 118 regardless of the actual spot rate on the value date, for example, US$/¥ 122.

(2) Exporter

Let us assume that the spot rate is US$/¥ 120, an export contract is concluded, and its collection date is three months later. If at that time the exchange rate falls, a foreign exchange loss occurs. To avoid the risk, the exporter makes a selling contract utilizing the forward rate of a maturity of three months. If the buying forward exchange rate of 3 months is US$/¥ 117, three months later, the exporter can make up for the loss by selling US$ by US$/¥ 117 according to the forward contract, regardless of the actual spot rate on the value date, for example, US$/¥ 115.

(3) Foreign Currency Debt Owner

For such companies, if an exchange rate rises a foreign exchange loss occurs and if the exchange rate falls a foreign exchange profit occurs. To make up for the loss caused by the rise of exchange rate a company can make a buying contract with a forward exchange rate. If an exchange rate rises, exchange rate loss will occur due to the rise of foreign currency debt, but the loss can be made up for by making forward exchange transactions (buying foreign currency). On the contrary, if the exchange rate falls, profit would be incurred due to the fall of foreign currency debt, but such chances to get profits will be offset through the forward exchange transactions (in selling foreign currency).

(4) Foreign Currency Asset Owner

For such companies, profits can be made when the value of currencies held are rising (the exchange rate is rising favorably) against the domestic currency, and losses could be realized when the value of currencies held is dropping against the domestic currency. To reduce asset depreciation by a drop in the exchange rate, the company can form a selling contract of domestic currency by implementing a forward exchange transaction. In the case of such forward transactions, irrespective of the whether the foreign currency's exchange rate rises or falls later, the assets will remain the same to those valued at the forward contracting date.

Speculation

While importers and exporters make forward exchange contracts to avoid assuming risk caused by exchange rate fluctuation, speculative dealers may deliberately assume the same risk to utilize forward exchange transactions to make profits from the exchange rate fluctuations. Dealing with currency exchange allows investors to make a highly leveraged margin account. This means that they can borrow more money from the broker than in trading normal stocks, and invest it with their own funds to create a greater chance of high profits or deep losses.

If the speculator having debt in US$ expects the exchange rate to rise, he can purchase that currency through a forward exchange transaction and "lock in" profits if the currency actually does go to the way he expects. Let us assume that the current forward rate for a maturity of three months is US$/¥ 118, and the speculator concludes a contract to buy US$, expecting the value of US$ to increase. If in three months the exchange rate has risen to 1 ¥ = 120, instead of paying ¥ 120 for 1 US$, the speculator only has to pay ¥ 118. By using a forward exchange transaction, he will have made a profit of 2 ¥ per 1 US$. On the other hand, if he speculates incorrectly, he could easily make a loss on his bet.

If the speculator expects the rate of US$ to ¥ will drop, he can make a selling forward exchange contract to take advantage of the depreciating US$. Let us assume the forward rate of three months is US$/¥ = 120. If in three months the spot rate has changed to US$/¥ = 117, the speculator can then make a profit of 3 ¥ per 1 US$. Another simple way for speculators to try to make gains in foreign exchange markets is to simply purchase a currency that he believes to be strengthened by spot exchange. Then, the speculator will hold the currency until he thinks it has risen to its peak, and try to sell the currency at that point to earn a profit.

8.2.4.3 Value Date of Forward Exchange Transactions

The maturity date of a forward exchange transaction can be set as standard or nonstandard. A standard rate means that the value date (maturity) is set and agreed on by calendar month (1 month, 3 months, 12 months, etc.), which bankers often use. A nonstandard or broken-term rate means that the terms are not stated in months, but simply in number of days (7 days, 50 days, etc.), and this type of rate is used more commonly for customers. Maturity dates or valued dates extending beyond one year are becoming more common, and for good bank customers, a maturity extending out to 5 and even as long as 10 years is possible.[14]

8.2.4.4 Foreign Exchange Position

In a financial institution or trading company, a foreign exchange position is defined as the difference in the selling value of a foreign currency and the buying value of a foreign currency for a certain period of time, as well as the difference between foreign currency assets and debt for a certain period of time. There are three basic

---

[14] Eun and Resnick (2009a, p. 123).

kinds of foreign exchange positions, that is, flat position, long position and short position.

Square/Flat Position

A perfectly flat position is the same as a perfect hedge, which means the investor has eliminated all of the potential risk, and therefore, eliminated all of the potential profit as well, which is a rare occurrence. This position is defined as "a situation where cash inflows match cash outflows in a given period of time." If an investor has a forward exchange position, he will have the exact opposite position to get rid of the change of risk.

Overbought/Long Position

To enter a long position means that an investor is purchasing a currency, commodity, share, or financial instrument in anticipation that the value of that currency will rise. An investor with a long position can also be called a "bull investor" for that particular currency. If the foreign currency depreciates during the period of time that it is held, the long investor will take a loss.

Oversold/Short Position

This is exactly the opposite of a long position, and is taken by "bear investors" who are anticipating that the currency they are investing in will go down. As can be imagined, if the currency value depreciates, the investor will earn profits, but if the value increases, the investor will take a loss.

8.2.5 Management of Exchange Risk

International trading companies and financial institutions maintaining foreign currency and debt nominated in foreign currency can have exchange losses or profits depending on their investment decisions and on exchange rate fluctuations. In order to minimize risk, investors and traders tend to hedge their portfolios, often by taking out positions in the futures or options markets.

8.2.5.1 Option

Making a futures contract is agreeing to buy or sell a currency at a specific future date at a certain price. Options are similar, but the movement of the currency has to be quite drastic to reach a break-even point – or the point at which the investor can start making money. An option is a contract giving the owner the right, but not the obligation, to buy or sell a given quantity of an asset at a specified price at some time in the future. An option to buy the underlying asset is a "call", and an option to sell the underlying asset is "put". Buying or selling the underlying asset via the option is known as "exercising the option".[15] A "call" option is made when it is

---

[15] Eun and Resnick (2009b, pp. 172–173).

predicted that the currency will rise in value (like going long) and a "put" option is made when it is predicted that the currency will fall (like taking a short position).

In case of the option for importers, for example, after buying a "call" option of foreign currency equivalent to the import price, the importer buys the foreign currency by exercising the option upon maturity if the exchange rate rises, and then pays the exporter. If the exchange rate falls, the importer will give up his option, take a loss, and purchase the currency by the spot market price to pay the exporter.

In case of the option for exporters, for example, after buying a "put" option of the foreign currency equivalent to the export price, the exporter sells the import foreign currency by exercising the option upon maturity if the exchange rate falls. But, if the exchange rate rises, the trader will take a loss, give up his option, and sell the export amount at the spot market rate.

8.2.5.2 Management of Foreign Currency Balance

Let us take as an example a foreign exchange position that is in an overbought position, that is, the foreign currency debt subtracting the foreign currency balance is positive, which means that the investor holds a surplus of the currency and an aggregate long position. In such case, in order to end the surplus to avoid the exchange risks, they can make a forward exchange selling contract, buy "put" options, or take a selling position through a futures or forward contract.

Let us take as an opposite example that of a foreign exchange position that is in an oversold position, being simply the opposite of the overbought position, which results in a net debt nominated by a foreign currency. To take a square position to avoid the exchange risks, they may buy currency through spot exchange and actually reimburse debts to the creditor, enter foreign exchange buying forward contracts, take buying positions in the futures exchange, or buy "call" options. Thus a foreign exchange in an overbought or in an oversold position can be managed by keeping a square position.

8.2.5.3 Matching

The matching strategy means that an investor will buy one liability (asset) in order to offset the risk of another asset (liability). For example, if a firm is open to a foreign exchange risk in a US$ receivable, it can be offset by buying goods from the United States to create an offsetting payable. This is typically utilized by multinational enterprises and trading companies, and is not a viable option for small-sized companies or individuals. Centralized risk management occurs when the two parties engage in ongoing trade and continually need to transfer one currency into another.

When it comes to the matching strategy, two types exist: natural matching and parallel matching. Natural matching is done in accordance with the times and costs of imports, while parallel matching is based on cash balances of payments in other currencies. The former is ideal and can achieve almost perfect hedging; in the case of the latter, however, perfect hedging is impossible as long as the fluctuations of the currencies are different.

8.2.5.4 Leading/Lagging

Leading and Lagging refer to altering the timing of cash flows within a firm (intercompany), or between companies (intracompany), in order to offset risk to foreign exchange exposures. Leading and lagging is more common when the firms are related, because they are more likely to embrace a common set of goals. Subsidiaries would like to ask their parent company to lag the payment, because the subsidiary is essentially to borrow the funds from the parent company for free.

With regard to the leading, if a parent firm is in short position of US$, it can accelerate its collection of US$ payments from its subsidiaries. By doing this, its US dollar account will start to level-out, resulting in less currency risk. With regard to the lagging, if a parent firm is in long position of US$, it can delay US$ collection from its subsidiaries. By doing this, its foreign currency, US dollar, account will start to level-out, resulting in less currency risk.

Assignment

1. Under the sales contract followed by the issuance of credit in previous chapters, try to manage the exchange position grouping into speculation in pursuit of the positive profit and hedge in pursuit for the stability and safety in foreign exchange transactions.

References

Eun CS, Resnick BG (2009a) International financial management. Mc Graw-Hill
Eun CS, Resnick BG (2009b) International financial management, 4th edn.

Supplemental Reading

Wright B (2001) The law of electronic commerce: edi, fax, and e-mail. Assn of Records Managers

Electronic Commerce

9

Learning Objectives

1. Development and practical use of Electronic Data Interchange (EDI) in international business transactions;
2. Importance and functions of standardization of EDI methods of communication from the viewpoints of promotion of facilitation in conducting international trade;
3. Function and importance of UNCITRAL model laws and conventions to promote international electronic commerce;
4. Factors to be considered in doing international electronic business transactions in comparison with the case of off-line transactions;
5. Efficiency and productivity in doing international electronic commerce compared with off-line commerce;
6. Factors to be considered in making transportation and cargo insurance contracts in international trade through electronic commerce compared with the case through off-line transactions;

9.1 Introduction

9.1.1 Development of EDI System

In the past two decades, e-commerce has emerged as an important issue in conjunction with improvement of national competitiveness under free trade of the WTO. Governments, academies, and companies in developed and developing countries have been making efforts to settle e-commerce data bases. International organizations especially concerned with settling international e-commerce regulations are the WTO, OECD, UNCITRAL, APEC, etc. Sharp increases in online transactions regardless of borders have propelled many countries into the age of e-commerce.

E.S. Lee, *Management of International Trade*,
DOI 10.1007/978-3-642-30403-3_9, © Springer-Verlag Berlin Heidelberg 2012

E-commerce is commonly understood as commerce conducted strictly over the Internet, but its scope is actually much broader: "Business conducted through the use of computers, telephones, fax machines, barcode readers, credit cards, automated teller machines (ATM) or other electronic appliances (whether or not using the Internet) without the exchange of paper-based documents." It includes activities such as procurement, order entry, transaction processing, payment, authentication and non-repudiation, inventory control, order fulfillment, and customer support.

When a buyer pays with a bank card swiped through a magnetic-stripe-reader, he is participating in e-commerce. The e-trade that is of particular concern to international trade is trade facilitated by the Internet, in which overseas buyers freely purchasing products from around the world. E-commerce has provided small and mid-sized companies with the means to make international trade negotiations without having a physical overseas network.

E-commerce has not completely replaced conventional means of trade, but is simply a new alternate means in which considerable time and money can be saved. International trade had been simplified due to the creation of standard forms by the representative establishment of UCP and Incoterms from the 1960s. Trade-simplifying projects have internationally and domestically been promoted to further simplify the trading process through expansion of deregulation on the basis of various standard forms from the 1970s–1980s.

Since the mid 1980s, the foundation of e-commerce began to be established with the predecessor of EDI (Electronic Data Interchange) system to e-commerce: EDI globally connected large firms to a computer network independent of the Internet. EDI proved to eliminate errors due to the necessity of retyping data, improved circulation time, and made just-in-time delivery possible. The principles of EDI have been applied to the Internet and other means of e-commerce.

EDI Agreement

"Electronic Data Interchange agreement; an agreement that governs the transfer or exchange of data, such as purchase orders, between parties by computer. • Electronic data transmitted under an EDI agreement is usually formatted according to an agreed standard, such as the American National Standards Institute ANSI X12 standard or the U.N. EDIFACT standard."

Source: Black's Law Dictionary (2009)

9.1.2   New Paradigm of International Trade

The digital revolution has been evaluated to dramatically transform the lives of human beings, constituting the third revolution after those of agriculture and industry. The speed and scope with which the Internet has transformed the world has unprecedently been increased and widened. But, the Internet alone is not sufficient to facilitate major trade deals, and a major IT infrastructure must continue to be developed worldwide for the continuous facilitation and cost-down of international trade.

The global economy is evermore becoming the Internet-based global economy, which demonstrates great developments in eliminating boundaries of time, money, commercial customs, and culture. The development of the Internet has accelerated the globalization of business activities and caused a shift in the trade paradigm by fundamentally changing the basic methods applied to trading activities. The Internet is capable of bearing the responsibilities of marketing, consulting, contract making, payment, and specifying details of delivery and transportation without the conventional limitations of time and space.

With VAN/EDI, paper documents were replaced with more standardized electronic documents. This can be considered a change in processing tools and methods of international trade transactions rather than a fundamental change in the process of trade. The Internet, on the other hand, has also fostered a fundamental change in international trading processes, such as the simplification of issuing a letter of credit to distribution of goods and settlement of payments – and, needless to say, the paper letter of credit of old has been replaced with an electronic letter of credit.

eUCP; What is the Last Case?

Integration is the Most Important Prerequisite for Active Use of e-Documents

"Electronic documents in future commercial life will be very active according to the vision of ICC – International Chamber of Commerce at the beginning of 2000. In this year a working group was formed for the electronic submission of documents attached to letters of credit. As a result eUCP (Supplement to UCP 600 for Electronic Presentation) brochure went into effect as of April 1, 2002. This development was considered to have come at the right time for investments in electronic commerce and as a good signal for the widespread use of e-Documents submitted under letters of credit.

However, many banks in the world still are not ready to execute transactions with electronic documents. This happens despite the fact that technological advances in Internet technologies and even legal infrastructure in many countries allow for the use of e-Documents. Why actually we cannot use e-Documents effectively is a question that deserves consideration. Perhaps the answer is this: Foreign trade operations represent a multilateral process. Importers, exporters, banks, insurance companies, customs agencies, transport companies, inspection companies, etc., are the parties included in a standard foreign trade transaction. Legal and technical problems may arise during one operation carried out with e-Documents. So as to solve these problems all the parties participating in the transaction should use the same

(continued)

system and a single reference format from the beginning to end. Unfortunately, today a global system (Internet-based) to meet these needs does not exist. That is the basis of all these problems.

Today, the number of institutions using e-Documents for foreign trade transactions is far less than expected. This case does not constitute an encouraging business environment. The reason for this situation needs to be examined. One reason for this slow transition to e-Documents is that International standards for paperless trade are as of yet unspecified. But the main reason is that there is not an integration system between institutions participating in a given foreign trade transaction. Another reason deserving mention is that coverage of eUCP is limited to letter of credit transactions.

Consequently, an integration system like trade points is the most Important prerequisite for active use of e-Documents."

Source: http://www.emrecivelek.com/eUCP-Supplement_to_UCP600_%20for_Electronic_Presentation.html

9.2   Process of Electronic Trade

The first step for selling of a product utilizing electronic systems is making potential customers aware of the product, and so exporters promote exports to potential buyers through various means. The second step is to engage in communication regarding a possible transaction in which parties agree on details about products, price, method of payment, transportation of delivery and insurance.

If the consultation progresses positively, the third step is taken for the terms agreed between the parties to be confirmed and binding. If a contract is concluded, both parties must take their respective steps in organizing delivery and payment. Typically a bank issues a letter of credit and under e-trade the letter of credit is issued and informed of electronically. A series of logistic operations such as shipment, transportation, discharging, inspection and clearance must be conducted physically, while registration and tracing can be done online.

More details are as follows:

9.2.1   Selection of Target Market

Before the advent of the Internet and the information age, it was common to use catalogues or promotional materials through trade fairs and conventions, or to make business trips to obtain important information about potential trading partners. Now, companies can easily and rapidly collect information about new products or customers and select the target markets domestically and internationally through traveling on the website.

9.2.2 Marketing

Similar to collecting information, business trips and catalogues or other promotional material have traditionally been used for marketing activities, but now exporters can send their web catalogues via the Internet, do marketing activities through e-mail, create informative websites, and quickly contact mailing lists about new advancements and products. Conventional marketing and credit inquiry are still important for many businesses, but the Internet has allowed entrepreneurs to participate in international business transactions, and screen the potential buyer through the credit inquiry by e-mail and etc. without a massive financial support for physical activities.

9.2.3 Negotiation and Agreement

E-trade has made negotiations and other points of contact more efficient and cheap through cyber conferencing, chat rooms, and e-mail.

9.2.4 Arrangement and Delivery

After a contract is made, the exporter must secure and deliver the contracted goods to the importer as specified. Digital products like e-books, music and software can be downloaded to the importers at any time according to contract specifications.

9.2.5 Payment

In order for the importer to fulfill his contractual obligations, he must make payment to the exporter as specified. Telegraphic transfer is generally used when the contract amount is small or the importer is credible, and payment through collection is used when the contract amount is large and the importer is credible. With e-trade, new methods including electronic letter of credit or trade cards can be utilized.

9.2.6 Follow-Up Management

The contract terminates when the payment is made and all shipments of goods have arrived to the importer. After termination is made, data-based marketing is needed for follow-up management, and trade disputes, if arises, will need to be resolved. Continuing management of trade partners will help any exporter grow a steady business by modifying products to tailor specifically to importers' needs. Long-term business relationships will save time and money in searching importers and marketing in the future.

9.3   Customer Research

9.3.1   Method to Find Customers

9.3.1.1 Using Trade-Related Organization

Specified trade-related organizations including the each country's importers' and exporters' associations can expedite a search for partners. Utilizing these sources, one can collect general information by looking through trade statistics, market trends, company directories of each country, and specific country's market data issued by export-and-import related banks or institutes. Potential importers can also be found through materials from government agencies, foreign diplomatic offices, or overseas official organizations like World Trade Center and International Chamber of Commerce.

9.3.1.2 Advertisement Through Overseas Media

To find customers, they can make catalogues for overseas promotion and distribute them to potential customers, or use domestic or international advertising media.

9.3.1.3 Use of Cyber-Marketplace

The cyber-marketplace is an efficient place to promote business transactions with products and find customers. It is a comprehensive information system providing information related to trade and supporting promotion, customer sourcing, and product information. Specific organizations providing cyber market place that can be advantageous to traders are Alibaba, Eceurope, Globalsources, Swissinfo, I-Trade, Tradecompass, and etc.

9.3.2   Searching for Customers Through Websites

9.3.2.1 Concepts

This is a way for trading companies to promote themselves and their products around the world using the website, and at the same time finding customers by searching or viewing information stored through website registrations. The websites supporting these functions are called e-marketplaces or trade sites, and various sites from trade-related organizations and private companies are developed and operated, which are avoidable to anyone who needs the specified conditions.

To use e-market places trading companies become members of the sites, post their home pages and product catalogues to appear themselves to the potential customers in their databases. A single site will likely have members from the domestic and foreign markets, further facilitating international traders' searching activities.

9.3.2.2 Process

The first step is to actually have the Internet, and then a company should develop an easily navigable homepage whose address can be attached to marketing material.

Promotion can be done by making e-catalogues and by mutually linking web sites, exchanging free advertisements with foreign web sites, and searching world famous e-market places.

Assignment

1. Making the scenario to enforce international trade contract which was formatted in previous Chaps. 3 and 4, through the electronic method of commerce, and make assessment of this electronic commerce compared with conventional off-line commerce, considering the fact that circumstance of international electronic commerce would be basically different from that of domestic commerce.
2. Checking lists to be considered when you enforced the international business transactions through electronic commerce and electronic data interchange focusing on the difference from the case of off-line physical transactions with the exporting items selected by the students.

Claim and Dispute Settlement

10

Learning Objectives

1. Difficulties and costs to pursue the enforcement of foreign judgments and arbitral awards in doing international trade;
2. Contractual element of arbitration with relation to the international trade contract;
3. Judicial element of arbitration with relation to the international trade contract;
4. Legal framework of arbitration with relation to the international trade contract;
5. Ad hoc and institutional arbitration with relation to the international trade contract;

10.1 Introduction

A trade-related claim is legal demand or assertion by one party for compensation, payment, or reimbursement for a loss or damage incurred due to the negligence or breach of the contract terms committed by the other party. The contents of a complaint are not only price reduction, contract avoidance and compensation for damage, but also include discrepancies, arguments, and disputes. Because of the wide range of possible claims, it is important to outline what claims are acceptable under the contract, and how the claims are to be made. Creating a clear path for claims is necessary, particularly, for the risk management in international trade. This path should clearly specify the period of time to present the official claim, causes for which claims are to be brought, and how to bring a claim. One type of claim that could take an exporter by surprise is termed the "market claim." This is the claim that the importer asks for damage compensation ostensibly due to only minor discrepancies in products delivered from those contracted, but the real cause of the claim is a decrease in market price of the imported products.

The buyer inspects the goods to insure that they are in accordance with the contract and clear discrepancies are not found. If any discrepancy is found or the

E.S. Lee, *Management of International Trade*,
DOI 10.1007/978-3-642-30403-3_10, © Springer-Verlag Berlin Heidelberg 2012

delivered quantity is short of the contracted quantity, the buyer should notify the problem to the seller immediately. The inspection and notification is the buyer's obligation. If he neglects this process, he loses the right to make legal claims.

It is advisable that the buyer inspects goods within as short a period as he can as far as circumstances permit,[1] as if he fails to send notification within a reasonable period of time despite a discrepancy, he loses the right to claim.[2]

10.2   Resolution of Trade Claims

10.2.1 Introduction

Trade claims are solved either amicably by parties or by intervention of a third party. The former solutions are made by waiver of claim, amicable settlement or compromise. When the contract party gets loss due to breach of contract committed by the other party, the damaged party does not exercise the right to claim, or simply gives up the claim, meaning that the damaged party will assume the incurred loss by himself. Amicable settlement or compromise is a solution found through compromise by independent negotiation and agreement.

As a solution by intervention of a third party, talks could be grouped into intercession or recommendation, conciliation or mediation, and arbitration and litigation:

In the case of intercession or recommendation, a third party has intervened in the dispute according to the request of one or both parties in order to suggest solutions or advice to determine a fair and unbiased compromise; In case of conciliation or mediation, an unbiased conciliator is selected according to a mutual decision, and this third party suggests a compromise. If both parties agree to the compromise, the claim is resolved; In case of arbitration, according to a mutual arbitral agreement, a fair arbitrator (not by legal action) is appointed and an arbitral tribunal takes place. Then, the arbitral award is submitted to the both parties unconditionally. The decision is irrevocable and nonnegotiable. Approval and enforcement of foreign arbitration are generally recognized among the countries. In case of litigation, the dispute is ruled by a judge, which resolves the claim according to the concerned country's law and judicial system.

Out of the dispute resolution, the simplest solution to a contract dispute is to contact and negotiate with the other party. With patience, understanding and flexibility, one can often solve conflicts to the satisfaction of both sides. If, however, negotiations fail and the sum involved is large enough to warrant the effort, a company should obtain the assistance and advice of its legal counsel and other qualified experts. If both parties can agree to take their dispute to an

---

[1] CISG, Art. 38.

[2] *Id.* Art. 39.

arbitration institute, this step is preferable to legal action because arbitration is often faster and less costly.[3]

Particularly, in Asia area including Japan and Korea, dissatisfied parties do not like to visit the court for litigation and therefore, sometimes, they would rather like to assume the damage than to bring the legal action to the court, which comes from the cultural feature of this area.

In such cultures, arbitration may prove "a 'face-saving' approach to dispute resolution." From a more practical perspective, litigation is an expensive process likely to permanently damage the business[4] relationship and is inherently unpredictable as to result. International litigation is often unduly delayed because of a lack of uniformity in procedural rules. For example, the liberalized nature of the United States investigation rules often meets with hostility in foreign courts.[5]

10.2.2 International Litigation

Dispute resolution through the recourse to public courts or tribunals is generally the slowest, most costly and most confrontational out of the various options to solve the disputes, which is the reason why the experienced trading companies try to avoid this approach by negotiating for the inclusion of alternative dispute resolution (ADR) or arbitration clauses in their contracts.[6] It is technically difficult and often requires specialized professional counsel.[7] In addition, there exists a risk of court bias when the court decision has to be enforced in the country of the party having the same nationality as the state court before whose enforcement is sought.[8]

With relation to the jurisdiction referring to the proper courts of the proper country where the claim can be brought to, if a contract is silent on the country of the proper court, the parties in a dispute case may want to invoke the jurisdiction of the national courts which maybe favorable to, or the courts which are convenient for them, which is known as "forum-shopping".[9] In order to avoid these problems, parties of the international trade contract are recommended to include a forum selection or choice of forum clause.[10]

---

[3] Dimatteo and Dhooge (2005, pp. 123–124).

[4] Nelson (1989, pp.187, 199).

[5] Dimatteo and Dhooge (2005, *supra* note 335, at 124–125).

[6] Ramberg (2008, *supra* note 48, at 66).

[7] *Id.*

[8] *Id.*

[9] *Id.*, at 67.

[10] *Id.*

Forum Shopping

"The practice of choosing the most favorable jurisdiction or court in which a claim might be heard. A plaintiff might engage in forum-shopping, for example, by filing suit in a jurisdiction with a reputation for high jury awards or by filing several similar suits and keeping the one with the preferred judge."

Source: Black's Law Dictionary (2009)

The parties may freely choose the governing law to their contract so long as it is not contrary to the public policy of the country where the legal action is brought.[11] If the contract does not specify the applicable law, or if the choice of law is unreasonable or contrary to public policy, then the court that hears the case will have to choose the applicable law, according to the principles of "conflict of laws".[12] According to the general and basic rules of conflict of laws the court will primarily look to the place where the contract was negotiated and/or signed, the place where it is to be performed and the domiciles of the parties involved.[13]

Conflicts of laws

"1. A difference between the laws of different states or countries in a case in which a transaction or occurrence central to the case has a connection to two or more jurisdictions. – Often shortened to conflict. Cf. choice of law.
2. The body of jurisprudence that undertakes to reconcile such differences or to decide what law is to govern in these situations; the principles of choice of law. – Often shortened (in sense 2) to conflicts. – Also termed (in international contexts) private international law; international private law. 'The phrase [conflict of laws], although inadequate, because it does not cover questions as to jurisdiction, or as to the execution of foreign judgments, is better than any other.'" Thomas E. Holland, The Elements of Jurisprudence 421 (13th ed. 1924).

Source: Black's Law Dictionary (2009)

---

[11] *Id.*
[12] *Id.*, at 68.
[13] *Id.*, at 67–68.

10.3 Commercial Arbitration

10.3.1 Alternative Dispute Resolution

Alternative dispute resolution (ADR) clause includes mediation, negotiation, conciliation, mini-trail, and expert determination clause.[14]

Conciliation

"1. A settlement of a dispute in an agreeable manner.
2. A process in which a neutral person meets with the parties to a dispute and explores how the dispute might be resolved; esp., a relatively unstructured method of dispute resolution in which a third party facilitates communication between parties in an attempt to help them settle their differences. Some jurisdictions, such as California, have Family Conciliation Courts to help resolve problems within the family. – Also termed (in sense 2) facilitation; conciliation procedure. CF. MEDIATION; ARBITRATION."

Source: Black's Law Dictionary (2009)

The mediation and conciliation processes make a neutral, independent and unbiased third party become involved in the dispute resolution process.[15] Concerned parties try to resolve the disputes without resorting to formal dispute resolution procedures including litigation or arbitration.[16] Mediation and conciliation are sometimes distinguished by the methodology used by mutual agreement upon the third party that will act as mediator or conciliator in the dispute[17]:

If the third party uses his skills to meet with each party on a separate basis and transmit and interpret their respective positions to others occasionally suggesting proposals for resolution of the issues, then the third party is acting as a mediator; However, if the third party is not only expected to perform this mediating role, but also to provide a formal written report of the issues and the successes or failure of their resolution, the process is usually referred to as conciliation.[18]

---

[14] Murray et al. (2007, *supra* note 8, at 538).

[15] *Id.*

[16] *Id.*

[17] *Id.*

[18] Willes and Willes (2005, p. 565).

Alternative Dispute Resolution

"ADR can be defined as encompassing all legally permitted processes of
dispute resolution other than litigation. While this definition (or something
like it) is widely used, ADR proponents may object to it on the ground that it
advocates litigation by giving the impression that litigation is aberrant or
deviant. That impression is false. Litigation is a relatively rarely used process
of dispute resolution. Alternative processes, especially negotiation, are used
far more frequently. Even disputes involving lawyers are resolved by negotiation far more often than litigation. So ADR is not defined as everything-but-
litigation because litigation is the norm. Litigation is not the norm. ADR is
defined as everything-but-litigation because litigation, as a matter of law, is
the default process of dispute resolution." Stephen J. Ware. Alternative
Dispute Resolution§ 1.5, at 5–6 (2001).

Source: Black's Law Dictionary (2009)

10.3.2 Arbitration

10.3.2.1 Concepts

Arbitration differs from litigation in that it is a consensual dispute resolution
process made by an agreement between the parties to refer their disputes to
arbitration, and choose a neutral party to resolve the dispute.[19] The agreement
may be set out in a clause of the main contract or may be an entirely distinct
contract.[20] The procedure adopted to resolve the dispute can, to a large extent, be
chosen by the parties, but most national laws and international agreements provide
that the procedure must contain a minimum requirement of due process.[21]

The culmination of the process of arbitration is the resolution of the dispute
between the parties by means of a decision of the tribunal.[22] The binding nature of
the award made by the arbitral tribunal may be seen as a consequence of the parties'
agreement to arbitrate and is often respected by national law or the United Nations
Convention on the Recognition and Enforcement of Foreign Arbitral Award of
1958 (The New York Convention).[23] An award, however, may not be binding in
circumstances where it was made without jurisdiction or if the process by which the
award was made was somehow defective or unfair.[24]

---

[19] Murray et al. (2007, *supra* note 8, at 538).

[20] *Id.*

[21] *Id.*

[22] *Id.*

[23] *Id.*

[24] *Id.*

10.3.2.2 Feature

Even though an arbitration panel can be composed of a tribunal of people who are not legal counsels and may likely judge the issues based on their own experience and ideas, judgments may be imperfect from the viewpoint of legality, and there can be a lack of predictability, arbitration that has the advantages compared to the litigation as follows:

First, peaceful atmosphere and informal procedure can be maintained by a civil arbitrator; second, arbitration is a single-trial system, and so cases can be settled promptly; third, since arbitration does not require lawyers, comparatively speaking, it is very cheap to be processed; fourth, arbitration is not publically open like court hearings, and therefore parties' confidentiality can be maintained; fifth, results of arbitral award are always binding, which are mandatorily enforced by foreign courts.

The New York Convention specifies mandatory enforcement in foreign countries. One of the most important and advantageous features of arbitration is that arbitrators are to be chosen by the concerned parties, which means that the dispute can be decided by panelists with specialized knowledge of a particular trade and commercial practice. This common framework of reference boosts the confidence and trust of businessmen in the proceedings and the resulting award. This is especially important in international commerce where parties come from different legal cultures.[25]

10.3.3 Arbitration Agreement

Arbitration agreements are mutual agreements to solve part or all of a dispute that already occurred, or is to occur about a certain legal relationship. There must be an arbitration agreement incorporated generally into the contract to solve disputes by arbitration. The objects to be treated by arbitration can be existing disputes or future disputes. A "submission agreement" is to be made for the arbitration about the existing disputes, an "agreement to refer" is an agreement to solve future disputes, and the arbitration agreement is generally made by incorporating arbitration clauses into the Agreement on General Terms and Conditions of International Business or Sales Contracts.

Standard arbitration is an arbitral agreement (as mandated) in writing. Oral agreements do not satisfy the conditions of a valid standard arbitral agreement. Arbitration law in the England and New York Convention outlines the principle that agreements must be in writing. Regarding the legal effect of arbitration agreements, certain legal systems including the New York Convention admit the "prohibition of

---

[25] Carr (1999, p. 317).

direct suit," and so if there is an arbitration agreement, the dispute must be resolved through arbitration and shall not be resolved through litigation.[26]

Arbitration Agreement

"Any dispute arising out of or in connection with this contract including any question regarding its existence, validity or termination shall be referred to and finally resolved by arbitration under the Rules of the London Court of International Arbitration which Rules are deemed to be incorporated by reference into this clause."

"If any dispute should arise in connection with the interpretation and fulfillment of this contract, the same shall be decided by arbitration in the city of Singapore and shall be referred to a single arbitrator to be appointed by the parties hereto. If the parties cannot agree upon the appointment of the single arbitrator, the dispute shall be settled by three arbitrators, each party appointing one arbitrator, the third being appointed by . . ."

10.3.4 Arbitral Tribunal

10.3.4.1 Concepts

An arbitral tribunal is a single arbitrator or a group of arbitrators organized provisionally for the purpose of hearing and ruling, and acts similarly to a court tribunal. As a court consisted by a judge and a collegiate group of judges, the arbitral tribunal is composed of a single arbitrator and a collegiate group of arbitrators. The type of tribunal selected – single or group – is dependent on the seriousness of the situation in terms of the financial amount in question. In typical cases, a tribunal is composed of three people, one of which is elected as the arbitrator in chief.

10.3.4.2 Selection of Arbitrators

First, the arbitrators must not be selected when they have any kind of legal or economic interests to the arbitrating outcome. When they have conflicts of interest with the disputes, their decisions could be severely biased and unfair. Arbitrators should also have a good understanding of the industry, and the items involved in the dispute. Arbitrators can be selected as specified in the parties' agreement, by a secretariat of the arbitration board, or by a court.

The selection can generally be made by the parties when they mutually agree on the selections. If parties fail to select the arbitrator, the secretariat of the arbitration board will assume the job of selecting. This process can also meet obstacles if both parties reject the selection, or if the arbitrator cannot do the job for any reason. In

---

[26] New York Convention, Art. 2.

this case, an arbitrator is designated in order of the list of arbitrators kept by the secretariat of the board. The last resort is for a party to turn to a court for selection.

10.3.5 Hearing/Awarding

10.3.5.1 Place of Arbitration

Selection of the place to carry out the arbitration is very important because it is a standard in selecting an arbitrator and deciding which procedures and governing laws to be applied. General arbitration laws and regulation decide the place to make arbitration considering various conditions of the case concerned including the concerned parties' convenience.

10.3.5.2 Method of Hearing

The most important aspect of the procedure is the actual hearing. In the hearing, an arbitral tribunal should give an arbitral award after reviewing statements, references, and other pertinent information. The process often involves both a written hearing and an oral hearing. Both methods are recommended, but they are not mandated. If parties do not agree as to whether the hearing should be written, oral, or both, the arbitral tribunal will decide upon it.

When the parties do not agree, the tribunal will necessitate at least an oral hearing, as it is considered the most important and informative. For speedy and exact procedures, an arbitral tribunal will often request parties to submit statements about arguments, evidence, and defending comments. It is a standard practice to present and inspect evidence while all parties are present. The arbitrators then judge the credibility of submitted evidence with their discretion.

An arbitral tribunal will decide the date, place and method for the hearing. If the tribunal has a satisfactory reason it can delay or expedite the hearing on his authority or by a party's request.

10.3.5.3 Presentation

It is each party's right and obligation to be present at the time of the hearing. If the arbitral tribunal determines that the procedure cannot promptly be undertaken because the applicant did not specify the purpose of application, or present the reason for application and verification method, or if it determines the procedure cannot be continued, it can terminate the hearing. This is considered a hearing termination due to concerned party's negligence. If one of party is absent or refuses to participate in the hearing in presence, the hearing can still proceed. However, if both parties are absent more than twice or refuse to attend the hearing in presence, the tribunal can declare the hearing terminated.

10.3.5.4 Termination

The arbitral tribunal cannot only terminate a hearing due to negligence of one or both parties, but can also make termination when it determines that the parties conducted all their arguments and verification properly. If summary statements are required, the tribunal considers the termination at the final date to submit the documents. The tribunal can resume the hearing at any time before the arbitration award completed on its own authority, or if one applies for resumption. In case of hearing resumption, the termination is made at the terminated date of the hearing.

10.3.5.5 Arbitral Award

The award should be granted within a certain period of time after the hearing termination, but can be delayed by the tribunal. A statement of arbitral award consists of requests and reasons to justify the specific issues awarded. If an arbitration award is fixed, its validity is the same as an irrevocable judgment in court, and is therefore a binding and enforceable determination. Since arbitration is a single-trial system, a party cannot apply for arbitration in the same country or overseas to reassess the decision.

When the arbitration award is completed, then the enforcement of arbitration is an extremely important issue. Arbitration, as a dispute settlement process, is rendered meaningless if it is not possible to enforce an award rendered by an arbitration tribunal. In international business transactions, the issue is whether an award made abroad is enforceable domestically, and whether an award made domestically is enforceable abroad. A number of international conventions including the New York Convention have made enforcement of arbitration awards concluded in the convention's member countries effective in their domestic domicile.

Arbitration Award

AWARD MADE IN CASE NO. 000 IN 2011
Arbitrator: Dr. Bruce Mckee (Australia)
Parties: Claimant: Kamas Nara Co. Ltd (USA)
    Respondent: Marine Trading Co, Ltd (Korea)
Subject matter: –Rescission of contract
        –Force majeure
Facts
In a contract made in 2006, Kamas Nara Co. Ltd. (hereafter Kamas Nara) granted to Marine Trading Co. Ltd. (hereafter Marine) the exclusive rights to reproduce, edit and distribute in Korean language the materials used in their USA magazine. The contract, concluded for the duration of five years, stated that the royalties to be paid by the Marine to Kamas Nara amounted to 5 % of the turnover of the Korean edition, with a minimum guarantee of approximately US$5,000 a month. The contract declared also if, with the exception of force majeure, the royalties were not paid within twenty days after the date of publication of an issue, Kamas Nara would have the right to rescind the contract without prejudice to its right to claim damages.

Although Kamas Nara several times sent materials to Marine, the Marine never paid the royalties. The latter used the materials, but it appeared that

Marine had prohibited publication for some time. In 2007 Kamas Nara requested Marine to pay the royalties and damages. Marine answered that the Korean version of the USA magazine had never been distributed in Korea. It recognized, however, that it owed some money, for various minor items, the total amount of which was approximately US$150,000. This answer did not satisfy Kamas Nara, and on the basis of the arbitral clause contained in the contract of 2006, it initiated arbitration, claiming approximately US$210,000.

The Court of Arbitration of the ICC designated an Australian national as sole arbitrator. The arbitration took place in Australia. Notwithstanding many notifications from the arbitrator, Marine did not participate in the arbitration. The arbitrator therefore proceeded in his absence.

Award

1. The arbitrator held first of all that Kamas Nara had not exercised its right of rescission, because it had asked for performance of the contract, failing which it would resort to arbitration. The royalties to be paid as well, as the damages, could therefore be taken account of during the entire contractual period of five years.

2. The arbitrator found further that no event of force majeure had occurred. Although the publication of two periodicals of Marine had been prohibited, the company still had a third periodical under publication, in which the material of the USA magazine could have been published. Moreover, the Marine had declared in a letter to Kamas Nara that the prohibition would be temporary.

The arbitrator also found that Marine had published materials of the USA magazine. In addition, Marine had not supplied any proof that, because of non-performance of Kamas Nara or force majeure, it was unable to publish materials in the years 2009–2010.

The arbitrator concluded that even if the obligation of Marine to pay royalties was temporarily suspended-which the arbitrator considered as uncertain-this obligation was entirely reestablished thereafter. Consequently, the arbitrator awarded to Kamas Nara the total amount claimed, and condemned Marine to pay the costs of the arbitration.

10.3.5.6 Prohibition of Lawsuit

A party cannot file a lawsuit after disobedience, but if there are any errors or discrepancies in the process or any breaches of the arbitration-related rules, a party can ask for relief by filing a suit of arbitral award avoidance.

Assignment

1. Under the presumption that your counterpart raised complaints against the breach of contract, for, example, relating to the quality specification, based on the contract established in Chap. 4 and followed by the issuance of credit in Chap. 5, proceed to communicate and negotiate with your counterpart to

resolve the complaints. You may choose to resolve them through the com-promise, commercial arbitration or legal litigation according to the provisions concerned under the sales contract.

2. Actual cases of recognizing and enforcing arbitration awards made by arbitral tribunals relating to international trade, and find out the difficulties, inconveniences and economic inefficiencies to be indemnified through the arbitration award, compared with the costs paid and investments made for the more complete risk management by your company during the process of preparing for exports.

References

Carr I (1999) Principles of International Trade Law, 2nd edn. Gavendish Publishing Ltd.
Dimatteo LA, Dhooge LJ (2005) International Business Law, 2ed edn., South-Western College
Nelson SC (1989) Alternatives to Litigation of International Disputees. International Lawyer 23
Willes JH, Willes JA (2005) Q.C, International Business Law. Mc Graw-Hill

Supplemental Reading

Carr I (2007) International Trade Law, 3rd edn. Cavendish Publishing, pp. 565–598
Fellmeth AX (2009) The Law of International Business Transactions. West, pp. 852–1004
Folsom RH, Gordon MW, Spanogle Jr. JA, Fitzgerald PL (2009) International Business Transactions: Contracting Across Borders. West, pp. 494–621
Kouladis N (2006) Principles of Law Relating to International Trade. Springer, pp. 41–62

Application to Practical Fields

11

11.1   Scenario for Practice

This chapter is designed to enhance students' ability to apply the knowledge and technical information gathered from the previous chapters to the practical fields of international trade: Illustrated application of the theoretical and legal principles and information is to be made by the processing steps according to the scenario of the actual business transactions between the exporting company named Kamas Nara Co., Ltd, Busan, Korea and the importing company named Chinese Marine Trading Co., Ltd with the LED lamp (Anion lamp) which is an environmentally-friendly item that purifies the air with anions. In this scenario, Kamas Nara Co. Ltd, as the specialized trading company in importing and exporting the environmental protection-related technologies and products, screened from world market, exports Anion Lamps manufactured in Korea to Chinese Marine Trading Co., Ltd. Herewith, the two companies have had a reliable and reasonable business relationship particularly through consulting with International Trade and Law Institute located in Korea.

International Trade and Law Institute, as the professional educating and consulting entity in the field of international business transactions, has consulted these two companies for the efficient and desirable management of international business transactions with environment-related items. Being consulted by the professional Institute, the two companies are assumed to concentrate on the practical activities of transactions for pursuing the maximization of the efficiency and productivity in implementing international business transactions without being concerned about the professionally required legal, financial or management knowledge and information.

E.S. Lee, *Management of International Trade*,   289
DOI 10.1007/978-3-642-30403-3_11, © Springer-Verlag Berlin Heidelberg 2012

International trade transactions are generally made step by step from the stage of formation of contract to the enforcement of contract. In the industrial field, several steps out of the following could be overlapped or be omitted, but the following generally covers the processed stages.

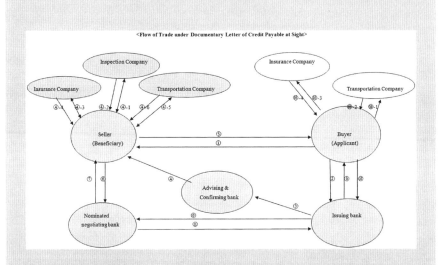

① Make a sales contract through the course of negotiation and discussion;
② Make an application for issuing a letter of credit according to the contract;
③ Swiftly deliver a message of advice and confirm issuing the letter of credit to the advising and confirming bank;
④ Advise and confirm the letter of credit under instructions from the issuing bank;
   ④-1 Make a contract for pre-shipment inspection with a pre-shipment inspection company;
   ④-2 Obtain the pre-shipment inspection certificate from the pre-shipment inspection company;
   ④-3 Make an insurance contract with an insurance company in accordance with the terms of the letter of credit;
   ④-4 Obtain the insurance policy from the insurance company;
   ④-5 Make a transportation contract with a transportation company;
   ④-6 Obtain the transportation documents from the transportation company;
⑤ Make a shipment according to the instructions stipulated in the letter of credit and sales contract;
⑥ Negotiate with the bank, submitting a bill of exchange accompanied by documents required under the letter of credit;

⑦ Pay the export price to the exporter when the documents and bill of exchange are submitted in accordance with the terms of the letter of credit;

⑧ Ask for a payment dispatching bill of exchange accompanied by documents to the issuing bank;

⑨ Present the proper documents to the importer and ask for payment at the import price;

⑩ Pay for the import price against the receipt of the transport documents;

　⑩-1 Present the transportation documents and ask for the delivery of the shipped cargo.

　⑩-2 Receive the goods against the transport documents from the transportation company;

　⑩-3 Make a claim for damage to the insurance company in accordance with the terms of the insurance policy;

　⑩-4 Receive the claimed amount from the insurance company;

⑪ Make reimbursement to the negotiating bank.

11.2 Specific Product Selection

The exporter selects the proper items to be exported to the specifically selected areas through market research using the information from trade statistics or other concerned entities. At this stage, Kamas Nara Co., Ltd (herein Kamas Nara, or Exporter) selects the Anion Lamp as the strategic export item for the proper market to be selected through the following market research. This product is not only used as a common LED lamp but can also be used as an air purifier producing anion to make the room clean and fresh.

China's war against sand

By Louisa Lim (BBC, Xinjiang)

China is fighting a war against its deserts, which are expanding and joining to create a massive dustbowl.

(continued)

It is a battle which is being waged in places where human habitation is scarce. But its success or failure will have environmental implications thousands of kilometers away. I drove 2,000 km through China's largest desert – the Taklamakan in north-western Xinjiang province – to see what was being done. Two thousand years ago, the ancient Chinese called the Taklamakan desert the Moving Sands. And their secrets lie buried in its depths – around 300 ancient cities swallowed by this sea of sand. Even today, life is a constant struggle for those living on the edges of China's deserts. They are people like farmer Imin Barat. The sand dunes are literally on his doorstep, and every year they creep closer. "The sand is burying the houses, so we've had to rebuild them. It's also burying our crops," he said. "By the time someone gets to 60 years old around here, they'll have had to move house three or four times on average." Imin Barat checked his precious herd of sheep. They are the main source of income for his family of eight, who have already lost two houses to the encroaching sands. But the irony is that herdsmen like Mr Barat are actually helping the desert advance. Their animals eat the plants which keep it in check. After the communists came to power in 1949, they resettled three million people in far flung Xinjiang. Their role is to populate the barren wasteland, protect the borders and dilute the restive local Uighur population. But the mass migration brought over ploughing and overgrazing, making the desert spread even faster. "Desertification and soil erosion is a huge issue in China and it is absolutely of global significance," said Juergen Voegele, an expert on desertification at the World Bank in Beijing. "China is one of the countries in the world with the highest soil erosion rates anywhere". If you look at the numbers you can say that about.... one quarter of the total land area in this country is in the process of active desertification and a large portion of that is actually irreversible, so we're not talking about a small problem. "We're talking about a very big problem which not only has consequences domestically, but also in the region," he said.

Creeping deserts

And those consequences can be seen each Spring when sandstorms darken the skies of China's eastern cities, thousands of kilometers away. Dust from China's western deserts even reach as far afield as Japan and South Korea. The sandstorms have been a wake-up call that the problem needs to be tackled, and urgently. To show what is being done we were taken to a plant research centre in the desert funded by the local Tarim oil company. It is a tiny spot of green amid a huge expanse of yellow sand. "We need to find plants that don't need a lot of water," said botanist Liu Bujun. And as we drive down the never-ending desert highway, it is clear that action is being taken to prevent the road being inundated, protecting important commercial interests. But much more still has to be done, according to Mr Voegele. "The government is taking the issue seriously. I do still think not seriously enough. They are looking at policies individually not comprehensively. "There is a large tree planting campaign going on for instance, which is helpful, but by itself it will not solve the problem. If it's not combined with better grazing management policies at the same time, those trees will not survive," he said. Deep into the desert we suddenly come across a small band of workers digging for water by the side of the road. "We're digging a well," their foreman said. "We're making this place green. In five years, there'll be red willow, poplars and date trees growing here. It'll be the longest green corridor in the world." It is a bold – you might say, crazy – statement from a man surrounded by rolling sand dunes. But China needs to take bold steps, and soon, to stop its moving sand."

Source : http://news.bbc.co.uk/2/hi/asia-pacific/3434069.stm

11.3   Overseas Market Research

The exporter completes market research for the efficient promotion of exports to the selected market making use of market research strategies and techniques. When exporters do market research, they can visit the targeted place physically or make use of second-hand information from international trade entities, and business-related media, including E-market place, databases, international trade bodies, countries' economic newspapers, journals of commerce, etc..

For the international business transaction to proceed successfully with reasonable profits, serious market research is needed to ensure that the item will have a high chance of success in its new markets. In the case of the Anion lamp, it was recognized by Korean and Japanese citizens that it is good for health and extended life expectancy due to its function to purify the polluted air, but if it could be exported to Cameroon, the results could fail as a large amount of the stock would remain without being sold. In Cameroon, generally speaking, they do not have to worry about the polluted atmosphere as currently their main industry is agriculture without using many chemicals or fertilizers. In the stage of making market research, they are recommended to collect and analyze data, and often make an agreement for a small shipment to "test the waters" before signing to a full-scale operation. This process of testing market is sometimes called a "pushcart."

The research will help to prove or disprove the theory that exportation of a particular product will be successful in its projected target market. "Target market" refers to the group of people who are targeted by the seller to be the main buyer(s). For example, the target market for high-priced, light-weight walking shoes, in general, are normally middle or elderly people, as they are the most likely to want to buy and use those products. Similarly, the Anion Lamp would be attractive to the highly-educated middle or elderly people, as they would generally be interested in pollution-free circumstances and health.

Determining the target market is essential in ensuring that the products are sold in the proper stores, the proper departments, and marketed through media that will reach that particular group of consumers. If the research renders a positive decision, the exporter will move forward using the available business connections as far as possible that can help facilitate the business transaction, through which they proceed to the next stage of marketing. At this stage, Kamas Nara selected China as the potentially proper market to export Anion lamp considering several factors derived from market research.

☞ **The following information is generally useful for the LED lamp to be exported to China.**

• **Import Tariffs**

"A comprehensive guide to China's customs regulations is The Customs Clearance Handbook (2007), compiled by the General Administration of Customs (China Customs). This guide contains the tariff schedule and national customs rules and regulations. This guide can be purchased at bookshops in China, or ordered from:
China Customs Publishing House,
No. 9A, Dong Tu Cheng Street,
Chaoyang District, Beijing, China 100013
Phone: (8610) 8527–1610;
Fax/Phone (8610) 8527–1611
Website: http://english.customs.gov.cn/publish/portal191/
1. Tariff Rates
     China Customs assesses and collects tariffs. Import tariff rates are divided into six categories: general rates, most-favored-nation rates, agreement rates, preferential rates, tariff rate quota rates and provisional rates. As a member of the WTO, imports from the United States are assessed at the most-favored-nation rate. The five Special Economic

Zones, open cities, and foreign trade zones within cities offer preferential duty reductions or exemptions. Companies doing business in these areas should consult the relevant regulations.

China may apply tariff rates significantly lower than the published MFN rate in the case of goods that the government has identified as necessary to the development of a key industry. For example, China's Customs Administration has occasionally announced preferential tariff rates for items in the automobile industry, steel, and chemical products.

2. Customs Valuation

   The dutiable value of an imported good is its Cost, Insurance and Freight (CIF) price, which includes the normal transaction price of the good, plus the cost of packing, freight, insurance, and seller's commission. On January 1, 2002, Customs Order 954, the Administrative Regulation on Examination and Determination of the Dutiable Value of Imported and Exported Goods, came into effect. Under the regulations, China Customs has been tasked with assessing a fair valuation to all imports. To assess a value, all Customs officers now have access to a valuation database that lists appropriate valuations for various imports, based on international market prices, foreign market prices and domestic prices. Customs officers check the price reported by the importer against this database. Normally, Customs officers will accept the importer's price. However, if the reported value is too far out of line with the database, the Customs officer will estimate the value of the goods based on methods listed in Article 7 of the PRC Administrative Regulations.

3. Tariff classification

   Before July 2004, China Customs exclusively used eight-digit codes in its harmonized tariff system, as opposed to a more detailed ten-digit code system. Without detailed codes, Customs officers have wide discretion to classify each import. On July 1, 2004, the Ministry of Commerce announced the use of ten-digit codes for certain items including rare earth, chemicals, internal combustion engines, pumps and automobiles.

• Trade Barriers

Following China's accession to the WTO in 2001 and during its subsequent transition period as a new WTO member, the Chinese Government took significant steps to revise its laws and regulations in a manner consistent with WTO obligations and strengthen its role in the global economy. Nevertheless, despite progress in many areas, significant barriers for U.S. companies exist. These include import barriers, an opaque and inconsistent legal system and limitations on market access. The U.S. Government strives to address these barriers through continuous bilateral dialogue and engagement, active export promotion, and enforcement

(continued)

of U.S. and international trade laws and obligations. For more information on specific barriers, please see the U.S. Government's National Trade Estimate Report on Foreign Trade Barriers at www.ustr.gov/ Document_Library/Reports_Publications/Section_Index.html.

- Temporary Entry
  1. Advertising Materials and Trade Samples
     Samples and advertising materials are exempt from customs duty and Value-Added Tax (VAT) if the item's value does not exceed RMB 200 (USD 30). Samples and advertising materials concerning certain electronic products, however, are subject to customs duty and VAT regardless of value.
  2. Warehouses
     Goods that are allowed to be stored at a bonded warehouse for up to one or two years, are limited to: materials and components to be used for domestic processing subject to re-exportation; goods imported under special Customs approval on terms of suspending the payment of import duties and VAT; goods in transit; spare parts for free maintenance of foreign products within the period of warranty; and fuel for aircraft and ships.
     At the end of the two-year period, the goods must be imported for processing and re-exported, licensed for import, or disposed of by Customs. Customs duties and VAT may be assessed depending upon the degree of processing done in China. Goods imported under normal import contracts are not allowed to be stored in bonded warehouses.
- Prohibited and Restricted Imports
  The following items are prohibited from entering China: arms, ammunition, and explosives of all kinds; counterfeit currencies and counterfeit negotiable securities; printed matter, magnetic media, films, or photographs which are deemed to be detrimental to the political, economic, cultural and moral interests of China; lethal poisons; illicit drugs; disease-carrying animals and plants; foods, medicines, and other articles coming from disease-stricken areas; old/used garments; and local currency (RMB). Food items containing certain food colorings and additives deemed harmful to human health by the Ministry of Health are also barred entry.
- Standards
  The Standardization Administration of China (SAC) is the central accrediting body for all activity related to developing and promulgating national standards in China. The China National Certification and Accreditation Administration (CNCA) coordinate compulsory certification and testing, including the China Compulsory Certification system. Both SAC

and CNCA are administratively under the General Administration of Quality Supervision, Inspection, and Quarantine (AQSIQ).

Standards in China fall into at least one of four broad categories: National Standards, Industry Standards, Local or Regional Standards, and Enterprise Standards for individual companies. National Standards can be either mandatory (technical regulations) or voluntary. In any case, they take precedence over all other types of standards."

Source: http://www.buyusainfo.net/docs/x_7668019.pdf

11.4 Marketing

Based on the market research, the exporter starts its marketing activities making use of trade and general portal website services, advertising agencies, out-posting, overseas Chambers of Commerce, general trading companies and agencies, etc. In China, advertising through out-posting and off-line marketing have proved to be efficient; therefore, Kamas Nara uses these methods, and then proceeds to the next stage.

☞ **The following is the advertising bulletin attached to the local import journal in China which is specifically designed to release the importing information to the journal's member companies.**

<LED Lamp Creating Pure Anions without Ozone Depleting Substances>

1. **Product:**
   LED Lamp Creating Pure Anions Without Ozone

2. **Features of the Products:**

   ◇ Unique air-purifying effect;
   ◇ Longer lasting than traditional incandescent lamps;
   ◇ Energy-saving and environmentally friendly;
   ◇ The lamp does not contain any ozone harming products, but only pure anions.
   ◇ The lamp contains a total of 42,253 anions/cc, which is even more than the 15,000-anion concentration per cc of the world-famous Niagara Falls!
   ◇ The lamp uses Nano Silver made from steel fibers; this special technology makes the lamp last such a long time that it can be considered a semi-permanent product.
   [LED Light Specifications]
   Function: Sleeping lamp

(continued)

Dimensions: 135 × 53 mm
Color: Green/Orange/Blue
Weight: 95 g
Regular Input Voltage: AC 220 V
Wattage: 4.5 W
[LED Lamp Features]

(1) Unique air-purifying effect:

The lamp has a very unique function which no other lamps have. Not only can it be used as a normal lighting fixture, but it also can be used as a wonderful air purifier which keeps the problems caused by excessive smoke, dust, air pollution in your home (recommended to be lit for 24 hours for good health), school, or office away from you. Therefore, while enjoying calm, warm lighting, at the same time, you can enjoy a healthy environment. When lighting is not necessary, it can work as a silent air-purifier. After using this unique light, you can most definitely expect noticeable improvements to your air space environment because as an air cleaner, it removes dirt, grime, smoke, germs, viruses and bad smells from the air for you.

(2) Longer lasting than traditional Incandescent Lamps:

The lamp is extremely energy efficient and long lasting. This efficient lamp uses just 2 watts of power which gives it an incredible, longer lasting life. It creates less heat than traditional incandescent lamps, which means it lasts significantly longer than traditional lamps (according to trial tests, almost 100 times longer). Due to its longer life, you need to purchase far fewer lamps, which means it can help you save on your lighting costs.

(3) Energy-saving and environmentally friendly:

The lamp uses less power with energy efficient lights, so it is cheaper to run and helps cut your energy bills. Furthermore, high efficiency creates less carbon emissions, so our lamps are better for the environment and your health. In addition, due to its longer life, you need to purchase fewer lamps, which means fewer lamps are produced, and fewer lamps go into landfills, which is also good for the overall environment.
[Comparison with Existing Lamps]

(1) Ozone

Most existing lamps contain Ozone damaging products, which are bad for human health. By special unique technology, the lamp does not contain any Ozone damaging products, but only pure anions.

(2) Anion concentration

At a distance of 30 cm, existing lamps contains few anions, while, at a distance of 2 m, through measuring, we obtained results showing that the lamp contains a total of 42253 anions/cc, which is even more than the 15,000-anion concentration per cc of the world-famous Niagara Falls!

(3) Lifetime

Existing lamps usually are made from carbon fibers. This means that, normally, they only can be used for 3 months at most. Different from existing lamps, this lamp uses Nano Silver made from steel fibers, this special technology makes the lamp last such a long time that it can be considered a semi-permanent product.

11.5   Finding/Screening Counterparts

The exporter finds and screens the importer by searching companies, attending expositions, e-mailing and faxing potential customers, receiving inquires and replying to them, consulting export management firms, etc. The exporter can use the branches of trade companies, general trading companies and trade agencies, Chamber of Commerce, World Trade Center and its associations, expositions, sales promotion fairs, etc.

In the case of China, for example, where reliability is regarded as very important in doing business, so utilizing existing business networks is likely to be a reliable choice, but if there are no current partners to work with, you can search for counterparts through trade directories of countries concerned, producer associations by item, or the proper Chambers of Commerce. At this stage, finding out the proper counterpart in China, Kamas Nara makes use of the Trading Promotion Center of Yang Fu Economic Zone in China along with existing business and personal networks established by its consulting institute, the International Trade and Law Institute.

Before an export manager makes a final choice, he or she is recommended to make a list of potential candidates and perform credit inquiries through credit inquiry agencies or other credit-related institutes in those companies' country. When making a credit inquiry, one should, at least, be informed of the character, capital, and capacity of the importer at issue.

Kamas Nara tries to investigate the character, capital, capacity, country, currency, etc., through major businesses, branches of the export insurance corporation, credit guarantee funds, trade promotion agencies, export and import banks, etc., in addition to the networked contact supplied by the International Trade and Law Institute. Judging from the reports from the inquiring sources, Kamas Nara screened Chinese Marine Trading Co., Ltd. as the potential buyer in China, considering the fact that it has been doing business very well for the past 35 years and enjoying a good reputation in its business fields.

☛ **To find out the best importer in China, Kamas Nara sent a letter to the Trade Promotion Center of Yang Fu Economic Zone, attaching the following company introduction.**

Kamas Nara Co., Ltd.

204-39, Onchen-dong, Geumjung-Gu

Busan, Korea

Tel: 82-51-583-9836

Fax: 82-51-582-9836

www.ksnara.com

April 5, 2013

Trade Promotion Center

Yang Fu Economic Zone

Hainan Province

Dear Manager,

We are pleased to ask you to introduce the proper importer of our products from Korea as shown

in the following table:

COMPANY INTRODUCTION

COMPANY NAME	Kamas Nara Co., Ltd.			
COMPANY ADDRESS (Homepage)	204-39, Onchen-dong, Geumjung-Gu, Busan, Korea (www.ksnara.com)			
BUSINESS FIELD	Application( ) Digital TV( ) DVR( ) Game( ) Handset( ) Mobilephone( ) –Mobile Solution( ) Network( ) PDA( ) Repeater( ) Security( ) Set-Top-Box( ) SI( ) TFT-LCD( ) Component( ) Others(0)			
CONTACT POINT	Name	S.W.Lee	E-Mail	swlee@hanmail.net
	Dept.	Overseas Business Transactions	Tel No.	82-51-583-9836
	Title	manager	Fax No.	82-51-582-9836

COMPANY INFORMATION			
YEAR OF FOUNDATION	1995		
NO. OF EMPLOYEES	100		
FINANCIAL STATUS	Year	Capital (US$)	Sales Revenue (US$)
	2009	30,000,000	150,000,000
PATENT APPLICATION			
PRODUCTS or TECHNOLOGY	Product/Technology/Description 1. Product : LED Lamp Creating Pure Anions Without Ozone 2. Features of the Products: • Unique air-purifying effect; • Longer lasting than traditional incandescent lamps; • Energy-saving and environmentally friendly; • The lamp does not produce any ozone damaging products, but only pure anions. • The lamp contains a total of 42,253 anions/cc, which is even more than the 15,000-anion concentration per cc of the world-famous Niagara Falls! • The lamp uses Nano Silver made from steel fibers, this special technology makes the lamp last such a long time that it can be considered a semi-permanent product. 3. LED Light Specifications • Function: Sleeping Lamp • Dimensions: 135 X 53mm • Color: Green/Orange/Blue • Weight: 95g • Regular Input Voltage: AC 220V • Wattage: 4.5W			

☞ **The following is the reply from Yang Fu Economic Zone to the request to find the best importer for Kamas Nara.**

Yang Fu Economic Zone

April 25, 2013
Kamas Nara Co., Ltd
204-39, Onchen-dong, Geumjung-Gu
Busan, Korea

Dear Mr. Lee,

We received your letter on April 15, 2013, expressing your desire to find qualified importers who would be in a position of handling your products in China.

We are pleased to inform you that the gist of your said letter will be inserted in the forth-coming issue of our weekly bulletin, "The Chamber of Commerce News," for circulation to our members.

Interested firms will contact you directly, and we also recommend a company, Chinese Marine Trading Co., Ltd., as a potential partner.

We hope that this arrangement we have made will result in your developing satisfactory business relations in our country and assure you of our cooperation at all times.

Very truly yours,

D.W.Pung/ Director

11.6　Making Business Proposals and Inquiries

Making trade inquiries is as important as credit verification in screening a final counterpart. A trade inquiry is a series of questions between an exporter and a potential importer, inquiring about the possibility of trade, asking for catalogues and product samples, and other general information about trade terms such as prices, transport options, and insurance requirements. Once a potential importer has passed potential importers' credit check standards and is selected as the company with which the exporter wishes to do business, the exporter should submit a business proposal. This proposal will outline the exporter's needs, likely be followed by negotiations, and ultimately (possibly) lead to an agreement. Most business proposals and inquiries will include the proposed details including items, transaction size, transaction area, company manual, and proposed main trade terms.

When making such a business proposal, it is important to keep the other party's interests of time and simplicity in mind. It is generally recommended to make the proposal with short concise sentences and only a few paragraphs. If the prospective business partner feels confused by the proposals, he will not be so convinced to do business with an inquirer. If the exporter is proposing to export a product which would newly be added to the prospective business partner's current import lines, efforts should be made to point out potential advantages for the importer.

Also, exporters should try to avoid exaggerations about their companies, because if the proposed company wishes to cut a business deal, they will certainly investigate the exporting company's status. Vague descriptions should be avoided, and expressions should be limited to facts and certainties. The composer of the e-mail or letter needs to present him or herself as the potential importer/exporter to be chosen to do business with. A company's accumulative experience in doing international business transactions will help to materialize any proposed business.

If one is looking for chances to export, it is recommended to briefly summarize the products' strong points in the new market, reflect specific potential-market research, and mention pricing and profit potential. In the proposal, likely-inaccurate expressions such as "we offer the most qualitative products at the lowest prices in the industry" should be avoided. Normally, it is unnecessary to send product samples before the potential importer shows interest in a particular product. It is also recommended to stress the mutual benefits of working together. A properly written proposal should influence the potential importer to realize the potential profit and to pursue further talks and negotiations. If the potential buyer determines to do business with the exporter, then at that point the exporter can choose whether or not to select him to be the buyer of the selected items.

☛ After the exporter selects the potential buyer from the available sources, the exporter can invite the selected importer for the negotiation as follows:

Kamas Nara Co., Ltd.

204-39, Onchen-dong, Geumjung-Gu

Busan, Korea

Tel: 82-51-583-9836

Fax: 82-51-582-9836

www.ksnara.com

May 1, 2013

Chinese Marine Trading Co., Ltd.

Floor 8, No.388, Yang Fu Port Management Building,

Yang Fu Economic Development Zone, Yang Fu, Hainan,

P.R. China

Gentlemen,

Your company has been recommended to us by the coordinator working with Yang Fu Economic Zone as one of the large importers of environmentally friendly goods in China. We are writing to you with a keen desire to open an account with you.

We have been established here for over ten years as one of the leading companies in Korea having exported and imported our environmentally friendly products and technologies to and from world markets since 2000s.

We have enjoyed a good reputation from domestic markets as well as from world markets due to the fact that all the technologies and products we have dealt in were all good for the end users and the enterprises and governments involved at the same time, because they have contributed to the health and life expectancy of human beings, environmental protection and energy saving.

Regarding the terms of settlement, it has been our basic policy to trade on an irrevocable letter of credit, under which we draw a draft at sight.

Our banking reference is Woori Bank Busan branch, who will furnish you with all the information you desire.

We are looking forward to your early and favorable reply.

Yours very truly,

Kamas Nara Co., Ltd

S. W. Lee/Manager

☞ **Accepting the invitation letter from the potential exporter, the potential importer can make inquiry to the referred bank as follows about the exporter's credit standing.**

Chinese Marine Trading Co., Ltd.

Floor 8, No.388, Yang Fu Port

Management Building,

Yang Fu Economic Development Zone, Yang Fu, Hainan,

P.R. China

May 2, 2013

Messrs.

Woori Bank

Busan branch

Gentlemen,

Your bank has been referred to us by Kamas Nara Co., Ltd. in their recent proposal to open a new account with us.

Should their business standing turn out unquestionable, we are prepared to accept their proposal. We would, therefore, be much obliged if you would give us such information as you may have or can secure for us regarding their financial standing and reliability.

We are particularly keen to know with which type of environmental goods they have mainly sold and to what their annual turn-over amounted on average for the last three or four years. And, if possible, please give us your candid opinion on their mode of doing business, willingness to meet obligations and general reputation they have enjoyed in your community.

Any expense to be incurred in connection with this inquiry, please charge to our account. Your prompt attention will be much appreciated, and we assure you that your information will be held in strict confidence.

Sincerely yours,

Chinese Marine Trading Co., Ltd.

Bruce Jin/Manager

☞ The bank would respond to the customer (potential buyer) about the credit standing of the potential exporter.

Woori Bank

247, Dongkwang-dong 1Ga, Jung-Gu,

Busan, Korea

Tel: 051-246-8000

Fax: 051-243-08001

May 6, 2013

Chinese Marine Trading Co., Ltd.

Floor 8, No.388, Yang Fu Port

Management Building,

Yang Fu Economic Development Zone, Yang Fu, Hainan,

P.R. China

Gentlemen,

We are pleased to report on the firm referred to in your letter of May 2 per below.

Kamas Nara Co., Ltd. was established in 1995 as an exporter and importer of handling environmentally friendly products, with a paid-up capital equivalent to US$30,000,000. The net worth at the end of last year exceeded the amount equivalent to US$150,000,000 about half of which is readily realizable.

Their main lines are in trade of environmentally friendly products and technologies. Their business policy has been very active and they have many business connections both at home and abroad.

They have maintained an account with us since 1997, always to our satisfaction and their latest financial statements show a very health condition. We are of opinion that they may be related as A1 and you would run the least risk in opening a connection with the firm.

For this information, we would not like to accept any responsibility but we shall be pleased to be of any further service to you. The enclosed note shows the charges which we have paid on your behalf, for which we ask you to settle soon.

Sincerely yours.

Woori Bank

Gil-Dong, Kim/Director

☞ **Being informed of the satisfactory credit standing of the exporter, the potential importer would begin negotiating with the exporter as follows:**

Chinese Marine Trading Co., Ltd.

Floor 8, No.388, Yang Fu Port

Management Building,

Yang Fu Economic Development Zone, Yang Fu, Hainan,

P.R. China

May, 10, 2013

Kamas Nara Co., Ltd.

204-39, Onchen-dong, Geumjung-Gu

Busan, Korea

Dear Mr. Lee,

We thank you very much for your letter of May, 1, 2013 in which you expressed your willingness to open an account with us.

We are glad to learn that you are especially interested in shipping the environmentally friendly Anions LED Lamp, and in this we may say that we are specialists.

We would appreciate receiving your best CIF Haikou on LED Lamp Creating Pure Anions without Ozone as well as several samples by air parcel post.

If your prices are competitive and merchandise is suitable for our trade, we will be able to place large orders.

We look forward to hearing from you soon.

Yours truly,

Kamas Nara Co., Ltd.

Bruce Jin/Manager

☛ **The above-mailed inquiry would be followed by the reply from the exporter as follows:**

Kamas Nara Co., Ltd.

204-39, Onchen-dong, Geumjung-Gu

Busan, Korea

Tel: 82-51-583-9836

Fax: 82-51-582-9836

www.ksnara.com

May 17, 2013

Chinese Marine Trading Co., Ltd.

Floor 8, No.388, YangFu Port Management Building,

YangFu Economic Development Zone, YangFu, Hainan,

P.R. China

Dear Mr. Jin,

Thank you very much for your inquiry of May 10.

As requested, we have already dispatched our most recent catalog and the price list with several samples by DHL service. Also please refer to our website (www.ksnara.com) where you can get more information of our products.

From the enclosed price list you will find that our prices are exceptionally low and such low quotation is entirely due to our recognition of the necessity for price cutting in order to develop our sales in your market.

Consequently, we can not keep the prices effective more than two weeks from the date of this letter and we wish to receive your order by return mail.

We hope that this will meet with your immediate approval.

Yours truly,

Kamas Nara Co., Ltd.

S. W. Lee/Manager

☛ **The exporter will not be able to meet the requirement from the potential buyer sometimes, for example, due to lack of stock, as follow:**

Kamas Nara Co., Ltd.

204-39, Onchen-dong, Geumjung-Gu

Busan, Korea

Tel: 82-51-583-9836

Fax: 82-51-582-9836

www.ksnara.com

May 18, 2013

Chinese Marine Trading Co., Ltd.

Floor 8, No.388, YangFu Port Management Building,

YangFu Economic Development Zone, YangFu, Hainan,

P.R. China

Dear Mr. Jin,

We thank you for your inquiry of May 10, 2013.

However, we regret to inform you that we are unable to quote you now, as we have no stock of these goods referred to, neither can we tell you how soon we can make delivery.

We sincerely regret our inability to be of service to you in this instance.

Yours truly,

Kamas Nara Co., Ltd.

S. W. Lee/ Manager

11.7   Consultation of Terms

The exporter and the screened potential buyer consult each other about settlement currency and exchange rate, foreign exchange risk aversion, settlement method, price, quality, quantity, shipment, adoption of Incoterms® 2010, logistics charge, sending samples, tariffs, market price, traveling and other relevant issues.

Usually, before they engage in further consultation, the counterpart company – if interested – will ask for samples in order to determine the practicality of the proposed transaction. Market research is also vital for the importer as in the case of the exporter to prepare for the transaction and to determine the scale of transaction.

☛ **The potential buyer would reply to the exporter to continue to negotiate for the trade conditions including price terms as follows:**

Chinese Marine Trading Co., Ltd.

Floor 8, No.388, Yang Fu Port

Management Building,

Yang Fu Economic Development Zone, Yang Fu, Hainan,

P.R. China

May 19, 2013

Kamas Nara Co., Ltd.

204-39, Onchen-dong, Geumjung-Gu

Busan, Korea

Dear Mr. Lee,

We have received your fax of May 17, 2013 with thanks.

Your samples (NE102) and other terms as shown in your catalog and specification sheet are quite acceptable to us.

However, we regret that we are unable to place an order with you at this time, as the prices are so high in applying to this area. In this market, our requirements for this line are fairly large, but competition is very strict. In view of this situation, we would like to request your best revised obtainable prices.

Your earliest favorable reply would be highly appreciated.

Sincerely yours,

Chinese Marine Trading Co., Ltd.

Bruce Jin/Manager

☞ **The exporter would suggest the price condition to the buyer as follows:**

Kamas Nara Co., Ltd.

204-39, Onchen-dong, Geumjung-Gu

Busan, Korea

Tel: 82-51-583-9836

Fax: 82-51-582-9836

www.ksnara.com

May 21, 2013

Chinese Marine Trading Co., Ltd.

Floor 8, No.388, Yang Fu Port Management Building,

Yang Fu Economic Development Zone, Yang Fu, Hainan,

P.R. China

Dear Mr. Jin,

We received your counter offer of May 19, 2013 and are pleased to offer you firm as follows:

1. Spec & Amount : NE102 (Anion Lamp) 100,000ea @ USD5.45 Total USD545,000.00
2. Price Term: CIF Haikou
3. Shipment: within one month after receipt of at sight letter of credit.

We hope you understand that the above quotations are final to us.

The above revised is the best price and therefore we are unable to make any further discount. So, unless you accept the price terms at this figure, no further business relations surrounding this item will be established.

We await your acceptance as soon as possible.

Yours very truly,

Kamas Nara Co., Ltd.

S. W. Lee/ Manager

☛ The potential importer would then want to take advantage of the discounted price as follows:

Chinese Marine Trading Co., Ltd.

Floor 8, No.388, Yang Fu Port

Management Building,

Yang Fu Economic Development Zone, Yang Fu, Hainan,

P.R. China

May 24, 2013

Kamas Nara Co., Ltd.

204-39, Onchen-dong, Geumjung-Gu

Busan, Korea

Dear Mr. Lee,

Thanks for your irrevocable offer of May 21, 2013.

In conclusion, we can accept your above dated offer subject to granting us USD0.05 more discount.

In view of the price ruling in this market, your price is rather stiff and your competitors are offering lower prices than yours.

If this proposal is acceptable to you, we will instruct our bank to issue a letter of credit according to your firm offer upon which the contract was formed. It would give us great pleasure to do business with you at this time.

We are looking forward to receiving your final confirmation.

Sincerely yours,

Chinese Marine Trading Co., Ltd.

Bruce Jin/manager

☞ **The following illustrates the case in which the exporter rejects the counterpart's suggestion to further discount the price.**

Kamas Nara Co., Ltd.

204-39, Onchen-dong, Geumjung-Gu

Busan, Korea

Tel: 82-51-583-9836

Fax: 82-51-582-9836

www.ksnara.com

May 25, 2013

Chinese Marine Trading Co., Ltd.

Floor 8, No.388, Yang Fu Port Management Building,

Yang Fu Economic Development Zone, Yang Fu, Hainan,

P.R. China

Dear Mr. Jin,

We have the pleasure of acknowledging your letter of May 21, 2013, requesting us to quote the most favorable price on Anion Lamps.

We regret that our prices were not low enough to meet your requirements.
But the previously revised one is the best price we can offer at present since the high quality of our goods cannot be maintained at lower prices.

In fact, our revised price is closely calculated, and we shall not be able to make any further price reduction in spite of our eagerness to do business with you.

We trust you will accept it without delay.

Yours very truly,

Kamas Nara Co., Ltd.

S. W. Lee/Manager

☞ The following illustrates the case in which the exporter accepts the counterpart's suggestion to further discount the price.

Kamas Nara Co., Ltd.

204-39, Onchen-dong, Geumjung-Gu

Busan, Korea

Tel: 82-51-583-9836

Fax: 82-51-582-9836

www.ksnara.com

May 25, 2013

Chinese Marine Trading Co., Ltd.

Floor 8, No.388, Yang Fu Port Management Building,

Yang Fu Economic Development Zone, Yang Fu, Hainan,

P.R. China

Dear Mr. Jin,

We accept and confirm your counter offer of May 24, 2013 to realize the first transaction with you.

We thank you for your efforts to expedite the business between us. Please note that the revised price, however, would appear impossible to produce the quality you require without raising the price for your future orders.

We shall do our best to execute this order to your entire satisfaction on receiving the advice of issuance for your letter of credit.

We are looking forward to being informed of your irrevocable letter of credit as soon as possible.

Yours very truly,

Kamas Nara Co., Ltd.

S. W. Lee/ Manager

11.8   Offer, Acceptance/Conclusion of Contract

The exporter makes an offer, a counter offer, negotiations and acceptance and finally concludes a contract with the importer by using any means of communication. The exporter and the importer, concluding a contract, make and exchange copies of the Agreement on General Terms and Conditions of Business Transactions, under which they make the specified sales contract.

☞ **If the concerned parties make agreement on the main conditions of transactions including price condition, they can make the following contract documents including: offer sheet, sales contract, general terms and conditions and purchase order, for the formation of contract: The following demonstrates the offer sheet made by Kamas Nara Co., Ltd. and dispatched to Chinese Marine Trading Co., Ltd.**

Kamas Nara Co., Ltd.

① 204-39, Onchen-dong, Geumjung-Gu

Busan, Korea

Tel: 82-51-583-9836

Fax: 82-51-582-9836

OFFER SHEET

② Messrs.   Chinese Marine Trading Co., LTD.

③ Offer No. KN110525

④ Date. May. 26, 2013

Gentleman :

⑤ We are pleased to offer you the following

⑥ Origin : REPUBLIC OF KOREA

⑦ Shipment   WITHIN 45 DAYS AFTER RECEIPT OF YOUR L/C.

⑧ Shipping Port : BUSAN, KOREA

⑨ Payment Terms : BY AN IRREVOCABLE AT SIGHT L/C TO BE OPENED IN OUR FAVOR.

⑩ Validity of Offer : BY June. 30. 2013

Item	⑪ Commodity & Description	⑫ Quantity	⑬ Unit Price	⑭ Total Amount
	Anion LED Lamp SIZE 135 X 53mm	⑮ CIF Haikou, china		
	Anion LED Lamp SIZE 135 X 53mm			
	Anion LED Lamp SIZE 135 X 53mm	100,000 PCS	@US$ 5.40	US$540,000.00
TOTAL : **		100,000 PCS *************	***************	US$540,000.00 ***************

⑯ Accepted by : _____   ⑰KAMAS NARA CO., LTD.

Date of acceptance _____   _____

☞ **The following is the sales contract made by Kamas Nara Co., Ltd. and accepted/countersigned by Chinese Marine Trading Co., Ltd.**

Kamas Nara Co., Ltd.

Address : 204-39, Onchen-dong,
Geumjung-Gu, Busan, Korea

Tel: 82-51-583-9836
Fax: 82-51-582-9836
www.ksnara.com

SALES CONTRACT

Kamas Nara Co., Ltd as Seller, hereby confirms having concluded the sales contract with Chinese Marine Trading Co., Ltd., as Buyer, to sell the following goods on the date and on the terms and conditions herein- after set forth. The Buyer is hereby requested to sign and return the original attached.

MESSRS	CONTRACT DATE		CONTRACT NO.
Chinese marine Trading Co., Ltd.	May,26, 2013		KN110501

COMMODITY DESCRIPTION	QUANTITY	UNIT PRICE	AMOUNT
Anions LED Lamp	100,000pcs	US$5.40	USD540,000.00

Time of Shipment : June, 30, 2013.

Port of Shipment : Busan, Korea

Port of Destination : Haikou, China

Payment : By an irrevocable, at sight L/C to be opened in favor of Kamas Nara. Co., Ltd.

Insurance : To be covered ICC (A/R) with War Risks and SRCC for 110% of invoice value.

        Insurance Policy shall be made out in China in the currency of US Dollars.

Packing : 100 pieces to be packed in a carton and each piece has to be packed with poly bag

Special Terms & Conditions :

Subject to the general terms and conditions set forth on back hereof :

Accepted by

(Buyer) Chinese Marine trading Co., Ltd.   (Seller) Kamas Nara Co., Ltd.

(Signature)   (Signature)
_____   _____

(Name &Title)   (Name & Title)
_____   _____

Date   Date

☞ The following is an example of the general terms and conditions to be made between Kamas Nara Co., Ltd. and Chinese Marine Trading Co., Ltd.

GENERAL TERMS AND CONDITIONS

All business hereunder shall be transacted between Buyer and Seller on a principal to principal basis and both parties agree to the following terms and conditions :

(1) Quantity : Quantity shall be subject to a variation of (10)% plus or minus at Seller's option.

(2) Shipment: Date of bill of lading shall be accepted as conclusive of the date of shipment.

Partial shipment and/or transhipment shall be not permitted. If shipment is prevented or delayed in whole or in party, by reason of Acts of God, or the consequence of, affecting Seller or any supplier to Seller of the goods sold hereunder or any manufacturer of the goods sold hereunder or any supplier to such manufacturer, such Acts of God to include but not limited to fire, flood, typhoon, earthquake, or by reason of riots, wars, hostilities, governmental restrictions, trade embargoes, strikes, lockouts, labor disputes, boycotting of Korean goods, unavailability of transportation or any other causes of a nature beyond Seller's control, then, Seller may, at its option, perform the contract of the unfulfilled portion here of within a reasonable time from the removal of the cause preventing or delaying performance, or rescind unconditionally and without liability this contract or the unfulfilled portion hereof.

(3) Payment: Irrevocable and confirmed letters of credit negotiable at sight draft shall be established through a prime bank satisfactory to Seller immediately after conclusion of contract with validity of at least 15 days after the last day of the month of shipment for negotiation of the relative draft. The amount of such letter of credit shall be sufficient to cover the contract amount and additional charges and/or expenses to be borne by Buyer. If Buyer fails to provide such letter of credit, Seller shall have the option of reselling the contracted goods for Buyer's account, holding the goods for Buyer's account and risk, and/or cancelling the contract and claiming for damages caused by Buyer's default.

(4) Inspection: The inspection of quantity shall be done according to the export regulation of the Republic of Korea and/or by the manufacturers which shall be considered as final. Should any specific inspector be designated by Buyer, all additional charges thereby incurred shall be borne by Buyer and shall be added to the invoice amount, for which the letter of credit stipulates accordingly.

(5) Packing: Packing shall be at the Seller's option. In case special instructions are necessary the same should be intimated to the Seller in time so as to enable the Seller to comply with it.

(6) Insurance: In case of CIF or CIP basis, 110% of the invoice amount will be insured unless otherwise agreed. Any additional premium for insurance coverage over 110% of the invoice amount, if so required, shall be borne by Buyer and shall be added to the invoice amount for which the letter of credit shall stipulate accordingly.

(7) Increased Costs: If Seller's costs of performance are increased after the date of this agreement by reason of increased freight rates, taxes or other governmental charges and insurance rates including war risk, or if any variation in rates of exchange increases Seller's costs or reduces Seller's return, Buyer agrees to compensate Seller of such increased cost or loss of income.

(8) Price: The price stated in the contract is subject to change and the actual price to be paid will be that of Seller's current price list ruling at the time of dispatch of the goods. Seller shall notify Buyer in writing or by telex, cable or telegram of any revised price which shall be applied to goods still to be shipped, unless Buyer cancels in writing or by cable or telex the undelivered balance within 15 days from such notification.

(9) Any Claim: Dispute, or complaint by Buyer of whatever nature arising under this contract, shall be made in cable within 10 days after arrival of the cargo in the destination port. Full particulars of such claim shall be made in writing and forwarded by airmail so as to reach Seller within 20 days after cabling. Buyer must submit with such particulars as Public Surveyor's report when the quality and quantity of merchandise is in dispute. A claim made after the said 30-day period shall have no effect and Seller shall not be obligated to honor it. Seller shall not under any circumstance be liable for indirect or consequential damages.

(10) Trade Terms: The trade terms used herein such as CIF, CIP and FOB shall be in accordance with Incoterms® 2010. In all other respects, this Contract shall be governed by and construed in accordance with the laws of Korea.

(11) Arbitration: All disputes, controversies, or differences which may arise between the parties out of or in relation to or in connection with this contract or for the breach thereof, shall be finally settled by arbitration in Seoul, Korea in accordance with the Commercial Arbitration Rules of the Korean Commercial Arbitration Board and under the Laws of Korea. The award rendered by arbitrator(s) shall be final and binding upon both parties concerned.

(12) Deduction: Buyer may not deduct any amount from the price without Seller's advance written authorization.

(13) Patents, Trade   Buyer is to hold Seller harmless from liability for any infringement with marks, Designs, etc.: regard to patent, trademark, copyright, design, pattern, construction, stamp, etc., originated or chosen by Buyer.

(14) Force Majeure: Seller shall not be responsible for non-delivery or delay in delivery resulting from causes beyond its control. In the event of such an occurrence, Seller may at its option either postpone delivery until removal of the causes, or cancel the balance of the order in the Contract.

IN WITNESS WHEREOF, the parties have caused this Agreement to be executed by their duly authorized representatives as of the date first above written :

For and on behalf of,

By :

Typed Name :

Title :

For and on behalf of,

By :

Typed Name :

Title :

☞ **The following is the purchase order made by Chinese Marine Trading Co., Ltd to Kamas Nara Co., Ltd.**

Chinese Marine Trading Co., Ltd.

Floor 8, No.388, Yang Fu Port Management Building,

Yang Fu Economic Development Zone, Yang Fu, Hainan,

P.R. China

PURCHASE ORDER

② Messrs.   ③ Your Ref : KN110525

Kamas Nara Co., Ltd.   ④ Our Ref : CMT20110503

204-39, Onchen-dong,   ⑤ Date & Place : May 28, 2013

Geumjung-Gu, Busan, Korea

⑥ Dear Sirs.

We, Chinese Marine Trading Co., Ltd., as Buyer, hereby confirm our purchase of the following goods in accordance with the terms and conditions given below.

⑦ DESCRIPTION	Anion LED Lamp 135 X 53mm
⑧ QUALITY	AS PER PREVIOUS SHIPMENT.
⑨ PACKING	EACH 100 PCS. TO BE PACKED INTO AN EXPORTABLE CARTON BOX. EXPORT STANDARD PACKING
⑩ QUANTITY	100,000 PCS. ONLY.
⑪ PRICE	CIF Hikou, China IN U.S. DOLLARS. NE102 @U$5.40/PCS
⑫ AMOUNT	TOTAL : US$540,000.00
⑬ INSURANCE	INSURANCE POLICY/CRETIFICATE BLANK ENDORSED FOR 110% OF C.I.F VALUE WITH CLAIMS PAYABLE IN JAPAN IN THE CURRENCY OF THE DRAFT INSURANCE TO INCLUDE I.C.C. (A) WITH INSTITUTE WAR CLAUSES, S.R.C.C CLAUSES.
⑭ PAYMENT	BY L/C AT SIGHT IN YOUR FAVOUR BY FULL CABLE. ADVISING THROUGH WOORI BANK, BUSAN, KOREA FROM THE CHINAI BANK, YANGFU. (INTEREST IS FOR SELLER'S ACCOUNT.)
⑮ SHIPMENT	SHIPMENT SHOULD BE EFFECTED DIRECTLY FROM BUSAN, KOREA TO HAIKOU CHINA BY DIRECT CONTAINER VESSEL AS FOLLOWS : BY JUNE/30/2013
MARKS & NO	TO BE MARKED ON BOTH SIDES OF EACH CARTON BOX AS FOLLOWS : C/NO.
REMARKS	ONE ORIGINAL CERTIFICATE OF ORIGIN FORM "A" & TWO COPIES OF NON-NEGOTIABLE B/L, INVOICE, PACKING LIST, INSURANCE POLICY SHOULD BE GIVEN BY YOU UNDER A CAPTAIN'S CARE FOR DELIVERY TO US.

Confirmed & accepted by :   Chinese Marine Trading Co., Ltd.

☞ The importer would inform the exporter of the issuing of a letter of credit, which would be followed by the preparation for exportation including export license as follows:

Chinese Marine Trading Co., Ltd.

Floor 8, No.388, Yang Fu Port

Management Building,

Yang Fu Economic Development Zone, Yang Fu, Hainan,

P.R. China

May 29, 2013

Kamas Nara Co., Ltd.

204-39, Onchen-dong, Geumjung-Gu

Busan, Korea

Gentlemen;

We would like to thank you for your fax of May 25, 2013, enclosing our purchase order No. CMT20130503. We are very glad to complete the first contract for mutual benefit and would like to ask you to do everything possible to ensure punctual shipment.

In order to cover this order, we have instructed our bank to issue an irrevocable at sight credit in your favor for the amount of this order and you will be duly advised it through the Woori Bank Busan.

Please inform us by return when you have completed the shipment and please sign this order and return it to us as an acknowledgement.

Sincerely yours,

Chinese Marine Trading Co., Ltd.

Bruce Jin/Manager

Export License (Application)

(The format and contents are different among governments. This is the case of the Korean government.)

	Handling Time : 1Day

(1)		671110	(4) Buyer or Principal of Contract
(Exporter)	(notification No)		Chinese Marine Trading Co., Ltd.

Name of firm, Address, Name of Rep.	(5) L/C or Contract No.
Kamas Nara Co., Ltd.	
204-39, Onchon-dong, Geumjung-gu	ILC10051234567
Busan, Korea	

(2)		(6) Total Amount
(Requester) (Business No.)		US$ 540,000

	(7) Period of Payment
	AT SIGHT
(Name of firm, Address, Name of Rep.)	
(Signature)	(8) Terms of Price
	C.I.F. HAIKOU CHINA

(3)Origin R.O.K	(9) Port of Arrival HAIKOU, CHINA

(10) HS Code	(11) Description/Size	(12) Unit/Quantity	(13) Unit Price	(14) Amount
	Anions LED Lamp			
9405.40.1000	NE102	100,000PCS	USD5.40	USD540,000

(15)Remarks to be filled out by an Approval Agency

(16)Period of Approval

(17)Approval No.

(18)No. of Approval Agency

(19)The undersigned hereby approves the above-mentioned goods in accordance with Article 14(2) of the Foreign Trade Act and Article 26(1) of the Enforcement Decree of the said Act.

11.9   Receipt of Letter of Credit for Export

To prepare for the letter of credit issuing, the importer should negotiate with the issuing bank, inter alia, to set a ceiling of credit extended to the importer. The importer should write all the conditions in the letter of credit application according to the sales contract terms (method of payment, loading port, arrival port, shipping period, expiration period, etc.) to submit to letter of credit issuing bank.

The letter of credit issuing banks should promptly notify exporters of letter of credit opening through advising banks as it issues the letter of credit. If the buyer issues and informs the letter of credits through the bank, the exporter reviews the letter of credit focusing on the safety of payment collection, whether it is the same as specified by the contract, whether there are poisonous articles, and the credit status of issuing banks.

☛ **In accordance with the sales contract, the importer would make application to issue the letter of credit and the issuing bank would inform of letter of credit issuing through SWIFT format to the advising bank located in the exporter's country as follows:**

APPLICATION FOR IRREVOCABLE DOCUMENTARY CREDIT

※1.Advising Bank Woori Bank	BIC CODE :
※2. Credit No. :	I10234567
3. Applicant :	Chinese Marine Trading Co., Ltd.
4. Beneficiary :	Kamas Nara Co., Ltd.
	204-39, Onchen-dong, Geumjung-Gu, Busan, Korea

5. Amount :	USD540.000.00	(Tolerance : +10 / -10)

6. Expiry Date :	07/31/2013 7. Latest date of shipment : 06/31/2013
8. Tenor of Draft	■At Sight (■Reimburse □Remittance)
	□Usance days □

9. For   %   of the invoice value (Usance L/C only :   □Banker's   □ Domestic)
                     □ Shipper's

┌──────────────────────────────────┐
│ DOCUMENTS REQUIRED (46A :)   │
└──────────────────────────────────┘

10.	Full set of clean on board ocean bills of lading made out to the order of WOORI BANK mal "Freight__Prepaid_____and notify (¦Accountee, □Other:_____ Air Waybills consigned to THE BANK OFCHI marke "Freight _____and "notify Accountee"
11.	Insurance Policy or certificate in duplicate endorsed in blank for 110% of the invoice value, stipulating that claims are payable in the currency of the draft and also indicating a claim setting agent in Korea. Insurance must include: the institute Cargo Clause _____
12.	Signed commercial invoice in Triplicate_____ 13. □ Certificate of analysis in_____
14.	Packing List in__Triplicate_____ 15. □ Certificate of weight in_____
16.	Certificate of origin in issued by
17. □	Inspection certificaten issued by
18. □	Other documents(if any)

19. Description of goods and/or services (45A:)   (Price Term)

Commodity Description	Quantity	Unit Price	Amount
(H.S CODE: 9505.40-1000)	10,000pcs	UD5.40	SD5,000.0

Country of Origin	Korea		Total	USD540,000.00

20.   Shipment Busan, Korea   Shipment To: Haikou, China
From:

21.   Partial ▫Allowed   ¦Prohibited   22.   ▫Allowed   ¦Prohibited
Shipment: Transhipment:

23.   ▫
Confirmation:

Confirmation charges:▫Beneficiary,   ▫Applicant

24 Transfer: ▫Allowed (Transfering)
                  Bank:

25. Documents must be presented within days after the date of shipment of B/L or
other transportation documents.

Additional Conditions (47A:)

▫   All banking charges(including postage, advising and payment commission,
    negotiation and reimbursement commission)

▫   outside Korea are for account of   ▫Beneficiary
¦   ▫Applicant

▫   Stale B/L AWB acceptable   ▫Charter Party B/L is acceptable

▫   ▫Third party B/L acceptable

▫   Third party document acceptable   ▫Combined shipment B/L is

▫   acceptable

▫   T/T Reimbursement: ▫Allowed

▫   ▫Prohibited

    Bills of lading should be issued by _____

    (House) Air Waybills should be issued by_____

    (   ) % More or less in quantity and amount to be acceptable

    The number of this credit must be indicated in all documents Other conditions:

※ Drawee Bank (42A):

※   Reimbursement

Bank(53A):

Except so far as otherwise expressly stated, This Documentary credit is subject to the
Uniform Customs and Practice for Documentary Credits (1993 Revision) International
Chamber of Commerce Publication N. 500

Address : Floor 8, No.388, Yang Fu
Port Management Building, Yang Fu
Economic Development Zone, Yang
Fu, Hainan, P.R. China

Applicant : Chinese Marine Trading
Co., Ltd

Case of issuing letter of credit through the format
of SWIFT MT780

Application header block :

: Input/Output Identifier	: I Outgoing Message
: Transaction Typer	: 700 issue of a documentary credit
: Transaction Priority	: n Normal
: From	: THE BANK Of CHINA, YANGFU
: To	: WOORI BANK
	BUSAN BRANCH. KOREA

Text Block :

/27 : sequence of total	: 1/1
/40A : form of documentary credit	: IRREVOCABLE
/20 : documentary credit number	: ILC10051234567
/31C : date of issue	: 13/06/24
/31D : date and place of expiry	: 13/07/31 KOREA
/50 : applicant	: CHINESE MARINE TRADING CO., LTD
/59 : beneficiary	: KAMAS NARA CO., LTD
/32B : currency code amount	: USD 540,000.00
/39A : pct credit amount tolerance	: 10/10
/41D : available with by name, address	: ANY BANK BY NEGOTIATION
/42C : drafts at	: AT SIGHT
/42A : drawee	: WOORI BANK, KOREA(ADDR 7, DONGGWANGDONG 1GA, CHUNG-GU, BUSAN, KOREA)
/43P : partial shipment	: NOT ALLOWED
/43T : transshipment	: NOT ALLOWED
/44A : on board/Disp/taking charge	: BUSAN, KOREA
/44B : for transportation to	: HAIKOU, CHINA
/44C : latest date of shipment	: 13/06/30

/45A : descr goods and/or services

Anions LED Lamp

135 X 53mm

C.I.F.HAIKOU.CHINA

/46A : documents required

+SIGNED COMMERCIAL INVOICE IN TRIPLICATE

+PACKING LIST IN TRIPLICATE

+FULL SET OF CLEAN ON BOARD OCEAN BILL OF LANDING MADE OUT TO THE ORDER OF

THE BANK OF CHINA MARKED FREIGHT PREPAID AND NOTIFY APPLICANT

+CERTIFICATE OF ORIGIN

/47A : additional conditions

ALL DOCUMENTS MUST BEAR OUR CREDIT NUMBER ILC10051234567

T/T REIMBURSEMENT NOT ALLOWED

OUANTITY 10PCT MORE OR LESS ALLOWED

+THIRD PARTY DOCUMENTS ACCEPTABLE

/71B : charges	: ALL BANKING COMMISSIONS AND CHARGES INCLUDING REIMBURSEMENT CHARGES OUTSIDE KOREA ARE FOR ACCOUNT OF BENEFICIARY
/49 : confirmation instructions	: WITHOUT
/53A : reimbursement bank	: WOORI BANK, KOREA(ADDR 7, DONGGWANGDONG 1GA, CHUNG-GU, BUSAN, KOREA)

/78 : instructions to the pay/acc/neg bk

DRAFTS MUST BE SENT TO DRAWEE BANK FOR YOUR REMBURSEMENT

AND ALL DOCUMENTS TO US BY COURIER SERVICE IN ONE LOT

/72 : sender to receiver information	: THIS CREDIT IS SUBJECT TO U.C.P(1993 REVISION) I.C.C. PUBLICATION NO. 600

11.10 Getting Export/Import Approval (if required by law)

Exporter checks whether the items are prohibited to be exported and, if it is required, should get approval of export from concerned authorities.

☞ **The importer would get the import license from the concerned authority, if it is legally required, as follows:**

Import License (Application)

		Handling Time : 1Day

(1)Importer Notification No.	671110	(5) Consignor
		Name of Firm, Address, Name of Rep.

Name of firm, Address, Name of Rep. Chinese Marine Trading Co., Ltd Floor 8, No.388, YangFu Port Management Building,YangFu Economic Development Zone, YangFu, Hainan, P.R. China	Kamas Nara Co., Ltd. 204-39, Onchen-dong, Geumjung-Gu, Busan, Kore

(2) Requestr Business No.	(6) Total Amount US$ 540,000.00
Name of firm, Address, Name of Rep. (Signature)	(7)Period of Payment AT SIGHT
	(8)Terms of Price C.I.F HAIKOU

(3)Origin REPUBLIC KOREA	(4)Port of Loading BUSAN, KOREA

(9) H.S Code	(10) Description/Size	(11) Unit/Quantity	(12) Unit Price	(13)Amount
9405.40.1000	Anions LED Lamp NE102 135-53mm	100,000PCS	US $5.40	US $540,000

(14)Remarks to be filled out by an Approval Agency

(15)Period of Approval

(16)Approval No.

(17)No. of Approval Agency

(18) The undersigned hereby approves the above-mentioned goods in accordance with Article 14(2) of the Foreign Trade Act and Article 26(1) of the Enforcement Decree of the said Act.

11.11   Manufacturing or Securing Contracted Items

The exporter manufactures or secures the finished products for export. In manufacturing or securing the contracted products, the employee in charge of export of the items is recommended to communicate efficiently and seriously with the manufacturing or securing section of the company to secure the products which are in accordance with the description and quality expressed and contracted under the sales contract and the letter of credit. Securing the proper products that are in the sales contract is the basic condition to be satisfied to avoid the trade disputes with the counterparts and to continue successfully to do business with the items.

11.12   Making Clearance/Arranging International Transport and Insurance

Arranging transportation and insurance contract with logistics companies and insurance companies, the exporter, in the case of maritime transportation, carries export goods to the Container Yard (CY) or Container Freight Station (CFS) in bonded areas for shipment, get the export permits from the customs authority after clearance, and get bill of lading before or after loading onboard, negotiating with logistics companies and marine insurance companies.

Meanwhile the importer, for receipt of the imported goods, secures required import permission or license (as seen in above stage) to legalize the transaction, and get pre-approval or recommendation from the proper authorities if it is required by the law concerned.

Container Yard (CY)

Port facility at which containers are accepted for loading onboard ships, and off-loaded containers are delivered to the consignees.

Source: http://www.businessdictionary.com/definition/container-yard-CY.html#ixzz-165P6rKYU

Container Freight Station (CFS)

Port facility for loading and unloading containerized cargo to and from ships. Also called container terminal.

Source: http://www.businessdictionary.com/definition/container-freight-station-CFS.html#ixzz165PjKX12

Bonded Area

Bounded or bonded area means the designated place where foreign merchandise is brought in without import duties, for further processing or re-exporting. Import-duty must be paid on these goods if they are released in the local market.

Source: http://www.businessdictionary.com/definition/duty-free-zone-DFZ.html#ixzz165Rqtknq

☞ The exporter would make application for the shipment to the transporting company and inform the importer of the shipment as follows:

Shipping Request				
Shipper/Export Kamas Nara Co., Ltd 204-39, Onchen -dong, Geumjung -Gu Busan, Korea		**L/C No. (or Contract No.)** ILC10051234567		
Consignee To the order of Bank of China, Yang Fu, China		**Forwarding Agent**		
Notify Party Chinese Marine Trading Co., Ltd Floor 8, No.388, Yang Fu Port Management Building, Yang Fu Economic Development Zone, YangFu, Hainan, P.R. China		**Another Notify Party**		
Place of Receipt HAIKOU, CHINA	**Pre-Carriage by**	**Country of Origin** MADE IN KOREA		
Vessel/Voyage HANJIN MALTA 0026W	**Port of Loading** BUSAN PORT KOREA	**Export Reference No.**		
Port of Discharge HAIKOU PORT, CHINA	**Place of Delivery** HAIKOU PORT, CHINA	**Final Destination**		
Container No. /Seal No. **Marks & No.**	**No. of** **package**	**Kind of Package** **Description of** **Goods**	**Total** **G.Weight(kg)**	**Total Meas.** **(CBM)**
HJCU7143514/435541 C/W 19,800kg MEA 31 CBM . China Marine Trading Shipment to Haikou C/N 1-2 Made in Korea	2CTNS IN A TOTAL 100,000 PCS OF ANIONS LED LAMP DETAILS ARE AS PER P/O NO. CMT20130503 L/C NO. : ILC10051234567 C.I.F. HAIKOU		19,800KG	31CMB

Kamas Nara Co., Ltd.

204-39, Onchen-dong, Geumjung-Gu

Busan, Korea

Tel: 82-51-583-9836

Fax: 82-51-582-9836

www.ksnara.com

June 10, 2013

Chinese Marine Trading Co., Ltd.

Floor 8, No.388, Yang Fu Port Management Building,

Yang Fu Economic Development Zone, Yang Fu, Hainan,

P.R. China

Dear Mr. Jin,

Shipment: Purchase order No. CMT20110503

We are pleased to inform you that we have shipped the above today by the m/s Hanjin Malta 0026w of Hanjin shipping Co., Ltd. leaving Busan.

According to your request, we enclose a copy of complete set of non-negotiable documents as shown in the credit.

We trust that they will reach you in good order and give you full satisfaction so that you may place us with repeat orders.

Yours very truly,

Kamas Nara Co., Ltd.

S. W. Lee/ Manager

☞ With a marine insurance company or its agent, or through the insurance broker such as Lloyd's broker, the exporter would make the marine cargo insurance contract as follows:

LG Insurance Co., Ltd.	
CERTIFICATE OF MARINE CARGO INSURANCE	
Assured(s), etc Kamas Nara Co., Ltd.	
Certificate No. 002599A65334	Ref. No. Invoice No. 1005
	L/C No. ILC10051234567
Claim, if any, payable at : Claims are payable in	Amount insured USD 540,000.- (USD540,000 XC 110%)
Survey should be approved by THE SAME AS ABOVE	Conditions
Local Vessel or Conveyance	⑨From(interior port or place of loading)	* INSTITUTE CARGO CLAUSE(A) 1982 * CLAIMS ARE PAYABLE IN AMERICA IN THE CURRENCY OF THE DRAFT.
Ship or Vessel called the HANJIN MALTA	Sailing on or about JUNE 30, 2013	
at and from BUSAN, KOREA	transshipped at	
arrived at HAIKOU, CHINA	thence to	
Goods and Merchandises ANIONS LED LAMP 135 x 53MM 100,000PCS	Subject to the following Clauses as per back hereof institute Cargo Clauses Institute War Clauses(Cargo) Institute War Cancellation Clauses(Cargo) Institute Strikes Riots and Civil Commotions Clauses Institute Air Cargo Clauses (All Risks) Institute Classification Clauses Special Replacement Clause (applying to machinery) Institute Radioactive Contamination Exclusion Clauses Co-Insurance Clause Marks and Numbers as
Place and Date signed in ⑰ SEOUL, KOREA June 30, 2013 No. of Certificates issued. ⑱ TWO	
⑳ This Certificate represents and takes the place of the Policy and conveys all rights of the original policyholder	

(for the purpose of collecting any loss or claim) as fully as if the property was covered by an Open Policy direct to the holder of this Certificate. This Company agrees losses, if any, shall be payable to the order of Assured on surrender of this Certificate. Settlement under one copy shall render all others null and void. Contrary to the wording of this form, this insurance is governed by the standard from of English Marine Insurance Policy.

In the event of loss or damage arising under this insurance, no claims will be admitted unless a survey has been held with the approval of this Company's office or Agents specified in this Certificate.

SEE IMPORTANT INSTRUCTIONS ON REVERSE

LG Insurance Co., Ltd.

AUTHORIZED SIGNATORY

This Certificate is not valid unless the Declaration be signed by an authorized representative of the Assured.

11.13 Negotiation for Payment Collection with Bank

The exporter prepares transport documents required by the terms of the letter of credit, reviews consistency between documents and the requirements under the letter of credit, and finally submits the documents accompanied by the bill of exchange to the bank for the payment collection.

The letter of credit opening bank receives the transportation documents and reviews for consistency between the letter of credit terms and the document terms, and sends the arrival notice of documents to importers. If in the case that imported goods arrive earlier than transport documents as they may come from neighboring countries or by air, the importer can receive cargo from the shipping company against the submission of a letter of guarantee (L/G), or air cargo delivery acceptance when exporters need clearance to release the cargo to the buyer.

Importers receive transportation documents, make payment immediately on sight in case of the "sight" drafts or make a payment on the due date in case of the "usance" drafts. The importer presents the bill of lading to the shipping company, carrying imported goods in bonded areas, and reports the import to the authority concerned through an electronic system or physically in-person. After making import declarations, importers submit delivery order (D/O) in order to pay import duties, process the import clearance, submit the clearance permission or delivery order (D/O) to the concerned authority and carry out imported goods from bonded areas.

☞ The exporter (beneficiary) would prepare for the negotiation with the bank for the collection of payment, securing the transportation documents required under the terms of letter of credit including bill of lading, commercial invoice, packing list, certificate of inspection, certificate of quality/quantity/weight, certificate of origin, etc., as follows:

Bill of Lading					
① Shipperp Shipper/Exporter Kamas Nara Co., Ltd		⑪ B/L No. ; But 1004			
② Consignee TO ORDER OF THE BANK OF CHINA					
③ Notify Party CHINESE MARINE TRADING CO., LTD					
Pre-Carriage by	⑥ Place of Receipt BUSAN, KOREA				
④ Ocean Vessel HANJIN MALTA	⑦ Voyage No.	⑫ Flag			
⑤ Port of Loading ⑧ Port of Discharge ⑨ Place of Delivery ⑩ Final Destination (For Merchant Ref.) BUSAN, KOREA HAIKOU, CHINA HAIKOU, CHINA HAIKOU, CHINA					
⑬ Container No. ⑭ Seal No. Marks & No		⑮ No. & Kinds of Containers or Packages	⑯ Description of Goods	⑰ Gross Weight	Measurement
Total No. of Containers or Packages(in words)		2 CNTRS	ANIONS LED LAMP (100,000 PCS)	19,800 KGS	31 CBM
⑱ Freight and Charges	⑲ Revenue tons	⑳ Rate	Per	Prepaid	Collect
Freight prepaid at	Freight payable at	Place and Date of Issue JUNE 30, 2013, BUSAN			
Total prepaid in	No. of original B/L	Signature			
Laden on board vessel Date Signature JUNE 30, 2013		Hanjin Shipping Co. Ltd. as agent for a carrier, zzz Liner Ltd.			

COMMERCIAL INVOICE

①Shipper/Seller	KRGILTRA159SEO	⑦ Invoice No. and date 1005 JULY. 05. 2013
KAMAS NARA CO., LTD. 204-39, ONCHEN-DONG, GEUMJUNG-GU, BUSAN, KOREA		⑧ L/C No. and date ILC10051234567 JUNE. 24. 2013
② Consignee CHINESE MARINE TRADING CO., LTD. 52FLOOR 8, NO.388, YANGFU PORT MANAGEMENT BUILDING, YANGFU ECONOMIC DEVELOPMENT ZONE, YANGFU, HAINA, PR. CHINA		⑨ Buyer (if other than consignee) CHINESE MARINE TRADING CO., LTD.
		Other references COUNTRY OF ORIGIN : REPUBLIC OF KOREA
③ Departure date JUNE. 30, 2013		
④ Vessel/flight ⑤ From HANJIN MALTA BUSAN, KOREA ⑥ To HAIKOU, CHINA		Terms of delivery and payment C.I.F HAIKOU, CHINA L/C AT SIGHT

Shipping Marks	No.& kind of packages	Description of Goods	Quantity	Unit price	Amount
Shipment to Haikou C/N 1-2 Made in Korea	2CTNS IN A TOTAL 100,000 PCS OF ANIONS LED LAMP DETAILS ARE AS PER P/O NO. CMT20110503 100,000PCS			US$5.40/M	US$540,000
				Signed by	

PACKING LIST

① Seller	⑦ Invoice No. and date
Kamas Nara Co., Ltd.	1005 JULY. 05. 2013

② Consignee	⑧ Buyer (if other than consignee)
Chinese Marine Trding Co., Ltd.	Chinese Marine Trading Co., Ltd
	⑨ Other references

③ Departure date	Country of Origin:
June. 30, 2013	Republic of Korea

④ Vessel/flight   ⑤ From
Hanjin Malta   BUSAN, KOREA

⑥ To
Haikou, China

⑩ Shipping Marks	⑪ No.&kind of packages	⑫ Goods description	⑬ Quantity or net weight	⑭ Gross Weight	⑮ Measurement
Shipment to haikou	135X53mm	Anions LED Lamp	100,000PCS	19,800kgs	31CBM
LOT NO			19,800 kgs.		
C/NO.1-2					
MADE IN KOREA					

///

	Signed by

CERTIFICATE OF INSPECTION

DATE : JULY, 02, 2013

AS PER L/C NO. ILC10051234567

SHIPPED BY KAMAS NARA CO., LTD

OF

TO CHINESE MARINE SHIPPING CO., LTD

THIS IS TO CERTIFY THAT OUR QUALITY CONTROLLER ATTENDED FOR INSPECTION
OF THE CAPTIONED SHIPMENT AT
AND SAMPLES TAKEN AT RANDOM FROM THIS SHIPMENT WERE INSPECTED AND
APPEARED TO BE SUCH AS TO WARRANT THE ISSUE OF THIS AUTHORIZATION.
THE ISSUE OF THIS CERTIFICATE OF INSPECTION TO SHIP THESE GOODS DOES NOT
IMPLY THAT THE GOODS ARE IN ACCORDANCE WITH THE CONTRACT AND DOES NOT
IN ANYWAY RELIEVE THE SELLERS OF THEIR RESPONSIBILITY TO SUPPLY THE
GOODS TO BE SHIPPED HEREWITH IN ENTIRE ACCORDANCE WITH THE CONTRACT.

MERCHANDISE INSPECTED BY :

QUALITY CONTROLLER :

_____

Authorized signature

CERTIFICATE OF QUALITY/QUANTITY/WEIGHT

DATE : JULY, 02. 2013

WE, THE MANUFACTURER,

HEREBY CERTIFY THAT QUALITY/QUANTITY/WEIGHT MENTION BELOW ARE IN GOOD

CONDITION AFTER ARE FULLY INSPECTED AT OUR FACTORY.

L/C NO. : ILC10051234567

INVOICE NO. : 1005

COMMODITY : ANIONS LED LAMP

QUANTITY : 100,000PCS

QUALITY

INSPECTION	PEC	JUDGEMENT	REMARKS

SIGNED BY _____

1. Exporter (Name, address, country)	ORIGINAL
KAMAS NARA CO., LTD. 204-39, Onchen-dong, Geumjung-Gu, Busan, Korea	CERTIFICATE OF ORIGIN issued by THE KOREA CHAMBER OF COMMERCE & INDUSTRY Seoul, Republic of Korea
2. Consignee (Name, address, country) Chinese Marine Trading Co., Ltd.	3. Country of Origin REPUBLIC OF KOREA
4. Transport details FROM : BUSAN, KOREA TO : HAIKOU, CHINA	5. Remarks CY 875-022-4 JUNE. 30, 2013

6. Marks & numbers ; number and kind of packages ; description of goods	7. Quantity
HJCU7143514/435541 C/W 19,800kg MEA 31 CBM 　　　　　　　2CTNS IN A TOTAL ．China Marine　　100,000 PCS OF ANIONS LED LAMP 　Trading ．　　　DETAILS ARE AS PER P/O NO. CMT20110503 Shipment to Haikou　/// C/N 1-2 Made in Korea /////////////////	100,000 PCS. /////////////////

8. Declaration by the Exporter (Signature) (Name)	9. Certification _____ Authorized Signatory
	Certificate No.

THE KOREA CHAMBER OF COMMERCE &
INDUSTRY

☞ The exporter (beneficiary) would make negotiation for payment collection by submitting the following bill of exchange accompanied by the above-prepared transport documents to the bank concerned.

BILL OF EXCHANGE

NO. ___123456___   BILL OF EXCHANGE, ② JULY 05, 2013 ③ BUSAN, KOREA

④ FOR US$540,000.–

⑤ AT xxxx SIGHT OF THIS ORIGINAL BILL OF EXCHANGE(SECOND OF THE SAME TENOR AND DATE BEING UNPAID)

PAY TO ⑥ WOORI BANK OR ORDER THE SUM OF

⑦ SAY US DOLLARS FIVE HUNDRED FORTY THOUSAND ONLY ;

VALUE RECEIVED AND CHARGE THE SAME TO ACCOUNT OF   ⑧ CHINESE MARINE TRADING CO., LTD.

⑨ DRAWN UNDER THE BANK OF CHINA, YANGFU, CHINA

⑩ L/C NO. ILC10051234567 _____   ⑪ DATED JUNE 24, 2013

⑫ TO THE BANK OF CHINA,

   YANGFU, CHINA

⑬ KAMAS NARA CO., LTD.

☞ The importer (applicant) would get the transportation documents including the bill of lading to receive the imported goods from the shipping company, but, if the transportation documents would not arrive yet even though the importer completed payment to the bank, the importer can claim the goods from the shipping company against the submission of the letter of guarantee issued by the importer and guaranteed by the bank, as follows:

LETTER OF GUARANTEE

Date : 2013.06.30

①Shipping Co. HANJIN shipping co.	⑥(L/C NO.) ILC10051234567			⑦(L/G NO.)
	⑧(B/L NO.)		BUT 1004	
②Shipper KAMAS NARA CO., LTD	⑨Vessel Name		HANJIN MALTA	
	⑩Arrival Date		JULY. 02, 2013	
	⑪Voyage No.			
③Invoice Value $540,000.00	⑫Port of Loading		BUSAN, KOREA	
	⑬Port of Discharge		HAIKOU, CHINA	
④Nos. & Marks	⑤Packages	⑭Description of Goods		
CHINESE MARINE TRADING CO., LTD P/NO. CMT20130503 Made in KOREA	100,000PCS 100PACKAGES	ANIONS LED LAMP 135 X 53MM		

Whereas you have issued a Bill of Lading covering the above shipment and the above cargo has been arrived at the above port of discharge (or the place of delivery), we hereby request you to give delivery of the said cargo to the above mentioned party without production of the original Bill of Lading.

In consideration of your complying with our above request, we hereby agree as follows :

1. To indemnify you, your servants and agents and to hold all of you harmless in respect of liability, loss, damage or expenses which you may sustain by reason of delivering the cargo in accordance with our request, provided that the undersigned Bank shall be exempt from liability for freight, demurrage or expenses in respect of the contract of carriage.

2. As soon as the original Bill of Lading corresponding to the above cargo comes into our possession, we shall surrender the same to you, whereupon our liability hereunder shall cease.

3. The liability of each and every person under this guarantee shall be joint and several and shall not be conditional upon your proceeding first against any person, whether or not such person is party to or liable under this guarantee.

4. This guarantee shall be governed by and construed in accordance with Korean law and the jurisdiction of the competent court in Korea.

Should the Bill of Lading holder file a claim or bring a lawsuit against you, you shall notify the undersigned Bank as soon as possible.

Yours faithfully

For and on behalf of   For and on behalf of

[Name of Requestor]   [Name of Bank]

Authorized Signature   Authorized Signature

11.14 Follow-up Management

If the buyer raises claims, the exporters should respond to such claims. The importer makes a claim for the loss caused by the damaged or defective products, and/or quantity inaccuracies. Solutions could be made through meditation, conciliation, arbitration, or lawsuits.

Trade claims can be made in a couple of different scenarios. First, a claim can be brought if there is a suspected breach of principles of good faith and diligence. Second, a claim can be brought if there is a delay in the performance of the contract, a rejection of performance, an impossibility of performance, incompletion of performance, or a delay of acceptance by creditors. The first efforts to settle the dispute is through amicable negotiations between the parties. This path is both the fastest and cheapest for the parties concerned. If these negotiations do not render a solution, mediation, conciliation, arbitration, or litigation might be needed.

☛ **If the received goods are not in accordance with the contract terms, the importer would bring claims as follows:**

Chinese Marine Trading Co., Ltd.

Floor 8, No.388, Yang Fu Port Management Building,

Yang Fu Economic Development Zone, Yang Fu, Hainan,

P.R. China

July 2, 2013

Kamas Nara Co., Ltd.

204-39, Onchen-dong, Geumjung-Gu

Busan, Korea

Dear Mr. Lee,

Two containers of Anions LED Lamps for our Order No. CMT20130503 have reached us, but we regret to have to inform you that their quality is inferior to the samples for which we placed the order.

Enclosed find sample from the goods we received. You will admit that your shipments do not come up to the quality of the sample.

We hope that you will correct the matter at once and let us know by return mail.

Yours truly,

Chinese Marine Trading Co., Ltd.

Brue Jin/Manager

☛ **If the contracting parties fail to make an amicable agreement to solve the claim dispute, then other solutions are to be sought. The following are for the case of requesting arbitration made by the exporter against the importer for the payment collection.**

Request for Arbitration

Claimant : KAMAS Nara Co., Ltd.

    204-39, Onchen-dong, Geumjung-Gu, Busan, Korea

    Representative Director: L.S. Hyang

Respondent : Chinese Marine Trading Co., Ltd.

    Floor 8, No.388, Yang Fu Port Management Building,

    Yang Fu Economic Development Zone, Yang Fu, Hainan, P.R. China

    Representative Director: Bruce Jin

Purport of Request

1. The Respondent shall pay to the Claimant the sum of US$540,000.00

2. The Arbitration Cost shall be borne by the Respondent.

Grounds for Request

The Claimant is a Korean Corporation engaged in environmental goods business.

The Claimant and the Respondent executed "Sales Contract" on May 26, 2013(see the attached Exhibit A-1),

Based on this "Sales Contract", the Claimant and the Respondent had established the amount of letter of credit to pay to Claimant within conclusion of contract with validity of 15 days.

The Respondent failed to make payment on the accounts outlined below and had no special

reasons. The exact calculation is as follows:

- Accounts amount : USD540,000.00

- Interest : USD540,000.00 X 3%(3 months) = USD16,200.00

- Total : USD556,200.00

The Respondent and the Claimant agreed that the Respondent would pay to the Claimant

USD540,000.00 before September 15, 2013 and that all disputes arising from the

Respondent's inability to fulfill the above obligations would be resolved by arbitration. (see the

attached Exhibit A-2).

The Respondent did not pay the amount. Accordingly, the Claimant requested arbitration to

be conducted by the Korean Commercial Arbitration Board as set forth in the Purport.

Method of Proof

Exhibit A-1 : Sales Contract

Exhibit A-2 : Certificate of outstanding payment to KAMAS Nara Co., Ltd.

Exhibit A-3 : Letter

Exhibit A-4 : Fax dated August 15, 2013

Exhibit A-5 : Mailing letter dated August 31, 2013

Exhibit A-6 : Fax dated September 3, 2013

KAMAS Nara Co., Ltd.

S. W. Lee/ Manager

SWIFT Message Type for issuing letter of credit
(MT700 Issue of Documentary Credit)

M/O	Tag	Field Name	Content/Options
M	27	Sequence of Total	1n/1n
M	40A	Form of Documentary Credit	24x
M	20	Documentary Credit Number	16x
O	23	Referenceto Pre-Advice	16x
O	31C	Date of Issue	6n
M	31D	Date and Place of Expiry	6n29x
O	51a	Applicant Bank	A or D
M	50	Applicant	4'35x
M	59	Beneficiary	[/34x]4'35x
M	32B	Currency Code, Amount	3a 15number
O	39A	Percentage Credit Amount Tolerance	2n/2n
O	39B	Maximum Credit Amount	13x
O	39C	Additional Amounts Covered	4'35x
M	41a	Available with … By …	A or D
O	42C	Draft at…	3'35x
O	42a	Drawee	A or D
O	42M	Mixed Payment Details	4'35x
O	42P	Deferred Payment Details	4'35x
O	43P	Partial Shipment	1'35x
O	43T	Transshipment	1'35x
O	44A	Loading on Board/Dispatch/Taking in Charge at/from…	1'65x
O	44B	For Transportion to…	1'65x
O	44C	Latest Date of Shipment	6n
O	44D	Shipment Period	6'65x

O	45A	Description of Goods and/or Services	50*65x
O	46A	Documents Required	50*65x
O	47A	Additional Conditions	50*65x
O	71B	Charges	6*35x
O	48	Period for Presentation	4*35x
M	49	Confirmation instructions	7x
O	53a	Reimbursement Bank	A or D
O	78	Instructions to the Paying/Accepting/Negotiating Bank	12*65x
O	57a	"Advise Through" Bank	A, B or D
O	72	Sender to Receiver Information	6*35x

Index

A

Acceptance, 38, 40–48, 65, 73, 74, 93, 94, 99, 100, 103, 105, 108, 110, 112, 126–127, 154, 158–160, 163, 170, 172, 179, 182, 212, 230, 311, 315–323, 344

Alternative dispute resolution, 279, 281–282

Arbitral award, 22, 23, 278, 282, 283, 285–287

Arbitral tribunal, 278, 282, 284–285

Arbitration, 5, 11, 16, 22, 23, 61, 86, 88, 90, 95, 101, 113, 181, 278, 279, 281–288, 319, 344–347

Arbitration agreement, 283–284

Assured, 11, 121, 219–222, 224, 225, 227–230, 232, 234, 235, 238, 240–245, 334, 335

Automated teller machines, 270

Autonomy of the letter of credit, 120–184

Avoidance of contract, 48, 54

B

Back-to-back and overriding credits, 130

Bank guarantees, 184

Bank indemnities, 159

Bare boat charter, 194

Bilateral contract, 38

Bill of exchange, 69, 73, 99, 127, 128, 153–155, 195, 290, 291, 342

Bill of lading, 69, 80, 97, 99, 103, 104, 107, 127, 132–136, 139, 141–142, 144, 145, 148, 149, 152, 156, 162, 163, 188, 189, 195–210, 212, 214–217, 233, 235, 250, 251, 318, 331, 335, 336, 343, 344

Breach of contract, 15, 49–56, 62, 278, 287

Buy-back agreement, 120, 130

C

Cancellation, 19, 41–43, 46, 54, 128, 177, 249, 334

Carriage and Insurance Paid (CIP), 21, 47, 66, 75, 79–82, 93, 98, 150, 151, 249, 318, 319

Carriage Paid (CPT), 21, 47, 66, 75, 79–82

CFR. *See* Cost and Freight (CFR)

Charterparty, 139, 141, 142, 144–145, 194, 207

CIF. *See* Cost insurance and freight (CIF)

CIP. *See* Carriage and Insurance Paid (CIP)

CISG (1980). *See* United Nations Convention on Contracts for the International Sale of Goods (CISG) (1980)

Claims, 2, 44, 61, 123, 187, 220, 259, 277, 291

Clean bill of lading, 195, 196

Combined transport document, 18, 136, 139–141

Commercial arbitration, 5, 23, 86, 90, 95, 101, 281–288, 319, 347

Confirmed and unconfirmed credits, 129

Consensual contract, 38

Consumer research, 26–27

Container bills of lading, 188–189, 194–210

Container operator, 202

Contract of insurance, 150, 220, 222, 226–228, 242, 243, 245, 253

Correspondent arrangement, 260

Cost and Freight (CFR), 21, 47, 66, 75, 79–82, 165, 168, 220

Cost Insurance and Freight (CIF), 15, 21, 47, 66, 75, 78–83, 93, 97, 98, 104, 109, 150, 151, 171, 174, 220–222, 228, 232, 248, 249, 295, 307, 311, 316, 318, 319, 321

Counter offer, 40–44, 46, 311, 314, 315

Course of business, 240, 241, 243, 244

CPT. *See* Carriage Paid (CPT)

Credit inquiry, 25, 32, 35–36, 182, 273, 299

Credit risk, 2, 4, 180, 181, 184

Customs clearance, 26, 30, 32, 33, 188

Customs territories, 1

Cyber-marketplace, 274

D

DAP. *See* Delivered at Place (DAP)

DAT. *See* Delivered at Terminal (DAT)

DDP. *See* Delivered Duty Paid (DDP)

E.S. Lee, *Management of International Trade*,
DOI 10.1007/978-3-642-30403-3, © Springer-Verlag Berlin Heidelberg 2012

Printed by Printforce, the Netherlands